The Workforce Engagement Equation

A Practitioner's Guide to Creating and
Sustaining High Performance

The Workforce Engagement Equation

A Practitioner's Guide to Creating and Sustaining High Performance

JAMISON J. MANION

CRC Press
Taylor & Francis Group
Boca Raton   London   New York

CRC Press is an imprint of the
Taylor & Francis Group, an **informa** business

A PRODUCTIVITY PRESS BOOK

CRC Press
Taylor & Francis Group
6000 Broken Sound Parkway NW, Suite 300
Boca Raton, FL 33487-2742

© 2012 by Taylor & Francis Group, LLC
CRC Press is an imprint of Taylor & Francis Group, an Informa business

No claim to original U.S. Government works

Printed in the United States of America on acid-free paper
Version Date: 20120409

International Standard Book Number: 978-1-4398-6809-6 (Paperback)

Library of Congress Cataloging-in-Publication Data

Manion, Jamison Jay.
   The workforce engagement equation : a practitioner's guide to creating and sustaining high performance / Jamison Jay Manion.
      p. cm.
   Includes bibliographical references and index.
   ISBN 978-1-4398-6809-6 (alk. paper)
   1. Employees--Rating of. 2. Employee motivation. 3. Leadership. I. Title.

HF5549.5.R3M254 2012
658.3'14--dc23   2012011247

Visit the Taylor & Francis Web site at
http://www.taylorandfrancis.com

and the CRC Press Web site at
http://www.crcpress.com

This book is dedicated to my wife, Starla, who has been my most faithful fan, ardent supporter, patient sounding post, and loving critic. And thanks to my daughters, Jayla and Aubrey, for the years of laughter and trials that have certainly shaped my understanding of human behavior and taught me that theory doesn't always work with family.

I'd also like to thank all those who have encouraged me and supported me through the years as I have navigated my own voyage of growth and discovery. A special thanks goes out to my customers and clients, who have been supportive and patient as we have discovered how best to apply the lessons of the Workforce Engagement Equation in their organizations. This is especially true for Mr. Nick Weber, who has trusted me as we've striven together to really make a difference.

And special thanks go to Dr. John Beck for starting me on my path to understanding leadership. I greatly appreciate all his support and encouragement in writing this book and the hours he spent reviewing and making editorial suggestions to the portions of the book relating to The Leader's Window.

Contents

Preface: Building on Solid Foundational Principles

Effective management is a thinking person's game where everyone within an organization enjoys the fruits of victory and experiences the losses of defeat. In effectively managed organizations, everyone is on the same team in which the common objective is to remain relevant and effective in a fast-moving world of change.

The Workforce Engagement Equation is a practitioner's guide that lays out the principles, tools, and techniques that have proven effective in leading and managing the "people side" of process improvement. It bridges the gap between strategies and tactics, allowing practitioners to take concrete actions to control ongoing operations sustainably. This step-by-step guide navigates through the complex waters of organizational change with easily understandable explanations, intuitive graphics, and real-world examples. It guides you to assess exactly where your organization is along the change continuum and which management and leadership techniques to apply to light the fire of true workforce engagement.

This work is targeted for practitioners. Theory is a good place to start, but unless it yields tangible, repeatable, and measurable results, you won't find it within the cover of this book. That doesn't mean that this work doesn't have a solid research foundation—far from it. This book builds upon centuries of thinking and experience. Fortunately, we can see further today because we stand on the shoulders of giants who have gone before us. Understanding the contribution of each gives us tools to choose from. The more tools we have in our toolkit, the more likely we'll be able to apply the one that is most appropriate for the situation at hand.

Table 0.1 lists the major conceptual pioneers that are credited with originating the concepts others have since built upon that have helped shape my understanding of Individual and Organizational Behavior.

I recognize and thank each of these pioneers for their insight and enlightenment that they have contributed to the discipline of organizational improvement and change management. I'd also like to readily acknowledge that this book is not the final word—scores of brilliant minds have built and continue to build upon the work of these pioneers. I encourage each reader to go back and review some of these original sources and continue to study the works of others that regularly contribute to this growing field of practice. When you find concepts and techniques that yield positive outcomes, add them to your toolkit and build them into your vessel of organizational improvement. In the meantime, The Workforce Engagement Equation™ will provide you with what you need to truly make a difference in the performance of your organization and the engagement of your workforce. I wish you success.

Table 0.1 Major Conceptual Pioneers of Individual and Organizational Behavior Theory

Theory	Originator/Major Contributor	Year
Economic Utility	Adam Smith	1759
Normal Emotions (DISC)	William M. Marston	1928
Hierarchy of Needs	Abraham Maslow	1943
Game Theory	John Nash	1950
Operant Conditioning	B. F. Skinner	1957
Group Development Stages	Bruce Tuckman	1965
Systems Theory	Ludwig von Bertalanffy	1969
Behavioral Economics	Daniel Kahneman	1973
Situational Approaches to Leadership	Dr. John Beck and Neil Yeager	1995
Leading Change	John Kotter	1996
The Path of Least Resistance	Robert Fritz	1999

What People Are Saying about The Workforce Engagement Equation

The Workforce Engagement Equation was formed in the trenches and on the front lines of business. It arose out of trials, errors, and adaptation evolving from project to project. Here are a few of the comments that practitioners who have experienced the power of workforce engagement are saying:

> "I have experienced more progress changing the culture in the two years since we started applying the principles of the Workforce Engagement Equation than I have seen in the past 25 years with the company. The statistics really support the process. Thanks for really helping to move the dial."

> **Nick W.**
> *Manager Work Equipment*

> "I just want to let you know the training was a great success. The team is working hard this week on the 'takeaways' from the class. Everyone has been talking about how it brought them together as a team and they are working in groups to accomplish all the tasks. I believe with the skills you taught us we will be successful once the line is installed and up and running."

> **Mike R.**
> *Production Manager*

> "I want you to know that your class will, and has, started to change my life for the better. It has been very informative and made me reevaluate how I treat others as well as what makes me the way I am. I wish this was common knowledge. I am honored to have been a part of [your] life, even for a week."

> **Jason L.**

> "Thank you for coming here and teaching us how to form into a team this week. I found you to be a very effective teacher. Some of us are 'Strong-Willed' people and that doesn't really matter for our behavioral style. There are strong-willed people in any style. The trick will be working together and growing on the strengths of each other as a group. And maybe we won't remember you in ten

years, but, hopefully all remember a lot of those things that you
have taught here."

Rufus B.

"Just wanted to say thanks for helping us see and realize what we
already had in each one of us. I've found myself using it in my
home life also. I'm just hoping it's a lasting impression."

Kerry S.

"Thank you so much! At first, I thought this class was going to
'SUCK'. I mean, 'Train us to work together? Haven't we been
already?' Well, I'm very happy we did it now because you came
in and showed everyone how to handle themselves in better
ways. Now we don't just have to deal with someone who is 'TOO
MUCH!'"

Ashton S.

"I've gotten the best Team-Building learning experience and I
enjoyed this class. You're on the level, so it makes learning fun."

Rustin T.

"I thoroughly enjoyed your class and got a lot out of it. I've needed
that class for a long time!"

Chad D.

A Note about the CD Accompanying this Book

The Workforce Engagement Equation is a handbook for practitioners—and
every craftsman needs good functional tools. To help you construct your
own organizational vessel and navigate the deep waters of organizational
change, I've included in the CD each assessment, form, and template contained in the book. When they are used, please acknowledge credit to *The
Workforce Engagement Equation*™ Copyright 2012, Workforce Engagement
Solutions, LLC.

Author

Having worked with scores of organizations throughout the United States and internationally, **Jamison J. Manion** brings a real-world, hands-on perspective to leadership, management, and organizational design. His unique background in operations, maintenance, and human resources combined with his education offers a complete package of technical, human resources, and business acumen. He has a proven track record leading organizational change and process improvement that he communicates with a rare blend of expertise and humor. Jamison's methods have proven effective in diverse industries, including both light and heavy manufacturing, energy and utilities, chemical, pharmaceutical, plastics, military and government agencies, and consumer products. As a Department of the Navy Certified Leadership Program Manager, he is able to provide contextual examples that transcend theory into real-world practical application. His passion for helping organizations bolster job security through aligned systems and improved organizational performance shines throughout the Workforce Engagement Equation. Applying the principles contained in this pragmatic and practical handbook will help any organization improve its chances for success (or at least explain why it crashed and burned). Enjoy your voyage!

Chapter 1

The Great Seattle Fire: An Analogy for Our Times

On June 6, 1889, in the frontier town of Seattle, WA, a cabinetmaker accidentally knocked over a pot of glue that started a fire. His attempts to extinguish the flames spread the grease-based glue. The fire spread to adjacent buildings, and by the time it had burned itself out, 25 city blocks of the bustling seaport town lay in ashes (Figure 1.1). Some could have been completely crushed by these events; the leaders among them recognized the opportunity.

Seattle before the fire was a thriving logging town, but it wasn't paradise. The city was built between a bountiful source of timber and a calm harbor with easy access to the sea. Daily, as the steady tides of Puget Sound ebbed and flowed, ships laden with timber sailed out to fuel the building boom of California's Gold Rush and the money flowed back in. Though prosperous and growing, the young city had its problems too. Like any union of land and water, Seattle had mud—lots and lots of mud. The streets were paved with it. Seattle's mud was legendary, the kind of stuff men and horses drown in, and some did, right in the middle of the city streets.

When the city leaders decided to rebuild, they wanted to improve. They proposed to regrade Seattle's foundation and raise the streets one to two stories higher than the original. It was a grand plan, and the population cheered—until they were told the cost. Many businessmen and shop owners decided that the mud was part of what gave Seattle its charm. They built upon the ashes at the exact same level. Undeterred by short-sighted thinkers only interested in quick profits, the city leaders wanted to invest in

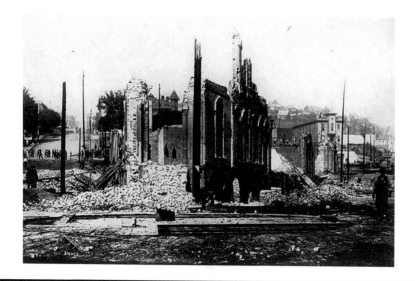

Figure 1.1 Aftermath of the Great Seattle Fire.

the future; they decided to improve the real estate owned by the city—the streets. Fill was brought in from the surrounding hillsides and quarries to raise Seattle's streets out of the muck between 12 and 30 feet higher than before.

Imagine the scene, buildings and sidewalks at sea level and streets towering between them like great, wide walls. Ladders were placed on corners so that pedestrians could climb up to cross to the other side. The city had cured the problem of potholes. No more would the embarrassment of men and horses drowning in the streets blight the shining city by the sea—problem solved! That is until a horse fell off the street and killed a passing pedestrian. As the horse discovered the "Law of Gravity," Seattle's founders discovered the "Law of Unintended Consequences." In response to this new challenge, the sidewalks were extended, and the ground floor of many buildings became basements; thus, Seattle Underground was born, and the bright new city of Seattle rose up from the mud upon which it was founded.

Thanks and credit for the brief history of Seattle are owed to the tour guides of Bill Speidel's Seattle Underground Tour and Bill Speidel's book, *Sons of the Profits: There's No Business Like Grow Business. The Seattle Story 1851–1901* (Nettle Creek Publishing Co., 1967).

Fire and Mud in the Twenty-First Century

The firestorm of the great recession of 2007–2008 burned up billions of dollars in equity, leaving many companies and lives in ruins and stuck in a stagnant economic quagmire. Like Seattle in 1889, there are those who want to rebuild on the same unstable foundation as the past, and there are others who want to see transformation—they want to lift their organizations out of the floodplains. They are advocates for positive change. On which side of history will your organization fall? Will you build upon higher ground? Seattle's story illustrates how visionary leadership can springboard progress from catastrophes and courageous leadership can overcome opposition—but it only happens when a clear vision of the future is built upon a solid foundation; it only happens when a vision is tenaciously pursued; it only happens when someone courageously chooses to lead.

Leadership Is a Choice—Rise Up, You Worthy Bastards, and Follow Me!

Leadership is a choice. Much has been written about leadership over the centuries, and the debate continues whether leaders are born or if they are made. In my experience, leaders choose to lead.

RISE UP, YOU WORTHY BASTARDS!: I met Dave working in a mill in a remote corner of rural Maine. He had taken the job after choosing to sell his beach house in a southern resort town. One bleak day in the middle of mud season, when freezing rain spread its gray veil over the land, Dave and I sat delaying our inevitable trek back out into the weather. "Why?" I asked him. He slowly turned toward me and said:

"When I started working at the southern mill, I had high hopes and principled ideals. I wanted to make a difference in the business and in the lives of the people I worked with. Years later, as I jogged along the ocean shore just outside my back door, I came to the realization that somewhere along the way, I had settled. I had lost my desire to make things better. I had decided that things were 'good enough.' I was no longer leading and no one was following. And if a brave champion in shining armor had ridden up to the gates of the mill on his powerful white charger and shouted, 'Rise up you worthy bastards and follow me!' I would have just sat there. I couldn't rise up anymore; I was no longer a 'worthy bastard'. I had become one of the disaffected rabbles I had sought to save. That's when I decided not to settle anymore. That is when I decided to go where I could make a difference."

Dave had made a choice. He chose not to settle and not to drift. He chose to lead. I don't know why he couldn't have chosen to lead from the beachhead of a tropical paradise, but hey, it wasn't for me to decide. And I respected him for it. So, wherever you're at in your life, your career, or your personal geography, you'll have to decide if you're willing to lead. You'll have to make the choice to be a "worthy bastard." Rise up, you worthy bastards, and follow me!

Seven Cardinal Sins of Change Leadership: Seven Reasons Why Things Don't Change

Having made the decision to lead, you'll need to prepare because the journey won't be easy—the clichés tell us so: "change is hard"; "nothing worth doing comes easily"; "if it were easy, it would already be done"; "Rome wasn't built in a day," nor was Seattle and neither will your vision of the future. Clichés are cliché because they also happen to be true—change is hard. The statistics bear witness to this truth; 75% of major change initiatives fail to achieve their stated objectives. Of those that are considered to be initial successes, almost 90% fail to sustain their gains one year later; *net–net, that's over a 97% chance of disappointment.* It's almost enough to discourage even the greatest optimist, but not me. Despite the numbers, I'm convinced that over 97% of all change initiatives can succeed if the organization is truly dedicated, affects the changes holistically and systematically, and then stays the course.

It could be construed that beginning a process improvement/change management book by discussing failure is to start on a discouraging note, but this book is for practitioners, the hands-on leaders who are engaged in the frontline of affecting change, those who have the bloody knuckles and bear the scars of past failed initiatives yet continue to persevere. I am confident that you are tough enough to take it. Besides, if you're going to drive the train successfully, it helps to know the things that will cause it to jump the track so you can avoid them. Or, putting it another way, if you don't know that a snake is venomous or realize just how poisonous it is, you may not take all the proper precautions to keep yourself from getting bitten. So let's begin by defining the problem and listing the seven major reasons I've seen behind organizations failing to sustain hard-won changes or failing to change altogether. At their root, each stems from failures of leadership; we'll call these *The Seven Cardinal Sins of Change Leadership*:

1. Profiting from the Status Quo: The Status Quo Exists to Serve the Status Quo
2. Saying Isn't Doing: I'm an "Idea Man"
3. Frequent Turnover: Manager of the Month
4. Majoring on the Minors: Rearranging Deck Chairs on the Titanic
5. Lack of a Holistic Solution: The Operation Was a Success, but the Patient Died
6. Failure to Stay the Course: Are We There Yet?
7. Attention Deficit Management: Dismantling What Works

1. The Status Quo Exists to Serve the Status Quo

There's a very good reason things are the way they are; the status quo exists because there are people who benefit from the status quo. When you seek to change the status quo, someone somewhere in the organization will experience a loss. It could be a loss of power; it could be a loss of freedom brought on by enhanced enforcement; it could be a loss of esteem; or it could be loss of security—i.e., "If they streamline the process, I may lose my job." It doesn't matter if the overall process will be healthier, more productive, or more sustainable, and it doesn't matter if the loss is real or perceived—there will be losses of some kind. Change involves shifting the dynamics of the situation and the reallocation of scarce resources. If nothing else, affecting change will require a greater amount of initial effort, and people will need to expend greater effort designing and implementing the change. As any economist will tell you, there are always costs associated with change.

Frequently, change initiatives fail because those benefitting from the status quo don't want things to change. I'm not just talking about people at the shop floor level of an organization—although they are the ones who are most frequently blamed for failed initiatives; I'm talking about people in the management and leadership positions. Some managers don't want to give up control by letting teams manage their processes. Some executives don't want to share data about the health and operation of the organization. And so it goes.

I had never really thought about it when I was younger; I just assumed that everyone would want to make things better—who wouldn't? I was wrong. I came to realize this ugly truth when I was effectively transported through time. I was working for a struggling company. Layoffs and threats of closure were just part of the daily routine. Every day, we worked on improvement initiatives. Year after year, I'd alternate between projects to address safety, then productivity, and then cost in a continuous vacillation until I was abruptly uprooted from my civilian job to wear my country's uniform fulltime when I was recalled to active duty after 9/11/2001. When my mobilization was complete, I returned home with a renewed sense of urgency and a deeply felt need to make a difference. I didn't just see the manufacturing facility as a place of business; I saw it as a lifeline for a thousand employees, their families, communities, and thousands of other families in the area. Energized and engaged, I attended my first team meeting and experienced a most profound sense of déjà vu. In the meeting, the team talked about the same people causing the same problems and the same production issues they were talking about before I had left. It wouldn't have mattered if I had just stepped out of that meeting for a minute or for a year—nothing had changed. After the Twin Towers came down, the world had changed, I had changed, but my company had not.

After the meeting, I immediately went to the plant manager's office to elicit his support to do things differently. He listened to me, indifferently checking e-mails and shuffling papers on his desk. When I finished, he looked up and said, "Everyone knows this plant will close—it's only a matter of time. And it really doesn't matter; I make so much money that if I lose my job tomorrow I could take a position as a greeter at a big box store and it wouldn't affect my quality of life." I expected a lot of things, but I never expected that. Stunned, I simply replied, "Sorry, I don't have that problem."

I left and thought long and hard about his words. Why should he change? He had worked his entire career to be promoted to his position, and he now enjoyed all the perks the system had to offer. Changes for him were just more work that distracted him from his recreation time. There was nothing I could say or do to change it.

Lesson learned: before you embark on a change initiative, ask yourself, "Does the organization truly have the desire to change? Is the leadership team willing to commit the time and expend the resources required to redesign and reshape? Given the fact that change entails loss and sacrifice, does the management team truly possess that level of commitment?"

> QUOTE: "It is difficult to get a man to understand something, when his salary depends upon his not understanding it!"
>
> **Upton Sinclair**
> *American Author and Journalist (1878–1968)*

2. Saying Isn't Doing: I'm an "Idea Man"

Not every manager is complacent and entrenched in the status quo. There are dedicated leaders and managers who truly want to improve things—but many of them don't really know how. Scores of leaders have decried obvious organizational problems and inspirationally proclaimed new visions and directions—far rarer are the ones who actually transform visions into reality. Just saying doesn't necessarily make it so—given that the status quo exists to perpetuate the status quo, changes won't just happen.

At an executive leadership retreat I was facilitating, I was asked, between the two, management and leadership, which I thought was most frequently absent in struggling organizations. My answer was counter to the prevailing opinion espoused in many contemporary business texts. I replied that in my experience, effective management is by far the rarer of the two. Don't get me wrong; leadership is important, and where you find ineffective organizations, you usually find a lack of both inspired leadership and effective management. But, when comparing the two, leadership is inspirational and energizing, whereas effective management is just plain hard work. It requires thought, proactive plans, close attention to detail, and the dogged determination to stay the course despite emergent crises *du jour* and ever-shifting priorities. Being an effective manager also requires a breadth of knowledge that spans multiple fields of expertise. Just having expertise in the primary activities of your organization is necessary but insufficient. Effective management requires an understanding of business and finance, economics, psychology, project management, and systems theory. To illustrate the point, I often retell an anecdote I heard as a kid growing up in Oklahoma about Will Rogers. I recall it went something like this:

Will Rogers was a cowboy humorist, movie icon, commentator, and philosopher, kind of the Jon Stewart of his day. During World War I, German U-boats were decimating allied shipping, and Rogers was allegedly asked what could be done. Slowly twirling his ever-present lariat, he thought for a moment and then smiled his gentle wry smile, "Boil the ocean; that would force them to the surface and our boys could pick 'em off like ducks on a pond."

Incredulously, the reporter followed up his first question with a second, "How would you propose to do that?"

Rogers replied, "I'm just the idea man here. Get someone else to work out the details."

This illustrates with humor that all too often, "idea people" make statements and commit their organizations to projects that they themselves have absolutely no clue how to implement or the amount of work that would be involved. Managers at every level make bold, sweeping statements about grand visions and impossible missions in the name of "leadership" and expect events to unfold like the changing of the seasons. It's not surprising that 75% of major change initiatives fail to achieve their objectives. Simply saying doesn't make it so.

Fortunately for the free world, there were some brilliant "detail people" who figured out how to boil the ocean—not the entire ocean, just the small piece of water that contained a U-boat. These little tea kettles, as the Brits called them, were depth charges, and they do boil the ocean. By using depth charges to "boil the ocean," U-boats were driven to the surface, where they were "picked off like ducks in a pond" just like Will Rogers had suggested.

Grandiose, seemingly impossible visions can be achieved, but only when they're accompanied by clear scopes of work, sufficient resources, and the application of a holistic change methodology for designing, developing, deploying, and sustaining the changes. Similar to how Thomas A. Edison observed that "Genius is 1% inspiration, 99% perspiration" (Thomas Edison taken by Mathew Brady in 1877), I have found that successful organizations contain 1% leadership, 99% management. Where you find struggling organizations, you will invariably encounter leaders who aren't engaged enough or even capable of effective management. I have met far too many executives and managers who want *important jobs* but not *hard jobs*.

As you work to achieve the goals and vision of your organization, always wear both your manager and your leader hats. Effective managers act in the best interest of the organization to help it accomplish its goals, protect its interests, and help ensure its long-term sustainability. To do this, they create and administer effective systems, consistently administer policies and procedures to establish the organizational conditions that incent effective behavior. At the same time, effective managers act in the interest of their employees by providing direction and resources. They create opportunities for their employees to achieve their potential in line with their capabilities and aspirations. Effective managers align organizational mission and goals with employee capabilities and interests using the following:

1. Communication
2. Coordination
3. Documentation

The greater the degree of alignment between an organization's mission and goals and employee capabilities and interests, the higher the organizational performance and employee satisfaction will be. The bottom line is that successful managers orchestrate the success of their organizations by helping their people efficiently accomplish the goals set for them.

Unfortunately, this is more easily said than done.

To be effective, managers must understand what compels behavior. People act to satisfy both internal and external "drives" in response to conditions. Effective managers work to align the conditions to the employees' capabilities and interests. Figure 1.2 represents how managers accomplish

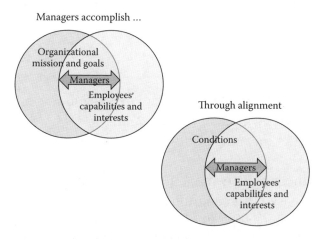

Figure 1.2   Aligning role of managers.

the mission and achieve the goals of the organization through the alignment of conditions with individual employees' capabilities and interests.

NOTE: Behavioral drivers are complex; we explore these drivers throughout the book in every stage of organizational change.

As compared to managing, leading is less about the mechanics of the organization and more about its purpose. Where management helps efficiently execute the vision, leadership defines it.

Just as managers do, leaders also act in the best interest of their organization. They do this through the following actions:

1. Establishing and articulating the vision
2. Setting the course
3. Championing the cause

Like effective managers, effective leaders act in the best interest of their people as well, but in more inspirational ways. The best leaders create hope, lead the way, and inspire higher performance. Almost everybody can think of a time when they achieved more than they thought possible when inspired by an effective leader.

Table 1.1 compares and contrasts the roles of effective leaders and managers.

So, which is more important to an organization? The answer is, of course, *both*!

Management without leadership is

■ Efficient, but not highly impactful
■ Marked by limited commitment—multiple agendas
■ Political infighting without a higher calling
■ Working without meaning and without inspiration

Leadership without management: Chaos! → Frustration! → Burnout!

Leaders set the vision and align the strategies while managers develop the plans and execute the tactics, all of which ideally result in the plan or project being accomplished on time and under budget! (See Table 1.2.)

Table 1.1   Role of Management Compared to Role of Leadership

Managers Act in the Interest of the Organization	Managers Accomplish This By
• Accomplish goals • Protect interests • Ensure sustainability	• Manage people and resources • Enforce policies • Navigate the organization's strengths, weaknesses, opportunities, and threats (SWOT)
Managers Act in the Interest of Employees	*Managers Accomplish This By*
• Provide direction • Provide resources and support • Provide opportunities	• Direction and communication • Facilitation and prioritization • Assessment, providing feedback, and mentoring
Leaders Act in the Interest of the Organization	*Leaders Accomplish This By*
• Establish a vision • Set a course • Champion the cause	• Seeking a higher purpose • Navigating obstacles • Rallying people around a common goal
Leaders Act in the Interest of Employees	*Leaders Accomplish This By*
• Ignite the flames of hope • Lead the way • Inspire higher performance	• Motivating action • Leading by example • Fostering a culture of trust, collaboration, and inclusion

Table 1.2   Leadership and Management Priorities

Leadership	Vision	• A sensible and appealing picture of the future
	Strategies	• A logic for how the vision can be achieved
Management	Plans and tactics	• Specific steps and timetables to implement the strategies
	Project management and budgets	• Plans converted to financial projections and goals

3. *Frequent Turnover: Manager of the Month*

Just as frequently and even more frustrating than having a manager who doesn't understand what it takes to make changes is having multiple managers in a string of successive changes. In the organizations I've worked with, the average tenure of leadership is two years. In some organizations, it is considerably shorter. Two factors drive the revolving leadership door: promotion or failure.

The promotion track requires managers to come on board, make their mark, and promote up to the next rung of the organizational ladder. The best analogy I've ever heard for this "manager of the month" syndrome was illustrated by one of the groups I was training in a leadership seminar. As an ice-breaking exercise, I asked the teams of participants to draw a vehicle that best represented their organization. The group drew a sad-looking dilapidated city bus. They explained that like other city buses, their bus stopped at every corner. But unlike typical buses, it wasn't passengers that got on and off at each stop, rather drivers. The spokesperson for the group explained, "We're riding along in the back of the bus with the windows painted over so we can't see outside of our own organization. We feel the bus slow and stop briefly—just long enough for a new driver to climb aboard. Without talking to us, he or she will reach up and rotate the destination placard and announce, 'Next stop, downtown.' 'Wait!' we'll all shout, 'We just came from downtown.' It doesn't matter, the driver turns the bus around and we cover the same route again as he claims the well-worn path as his new direction for progress. When we're finally making some headway, the bus will come to another stop and the next manager takes the wheel, proclaiming, 'We're heading uptown!'"

Other managers rotate out after making their mark but not the kind of marks they were intending. A common assumption guiding the decisions to promote an effective employee presupposes that those who perform the work well will be able to develop others to become as effective as they were. Unfortunately, just because you can perform a task doesn't mean that you can get others to perform it equally well. Too often, supervisors become "Super Operators." Instead of delegating and working through others, they end up doing the work themselves. Just giving a new title or strapping a radio to the belt does not qualify someone to manage others; managing others requires an entirely different set of competencies than those involved in performing the job tasks. Too often, effective employees are promoted without additional training or preparation to a point where they become less effective. This concept was explained quite eloquently and humorously by Lawrence J. Peter, PhD, and Raymond Hull in *The Peter Principle: Why Things Always Go Wrong* (1993–2002, Buccaneer Books). The authors describe how people are promoted to their level of incompetence. For example, a super competent mechanic is promoted to become a competent supervisor and then gets promoted again to become an incompetent general manager. This manager will either be forced out of the organization or linger at his or her achieved level of incompetence.

And so it goes, managers cycle in and out, expending scarce resources without affecting transformational organizational change—and yet, every one transferring out to a promotion or new assignment declares "mission accomplished" and touts their achievements with bright and shining superlatives as those left behind remain obscured in the swirling dust and debris left in the outgoing manager's wake.

4. Rearranging Deck Chairs on the Titanic: Majoring on the Minors

Management and leadership aside, organizations are frequently very busy changing things that have very little impact on the organization's triple bottom line of sustainability: people, profit, and planet. Organizations can spend significant time and resources changing things that don't matter. Members of the organization are very busy accomplishing the tasks assigned without a view to the overarching purpose that those tasks support. As a result, they "major on the minors." The most common cause of these ineffectual activities is a lack of systems thinking—they are affecting outputs, not outcomes.

An output is the direct result of an activity. An outcome is the overall end result achieved. For instance, I may want to provide training, but having well-trained people is not the actual goal. The actual goal is to have people who behave differently, people who work efficiently to maximize the organization's bottom line. Just because people are trained doesn't mean they actually behave differently. Most people in developed nations have learned that if they eat less and exercise more, they'll typically be healthier, have more energy, live longer, and, if asked, repeat this advice. Unfortunately, far more people know this principle than those actually putting it into practice. That is the difference between outputs and outcomes. The difference between knowing something and acting on it entails a set of drivers and restrainers that are more complex than simple training can effect. Systems thinking helps explain the myriad of factors that drive and restrain behavior. Training is necessary but insufficient to guarantee the desired outcome.

Individuals and organizations can produce desired outputs without achieving a desirable outcome.

5. Lack of Holistic Solutions: The Operation Was a Success but the Patient Died

Even if you are focused on effecting outcomes, it may not be sufficient if you apply the wrong solution. To a hammer, everything looks like a nail. Putting it another way, inexperienced or uninformed managers tend to implement the solutions they happen to be familiar with to any given problem they encounter. If a manager doesn't have a broad understanding of everything involved in changing both processes and behavior, they are likely to apply inappropriate or insufficient solutions. Effective managers need to have what Thomas W. Ross, President of the University of North Carolina, described at the 2011 International Economic Development Council's annual conference as "T" shaped skill sets—managers must have both a breadth of knowledge in multiple disciplines in addition to a significant depth of expertise in their own organization's core competencies of operation. Without both breadth and depth, their solutions will be limited in impact and have limited chances of success.

To illustrate this concept, consider how organizations often apply the latest program that is in vogue, case in point, Lean and Six Sigma (LSS). I am a strong proponent of LSS methods; many of the organizations utilizing the practices and tools of LSS have realized significant increases in productivity and cost savings.

The LSS methodology is founded upon a systems approach and uses the DMAIC Process: Design, Measure, Analyze, Implement, and Control (Figure 1.3) to understand, measure, and implement improvements. In concert with

Figure 1.3   DMAIC process.

the LSS tools, effective project management must be applied for successful process improvement. Without it, process improvement can become an end-less cycle of chaos. There are many project management models, and each of them generally contains the following steps:

Plan → Design/Prepare
Do → Develop/Deploy
Check → Measure
Act → Sustain

Combining the DMAIC process with effective project management helps ensure that the planned changes are implemented and that productivity improves.

The first three steps, Design, Measure, and Analyze, have very detailed tools and prescriptive methodologies that routinely yield initial success when performed rigorously in concert with effective project management. But (there's almost always a "but"), as every LSS practitioner will tell you, these hard-fought gains are difficult to sustain. Organizations backslide. This occurs in many organizations because, unlike the prescriptive first three steps, Implementation and Control stubbornly remain in the realm of the "Art of Management." My experience and observations lead me to believe that this is because the first three steps are tightly tied to operations and processes—tangible things that lend themselves to metrics and measure-ment. Implementation and Control lay squarely in the human resources camp where things aren't so structured. This is the squishy realm of organi-zational change management.

Organizational change is a continuous and complex journey that is a dynamic, on-going process. Because of the interconnectivity of all elements in a system, altering one element usually results in changes in others. For instance, if you implement a new technology, there will usually be changes in the functional and social aspects of the organization as well. Some consequences are easier to predict than others. For instance, if the speed of a machine is increased, vibration and heat associated with the increased speed could cause other mechanical and electrical problems, so it is important to design solutions for these anticipated consequences. Another example might be if the time to process an order increases, as it might when an enterprise resource planning (ERP) system is implemented, then less time will be available for other func-tions and will need to be planned for accordingly. Unfortunately, even well-planned changes can result in unexpected and unintended results. These are referred to as "unintended consequences." It's the unintended consequences that make process improvement so difficult to sustain.

> DEFINITION: The Law of Unintended Consequences—altering any element of a complex system results in other unexpected changes.
>
> **EXAMPLE 1.1**
> ACTION: A company implements a sales incentive program focused on obtaining new clients.
> UNINTENDED CONSEQUENCE: So much focus is placed on gaining new prospects that established clients no longer receive the attention they expect and move their accounts to competitors, resulting in lower overall revenues.
>
> **EXAMPLE 1.2**
> ACTION: An improvement in production efficiency exceeds sales volume leading to a buildup of inventory.
> UNINTENDED CONSEQUENCE: The shutdown of the machine line and the lay-offs of the same employees who worked diligently to improve production.
> COUNTERDEFINITION: No good deed goes unpunished.

Of all the unintended consequences, the ones associated with people are the hardest to foresee. That's why experienced change practitioners say, "The soft stuff is the hard stuff." To manage the people side of process and organizational improvement, it is necessary to establish a rigorous methodology that captures the "art of management" to consistently achieve Implementation and Control. The methodology must be a sufficiently detailed, repeatable, and measurable process similar to what is prescriptively detailed for Design, Measure, and Analyze. You could say that LSS is necessary but insufficient.

Bringing structure to Implementation and Control is one of the main focuses of the Workforce Engagement Equation©. Utilizing the principles contained in this book improves implementation and control. The DMAIC methodology becomes a continuous cycle with no beginning and no end, as shown in Figure 1.4. When a process change is implemented, subsequent behavior changes necessitate further Design, Measurement, Analysis, Implementations, and Controls. It is a continuous journey of process improvement with backsliding and side trips along the way. The real trick to continuous improvement is that even though it's a cycle, you don't want

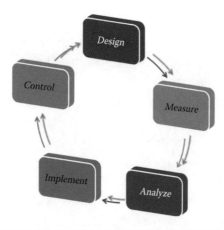

Figure 1.4　DMAIC cycle.

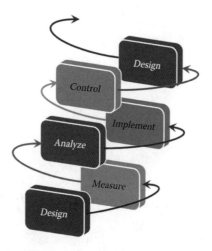

Figure 1.5　DMAIC upward spiral.

to end up back in the same place you started. You want the process to become an upward spiral of continuous improvement, as shown in Figure 1.5. Utilization of the tools and techniques of the Workforce Engagement Equation creates that upward spiral of continuous process improvement.

6. *Failure to Stay the Course: Are We There Yet?*

The sixth reason that changes fail is lack of understanding or anticipation of the amount of time needed to affect changes. In today's economy, the market demands rapid response. This is particularly true for publicly traded companies. Despite the speed of technology, people often require more time to change than the technical aspects of a project. When an organization spends its time chasing short-term results, the organization is whip-sawed back and forth, making sustained progress nearly impossible, as the company shifts to the next project before it has fully integrated the first into its culture.

I was working with a transportation company that had been trying to create engagement through an internal branding and marketing campaign. They wanted their mechanics to see themselves as professionals. The communications department devised logos, slogans, and an extensive advertising campaign. After a time, the mechanics started to adopt this language and make it their own. They designed patches with the catch phrases and incorporated the logos and slogans into the headings of their procedures. Unfortunately, by the time they had started this, corporate communications had already moved on. Not seeing the results they wanted in the short term, corporate communications scrapped the campaign and began initiating a different branding initiative. The mechanics were told to stop using the logos and slogans that they now considered their own. The mechanics became frustrated and resentful—the exact opposite of the desired outcome of creating employee engagement.

It is far better to focus on a few initiatives and stay the course than working by the "spray and pray" approach in which you throw everything against the wall and hope that some of it sticks.

7. Attention Deficit Management: Dismantling What Works

The seventh and final cardinal sin of change leadership is what I like to refer to as Attention Deficit Management. In 1905, George Santayana wrote, "Those who can't remember the past are condemned to repeat it." It's just as true in the twenty-first century as it was in the twentieth. Many organizations I've worked with manage their business as though they are in a dark closet with only a flashlight—whatever the narrow beam illuminates gets managed. If safety is in the spotlight, the major focus of management's attention is on safety. If the beam falls on high costs, they focus on cost reductions. If it falls on quality, nothing else matters at the moment. It is truly as though the company has an attention deficit disorder. Management of single focal points is better known as "firefighting" and keeps the organization in a constant state of turmoil.

My experiences have led me to conclude that one of the significant drivers of Attention Deficit Management is failure to maintain a long-term perspective resulting in insufficient preparation for the future. For example, whenever times get tough and costs need to be cut, training is invariably one of the first casualties. When times are good and the organization wants to implement a change, they pour large resources into training. Once the change is made, training is intentionally shelved or simply allowed to fade away due to neglect. Just as those of us who took a foreign language in school realize, without ongoing practice and use, those language skills atrophy like unused muscles. When we need them next, we have to work even harder to ramp up our skills just to gain back a portion of the ground we lost.

Organizations that don't remain focused on all the aspects required for success remain in a continuous condition of flux. What's more, the reactionary responses to emerging crises are frequently overreactions. These knee-jerk reactions consume precious resources and burn out the organization.

Don't Abandon Hope—There Is a Solution

Now that we've explored the seven reasons changes fail, let's turn our attention to how to make changes succeed. The important lessons to draw from this list of The Seven Cardinal Sins of Change Leadership form the foundation for mastering the human elements of implementing and sustaining process improvement and organizational change.

Stages of Organizational Development

Over the course of decades implementing process improvements and then observing the resultant outcomes, responses, and unintended consequences, patterns begin to emerge. Learning to recognize these patterns allows the process improvement practitioner to understand the drivers and root causes of organizational behavior. With this understanding, effective management and leadership responses can be applied to maximize organizational effectiveness and avoid unintended consequences.

Like process improvement, improving organizational effectiveness is a continuous journey. Like any journey, the process has a beginning, a path, and a destination. And like other journeys, it helps to have a map that outlines the milestones you'll pass along the way to reassure you that you are on the right path or indicate that you may be headed somewhere you don't want to go.

Probably the most widely cited model describing the stages of group development was introduced by Bruce Tuckman in 1965. His article, "Developmental Sequence in Small Groups" (1965, by the American Psychological Association;

Psychological Bulletin, Volume 63, Number 6) outlined a four-stage model: Forming → Storming → Norming → Performing. He amended this model in 1977 by adding a fifth stage: "Adjourning." We'll build upon this model to outline appropriate timing, tools, and techniques for the practitioner to apply.

In the 1990s, John Beck and Neil Yeager refined Tuckman's model with the assertion that Storming is not a foregone conclusion and the stage could be minimized or eliminated altogether with effective leadership. In their work contained in *The Leader's Window* (1994, John Wiley & Sons; 2001, Davies-Black), they modified the model to be Forming → *Focusing* → Performing → *Leveling*. In this new model, Storming only occurs when there is lack of direction and a clear understanding of roles and responsibilities— when the leader hasn't done a good job of Forming and Focusing the team. The Leveling Stage recognizes that if a group doesn't continuously adapt and change to match the shifting competitive landscape, performance plateaus, requiring a new intervention to chart a path of continuous improvement. If an organization doesn't continuously renew itself and adapt, leveling will occur.

Beck and Yeager's research focused on smaller groups and teams. I have adapted the principles observed in small groups to understand and guide larger organizational changes—after all, organizations are larger groups made up of groups of groups.

NOTE: The terms "group," "team," and "organization" are used throughout the book. There are differences between each of these terms; not all groups are teams and not all groups of teams form coherent functioning organizations. To help clarify, the terms "group" and "team" relate to the human factors and their associated needs. The terms "organization" and "organizational" relate to the systems and processes that allow individuals to function as teams and teams to function cohesively as an organization. And, from a practical and pragmatic point of view, just as most projects don't require computations involving Pi to be written out to nine decimal places, 3.14 yields perfectly acceptable results; for the practitioner's toolkit, the differences between functioning groups and organization are really a matter of degree. We will focus on how groups become teams and how multiple teams form functional organizations through interoperable systems. When there are significant differences that affect implementation, they are clearly specified.

So whether your focus is a small team or an entire organization, under-standing these principles enables the practitioner to understand what is occurring within the group and make course corrections to guide the orga-nization to a higher level of performance. Based upon my own observa-tions and experience in implementing team development and organizational changes, I've adapted Beck and Yeager's model further. When evaluating group development, think of each stage as a juncture point through which the group must navigate. Refer to Figure 1.6 as we explore the Stages of Group Development.

Forming → Focusing → Committing → Sustained Performance → Renewal

If the group successfully navigates a stage, it moves to a higher level of cohesiveness and effectiveness. If the stage is not effectively traversed, then group cohesiveness and productivity is impacted. As the group develops, each subsequent stage must be successfully navigated to continue reaching higher levels of effectiveness.

When a stage is not successfully navigated, the group experiences confu-sion, frustration, and lowered productivity. The group cannot simply keep plowing ahead believing that it will all somehow work itself out. Hope is not a strategy. Instead, the group needs to backtrack to explore why the previous stage was not implemented well. When a stage of group develop-ment is not well traversed, the group experiences an alternate, less effective, stage:

Stumbling → Fragmenting → Inconsistent Performance → Leveling

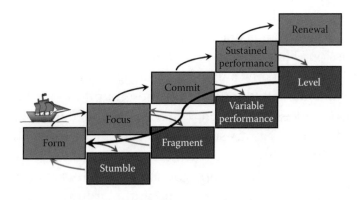

Figure 1.6   Stages of group development.

Intuitive Assessment of Group Developmental Stages

Before we delve deeply into group, team, and organizational development; leadership; and management, let's set a contextual pragmatic foundation. The best management tools are practical enough to use from day to day without requiring unsustainable effort or additional layers of complexity. The reality of our daily work lives is so busy and hectic that managers don't pause to say, "Hmm, I wonder what stage my team is at today?" You have to work and make decisions on the fly, "building the airplane while flying it." That's the strength of this group development model—it's intuitive. Just think about it for a minute: when a group initially forms, it has multiple individual and group needs that must be met for group formation to progress to a higher level of cohesiveness and productivity. Chief among these needs are orientation, trust, and the development of a common vision. If the managers effectively lead the organization through forming, the group begins to focus on the tasks at hand. If the group doesn't form well, they stumble, experiencing internal conflict, frustration, and stalled progress. To quit Stumbling, the needs of the Forming Stage must be readdressed; high-performing groups will not form without meeting the essentials. You can't just assume that these needs will take care of themselves. Too often, managers assume that conflict, power struggles, false starts, and frustration are just a part of normal group dynamics. Assuming that stumbling is just a normal part of group dynamics that will work itself out is one reason that many organizations fail to achieve the results they seek. Granted, stumbling occurs so often it feels like it is just a normal part of group development. I contend that stumbling occurs so often because managers frequently fail to navigate their group through Forming well. They don't take the time to clearly communicate the vision, provide orientation, and build trust. They take these elements for granted and assume that each individual understands and is aligned and committed to their vaguely articulated mission. They also assume that the group norms, standards of behavior, and group dynamics that form during a contentious period will somehow become a solid foundation for the group to move toward sustainable high performance. More often, I've seen dysfunctional norms grow out of unmanaged conflict. Norms such as mistrust, guarded communications, fragmentation, cliques, backbiting, withdrawal, lowered morale, and factional infighting become the group's foundation. Unless resolved effectively, these dynamics linger and fester, preventing the group from ever achieving their objectives.

Every stage in the logic model presented in this book is built upon similar intuitive principles that allow you to sense where the group is at. Each section of this book does contain an in-depth assessment of the stage being evaluated—but once you understand the principles, you don't have to continuously refer back to the detailed evaluation. Use your intuition; be more "directionally correct" than "management micrometer." Sensing where your group is at allows you to understand their needs and what may be lacking as well as what is coming next. This intuition enables you to apply appropriate tools and techniques that help to avoid many of the common pitfalls groups and organizations encounter and helps you build the group and organizational cohesiveness and effectiveness necessary to achieve higher levels of performance.

Parallel Paths—Group Development and Project Management

Addressing only the group's stages of development will not effectively navigate the waters of change. You'll also need to have effective project management skills. Project management needs to be woven into the group development and vice versa. One without the other will not achieve sustainable high performance. To address the project, we'll use a five-stage project management model in parallel with the stages of group development:

Design → Develop → Deploy → Sustain → Continuous Improvement

Combining the parallel paths of project management and group development as shown in Figure 1.7 helps us understand effective navigation of each

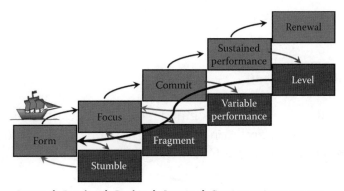

Design → Develop → Deploy → Sustain → Continuous improvement

Figure 1.7 Stages of group development and project management.

stage. Both project management and group development require appropriate management and leadership responses to satisfy the evolving organizational systems' needs as well as the group's needs that emerge during dynamic change initiatives. Remember, each stage is characterized by its own unique set of needs that fall into one of two categories:

1. Team needs
2. Organizational needs

Each set of needs can be satisfied by applying the appropriate set of tools and tactics:

1. Effective management responses
2. Effective leadership responses
3. Effective tools and techniques to analyze and employ

Each stage has desirable outcomes and observable characteristics. These indicators become navigational aids that reveal where the organization is and where it's heading. Without an understanding of the signs, one can become as lost as an inexperienced sailor circumnavigating the globe without even a compass or a sextant let alone a global positioning system. Throughout this book, we will examine the needs of each stage, their indicators, and the tools and techniques that—experience has shown—most efficiently move the group to a higher level of organizational performance. We'll also explore how to recognize when you've begun to drift and how to adjust your organizational sails to the correct course. And just in case, we'll provide you with damage control kits to employ when you've been completely blown off course and are headed toward the rocks of failure.

Book Layout

This book is laid out in discreet segments that align to the stages of group/organizational development. Consider each segment to be an "OAK" plank in your construction. Each plank is made of three sections:

Overview and Assessment
Analysis
Key Takeaways

INTERESTING FACT: We have compared organizational development to a voyage. Throughout this book, we'll continue using the sailing ship analogy. To weather the rough conditions of the open sea, sailing ships need to be built of the strongest and most durable wood available. One of the most effective woods used is oak. Much of the hull, timbers, and spars of the *USS Constitution* were made from oak. The sturdy oak withstood cannon fire so well they nicknamed the Constitution "Old Ironsides." To build a worthy vessel for your own organizational development voyage (and survive the cannon fire you're sure to encounter), we're also going to use OAK (Overview and Assessment, Analysis, and Key Takeaways).

Overview and Assessment begins with a 10-question evaluation. Complete the assessment for your organization. Based upon the results, you will be able to make a quick determination of where your organization is operating along the performance continuum. The assessment will also help you determine which strategies and tactics will help you address areas of performance. The overview section contains a table that summarizes the key indicators, desired outcomes, and a list of individual needs that must be satisfied to successfully navigate the organizational stage. The table cross-references the needs with the tools or techniques that have been shown to effectively satisfy each need.

Analysis examines each organizational stage, the drivers, and provides a step-by-step process to successfully navigate the stage utilizing tools and templates. The Analysis section contains examples and lessons learned.

Key Takeaways contains two tables for each stage. The Project Planning Checklist outlines the project steps that have proven effective navigating through the stage of organizational development previously discussed. The Key Takeaways section concludes with a concept summary table that provides a quick reference and review of the stage's indicators, organizational and individual needs, effective leadership and management responses, and lists of tools and templates applicable for use in navigating that stage. You will be able to refer back to the Key Takeaways section to refresh your memory and as a quick checklist for planning and navigating your voyage.

The book can be read in order, or you can skip between segments to address specific issues or topics according to your interests or needs; the choice is yours.

Breadth versus Depth

One final note about the contents of this book: You will find a broad range of topics covered, many of which can and have filled entire books in and of themselves. It is not the intent to cover all of these topics to the exclusion of other sources. Each topic is discussed in just enough detail to familiarize you with it and to provide some key lessons learned to help you understand when and where the tool or technique can be applied to best navigate the various stages of group and organizational development. Knowing which tool has been shown to be beneficial during particular phases of group development will help you become more effective. If you are not familiar with the tool, seek out references that focus on that tool in sufficient depth to effectively apply it.

Another consideration for you as you learn about the Workforce Engagement Equation is that there are many other excellent tools, techniques, and concepts out there that are not discussed. I encourage you to use your experiences and tools that have worked well in the past along with other sources and build them all into your own vessel of organizational success. Every effective management tool and technique can be built into the Workforce Engagement Equation's Stages of Organizational Development— you the practitioner will have to make the determination when and where.

In addition to a wide variety of topics discussed, at various points you will find that some topics or tools are addressed more than once throughout the book. This is intentional. It is my experience as a practitioner that it is often necessary to readdress, reinforce, and build upon processes, tools, and techniques introduced in an earlier stage of organizational development—this is done to provide just enough just in time. For instance, training is described in several stages, but with each stage, the depth of training increasingly bores down deeper and deeper. When you first introduce a topic, the individual needs to understand the basics. Once they have had a chance to spend some time utilizing the technique, they will be ready to learn more. Each time it is reintroduced, they know it more broadly and deeply. Similarly, other topics are discussed in different stages, addressing different aspects and drilling deeper. Just as different structural elements are constructed within the architecture of a ship, different elements are built into your vessel of organizational success. A foundational keel is laid, then another complementary beam is introduced, and then, at the appropriate time, we'll go back and build further upon the first to construct the intricate patterns necessary to develop the solid vessel of a well-run organization.

Bon voyage!

Chapter 2

Stage 1—Forming: Preparing for the Voyage and Assembling the Crew

Overview and Assessment: Forming

Forming, the first stage of group/organizational development, occurs during the Design Stage of Project Management. When people first come together, they are not a team; they are a group of individuals. When they join the organization or are assigned to a project, they may not fully understand the reason why they are being assigned, nor do they know what part they'll play. They certainly don't know the details of the plan and what they'll gain from their involvement. They may have some initial thoughts, but nothing is well defined for them. They may not have a high degree of trust depending upon their own temperament and past experiences. Even if they are cautiously optimistic and open to join the group, they won't have commitment to the group's function or to the other members of the group.

To move beyond forming so the team could focus on mission accomplishment, the team will need to develop a shared purpose, identity, and commitment. They'll need to gain a widespread understanding of the team's mission and vision. As this information becomes widely known throughout the team, you'll notice a growing sense of excitement as each team member begins to envision how their involvement will impact the team and, in turn, satisfy their own individual needs.

Assessing Where You Are or Where You Want to Go

If you are part of an existing organization, complete the assessment contained in Table 2.1 based upon the general characteristics typically experienced. If you are just developing an organization or a team, you won't have concrete examples on which to base your assessment; in that case, use Table 2.1 to familiarize yourself with the organizational indicators that will help guide you as you navigate your team through the Forming Stage. As your team coalesces, you'll be able to refer back to Table 2.1 to help you navigate along your route toward sustained high performance.

WHAT'S YOUR VIEW OF THE PARADE: One thing I ask clients to keep in mind when performing an assessment is not everyone in the organization will have the same view to the parade. Executives may believe everything is moving along well while frontline workers hold an entirely different opinion. To illustrate this point, imagine we are going to go see Macy's Thanksgiving Day Parade. I arrive early and get pretty good seats on Central Park West just before the 59th Street Columbus Circle. You, on the other hand, have a great view! You were the lucky winner of a contest and are riding high and comfortably in the Goodyear Blimp. After the parade, we meet up and compare notes.

"What did you think?" you ask me.

"It was good; I had a good view of each float, marching band, and troupe of clowns as they cavorted down the parade route. I couldn't really see what was coming up behind each group, and once they travel around Columbus Circle, I lost sight of them as well. But, all in all, I really enjoyed the parade. How was your view?"

"It was amazing! We sat in climate-controlled comfort, sipping mimosas and dining on gourmet cheeses. We had a complete view of the parade and could see it starting on 77th street and marching its way down to 34th street. In addition to that, we had live feed from cameras set up along the route so we saw every detail in high definition on a bank of mounted screens. I loved it! And what did you think of the parade?" you ask a little boy standing nearby.

"It sucked! I couldn't see a thing. It was cold and I was stuck behind a great big guy with gas. I spent the entire parade staring up at his butt trying to get a glimpse of the parade. I will never get up at 4:00 AM to go see that crappy parade ever again!"

These are three views with three very different opinions of the same parade. Keep this in mind as you assess how your team is forming and how systems are working; solicit input from all levels of the organization and from every department and functional area so that you gain a broad view and a truer understanding. Limiting your view to one source or one perspective will limit your ability to effectively manage and lead.

Table 2.1   Forming Assessment

For each of the paired statements or groups of statement below, decide which statement most accurately describes your experiences in the day-to-day work activities within your organization. For the statement that is chosen, check to what degree you believe the statement is either Most or Somewhat like your routine experience within your organization's work activities.

Check only one statement per paired question.

Assessment (Select One)			*Choose the Statement that Best Describes Your Organization*
1	4	Most Like Us	The organization's mission is clearly defined and aligned with the needs of customers, stakeholders, and suppliers.
	2	Somewhat Like Us	
	−2	Somewhat Like Us	The organization is driven less by an overall guiding mission and purpose but is more controlled by individual agendas and disparate, misaligned activities. Rules govern action, not purpose and outcomes.
	−4	Most Like Us	
2	4	Most Like Us	Initiatives are appropriately prioritized and sponsored by senior-level decision makers and staffed with influencers who are key linking pins in the organization such that initiatives carry weight enough to be accomplished, gain buy-in, and be cascaded down through the organization.
	2	Somewhat Like Us	The organization is staffed by individuals with the appropriate competencies and motivations necessary for mission accomplishment.

(continued)

Table 2.1   Forming Assessment (Continued)

Assessment (Select One)			Choose the Statement that Best Describes Your Organization
	−2	Somewhat Like Us	Initiatives do not have adequate senior sponsorship—those responsible for implementing initiatives are not key influencers and do not have sufficient authority within their own department (or across multiple departments if necessary) to garner sufficient support necessary to affect change.
	−4	Most Like Us	
			Members have been assigned in addition to their regular jobs creating ongoing conflicts with other priorities and goals.
3	4	Most Like Us	The organization appropriately prioritizes goals aligned to objectives and outcomes such that sufficient resources (money, materials, manpower, and sponsorship) are applied to maximize the impact and chances for success of initiatives.
	2	Somewhat Like Us	
	−2	Somewhat Like Us	The organization does not adequately resource initiatives either because there are too many initiatives or poor prioritization. The result is that many initiatives are started that peter out due to apathy or change in direction or initiatives struggle along anemically, draining resources while having little significant impact.
	−4	Most Like Us	
4	4	Most Like Us	There is a general climate of trust in the organization. People enter into relations and situations "assuming good intent." Most members know other members as persons. Communication is open and honest among team members. Team members are comfortable sharing information with other organization members.
	2	Somewhat Like Us	
			Relationships are based on trust, mutual respect, and mutual success.
	−2	Somewhat Like Us	Communication is guarded and mostly comes from the top down. Intent is always in question. There is a pervasive judgmental environment where certain characteristics are valued and others are marginalized.
	−4	Most Like Us	
			Relationships are competitive and can become destructive. Weaknesses are something to be hidden, not as opportunities for mutual support.

(continued)

Table 2.1   Forming Assessment (Continued)

Assessment (Select One)			Choose the Statement that Best Describes Your Organization
5	4	Most Like Us	Team members and the team leader know and value each other's styles, strengths, and preferences. They work collaboratively to maximize each member's contributions.
	2	Somewhat Like Us	
			Team members understand and respect the personal values and goals of the other organization members.
			The organization members recognize the particular strengths and potential contribution of each team member creating a mutually supportive environment where members feel valued and vital to mission success.
	−2	Somewhat Like Us	There is little understanding nor concern for individual styles, strengths, and preferences. Team members do not support and at times exploit differences for individual gains.
	−4	Most Like Us	
			Members do not value diversity of ideas, approaches, or styles. Cliques form and there are delineation of who is "in" and who is "out."
			Assignments are given with little regard for individual aptitude, interest, or growth opportunities. With no consideration given to differences and preferences, some individuals are misplaced and struggle in their roles growing frustrated and more and more alienated.
6	4	Most Like Us	Leaders set the tone for effective communication—open and inclusive with clear expectations.
	2	Somewhat Like Us	Leaders adapt their style to the situation matching both the needs of the organization and the needs, abilities, motivation, and confidence of the members of the group.
	−2	Somewhat Like Us	Leaders block or limit communication within the team—creating silos and limiting the "big picture" for themselves in attempts to maintain or increase their own power and control. Leaders often play one member against another creating a climate of mistrust.
	−4	Most Like Us	

(continued)

Table 2.1   Forming Assessment (Continued)

Assessment (Select One)			Choose the Statement that Best Describes Your Organization
7	4	Most Like Us	Structures exist for written and verbal communication along with feedback mechanisms to ensure that communications are cascaded throughout the organization in a timely manner. Key messages are conscientiously crafted with talking points and frequently asked questions such that managers and leaders at all levels can disseminate messages consistently and with adequate detail.
	2	Somewhat Like Us	
	−2	Somewhat Like Us	Communication is haphazard and indirect. People not present in meetings aren't informed in a timely manner. Information is circulated through the "rumor mill," fueling division and a climate of fear or mistrust.
	−4	Most Like Us	
8	4	Most Like Us	The organization has developed and routinely utilizes ground rules on how the organization will function and how members behave and interact. Unconstructive behaviors are dealt with openly in a timely manner with a focus on solving the problems and promoting continuing cohesiveness and effectiveness of the group.
	2	Somewhat Like Us	
	−2	Somewhat Like Us	No clear behavioral expectations exist; organizational norms and standards of behavior are implied, or they are simply "words on the wall." Violations of the group's behavioral norms are not addressed in an open and constructive manner. A double standard may exist where allowances are made for select groups' or individuals' behaviors.
	−4	Most Like Us	
9	4	Most Like Us	Meetings are well planned and adequate time, details, and notification are given such that members come to meetings informed of the purpose and with a good idea of the topic(s) to be covered such that they are prepared to contribute.
	2	Somewhat Like Us	
	−2	Somewhat Like Us	Meetings topics are a mystery until the meeting occurs, leaving members little time to understand the issues, prepare, and unable to make significant thoughtful contributions.
	−4	Most Like Us	

(*continued*)

Table 2.1 Forming Assessment (Continued)

Assessment (Select One)			Choose the Statement that Best Describes Your Organization
10	4	Most Like Us	Each meeting has a designated facilitator. Most of the organization members are effective group meeting facilitators such that if the designated facilitator is unable to attend, another member will step forward to facilitate the meeting ensuring forward progress of the group.
	2	Somewhat Like Us	
			People participate in meetings, contributing productively. Every member knows and feels comfortable intervening if needed to help keep a meeting on track.
			When an organization meeting is over, each member is clear about who will do what and by when.
			Someone is designated as recorder (scribe) whenever a meeting is held and the results of each meeting are shared with all interested parties, including decisions made, actions needed, who is responsible, and projected completion dates.
	−2	Somewhat Like Us	Meetings are generally unstructured, and administrative functions or meetings are not routinely held.
	−4	Most Like Us	Meetings are mostly "tell" events where members listen passively with little input and decisions are basically a foregone conclusion. Meetings routinely stray from main topics to be covered, resulting in excessively long meetings or just not getting to all the topics scheduled to be covered.
			If the designated facilitator is absent, meetings are ineffective or are cancelled because no other team members feel empowered, comfortable, or have sufficient skills to facilitate.
			Meetings end without clear assignments and time constraints, resulting in slow group progress and frequently missed deadlines. It is not uncommon to attend a meeting without having any action taken from previous meetings.

Once you've completed the Forming Assessment Table, transfer your scores into the Forming Scoring Matrix contained in Table 2.2:

Total up your score. The final score will fall between +40 to −40. If your organization scored between 30 and 40, congratulations, you can feel fairly confident that your organization has a well articulated and well understood mission. Less than 30, but more than 20, indicates that there are areas that

Table 2.2 Scoring Matrix—Forming

No.	Score	Element of Forming	Effective Leadership	Effective Management	Tools and Techniques
1		Setting a clear vision for the organization	Defining and communicating a clear vision for the organization	Outlining how the mission will enable the vision	Value proposition
2		Senior leadership involvement	Participating and setting expectations for other senior leadership involvement	Prioritization of initiatives and delegation of authority	Staffing plans and schedules
3		Resource allocation and strategic staffing	Limiting scope of work within limits of resources	Resource allocation and strategic staffing	Dual staffing plans (Teams "P" and "F")
4		Climate of trust, mutual respect, and mutual success	Demonstrating valuing of diversity	Open dialogues and addressing counterproductive behaviors	Johari Window Communications and feedback
5		Team members and the team leader know and value each other's styles, strengths, and preferences	Modeling inclusion	Strength-based delegation	DISC temperaments

		Adaptive situationally based leadership	Expectation setting	Situationally based adaptive leadership
6	Leaders set the tone for effective, open, and inclusive communication	Adaptive situationally based leadership	Expectation setting	Situationally based adaptive leadership
7	Communications are planned, deliberate, and broad reaching	Frequent and direct communication	Planning communications and orientation meetings	Strategic and tactical communications plans and templates
8	Clear behavioral norms are established and broadly observed	Leading by example	Facilitation of team building	Team charters and team ground rules
9	Meetings are well planned in advance and appropriate notification is given	Meeting expectations and participation	Planning meetings	Meeting agendas and notifications
10	Meetings are well run, structured, and productive	Meeting moderation and decision making	Delegation of work assignments	Meeting management, notes and assignments
	Cumulative Forming Score			

need improvement in communication and coordination. As you review the scoring matrix, you will probably find areas where you've scored low. These indicate elements that are missing or not widely applied within your organization. It goes without saying that the lower your organizational score, the stronger the indication that there is not a well defined and cohesive driving strategy guiding your organization and interpersonal communications and interactions may need improvement.

> NOTE: View this, and all other assessments as general directional indicators. They are not designed to provide a statistically validated survey instrument. What this instrument does is helps you ascertain areas where the organization could be strengthened. So, instead of trying to determine if the direction is exactly NNW or NNE, you'll know that the organizational direction is generally northerly and you are heading along a path that will take you closer to your destination or heading in a path counter to your objectives. The reason I don't sweat fractional details is because even very detailed and complex assessments containing hundreds of questions show variation and will be affected depending upon the day and any recent events affecting the organization. If you completed the assessment the day after you win a big contract, the score would be quite different as compared to assessing the organization the day you lose a major customer. Accordingly, use this and all other instruments that follow as directional indicators. They'll help you understand and help you move toward a more functional organization; just don't get bogged down majoring on the minors.

Analysis: Forming

Assembling the Crew

When a group is first assembled, they are not a team, just a group of individuals gathered together. Consider the first time you attended a meeting you'd been "voluntold" to attend. You walked into the room and saw a dozen people sitting around the table. You may have known some of them. Some seemed to know each other. As you sat down you may have been wondering "Why am I here? Who are these people? Will this be a worthwhile use of my time—or will I be one hour closer to death with nothing to show for it?" Chances were that others in the room had the same questions and concerns. To shape a group of individuals into a high-performing

Table 2.3   Summary of Indicators: Forming

	Focus	Commit	Sustained Performance	Renewal
Form	Stumble	Fragment	Variable Performance	Level

Forming: Occurs after individuals first come together as a group and begin to transition from a group of individuals into a nascent team

Team Needs: Individuals joining a new team need
• Orientation
• A sense of purpose
• Building trust

Indicators of Effective Navigation	**Indicators of Ineffective Navigation**
• Shared purpose and identity • Widespread understanding of the team's mission • Growing excitement	• Lack of understanding • Mistrust guarded communication • Anxiety and apprehension

organization these questions need to be answered and their concerns addressed. Table 2.3 summarizes the navigational markers including the team's needs and indicators of successful and unsuccessful navigation associated with forming.

Forging the team from a disparate group of individuals and effectively navigating the Forming Stage requires leadership. Legendary football coach Lou Holz once listed three reasons why someone follows a leader:

1. Can I trust you?
2. Do you care about me?
3. Are you committed to excellence?

I've added a fourth:

4. Are you going somewhere I want to go?

In order for people to follow your leadership you'll need to answers these four essential questions. Addressing the ten elements contained in the Forming Assessment Table will effectively demonstrate to the organization that the answer to each of these four questions is a resounding, "Yes!"

Forming Element 1: Setting a Clear Vision for the Organization

The first element on the Forming Assessment Table asks whether the organization's mission is clearly aligned with the needs of customers, stakeholders, and suppliers. This is the first question to ask when evaluating the effectiveness of your organization because it gets to the heart of organizational leadership; it speaks to the direction the organization is heading. The childhood game of "Follow the Leader" reveals two fundamental characteristics that define someone as a leader; the first is that leaders are going someplace. Leadership involves motion. If there's no motion, then there is no need for anyone to lead. The second fundamental characteristic that defines a leader is that people are following. If no one is following, you're not leading. A game of "Stand around Staring at Each Other Wondering What We Should Do Next" is not nearly as much fun as "Follow the Leader"—although when raising teenagers, you may see this game played more often. In order to lead, you'll need a direction, so we will start by setting a course by defining your value proposition.

Setting a Course: Leading Your Way to Higher Performance—Value Proposition

Let's imagine that we're going to take the best vacation ever. It will be fun, exciting, and completely unforgettable. We are so excited to get started that, without any further discussion, we jump into our separate vehicles and take off without maps in separate directions and at different times. What's the chance that we'll arrive at the same place at the same time? Slim to none. Leading an organization is the same. Before embarking on a journey, you have to determine the destination. For a team to be effective they need to share a common direction and an overarching vision that will coordinate their activities and help shape their decisions through the establishment of priorities.

Most organizations I've worked with had been very busy going about the activities of performing tasks and executing projects; however, many of the activities had very little interaction with each other. These organizations were operating in what is commonly referred to as "silo mentality." Organizational areas often worked within their boundaries and accomplished their assignments with minimal cross-connection and coordination.

In such an organizational condition, even when each independent department is operating efficiently, the organization won't be optimized. There will invariably be redundant activities and inefficient utilization of resources. In addition to being less than optimal, siloed organizations are incubators for conflict. With each organizational structure focusing on its internal activities and priorities there won't be conflicts as long as there are sufficient resources for every disparate area to support its operation. However, as soon as resources become limited, the misaligned needs of the organizational areas will lead to conflict as each entity battles for its own survival. To optimize the organization and minimize internal conflicts organizations need an overarching purpose toward which every activity in every area is aligned; they need an organizational value proposition.

A value proposition is the term that justifies the overall worth of the products, services, or even the mere existance an entity. Every activity consumes resources; the question that remains is whether the resultant outcome of the activity is of greater value than the resources consumed. If yes, value is added; if no, value is lost. Consider the manufacturing process for paper; trees, chemicals, water, energy, manpower, real estate, capital, and time are all consumed in the process. If the resultant value of the rolls or reams of paper is of greater value than the trees left undisturbed in the forest, value is added. However if the the resultant products don't cover the costs of raw materials and manufacturing costs, it would be more profitable to just sell the land.

This example of a value proposition gives only a partial view. Think broader of your organization's value proposition by describing how the activities performed by each area of your organization add value to its customers and stakeholders. Do the activities, products, and/or services of each area add value customers and stakeholders are willing to pay for? Don't fall into the trap of limiting your thoughts to whether the activities benefit the organization—although that is certainly a consideration. Limiting your thoughts to internal users won't act as a catalyst to focus and align the entire organization's activities. Some organizations are so internally focussed they are comparable to self-licking ice cream cones—existing for their own gratification, satisfying nobody else.

An example of failing to consider the value proposition was a community group that met weekly to set up a business incubator. They had a building identified and had spent weeks listing the services, facilities, and activities that would be part of the incubator. I was asked to provide input. After hearing their ideas and thinking about what I had gone through starting up a small business I couldn't think of anything they were proposing that would have been valuable enough to me to join the incubator. They began their equation with what they needed to cover their costs and the costs of the building—not what a potential client would be willing to pay. Prior to that point in time, the group had not met with a single emerging business to ask the fundamental question, "If we build this, would you come?"

To help you determine your organization's or area's value proposition, think about why someone would pay to utilize your services—even if the services you offer are free of charge, they are not free of costs. It takes time and effort to use your services and if they are not adding sufficient value, it's not worth their time and effort to seek you out. There are plenty of nonprofit organizations waiting and hoping for someone to utilize their free services. In very general terms, value proposition falls into one of three categories:

■ Makes money
■ Saves money
■ Solves problems

If your product or service will allow me to make more money than it costs me, it is value added. If your product or service is one I'd use and it's cheaper than other alternatives, it too is value added. And finally, if your product or service solves my problems, than it is value added. Sometimes convenience is seen as value added, "The gas on the corner is a little more expensive, but, it's really close and on the way." I consider that under the category of solving problems. It could also be considered to be lower cost in terms of time and effort.

Two significant exceptions to these three categories come to mind:

■ Brand value—some people may pay more for a Versace purse because of the brand.
■ Charitable value—people often donate to charities or buy products to benefit good causes because they feel that their efforts benefit a greater cause and believe it is worth the cost.

Other than a few exceptions, to create a sustainable organization it is necessary to define the value you add in the common terms. When times get tough, people tend to give less to charities and they don't spend more on luxury items.

Table 2.4   Value Proposition Worksheet

Product or Service	Why Would Anyone Use It?	Is It Worth It?

To define your organization's or area's value proposition take a few minutes to consider your organization's products or services in terms of the customer's or stakeholders perspective. To facilitate the definition process, complete Table 2.4.

Having defined your organization's value proposition, you are now ready to begin constructing a sustainability engine.

Building a Sustainability Engine—Part 1: Forming

Organizations that are most competitive and sustainable have a well-defined value proposition. However, particularly in turbulent times of global competition, there are no guarantees that simply having an overarching purpose alone will assure survival of the organization. A value proposition is not valuable unless the organization or area is able to consistently deliver on that value proposition. Recall that the second cardinal sin of change leadership described "idea people"—those individuals who have big ideas but don't know how to translate those big ideas into reality. They are unable to effectively transform ideas into broad strategies that are then achieved through tactics but naively expect the organization to transform around their ideas like spring follows winter—this rarely happens. If you are seen as an "idea person" with grand schemes and visions that needlessly consume time and resources, your credibility will suffer, and people won't trust you enough to follow.

Transforming visions into a new reality is most effeciently accomplished utilizing a systematic approach of applying project management skills in concert with your leadership. The sustainability engine shown in Figure 2.1

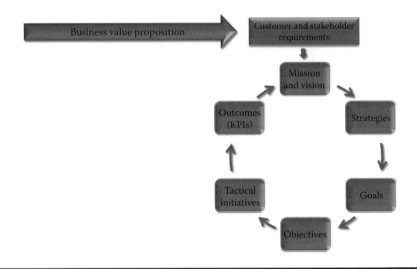

Figure 2.1   Simple sustainability engine.

is a diagrammatic model that helps think through how organizations align around the value proposition and convert the strategies into day-to-day activities. Each step in the engine's cycle breaks down the preceding step into finer, more granular details that are both measurable and directly actionable.

Once you've defined your value proposition, describe it in terms of customer and stakeholder requirements. These requirements will help you then define your mission and vision. The mission and vision is subsequently broken down into strategies. Goals are created to accomplish the strategies. Individuals are assigned objectives to accomplish the goals. Tactical initiatives in the form of projects and or activities are performed which will yield outcomes. The effectiveness of these outcomes is measured in terms of key performance indicators (KPI). The KPIs are evaluated to determine how effectively the mission was accomplished and to what degree the vision was achieved. We'll outline in detail how to break the vision and mission down into actionable goals and activities in the Focusing Stage, but first, let's explore the number one essential question asked of leaders, "Can I trust you?"

Forming Element 2: Senior Leadership Involvement

Forming Element 1 evaluated whether you could describe your organization's destination so that people understand it. Even if they understand it, people will only follow if the destination aligns with their personal values and aspirations. We won't spend too much time talking about this; I'll leave it to you to determine if your organizational destination is desirable to your team members. Let's assume your destination is a worthy one; next, people will only willingly follow if they trust.

Trust is the currency of change. If people are going to step out of their comfort zone and abandon the status quo, they have to trust that the journey will be worth it. Trust is one of those elements that are hard to quantify but people "know it when they see it." Trust involves aspects both personal as well as professional. It is the confidence that your actions are consistent with your words. On the professional front, trust depends upon the degree to which others respect and value your skills and judgment. Prior to people putting their trust in you personally, they have to first trust that the organization itself is supportive of the change. They may trust that you are an honest person with good intentions, but they won't be willing to take risks and go the distance if they don't believe you have the capacity to deliver. Trust in the organization relies on the prioritization of resources: staffing and projects.

A large part of people's willingness to trust and commit to a change initiative will depend upon who is involved. Element 2 in the Forming Assessment Table ranked whether the organization was staffed with individuals who have the appropriate competencies and motivations necessary for mission accomplishment. Too often project teams are staffed by default or with people whose absence will have the least impact on their area's day-to-day operations. Very often managers want to keep their "A-Team" under their direct control doing the work they believe is most important. Consequently, when called upon to staff special projects they send the individuals they feel they can most live without. Anyone who has been with the organization for any length of time will recognize when key influencers and decision makers are not supportive of the project. Too often, senior staff members take a "wait and see" approach to change initiatives. They are too cautious and more concerned about how appearances will affect their personal career aspirations. If the project turns out to be a "stinker" they don't want to get any on themselves. So, instead of taking a risk to change, they apply platitudes and lip service to changes. In this way they maintain a level of plausible deniability. If the project succeeds, they can ride the coattails to success; if it fails, they will not be guilty by association. To maximize the chances of a project succeeding, senior managers need to be involved and visibly committed.

Appropriate Delegation of Authority

How many times have you had accountability without the appropriate level of authority? Too often initiatives are assigned to junior staff members that don't have the organizational authority to harness the resources required to affect change (this is particularly true when changes affect multiple departments outside the project leader's jurisdiction). The project leader is assigned to change procedures and affect behaviors where they don't have the authority or influence to affect the changes. In addition, the reward structures in the other departments often remain aligned to the status quo. People don't see any substantial benefit for working on projects outside their primary roles and responsibilities for which their performance is primarily evaluated.

This often occurs with "grass roots" initiatives. It's not that getting involvement at the operations level is not critical to success, but, grass roots alone rarely have the organizational firepower required to modify entrenched organizational behaviors. This is why it is essential that senior level leadership is directly involved and directly accountable for accomplishing change initiatives. The greater the degree of change, the higher the level of authority will be required to affect the change. If the change initiative is to be successful, ensure that it has appropriate sponsorship and leadership.

Project Charters

One effective tool that helps ensure the appropriate sponsorship, leadership, scope, and authority of a newly forming team is the development of a *team charter*. Team charters have gotten a pretty bad reputation in many organizations. They are sometimes seen as a pointless exercise in which a large amount of time and effort is expended "wordsmithing" verbose sentences full of buzz words, jargon, and cliché statements about quality, productivity, and efficiency that then get filed away and serve no further purpose. Unfortunately, reality too often supports this perception. If the only point of crafting a charter is to check a box—don't waste your time. However, if you look to the intent of the charter it can serve a critical role setting expectations and defining the scope of the team. Table 2.5 defines the elements of an effective team charter.

Team Charters and Organizational Stages

Once the charter is developed and approved, it will significantly help navigate the forming process by facilitating the team's understanding of the

Table 2.5 Elements of a Team Charter

Vision statement	The vision statement explains the future state to which the team's activities aspire to take the organization.
Objective statement	The objective statement is the immediate outcomes the team will accomplish. This statement forms the basis by which the team's effectiveness will be measured.
Scope of work	The scope of work defines the span of impact for the team's activities. Establishing a challenging yet realistic scope of work is essential to the team's ultimate success.
Key stakeholders	Key stakeholders define the individuals and groups who will be directly affected by the team's activities. Typically, stakeholders include customers, suppliers, leadership, and operations.
Partners and resources	Partners are the groups with whom the team will work. Resources are the financial, material, and human capital that will be made available to the team.
Deliverables	Deliverables define the products, services, decisions, and other activities that will be a direct output of the team's activities.
Communication plan	It is important to outline the communications plan that will be crucial to keeping stakeholders and partners informed of the team's activities, needs, decisions, and progress. The communications plan should also define feedback channels to ensure that information is flowing both from and to the team.
Key challenges and assumptions	It is important for the team to identify the challenges the team will face along with the assumptions the team has made as it makes its plans. At a minimum, assumptions will usually include the support the team will receive, the resources that will be made available, and degree of authority with which they are empowered.
Team sponsor(s)	The team sponsor defines which executive leader or leaders will be directly accountable for supporting the team, defining priorities, ensuring resources, helping to resolve conflicts and remove barriers as well as provide the ultimate assessment of the quality and effectiveness of the team's accomplishments.
Team leader(s)	The team leader(s) is the individual(s) directly responsible for guiding the members and supporting the team's day-to-day activities.
Team members	The list of team members should include both full- and part-time team members as well as the expected available time that each will have to work on the project.

vision, the scope, the resources, and project's importance—all things critical to forming well. But the Forming Stage is not the only time in which the charter will be useful; in fact, it often proves more important in later stages.

Purpose of the Team Charter during Focusing

Having a charter that all team members have ownership of will be important when the crew is in the Focusing Stage. During the Focusing Stage, the team conflicts really begin to surface—you're past the polite "honeymoon" stage and are getting down to the work of the team. If you have taken the time to develop the charter, it will help ensure that people stay on point as focusing proceeds along. However, when differences of opinion, style, approach, or prioritization arise, having a well-crafted charter will help the team weigh the two conflicting elements and select the one that most effectively moves them toward the stated objective agreed to in the charter. Think of a charter as building bridges before the flood.

Purpose of the Team Charter during Committing

The team charter will also play a role during the Committing Stage. Commitment forms when people embrace the mission of the organization as their own while working toward clear integrated goals within a culture of inclusion. Referring back to the charter during this stage helps assure people that they are indeed on track. Their confidence rises as they see that the systems developed during the Focusing Stage are indeed moving them closer to their objectives; as their confidence increases, so does their commitment.

Purpose of the Team Charter during Sustaining Performance

Aboard ship we had a saying, "The more you work, the more you work." This humorous, cynical, and rather sarcastic observation of the individual rewards that come from hard work was actually an acknowledgment of "scope creep." As the team proves effective and makes progress, other managers, leaders, and departments will want to get a piece of the action. "Special projects" are assigned that have less and less alignment to the core mission of the team. As individuals are pulled in competing directions, their overall effectiveness becomes degraded. As they try to satisfy everyone, they end up satisfying no one. Use the charter as a shield to keep these distracters away from the team. If the projects make sense and add to the organization's value proposition, you have three choices:

1. Add the new work to the team as an enhancement and refine the charter to reflect the expanded mission. If this option is chosen, ensure that the timeline and available resources are also adequately adjusted as well as any other element of the charter that is impacted by the added scope of work.
2. Create a separate project team with adequate resources to accomplish the project without diverting the primary team from continuing to accomplish the primary mission.
3. Direct the project to the organizational team or department whose mission is aligned to the new project so that those who should be accountable for the work are responsible for completing it.

Option 3 usually requires the executive sponsor to push back against the infringing scope creep when outside managers seek to have others accomplish the tasks for which they are rightly accountable. Consider this parallel military axiom: "For all those people who are willing to work there are others who are willing to let them." Too often, effective teams become overburdened with ancillary tasks and assignments that are beyond their responsibility. We will discuss this more when we discuss the ineffective management style of "riding the good horse" in Committing Element 6.

Purpose of the Team Charter during Renewal

Just as the team charter is important to Forming, it is equally important for Renewal. As new members join the crew, they'll need to become oriented, and the team charter is a solid base for maintaining message continuity. Even without the addition of new members, the charter is important to help the group remain effective. Over time, the organizations can drift. It's helpful to pull out the charter on occasion, dust it off, and ask, "Are we still effectively accomplishing our objective?" If the answer is, "not so much," then, the group will need to reform, refocus, and recommit to ensure ongoing effectiveness.

Take a few minutes to review the blank charter template contained in Table 2.6. What's your organization's vision? Objective? Is the scope of work appropriate? This template will help develop your team's charter.

NOTE: A team charter template is contained in the companion CD, which can be utilized and modified to support the formation of your team.

Table 2.6   Team Charter Template

Vision statement	
Objective statement	
Scope of work	
Key stakeholders	
Partners and resources	
Deliverables	
Communication plan	
Key challenges and assumptions	
Team sponsor	
Team leader	
Team members	

Forming Element 3: Resource Allocation and Strategic Staffing

Along with senior-level sponsorship, change initiatives need to be staffed with a talented team. Without the appropriate people on the team, the decisions and design may not be of sufficient quality and may lack the credibility essential to their being implemented. If the project is worth expending time and resources on, ensure that the team is staffed with those capable of effecting the required changes. If it's not worth staffing appropriately, it's not worth doing.

Given the finite supply of effective change agents and resources, it is particularly important to limit the number of projects and initiatives to those that will make a substantial impact. There is a German proverb that states "He that attempts too much accomplishes too little." Too often, organizations take a shotgun approach to change. They try to change everything all at once. Entertaining everyone's priorities and initiatives needlessly expends scarce resources with little positive impact. It is far better to work on the few key elements that directly improves the value proposition rather than working on everyone's pet project in a misguided attempt to not offend.

Dual Staffing Plan (Team "P" and Team "F")

Most change initatives occur within existing organizations. At the same time that the new future state is being defined and the organization is being redesigned, the organization is expected to continue to operate and accomplish its core mission. The organization is essentially rebuilding the airplane while flying it. Adding complexity, some change initiatives are not specially staffed; instead, the projects fall under current staffing objectives as "other duties as assigned." Depending upon the scope and degree of change, this requires individuals to wear multiple hats and juggle competing priorities. Granted, it is typically within every manager's expected responsibilities to improve the effeciency and productivity of their area of operations. However, depending on the scope and breadth of the change, these competing priorities can become overwhelming, and the quality of their current work declines or the change initiative is abandoned. Lack of resources and competing priorities are significant barriers to successful change initiatives. Accordingly, if the need to change is compelling enough and the span of impact is broad enough, then two teams should be formed: Team "P" and Team "F."

Team "P" is responsible for maintaining present operations. Team "F" is all about reshaping the future. Forming two teams engages the entire organization and utilizes everyone's talents by meaningfully engaging them in either improving present operations or crafting future operations, processes, and products. When prioritizing work, the organization will need to support both teams at once. Team "P" feeds Team "F" until the enterprise's future vision becomes the present reality.

Essential Framework of Teams

Since much of the work of the organization will be performed through collaborative work teams, it is important to understand the five structural timbers that form the framework of effective teams, shown in Figure 2.2

1. Team composition
2. Communication and coordination
3. Team working approach
4. Systems, procedures, and roles
5. Mutual accountability

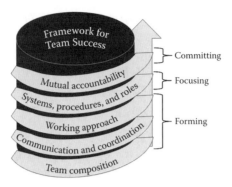

Figure 2.2   Framework for team success.

The first three timbers are laid down during the Forming Stage of organizational development. Systems and procedures will be developed during the Focusing Stage. As the systems and procedures are developed, the team's working approach, communications and coordination, and even its composition may be altered to focus the team on the work at hand. Although you will see signs of it during each stage, mutual accountability really won't become fully apparent until the Committing Stage.

Teams are made up of individuals. For the team to accomplish its work, each individual must possess the necessary skills to complement each other's and to fulfill the tasks assigned in order to realize the team's purpose. Assigning individuals to teams should be deliberate, with due consideration given to what each individual will contribute to the accomplishment of the mission. Because of its critical importance, we will return to explore the elements of team composition repeatedly.

Forming Element 4: Climate of Trust, Mutual Respect, and Mutual Success

One of the dangers of forming two teams is the accompanying assignment of value judgments. Many times the team selected for crafting the future are seen as special. They get to attend special meetings, eat special food, wear special jackets, and get special access to organizational leaders and knowledge. This special focus can leave those left to attend to day-to-day operations feeling second rate, frustrated, and resentful (especially if the manager staffed Team "F" for convenience and kept the most qualified workers tending to their primary jobs). These feelings of resentment can lead to lower productivity and maladaptive behaviors. Team "P" can undermine the work of Team "F" through noncompliance or even outright sabotage.

Avoiding dysfunctional internal competition will require special focus and effective leadership. Team "P" needs to understand the reason for the change initiatives and understand the integral role they play in shaping the organization's future. Leadership must ensure appropriate communications and involvement that engage Team "P" and help ensure widespread understanding and buy-in into the change initiatives.

Role of Communications in Building Trust

The second timber in the Framework for Team Success shown in Figure 2.2 is communication and coordination. Almost every leader and manager I've worked with lists poor communications as a significant barrier to effective operations. Two factors seem to contribute most significantly to this pervasive problem: assumptions and lack of time.

When an organization is going through the upheaval of change, people get stressed and the level of activity becomes frenetic. Since people are inherently "sense making," they try to make sense of the activities they see around them by making assumptions and assigning motives to the actions of others. "I wasn't invited to that meeting because…"—people fill in the gaps of what they don't know with assumptions. Without a strong climate of trust, the motives assigned to others tend to be more negative. To gauge your organizational climate compare and contrast your organization with descriptions of climates of trust versus mistrust contained in Table 2.7.

Cultures grow from fact and from perception. It should go without saying, but the most important element to help develop a climate of trust is to be trustworthy. This truth seems so obvious that it need not be stated; however, in reality, it is more complex than simplistic because people have an innate ability to justify their own behaviors. *We tend to judge others by their actions and judge ourselves by our intentions*—two very different standards. Compare what is said about others to what we think about ourselves.

> "He was late for our meeting so obviously he doesn't value other people's time."
> "I was running late because I got caught up in a previous meeting scheduled across town and there was traffic and…"

Table 2.7   Climates of Trust and Mistrust

Climate of Trust	Climate of Mistrust
• Communication is open and honest among team members.	• Communication is guarded and mostly comes from the top down.
• Mutual regard forthrightness—most members know other members as persons and appreciate the differences between styles and approaches.	• Diversity of personality, temperament, and styles are not valued so people build and maintain defensive facades.
• Team members are comfortable sharing information with other organization members.	• There is a pervasive judgmental environment where certain characteristics are valued and all others are marginalized.
• Relationships are based on trust, mutual respect, and mutual success	• Relationships are competitive and can become destructive.
• Team members rely on each other and trust that others will live up to their commitments and obligations.	• Individuals do not trust that others will fulfill obligations and commitments, and the quality of what is delivered is suspect.
• Risk taking is encouraged.	• Debilitating caution is pervasive— weakness is not allowed.

Creating mutual awareness and mutual respect goes a long way toward building trust. The most elegant and insightful model I have worked with for examining our relationships with others was first introduced in 1955, when Joseph Luft and Harry Ingham published a model of human interaction they called the Johari Window—the name is a combination of Joe and Harry (Luft, J. and Ingham, H. 1955. The Johari Window, a graphic model of interpersonal awareness. *Proceedings of the Western Training Laboratory in Group Development.* Los Angeles: UCLA).

Opening the Johari Windows

I like boxes. Boxes keep everything neat and organized. In a matter of minutes, a completely disorganized mess can look great through the magic of boxing stuff up (granted, the mess has just been transferred to the inside of a disorganized box and you may not be able to find anything—but, dang, it sure looks better!). Because I like boxes, I really like the Johari Window. Everything that is known, is not known, will be known, and will never be known in the universe can be packed neatly into four little boxes. Don't believe it? Just look at Figure 2.3. Wouldn't you agree that when it comes to all the knowledge in the universe, you either know it or you don't? You may learn it or you may have forgotten it, but at that moment, you either know it or you don't. And, wouldn't you agree that others know it or they don't? So, applying these headers, everything gets packed into four little boxes. At this point you may be thinking, "So what?" Fair enough, let me explain how these four little boxes really help to understand personal relations and the development of trust.

Look at the upper left quadrant of the Johari Window shown in Figure 2.4. If something is known by you and known by another person,

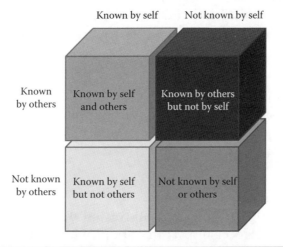

Figure 2.3   Universal storage boxes.

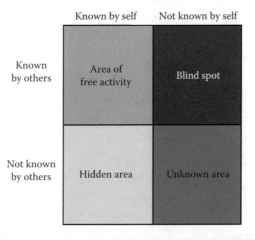

Figure 2.4   Johari Window.

then you can talk about it. This is an area of *free activity*. Items in this quadrant can be talked about and explored because both parties involved already know the facts so there is no reason to hide or avoid them.

Moving to the upper right quadrant you have information that is known to others but not known to yourself. This is a blind spot. Others can see it, but you can't. It could be something physical like that spinach in your teeth, your zipper hanging wide open, or the way you made a fool of yourself angering all the other team members when you went on and on about how your idea is the best when a decision had already been made. Everyone else is well aware of it, but you can't see it.

The lower left quadrant represents items you know that others don't. This is the hidden area. It may be hidden by design, or it may just have never come up; either way, it is hidden nonetheless.

The lower right quadrant is the unknown area—unknown to self and unknown to others. This may come into play when you have a strong emotional reaction to something that is said or done. The others involved say, "Wow, we had no idea you felt so strongly about that." And you, somewhat embarrassed, respond, "Me neither, but from now on, let's never order sushi from Joe's Dog Stand ever again."

Shifting Boxes

The power of the Johari Window comes from understanding the shifting dynamics in a relationship. Think about what is known between two strangers when they first meet. The only thing known by both that is safe to talk about is the weather. Most people typically don't want to strike up a conversation with a stranger to discuss politics or religion. And if they do, it becomes "awkward"! For strangers, the window of free activity is very small as shown in Figure 2.5. As you get to know someone, the window begins to open more and more as the relationship evolves and deepens. Think about a significant relationship in your own life. There are things you feel freely talking about with them that you would never share with others—your hopes, your fears, that weird mole on your left buttocks.

For a relationship to be really healthy, the area of free activity must be quite large as shown in Figure 2.6. It will never be 100%, nor would you want it to be. There will always be some things that you keep to yourself; there will always be some blind spots we maintain as defense mechanisms (if there weren't, we probably would never get out of bed in the morning);

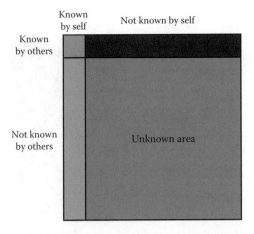

Figure 2.5   Johari Window—Strangers.

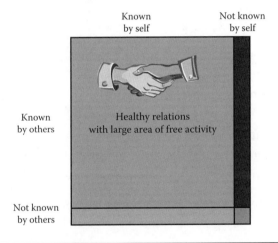

Figure 2.6   Johari Window—Healthy relations.

there will always be the mysteries in life that we will never know. This is as it should be.

Where relationships get strained is when the window of free activity remains small and another window dominates. For instance, you have probably worked with someone that seems to be utterly oblivious to how their behavior affects others. As shown in Figure 2.7, they are like an elephant in a china shop stomping around, damaging fragile relations, creating tension, hurting feelings, and destroying the ability of the team to work harmoniously.

Equally destructive to effective relations is the individual whose motives remains hidden like a venomous snake concealed in the tall grass

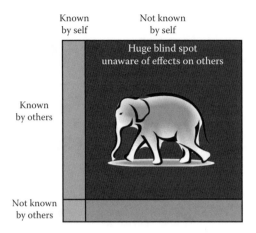

Figure 2.7   Johari Window—Blind spots.

(Figure 2.8). You've probably worked with individuals who obviously know much more than they are willing to share or seem to be working toward a hidden agenda. When you sense that the other may have ulterior motives, you don't trust them. And you certainly aren't willing to give them any more information if you can help it.

The last category represents those individuals that seem to have very little awareness about themselves or anyone else. They are like the ostrich shown

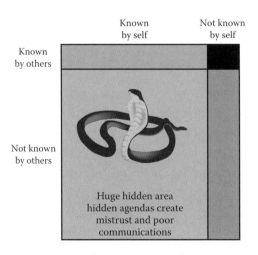

Figure 2.8   Johari Window—Hidden agendas.

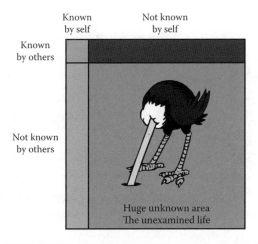

Figure 2.9   Johari Window—The life unexamined.

in Figure 2.9; they keep their head in the sand such that you may wonder, "How have they lived so long and know so very little?"

Opening Windows

To develop healthy, trusting relationships requires the increase of the area of free activity of the Johari Window to become closer to the ideal. This requires that you push down the barriers of what's not known by others and push back what's not known by the self, as shown in Figure 2.10.

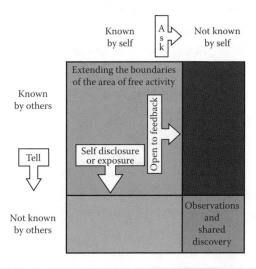

Figure 2.10   Johari Window—Keys to open and healthy relations.

You reduce what's not known to others by talking, by sharing information freely, and by being candid. Be open with people. Tell them what you can. If you can't tell them something, be up front about it. People recognize that you may not be able to share everything for a variety of reasons from confidentiality to nondisclosure agreements, but being as open as you can promotes trust. Answering "I know but just can't talk about it" is more acceptable then being evasive.

You reduce what's not known by the self by listening, by being open to feedback, and by observing. Be aware of the reactions that others are having. Be observant of body language, tone of voice, and the many unspoken cues people give about how they are receiving you and how they are feeling. This will help you gauge your own effectiveness. In addition, being open invites others to give you feedback. Believe me, it is far, far better to find out early that your zipper is undone rather than give your entire presentation with people focusing on something other than your message.

Forming Element 5: Team Members and the Team Leader Know and Value Each Other's Styles, Strengths, and Preferences

We've talked about staffing two teams, Team "P" and Team "F"; we've also talked about the need to communicate and involve all levels of the organization in designing the new organizational structure. Think about the first three timbers of the Framework for Team Success, shown again in Figure 2.11. The success of teams in achieving the change initiative will greatly depend upon who staffs the different teams (team composition), how

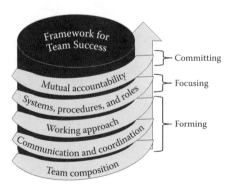

Figure 2.11   Framework for team success.

the two teams interact with each other (communications and coordination), and how the individual team members collaborate to solve problems and interact among themselves (working approach). This requires that each and every team member must first be self-aware and each must be aware and appreciative of the differences of others. An effective method to expand both self-awareness and the awareness of others is through education of temperament styles and preferences. This awareness of inherent strengths, blind spots, and limitations will also help in making the decision of how to staff the teams such that the organization plays to the inherent strengths of its members.

Self-Awareness: DISC—Personality Temperaments and Preferences

NOTE: The quick overview of the DISC personality model and principles is not intended to be an all inclusive study of the topic—that would require a book unto itself. The intent is to become familiar with these concepts to form a common language that will be referred to extensively throughout the remainder of the book.

For your own organizational work, I recommend that if understanding self and others is needed, you may want to work with one of the many excellent firms that specialize in training the DISC concepts.

Socrates famously exhorted each of his students to, "Know thyself" as the first tread on the path to wisdom. Knowing yourself begins with self-awareness. When you understand yourself, you recognize and accept your natural tendencies, your strengths, and your weaknesses. This level of understanding helps you become aware of your inherent blind spots. Being aware of your blind spots won't change the fact you have them, but it will allow you the opportunity to put controls and feedback mechanisms in place so that you are not blindsided by them as frequently. As your self-awareness increases, you will find that you have more conscious control of your behavior and, to some extent, your emotions. You'll be better able to adjust your behavior to various situations to better affect desirable outcomes. You'll also be able to communicate your needs and desires more effectively, thereby improving collaboration and productivity and reducing conflict with others.

Behavioral-Based Model of Temperaments and Preferences

Since you first became aware that you were an independent little person, separate from your mother, you've come to recognize that you are not the same as other people. There are some who are similar to you with whom you relate and easily establish relationships, and there are others that are so alien to you, even simple interactions are tense and strained; you struggle to understand why they act the way they do, and you may become frustrated and withdraw from them or become angry and attack them. These interactions color future interactions creating a downward spiral of misunderstanding. Fueling this frustration is our tendency to assign our motives to others actions. To be perfectly honest, we really have no idea why others speak and act as they do; but that doesn't stop us from interpreting those actions and assigning the motives that, we believe, account for the observed behavior. Frequently, we're wrong.

VALUING DIVERSITY: In today's landscape of "political correctness," valuing diversity mainly refers to race—it has been expanded to gender, sexual preference, and religious beliefs to some degree. In my experience, this focus is actually counterproductive and has very little impact in changing someone's prejudices. Highlighting differences accentuates those differences—I see what I'm looking for. Truly valuing diversity focuses on our similarities and our strengths—what each of us brings to the table. When we all begin to understand the differences in temperament and working approach, we see that regardless of race, color, creed, or sexual orientation, we all have something we bring that strengthens our organization and helps each of us achieve our overall goals. Only when we do this do we overlook the physical differences and bond together in mutual support toward mutual success; only then will we ever achieve Dr. Martin Luther King Jr.'s dream.

FAMOUS QUOTE: "I have a dream that my four little children will one day live in a nation where they will not be judged by the color of their skin but by the content of their character."

—Martin Luther King Jr. (August 28, 1963)
American Civil Rights Activist (1929–1968)

To improve your ability to interact with a wider variety of diverse people, it helps to have framework to characterize and categorize general personality types. By understanding the different personality types, or temperaments, foundational guidelines can be outlined for becoming more effective with each. There are many very good personality profile models in use today: The Big Five Factors, Four-Quadrant Models, Myers–Briggs, Keirsey, and Marston just to name a few. Over the course of years, I've utilized assessments and team profilers based on various models and found that each provides some useful insight and each overlaps the other as they seek to explain human interactions. It's been my experience that it doesn't matter which model you use just as long as the theory lends itself to practical application and benefits:

- Provides insight into individual temperament and interpersonal relations
- Improves communications through the use of a common language that enhances working relations
- Integrates diverse personalities into the work flow and improves group decision making
- Aids in conflict resolution

Some models are more complex than others, and some tend to be more theoretical rather than practical. Each of these models has various measures and degrees to assess where an individual's traits fall along a spectrum from one extreme to another.

CAUTION: Many personality profilers are seen as "pop psychology" that don't have a clinical basis sufficient to be considered true validated psychological testing instruments like the Minnesota Multiphasic Personality Inventory (MMPI) or the California Psychological Inventory (CPI). I agree. What's more, these trait assessments should never be used in order to "fix a defective employee." I've seen too many managers forge an ounce of psychology into a career-killing weapon used to vindicate their own pet peeves and narrow-minded preconceived ideas and prejudices—"Sally won't get promoted to be a director because she doesn't have the right stuff," i.e., she's not like me so she must not be fit to lead. The interpretation of psychological tests requires considerable training to score and interpret. Making decisions that affect others' careers should never be done casually.

That being said, it doesn't mean that these instruments aren't beneficial tools when used appropriately and with good intent to build stronger, more functional relationships. In fact, I contend that understanding personality is essential to your success as a manager, as a leader, as a parent, and in life in general. I just caution you to use such instruments within the limits of their capability and only for the edification of others.

Personally, I've always enjoyed studying the Myers–Briggs temperament model (in case you're wondering, I'm an ENTP—an **E**xtraverted, **In**tuitive, **T**hinking, **P**erceiver for what that's worth). As much as I like Myers–Briggs, within my own experience, I've had more success helping individuals and teams understand each other, improve relations, and effect more lasting changes utilizing the DISC model. Whereas the Myers–Briggs model is predicated upon intrinsic, unseen drivers, in contrast, the DISC methodology is based upon observable behavior. This removes the need to assign our motives to others' actions from the equation. It doesn't matter why they did it; the fact is they did it.

The DISC model is a four-quadrant methodology derived from the intersection of two axes: relative power versus priority of focus. The DISC model was first proposed by William Moulton Marston in his 1928 work (Marston, W. 1928. *Emotions of normal people*). At a time when most of his contemporaries were viewing psychology through the perspective of Sigmund Freud and his focus on abnormal and aberrant behaviors, Marston wanted to understand normal people. While the disciples of Freud were busy defining psychoses, neuroses, and just plain nuts, Marston wanted to better understand those of us who weren't tilted toward the extremes. He set out to study those who didn't want to kill their fathers and weren't fixated on anal retention. You know the ones, those people who get up every day, go to work, manage to pay the mortgage, walk the dog, raise their kids, and take a trip to the shore every other year or so.

Marston began his observations exploring why people took action or refrained from acting. In general, he found that people took action when they felt that the odds were in their favor to effect an outcome they desired. When people didn't feel that the odds favored them, they didn't act. This concept can be illustrated along an axis, as shown in Figure 2.12. Marston viewed one element of behavior as the balance of personal power as compared to the environment. If you believe you are more powerful than the situation you are

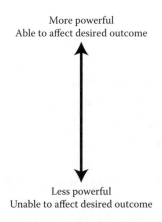

Figure 2.12   Original DISC perspective: balance of power.

in, you will tend to act; if you feel less powerful, you will tend to refrain from acting. Now situations can change from moment to moment, but on average, some people tend to see themselves as generally powerful and able to shape the world they live in to conform to their will; others are more cautious in their estimation of their personal power and conclude that, on average, they are less powerful than the forces that shape the world; therefore, they are less prone to act or act only after deeper consideration.

Marston considered the second element that affected temperament along a horizontal axis that represented the degree to which a person viewed the world as a favorable and accepting place or as a hostile and challenging place. The DISC model considers these two axes perpendicular to each other, as shown in Figure 2.13. Marston's hypothesis asserted that the relative balance of these two perspectives interacted with each other to shape four

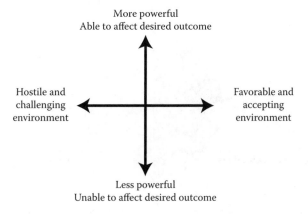

Figure 2.13   Perception of relative power versus perception of the environment.

basic DISC temperaments. Imagining how someone would act according to these two intersecting perspectives helps make the DISC model quite intuitive, as shown in Figure 2.14.

If I imagine myself as more powerful than the environment (area above the horizontal axis) and I view that environment as adversarial or hostile (to the left of the vertical axis), I will act to dominate my situation. Marston labeled this combination *dominance*. The upper left quadrant is labeled as "D" for dominance.

Consider the upper right quadrant. Again, I see myself as more powerful than my environment (above the horizontal axis), but unlike the "dominant" view, I see the world as favorable (to the right of the vertical axis); I am dominant and I believe the world is accepting of me; I won't tend to dominate it; instead, I will affect my will upon the world through inducement or influence. Marston labeled this combination as "I" for *inducement*. Today, most DISC practitioners use the term *influence*.

If I see myself as less powerful than the world (below the horizontal axis), I wouldn't attempt to act to directly change what I had no capability to alter. Now, if I believe I can't alter my environment but I see the world as favorable to me (right of the vertical axis), that's OK; I wouldn't want to change it anyway. I'd want to sustain it just the way it is—steady as she goes. Marston labeled this combination of traits as "S" for *steadiness*. Practitioners I have worked with are about evenly split between whether they refer to the "S" type as *steadiness* or *sustaining*.

And if, like the "S" perspective, I doubted my own capability to affect a desirable change upon the world (below the horizontal axis), I too would refrain from acting. However, unlike the "S" perspective, if I viewed the world

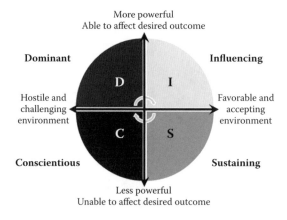

Figure 2.14   Original DISC temperaments.

as unfavorable or even antagonistic to me (left of the vertical axis), I wouldn't want to sustain it; I'd just want to survive it. And how do people without power survive in a hostile environment? They act compliantly to the powers that govern them. Marston labeled the temperament that perceived self to be less powerful and existing in a hostile-unfavorable environment as "C" for *compliance.* As a practitioner, I like to think of "C" more as *conscientiousness.*

Observable Traits of DISC Styles

When we began the discussion of the DISC temperament model, I stated that it was based upon observable behavior. The two axes of "view of personal power" and "view of the environmental climate" are anything but observable, and speculation about someone else's perspective would just be conjecture. To make DISC useful for the daily practitioner, let's change the axes to reflect observable characteristics (refer to Figure 2.15).

People seeking change are active. They are directly doing something to affect the changes they desire. If they're not seeking change, they are usually more reserved. Their activities have more to do with maintaining rather than changing. The vertical axis becomes a spectrum between outgoing versus reserved. People who are outgoing, action oriented, and fast paced fall on the higher end of this spectrum. People on the opposite end of the spectrum tend to be more reserved and thoughtful. They act with a more measured pace. Gauging another's level of activity is pretty straightforward. Do they talk fast? Do they act promptly? Or do they tend to think things through in a measured, deliberate manner.

Whereas activity level is readily apparent, can the same be said for someone's world view? Sometimes this can be determined by the level of optimism or pessimism. If someone is vocal about the many faults in a system

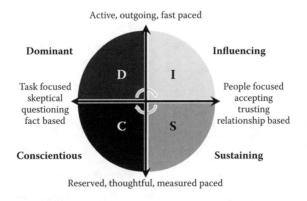

Figure 2.15   Observable DISC behaviors.

and how frustrating the world is, they may view the world as an antagonistic, hostile place or they could be reacting to a current situation that has resulted in a setback. To be considered a temperament type and not just a temporary state of mind, the world view can't be based upon transient conditions; it should be a prevalent theme. As such, degree of optimism or pessimism isn't always a reliable indicator of world view. So what is? As a practitioner, the easiest way to gauge the spectrum spanning the horizontal axis is through the determination of whether a person is task or relationship focused. At first blush, this may seem as nebulous as optimism and pessimism, but from a practical point of view, it is a reliable indicator. If people tend to think of the world as antagonistic and challenging, they won't accept things on face value. They'll need to question things. They'll have a more skeptical outlook, and, viewing facts more reliable than people, they want to have facts to validate positions and opinions. If people generally see something as positive and supportive, they'll tend to accept things more at face value. They'll need fewer facts to confirm what they already believe about the situation. Think of a trusted friend; when he or she says something, you generally believe it without the need to question, speculate, or second guess. Compare that to when you are negotiating with a particularly aggressive individual who clearly is out to get the most out of the situation regardless of what it may cost you. You will question every statement, scrutinize the fine print, and run the numbers multiple times to determine the true cost and try to ferret out any loopholes or hidden agendas that you will come to regret later after it is too late. In that situation, you are not about establishing a relationship; you are focused on protecting your own interests.

Now we have observable characteristics of each spectrum. Combining the two sets of variables defines the characteristics of the four DISC styles. Refer to Table 2.8.

Table 2.8   Summary of DISC Styles

Dominant (D)	*Influencing (I)*
Active, outgoing, fast paced	Active, outgoing, fast paced
Task focused Skeptical, questioning, fact based	People focused Accepting, relationship based
Conscientious (C)	*Sustaining (S)*
Measured pace, reserved, thoughtful	Measured pace, reserved, thoughtful
Task focused Skeptical, questioning, fact based	People focused Accepting, relationship based

NOTE: When learning new concepts, it is easier to study single focus elements before combining multiple dimensions. For DISC, this means looking at the extreme ends of the spectrums. The discussions below are generalities regarding tendencies and traits. We'll look at each of the four styles in isolation. Recognize that, in reality, every person has a little bit of every temperament and can consciously alter their behaviors at times as they deem to be most appropriate to achieve their desired goal. It helps to think in terms of *natural behaviors* as compared to *adapted behaviors*. People may have a natural tendency to be outgoing and talkative, but, depending upon the situation, they can be reserved and refrain from talking. In DISC, people are classified according to their natural behaviors.

Quick and Dirty DISC Assessment

You may have already taken a DISC assessment and know what your dominant temperament is. If you have never taken a formal assessment and you'd like a "quick and dirty" determination of where you fall on the DISC spectrum, complete this simple exercise.

The DISC self-assessment is done in two parts, contained in Tables 2.9 and 2.11. Each section assesses one of Marston's determinants of temperament. Each table contains two columns. Table 2.9, the first assessment, gives you a relative view of how outgoing or reserved you are as compared to others. To some degree, this is related to your general degree of extraversion or introversion. But, it also relates to how you generally interact with your environment—whether you tend to be more assertive or more passive.

Table 2.9 is set up such that each row has a pair of juxtaposed statements, one in each column. Read each pair of statements and rate the degree to which each of the statements describes you by allocating 11 points between Column "O" and Column "R." Don't try and overanalyze each statement; just go with your gut. For example, the first statement reads,

> "Do you become more energized spending time with other people? You find that your energy levels increase with more interaction. Spending excessive time alone you become restless and need to seek out others."

Compare the first statement to its counterpart:

"Do you become reenergized spending time alone? You find that interacting with other people is taxing and after being around people for a while, you need time alone to recharge."

If you think the first statement sounds more like you but there are times you feel like the second statement, you might divide your 11 points 6 to 5. You would write a 6 next to the first statement in Column "O" and mark a 5 next to the statement in Column "R." Do the same for each of 11 pairs of statements. When you have finished ranking the 11 paired statements, add up each of the columns and record the total below each column. The sums of both columns add up to 121 points. Divide each of these sums by 10 by placing a decimal point just to the left of the last digit, giving you scores between 0 and 12.1.

NOTE: This is not an average; the division by 10 is simply done to decrease the scale of the DISC plot for easier plotting and visibility.

Table 2.10 shows how I ranked myself on the Outgoing versus Reserved comparison. My self-assessment shows that I tend to be more outgoing (9.3) as compared to being reserved (2.8).

Table 2.9 Outgoing versus Reserved

Column "O"—Outgoing		Column "R"—Reserved	
1. Do you become more energized spending time with other people? You find that your energy levels increase with more interaction. Spending excessive time alone you become restless and need to seek out others.	____	Do you become reenergized spending time alone? You find that interacting with other people is taxing and after being around people for a while, you need time alone to recharge.	____
2. Do you enjoy being the center of attention—in a good way? Being on stage in a crowd is exciting and fun.	____	Do you avoid being the center of attention? Being the center of attention is embarrassing and you're much more comfortable without a spotlight on you.	____

(continued)

Table 2.9 Outgoing versus Reserved (Continued)

Column "O"—Outgoing		*Column "R"—Reserved*	
3. Do you tend to act before you think?	____	Do you generally think before you act?	____
4. Do you find yourself thinking out loud?	____	Do you tend to think things through inside your head?	____
5. Are you easy to "read" and know? People know where you stand because you tell people what you think.	____	Are you more private; you share information with a select few people?	____
6. Do you tend to talk more than listen?	____	Do you tend to listen more than talk?	____
7. Do you communicate with enthusiasm?	____	Do you generally keep your enthusiasm to yourself?	____
8. Do you generally respond quickly? Enjoy a fast pace?	____	Do you tend to respond in a measured, thoughtful manner? Enjoy a calmer pace?	____
9. In general, are you interested in learning a little about many subjects and topics? You prefer to understand the big picture in broad brush strokes. Don't get mired in the minutia.	____	Do you prefer to learn everything there is to know including fine details about subjects and topics that interest you? There is elegance in the details.	____
10. Would people tend to see you as assertive and bold?	____	Would people tend to see you as careful and calm?	____
11. Do you feel the urge to speak your mind? It is as difficult as keeping a hot coal on your tongue as it is to remain quiet when you have something to say.	____	You don't feel the need to say everything that pops into your head. In fact, there are times when people don't know what you're thinking and push you to express yourself and say what you think.	____
Total Count Column "O"/10	____	Total Count Column "R"/10	____

_____	–	_____	=	_____
Column "O"/10	Minus	Column "R"/10	Equals	Vertical Differential

Table 2.10 Manion's Outgoing versus Reserved

Column "O"—Outgoing		Column "R"—Reserved	
1. Do you become more energized spending time with other people? You find that your energy levels increase with more interaction. Spending excessive time alone you become restless and need to seek out others.	6	Do you become reenergized spending time alone? You find that interacting with other people is taxing and after being around people for a while, you need time alone to recharge.	5
2. Do you enjoy being the center of attention—in a good way? Being on stage in a crowd is exciting and fun.	10	Do you avoid being the center of attention? Being the center of attention is embarrassing and you're much more comfortable without a spotlight on you.	1
3. Do you tend to act before you think?	8	Do you generally think before you act?	3
4. Do you find yourself thinking out loud?	9	Do you tend to think things through inside your head?	2
5. Are you easy to "read" and know? People know where you stand because you tell people what you think.	7	Are you more private; you share information with a select few people?	4
6. Do you tend to talk more than listen?	7	Do you tend to listen more than talk?	4
7. Do you communicate with enthusiasm?	10	Do you generally keep your enthusiasm to yourself?	1
8. Do you generally respond quickly? Enjoy a fast pace?	10	Do you tend to respond in a measured, thoughtful manner? Enjoy a calmer pace?	1
9. In general, are you interested in learning a little about many subjects and topics? You prefer to understand the big picture in broad brush strokes. Don't get mired in the minutia.	9	Do you prefer to learn everything there is to know including fine details about subjects and topics that interest you? There is elegance in the details.	2
10. Would people tend to see you as assertive and bold?	9	Would people tend to see you as careful and calm?	2

(continued)

Table 2.10   Manion's Outgoing versus Reserved (Continued)

Column "O"—Outgoing		*Column "R"—Reserved*	
11. Do you feel the urge to speak your mind? It is as difficult as keeping a hot coal on your tongue as it is to remain quiet when you have something to say.	8	You don't feel the need to say everything that pops into your head. In fact, there are times when people don't know what you're thinking and push you to express yourself and say what you think.	3
Total Count Column "O"/10	9.3	Total Count Column "R"/10	2.8

9.3	–	2.8	=	6.5
Column "O"/10	Minus	Column "R"/10	Equals	Vertical Differential

In Figure 2.16, plot where you fall on the vertical axis. Plot the result of Column "O"/10 on the vertical axis labeled O1–O12 above the horizontal axis. Plot the result of Column "R"/10 on the vertical axis labeled R1–R12.1 below the horizontal axis. Figure 2.16a shows how I plotted my Outgoing (9.3) and Reserved (2.8) scores.

Now subtract the sum of Column "R"/10 from the sum of Column "O"/10. This will give you a number between +12.1 and −12.1. Record this number

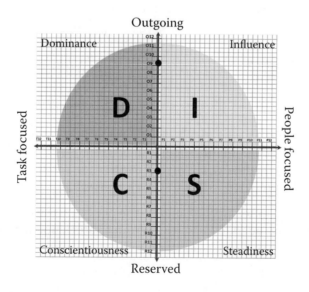

Figure 2.16a   DISC grid. Manion's DISC—vertical plot.

in Table 2.13. This represents the *vertical differential*, which will be used later to plot your DISC profile. My vertical differential equaled 6.5.

$$\text{"O"}/10 - \text{"R"}/10 = \text{Vertical Differential}$$

$$9.3 - 2.8 = 6.5$$

Depending on how you scored yourself, your vertical differential may be a negative number.

The second assessment table (Table 2.11) explores whether you tend to be more "task" or more "people" focused. Just as you did for the first portion of the assessment, read each pair of statements and allocate 11 points between the statement in Column "T" and the statement in Column "P" depending on how closely you generally align with each of the two statements. Again, don't overanalyze each statement; go with your gut.

Sum the total of each column and divide by 10.

NOTE: Again, this not an average of the column numbers; it is simply done to reduce the scale range of the assessment for ease of plotting and viewing.

Table 2.11 Task Focused versus People Focused

Column T—Task Focused		Column P—People Focused	
1. You generally tend to apply impersonal analysis to problems.	___	You are naturally sensitive to emotions. You instinctively consider the effect your actions may have on others.	___
2. You value logic, justice, and fairness; there is one standard for all—if they did the crime, they must do the time.	___	There are exceptions to rules and justice is best served when you weigh each case on its merits and circumstances.	___
3. You naturally tend to see flaws and usually feel the need to point them out.	___	You like to please others—show your appreciation instinctively.	___

(continued)

Table 2.11 Task Focused versus People Focused (Continued)

Column T—Task Focused		*Column P—People Focused*	
4. You can be harsh when you are in an argument. At times you have been accused of being insensitive or uncaring.	___	During stressful times, you can become quite emotional and have been accused of being overly sensitive?	___
5. As a general rule, it is more important to be truthful than tactful—sometimes the truth hurts.	___	You are naturally tactful and diplomatic. It is just as important to be tactful as well as truthful.	___
6. You pride yourself on logic and keeping a clear head during times of stress. Feelings are valid when they are logical. It is frustrating dealing with people whose logic is clouded by their emotions.	___	You naturally accept your feelings and the feelings of others. Feelings are valid whether they make sense or not. Your emotions serve as a compass that guides you through stressful times.	___
7. Primarily, you are motivated by personal achievement and accomplishment.	___	A desire to be appreciated and valued motivates you.	___
8. You tend to be skeptical and questioning of new people, plans and ideas. People need to prove themselves and earn their place.	___	You tend to be more receptive and accepting of new people, plans, and ideas. You accept people at face value unless they give you a reason to doubt them.	___
9. You focus most of your attention on the facts, tasks, and results.	___	The impact events will have on people is foremost in your mind when making your plans.	___
10. You generally tend to be objective in your analysis.	___	You frequently find yourself empathizing with people in your analysis.	___
11. You value tangible results.	___	You value empathy and harmony.	___
Total Count Column "T"/10	___	Total Count Column "P"/10	___

_____	– Minus	_____	= Equals	_____
Column P/10		Column T/10		Horizontal Differential

Table 2.12 Manion's Task Focused versus People Focused

Column T—Task Focused		Column P—People Focused	
1. You generally tend to apply impersonal analysis to problems.	6	You are naturally sensitive to emotions. You instinctively consider the effect your actions may have on others.	5
2. You value logic, justice, and fairness; there is one standard for all—if they did the crime, they must do the time.	6	There are exceptions to rules and justice is best served when you weigh each case on its merits and circumstances.	5
3. You naturally tend to see flaws and usually feel the need to point them out.	7	You like to please others—show your appreciation instinctively.	4
4. You can be harsh when you are in an argument. At times you have been accused of being insensitive or uncaring.	8	During stressful times, you can become quite emotional and have been accused of being overly sensitive?	3
5. As a general rule, it is more important to be truthful than tactful—sometimes the truth hurts.	7	You are naturally tactful and diplomatic. It is just as important to be tactful as well as truthful.	4
6. You pride yourself on logic and keeping a clear head during times of stress. Feelings are valid when they are logical. It is frustrating dealing with people whose logic is clouded by their emotions.	6	You naturally accept your feelings and the feelings of others. Feelings are valid whether they make sense or not. Your emotions serve as a compass that guides you through stressful times.	5
7. Primarily, you are motivated by personal achievement and accomplishment.	6	A desire to be appreciated and valued motivates you.	5
8. You tend to be skeptical and questioning of new people, plans and ideas. People need to prove themselves and earn their place.	8	You tend to be more receptive and accepting of new people, plans, and ideas. You accept people at face value unless they give you a reason to doubt them.	3
9. You focus most of your attention on the facts, tasks, and results.	7	The impact events will have on people is foremost in your mind when making your plans.	4

(continued)

Table 2.12   Manion's Task Focused versus People Focused (Continued)

Column T—Task Focused		Column P—People Focused	
10. You generally tend to be objective in your analysis.	5	You frequently find yourself empathizing with people in your analysis.	6
11. You value tangible results.	8	You value empathy and harmony.	3
Total Count Column "T"/10	7.4	Total Count Column "P"/10	4.7

4.7	–	7.4	=	−2.7
Column P/10	Minus	Column T/10	Equals	Horizontal Differential

Table 2.12 shows how I ranked myself on the Task Focused versus People Focused assessment.

In Figure 2.16, plot where you fall on the horizontal axis. Plot the result of Column "T"/10 on the horizontal axis labeled T1–T12 to the left of the vertical axis. Plot the result of Column "P"/10 on the horizontal axis labeled P1–P12.1 to the right of the vertical axis. Figure 2.16b shows how I plotted my Task Focused (7.4) and People Focused (4.7) scores.

Now subtract the sum of Column "T"/10 from the sum of Column "P"/10. This will give you a number between +12.1 and −12.1.

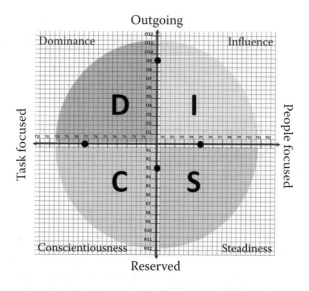

Figure 2.16b   Manion's DISC—horizontal plot.

NOTE: Subtract the total of the column on the *left* from the column on the *right*—this requires you to reverse the numbers in the equation as compared to the first assessment.

The differential between the People Focused and Task Focused is your *horizontal differential*. The horizontal differential will be paired with the vertical differential to plot your DISC profile.

My horizontal differential equaled –2.7. Record your horizontal differential in Table 2.13.

$$\text{``P''}/10 - \text{``T''}/10 = \text{Horizontal Differential}$$

$$4.7 - 7.4 = -2.7$$

Pair the horizontal differential you just calculated with the vertical differential in Table 2.13.

Plot your Rise versus Run in Figure 2.16. If your Rise is a positive number, start at the origin (0, 0) of the grid and move up. If your calculated Rise is a negative number, start at the origin of the grid and move down. From this point, move to the right of the vertical axis if you have a positive Run; move to the left of the vertical axis if you have a negative Run. Where your Rise and Run places you on the grid represents your dominant DISC quadrant.

For me, my Rise versus Run came out to be Rise = 6.5 and Run = –2.7 (Table 2.14). Figure 2.16c shows that plotting my Rise of 6.5 and a Run of –2.7 places me into the "D" quadrant. Dominance is my prevalent DISC tem-

Table 2.13   Rise versus Run

Vertical Differential (Rise)	*Horizontal Differential (Run)*

Table 2.14   Manion's Rise versus Run

Vertical Differential (Rise)	*Horizontal Differential (Run)*
6.5	–2.7

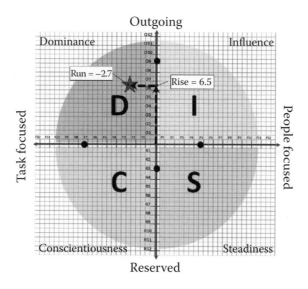

Figure 2.16c   Manion's DISC profile.

perament. Now that you've determined which quadrant you tend to be, let's examine the characteristics of each of the four DISC temperaments.

"D"—Dominant: Entrepreneurs, Adventurers, and Change Agents

Dominant personality types have a bias toward action with more focus generally directed toward the tasks that confront them rather than the relationships that surround them. The "D" type seeks out challenges and enjoys competition—sometimes to the point of inciting conflict. "D"s exude self-confidence—even when they have limited experience in a subject. Sometimes this is seen as overconfidence and can get a "D" in trouble. "D"s are generally convinced that they can achieve their objectives through logic and the strength of their arguments. If that fails them, they will continue to argue for their point through the sheer force of their indomitable willpower.

Communicating with a "D"

When you communicate with a "D," speak to the facts and focus on actions. Recognize that "D"s may become restless with too many details. "D"s typically have no problem making decisions. In fact, they feel better after decisions have been made and they can continue to move toward their objectives. "D"s tend to gravitate toward positions of leadership. They are valuable members of a team when you need to get things done.

Potential Blind Spots and Weaknesses of "D"s

"D"s get things done. However, "D"s can act so quickly and decisively they may not necessarily wait for all the facts. They can sometimes get themselves into trouble when they jump into projects and situations without fully comprehending all of the hazards or complexities involved. You might say that "D"s can be "frequently wrong, but never in doubt"! At times "D"s can confuse what they "think" with what they "know." This can cause them to jump to conclusions and act swiftly to execute decisions ignoring other input. This can overwhelm and frustrate others who prefer to know what they are getting into before they commit.

Motivation for "D"s

"D"s seek to increase their control over situations and power over others. Power and control are essential elements that enable "D"s to achieve their goals. "D"s can sometimes be seen as dictating, arrogant, and self-serving if they don't take the time to engage others and consider the thoughts, needs, and perspectives of others.

"I"—Influencer: Politicians, Social Directors, and Entertainers

Influencing personality types tend to have a bias toward action with more focus generally directed toward the relationships that surround them rather than the tasks that confront them. The "I" type thrives on dynamic, fun, fast paced relationships. They have a visceral need to socialize. When working for long periods in isolation without the opportunity to collaborate with others, "I"s can become discouraged and their productivity can suffer. Part of the reason this occurs is "I"s are extroverts.

Introversion as Compared to Extroversion

When people compare extroverts to introverts, they tend to describe observable traits: talkative as compared to more reserved—gregarious and outgoing versus shy. It is true that extraverts are generally more talkative and outgoing, but, from a working perspective, how they process information is a far deeper and more significant difference between extroverts and introverts. Extraverts process information using the auditory and speech areas of the brain. They talk through their thoughts and through speech, the ideas become more clarified and more concrete. Compare this with intro-verts. Introverts take in the information and then process the information internally—they then tell you what they think. These fundamental differ-ences of how the two mind variations work has more profound workplace implications than the degree to which people are outgoing. Imagine a scene where an introvert and an extrovert are discussing the pros and cons of a particular decision:

Extravert: "OK, I think that covers the issue; let's make a decision."
Introvert: "No, we need to think about it."
Extravert: "What do you mean, 'we need to think about it?' we just thought about it. That's what we've been doing."
Introvert: "No, we've been talking about it; now we need to think about it."
Extravert: "What have we been doing for the past hour? I just don't under-stand you."

The two part ways frustrated. If they understood that they each pro-cessed information differently then each could respect the other's process as equally valid and they could have a more harmonious working relationship.

WORK EXAMPLE: I worked with a northwestern paper manufacturing facility with low efficiencies and poor morale. I was new to the job and eager to help. My new boss was brilliant, but extremely introverted. Daily, I would enter her office and start "bouncing" ideas off of her. The conversations were never productive and I could see she was becoming more and more frustrated with me. I'm certain that she was questioning her hiring decision. Frustrated myself, I thought about the old adage: "Insanity is doing the same thing over and over again and expecting different results." I stepped back and tried to apply some of that psy-chology stuff I'd learned.

I went back to my office and sat at the keyboard and typed out all of my ideas into a lengthy proposal and work plan. The next day, instead of my usual bouncing off the walls, I knocked on the door and handed my boss the concept paper. "Here are some thoughts I have on increas-ing productivity. Could you take some time and read them over? I'll check back with you early next week." Shocked, obviously not expect-ing this from me; she thanked me and took the paper. The following week I stopped by her office at the appointed time. She was visibly more relaxed and enthusiastic. She had set two chairs at the table and copies of my concept paper were laid out for review. There were notes and marks, highlights and annotations throughout the paper. We talked for the next two hours about my ideas and hers. Together we came up with some refinements to my proposals and many ideas that neither of us would have thought of alone. That was a watershed event in our working relationship. From that point forward our working relationship was very productive and mutually rewarding.

Please recognize that I'm a pretty severe extrovert. People often ask me, "Did you think about that before you said it?" And I happily reply, "Nope, I thought of it as I said it!" The act of sitting alone coalescing my thoughts with just me and the blank screen—"mano-a-keyboard"—is not my favorite way of working. It was even more of a struggle when I was younger. But, in that instance, I needed to change my methods for the sake of effectiveness and the relationship—not to mention keeping my job.

Both "D"s and "I"s tend to be extroverts. They both process information verbally, but, whereas a "D" will be more directive, the "I" tends to work to achieve goals through collaboration and influence.

Motivation for "I"s

Because "I"s are social by nature, they are motivated by inclusion. They value praise and usually enjoy public recognition when the recognition is sincere and recognizes them for their contributions. When you communicate with an "I," show your enthusiasm; address the human side of the situation. Like "D"s, "I"s can also become restless with the many details.

Potential Blind Spots and Weaknesses of "I"s

Like "D"s, "I"s can get into trouble when their natural tendencies are allowed to dominate without appropriate counterbalance. When they dial up the "I" too high, they may lack follow-through and attention to details. "I"s may struggle when they have to make a quick decision. Because of their desire to collaborate, they may work excessively hard getting multiple inputs and gathering support. Consequently, deadlines may slip because critical decisions may not be made in an expeditious manner.

"S"—Sustainer: Administrators, Mediators, and Counselors

Sustaining personality types value stability and harmony and an environment free from conflict. "S"s believe that collaboration and mutual support are the most effective ways to maintain the stability they seek. "S"s may be seen as change averse. Their motto might be, "if it ain't broke, don't fix it." This is frustrating to "D"s who can be change junkies who think, "if it ain't broke, break it, reform the pieces into a better faster version, throw away what doesn't fit, and move on quickly to the next exciting challenge." Consequently, "D"s can be very frustrated with "S"s and "S"s can become completely exasperated with "D"s.

In today's fast paced, technology accelerated, 24 × 7 world, "S"s can become overwhelmed. I've heard more than one "D" manager say, "Get on the train or get run over by it." To me, this attitude is very short sighted. "D"s need "S"s—and not just for someone to blindly carry out their orders without question. Think about this, I'm a "D" and I like to solve problems. I like to design systems and see them implemented. There is no better feeling than to see a solution I've implemented effectively working to solve the problems it was designed to correct. As much as I love to see my solutions working, I believe the second ring of hell would be me sitting for eternity accurately inputting data maintaining a system that I designed. It would drive me nuts! So, as a manager, I love working with someone who is completely satisfied having routine in their lives where they come in every day, enter the data, find the errors, and keep the system running accurately and efficiently. Change agents like "D"s need to recognize that once the changes have been made, systems need to be maintained.

Potential Blind Spots and Weaknesses of "S"s

"S"s seek stability and harmony. A key attribute of "S"s is that they are "people pleasers." They genuinely enjoy and feel rewarded serving the needs of others. They can be compassionate and giving. In most situations, these are admirable attributes; it becomes problematic when "S"s spend so much time serving others that they neglect their own needs. They can become so caught up doing for others that they allow their own needs and requirements to go unsatisfied thereby increasing their stress levels and eventually burning out. "S"s need to be aware of their own limitations and capacity to serve and learn to accept that it is sometimes OK, even essential, to say "No."

One area that "S"s too often have no problem saying no to is change. Because they value stability and are traditionalist by nature, "S"s may resist changes that are essential to remain competitive. "S"s can best serve the team by embracing change while still respecting the value of systems and processes that work. By braiding what is good about the present into the vision for the future, "S"s can help craft more affective change solutions.

Communicating with "S"s

"S"s do not like being singled out as the center of attention. They enjoy praise most when it is sincere and discreet. They thrive on being needed and valued for the services they provide. Respect their contributions and their positions.

When changes are required, explain how the changes are anchored in and enhance what works well in the current systems. "S"s like to have time to practice. When changes are made, build in the training and practice required to allow mastery of the new systems. In this way "S"s will play a very essential role ensuring success.

"C"—Conscientious: Scientists, Engineers, and Accountants

Conscientious temperament types are task focused and have very little need to socialize. They value accuracy and attention to detail. "C"s rely on in-depth knowledge and attention to details to succeed. Within an organization, "C"s are most satisfied with clearly defined rules and structured rewards based upon quality, accuracy and individual contribution.

Potential Blind Spots and Limitations of "C"s

"C"s can usually see the flaws in the logic of plans once they've had the time to thoroughly analyze the details. But don't expect snap decisions from a "C." Because "C"s are introverted by nature, they process information internally. Flooding a "C" with details without allowing them time to process, compare, and synthesize the details, "C"s can become frustrated and discouraged. So remember, for "C"s to be most effective, the time to analyze is crucial. This can be quite exasperating for quick-acting "D"s who are ready to make a decision and move on while the detail people want more information and more time. At times, "C"s are accused of "paralysis by analysis." It's important to strike a balance between the need to act quickly and the need for accuracy.

A TALE OF TWO CULTURES—BALANCING EFFICIENCY AGAINST CREATIVITY: "D"s and "I"s flourish within creative chaos; "S"s and "C"s thrive within a more structured routine. It's challenging for these dichotomies to coexist within a single organizational culture. A highly structured environment will be welcomed by some and shunned by others. As the Lean and Six Sigma (LSS) revolution took root in many organizations, the highly structured methodology reduced waste and raised efficiencies, resulting in increased quality and profitability. "The Art" was replaced with "The Science." The detailed DMAIC process required weeks or months of measurement, study, and analysis before projects were approved. No longer were engineers permitted to just "wing it." Unfortunately, this had some unintended consequences. A lot of very profitable inventions came from pure happenstance and serendipity. The LSS process isn't big on happenstance and serendipity. The messy "sausage-making" process of back room invention was abandoned.

3M is one of the companies that struggled with this balance. When CEO James McNerney introduced Six Sigma efficiencies, the company's free-for-all culture became structured and highly efficient. 3M shareholders initially profited from this revolution (although you could say that the 8000+ employees sacked in the process probably didn't appreciate the change). However, after a period of time, 3M's pipeline of innovations dried up. The company that had become famous for revolutionary products slowed to an incremental pace (Hindo, B. 2007. At 3M, a struggle between efficiency and creativity. *Business Week*. June 11, 2007).

So, as you move forward with any improvement process, work to maintain the balance between the extremes and make room in your culture for all types to thrive and contribute to your organization's present and future successes.

Natural versus Adapted Behaviors

As you read about the four DISC temperaments, you probably thought, well that's a little bit like me; but that also applies to me too. This is understandable and expected because very few people are strictly "Pure" "D"s or "Pure" "C"s or "Pure" any single style. Each of us has a mix of characteristics that blend and flow. Even the most extreme personalities have characteristics from all four temperaments. Just because you are an "S" doesn't mean that you can't be dominant on occasion or analytic in your approach. Your dominant DISC temperament reflects a general preference—not an absolute standard. Think of each temperament as a color. For every pure color, there are thousands of variations of hue and shade. There is a wide variation between pale sky blue and ultra dark navy blue.

Our DISC temperaments reflect our natural preferences—our comfort zones. It helps to think of natural as compared to adapted style. Your natural style reflects the behaviors that are most comfortable for you. It's what you feel like doing at the time. Natural behavior is how you would act given your absolute control over a situation with no consequences one way or another. It's how you'd act when you were all by yourself, with no one else's expectation or requirements.

Adapted behavior is how you act that is most appropriate or effective for the given situation. Imagine you are asked to attend a meeting of the board of directors for your company as a guest. Typically, you may be quite assertive and talkative by nature; however, when you are sitting in room full of senior directors you may be quieter than usual. If you did decide to speak, you would probably choose your words more carefully and listen more than you typically would. You may really want to speak up and correct your boss when he gets the facts a little off, but, given the situation, you decide to hold your tongue—even though it is burning in the back of your throat trying to blurt forth.

DISC Space

Adapting your style from what is natural to what is most appropriate for the situation can be quite taxing—particularly if the style you're adapting to is a far stretch from your natural style. For instance, consider Susan who has a "C" temperament. Like other "C"s, Susan is reserved and private by nature. On this day, Susan is attending a family reunion with fifty of her relatives. Each aunt, uncle, and distant cousin wants to find out everything that has happened to Susan since they saw her last when she was two years old. The party continues on throughout the day and late into the night. Susan has a good time but, as the night wears on, Susan's energy levels are dropping by the hour. By the time she is able to politely step away and return to her room, all of her reserves are gone and she is running on empty. She can hear the party continuing on as other, more extraverted relatives keep on going and going with seemingly endless levels of energy. The only thing

Susan wants to do is draw a hot bath and sit quietly alone. Susan enjoyed the party, but it took a lot out of her.

Susan's story illustrates a key aspect of DISC behavioral temperaments. People can display the characteristics of any of the four temperament types, but it requires more energy to step out of your natural style into an adapted one. When you think of tasks at work, the same concept applies. If you are an "I" by nature, you probably don't care much for long, in-depth calculations and the tedious details of bookkeeping. That doesn't mean you can't do it; it just requires you to focus more and work at it a little harder than someone with a "C" personality who really enjoys digging into the details. How extreme you are on the spectrums of your behaviors will determine just how taxing stepping out of your comfort zone and into another quadrant can be.

MY FRIEND JEFF THE "C": I have a very dear friend whom I've known for years who is a pretty high "C." When I first met Jeff in a barracks room we were to share, he was happily pouring over reams of paper with complex calculus equations and no calculator. "Doing homework?" I asked. "Nope, I just like doing calculus equations." Not relaxing for me but definitely enjoyable for many "C"s out there.

To illustrate your own range of behavior, let's plot out your DISC space. Turn back to Figure 2.16 and draw lines connecting the dots on your DISC grid between "O," "P," "R," and "T." When you have finished, you will have a figure that represents your DISC space. Figure 2.16d represents my DISC space.

Think of your DISC space as your comfort region. Almost everyone will have a little bit of each quadrant in their DISC space. As you can see in Figure 2.16d, although I tend to be a "D," I have a significant area of my personality that extends into the "I" quadrant. I enjoy the social side of work almost as much as I enjoy accomplishing my goals. I can also be detailed and analytical—but it is not my strongest suite. I have to focus on it and double check my work because I enjoy the big picture more—I tend to paint with very broad brush strokes.

The smallest quadrant I have represented is "S." There isn't much in my life that I'm not trying to fix, change, or control. I tend to be restless by nature and always have some kind of project in the works—and usually, too many. The amount of projects going in my life can become overwhelming. After running at my typical pace, I'll get the urge to just sit, be quiet, and enjoy the

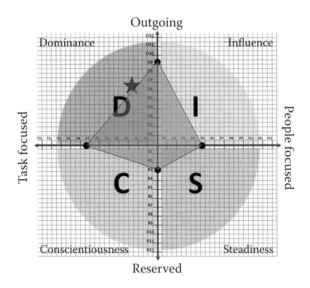

Figure 2.16d   Manion's DISC space.

status quo for a while. I tell my wife, "Let's go on vacation and just sit quietly by the beach." Invariably, after a few hours, a day at the most, I'll be restless and going stir crazy! "Come on; let's go do something—I'm going nuts!"

This is who I am. Over the years, with concerted effort, study, and ample feedback from people who genuinely care about me, I've learned to accept my strengths and recognize my many weaknesses. What's even more important is that I've learned to appreciate the strengths and weaknesses in others. I am most effective when I have a diverse team with different DISC temperaments that complement mine, give me perspective, and fill in the gaps.

Examine your DISC space that you plotted out in Figure 2.16. What are your strengths? What behaviors lie outside of your comfort zones? How can other temperaments complement yours to make a more effective team?

General Guidelines for Working with DISC Temperaments

To increase your effectiveness with others, it helps to understand each DISC style and recognize key aspects of each style affect behavior and can be best integrated into a diverse team. For each of the four DISC temperaments, consider the following:

1. Communication patterns
2. How information is processed

3. Work pace
4. Priorities and goals
5. Fears and stressors

Working with Dominant Personality Types—"D"s

"D"s shape their environment by confronting it head-on to overcome barriers, opposition, and solve problems. They enjoy taking action and getting quick results. "D"s accept challenges—sometimes even challenges that they are not fully qualified to confront. They give and like to get direct answers. Sometimes, they can appear blunt, tactless, and even rude with their directness.

"D"s are motivated by a need to gain power and authority. They thrive on opportunities for individual accomplishments in environments free from direct control. For a "D," rules are just guidelines that may or may not apply to them. When working with a "D," you will notice an air of confidence about them. Some would even see this as arrogance.

"D"s tend to make quick decisions even when they don't have all the details. Once they have made a decision, they act quickly on their decisions. They are risk takers. "D"s can become restless and frustrated if they perceive that things aren't happening as fast as they would like. "D"s get bored after the challenges have been accomplished—even if all the details haven't been worked out yet. They enjoy new and varied activities. They are continuously looking toward what's coming next.

"D"s fear loss of control or being taken advantage of. They bristle when their authority is questioned or challenged. If their natural tendencies are not tempered by self-control, sound judgment, and an accurate assessment of the situation, "D"s can take excessive risks. At times, they may show impatience and lack of concern for others as they rush forward with their plans without considering outcomes, follow-through, or the systems that need to be put in place to sustain their plans over the long haul.

Working with Influencing Personality Types—"I"s

"I"s enjoy shaping their environments through persuasion and influence. They are "people" who need to be involved with other personable and outgoing people. "I"s work to make a favorable impression when they first meet you. They exhibit boundless enthusiasm. They can be very charming and entertaining and enjoy group participation—particularly when they are the center of attention.

When you approach an "I," recognize what is important to them. They thrive in group activities. They typically have and maintain many relationships. "I have 5000 friends on Facebook®" "I"s are motivated by their need for inclusion and recognition. They enjoy having the freedom to express themselves and freedom from control. "I"s can be effusive in their conversations and freely express their emotions.

"I"s don't like to be bogged down with details. They can become frustrated when the situation requires long periods working alone and focusing on details. "I"s fear social rejection, disapproval, loss of influence, and public embarrassment. At times, "I"s can be impulsive, disorganized, and lack follow-through with the details of a project.

Working with Sustaining Personality Types—"S"s

"S"s accomplish tasks by cooperating with others to achieve stability. They tend to be easy-going, calm, patient, loyal, and good listeners. "S"s can be very good team players when they understand their roles and responsibilities.

"S"s are motivated to please others and thrive on sincere appreciation and being part of a cohesive team. "S"s frequently play the role of peacemaker in a group. They can be good counselors. At times, "S"s' concern for others can cause them to become overtaxed as they work hard to satisfy everyone else's desires, putting their own needs last.

"S"s prefer to work in a methodical manner using traditional, tried and true methods. "S"s accept change best when it is incremental in nature and clearly anchored to existing procedures. Rapid, continuous, and/or chaotic changes can be overwhelming to "S"s particularly if the logic necessitating the changes is not clearly explained. When change is required, they desire to work through it with ample time to practice and learn the new procedures in depth. When you communicate with an "S," link the plans to what works well in the present. "S"s like details to be explained in a linear organized manner.

Working with Conscientious Personality Types—"C"s

"C"s use their analytical minds to work through problems and strive for quality. They generally work well within established rules and structures. "C"s work best when expectations and performance standards are clearly defined and where quality and accuracy are valued. "C"s are generally dip-lomatic. They prefer a reserved business-like atmosphere where roles and responsibilities are respected.

"C"s are meticulous in their approach and pay close attention to fine details and subtle nuances. Their need to analyze and double check can be seen as overly cautious and perfectionistic. "C"s fear slipshod methods. They bristle when their work is criticized especially from others they don't respect as subject matter experts.

"C"s' propensity to follow set rules and established methods may limit creativity in problem solving. When faced with conflict, "C"s rely on known facts and details to argue their point. The emotional perspective holds little sway with a "C" and will never trump the known facts. They become frus-trated when others become emotionally out of control. "C"s can be overly critical of others and of themselves. Their desire to be absolutely certain can cause them to be indecisive as they delay action to collect and analyze more data.

DISC at a Glance

As your understanding of the general nature, tendencies, and limitations of the four DISC temperaments improves, so will your effectiveness working with a wide variety of people. The quick and dirty DISC assessment is not a quantitatively accurate instrument. I have found that attempts to meticu-lously measure the degree of "D"-ness" or "S"-nicity of a person are generally unproductive. What is essential for managing and leading others is to have insight into the personality preferences and the general attributes of each style and truly valuing the strengths while understanding the limitations of each. When you do, you will be better able to assemble well-rounded teams in which roles and responsibilities are allocated such that the work plays to people's inherent strengths while shoring up their limitations within a mutu-ally supportive organizational structure.

With study and practice, you won't even need an assessment instrument to recognize someone else's DISC style. Within a few minutes of meeting anyone, you will be able to ascertain their general temperament and adapt your approach to interact most effectively with them.

To determine other people's DISC style, begin by first observing their pace of speech and level of enthusiasm. As illustrated in Figure 2.17, if they are active and quick, they fall into the "D" or "I" category. Next, determine

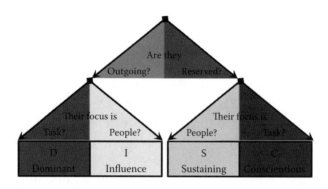

Figure 2.17 DISC at a glance.

if they are focusing on the people or on facts and tasks. If they are task based, they fall into the "D" quadrant. If people and relationships are their focus, they would fall into the "I" quadrant.

If, as you interact with people you have just met, they appear more reserved and moderate, choosing their words carefully, they fall into either the "S" or "C" quadrant. Now determine if they are focusing on the people or on facts and tasks. If people and relationships are their focus and they are reserved, they would fall into the "S" quadrant. If they are task based and reserved, they fall into the "C" quadrant.

You might be thinking, well, what if they are really a "D" or an "I" but they are just not feeling as energetic as they normally do? Couldn't they just be having an off day? Sure, but that's not a problem. The goal of DISC is to improve your communications effectiveness. If someone is feeling a little more subdued than usual, they probably aren't going to much feel like dealing with someone with boundless energy at the moment, so, if you are naturally a "D" or an "I" and you dial back your enthusiasm a bit, they'll relate to you just fine. The goal here is *connection, not perfection.*

CAUTION: AN OUNCE OF POP PSYCHOLOGY: The entire goal of DISC is to improve your communications effectiveness and to increase your ability to work with a broad spectrum of people. DISC is not intended to label, stereotype, or pigeon-hole people. If you do, your efforts to improve your effectiveness with people will be defeated and you will not be trusted. When I was younger, I had a manager that fancied himself an expert on people. He took the latest psychology and business books and labeled all his people. Once he labeled you, you stayed labeled in his narrow mind regardless of performance to the contrary. Unfortunately, I learned this too late. Within my first week on the job, the manager invited me into his office. "Sit down, make yourself at ease." He said amiably. Naively, I did. I sat on his couch—not the little chair he had perched in front of his oversized desk—making myself comfortable. We had what I thought was a very nice conversation. I left thinking we were on very good terms. I was wrong. A few months later, I became involved in a conflict with another staff member regarding a procedural practice. My coworker ran to the manager. They returned together. Without even allowing me to explain my perspective, the manager proceeded into a screaming tirade, "I knew you were trouble the moment you walked into my office and sat down like you owned the place. I nailed your type right away and knew it was only a matter of time before you'd cross the line and cause trouble." I was convicted and executed before I had ever left his office when I first joined the organization; he had only waited for an opportune time to carry out the sentence.

Learning from this painful chapter, my advice to you is don't assume that someone who invites you to "make yourself comfortable" really means it. And, if you are a manager, don't utilize DISC or any other assessment tool or theory as a weapon. DISC and other tools like it should be used to edify your staff, improve communications, and grow a more effective organization—not to justify your own prejudices and personal agendas.

The most beneficial concept you can take away from this discussion on DISC temperaments is that each of us has natural tendencies and others will differ from our own. Figure 2.18 summarizes the four DISC temperament styles showing strengths and potential limitations for each style. If you take a balanced view, you'll come to accept that there is no *best style*; each has strengths, and each can contribute to the overall effectiveness of the organization. The truly wise manager will find a way to utilize each crew member's talents to improve the overall effectiveness of the organization.

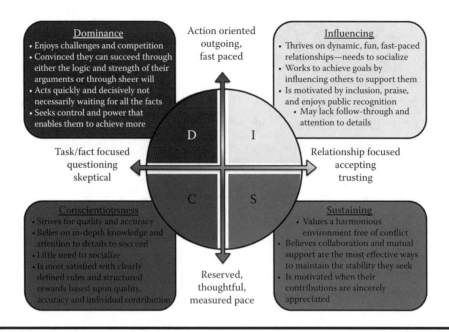

Figure 2.18   Summary of DISC styles.

DISC Temperaments and Team Strengths

Earlier, in the analysis of Forming Element 3, we discussed the two teams that are needed to effectively navigate a substantial organizational change initiative: Team "P" (for present) and Team "F" (for future). Team "P" needs to focus every day on keeping the wheels on the bus, making sure quality is maintained, and the day-to-day routine of the organization is carried out. While Team "P" is maintaining, Team "F" should be looking ahead at what needs to happen to remain competitive in the ever-changing global marketplace. When Team "F" has worked out the plans for the future, they work with Team "P" to implement the changes into ongoing operations. Team "F" should never be working in a vacuum from Team "P." If they do, they may design solutions that have no basis in reality or curtail current processes and systems that are essential to effective operations. When Team "F" has improvements to introduce into the organization, they should utilize an effective process to integrate the changes with minimal disruption such that the present becomes the future and is steadily and reliably maintained day in and day out. Staffing Team "F" entirely with "S"s or Team "P" entirely with "D"s would be frustrating for everyone involved. In fact, staffing any team with all of one type and none of the other to counter potential blind spots and limitations is equally ineffective.

Widespread understanding of the inherent difference in the preference of each style allows each style to contribute to the overall health of the organization. For example, "S"s are motivated when their contributions are sincerely appreciated. They enjoy working with "D"s that value and respect their contributions and the stabilizing influence they provide.

When undertaking a major project or organizational transformation, you want to consider the strengths of the people on your team. Certainly you want to have some "D"s on the team to drive the project—but what will happen if you have a team of all "D"s? Probably a lot of infighting and power struggles—definitely not a recipe for progress. You'll need some team members who enjoy following direction and following a good leader—you'll need some "S"s. But, remember, you'll need to give them time to accept the changes. "S"s will also help you not "throw the baby out with the bath." There are things about every organization that work well and should be maintained. "S"s help you understand the history and keep the elements that add continuity to the change initiative. You'll also want some "I"s on the team to motivate and influence the team. "I"s desire changes, but they are also focused on the relationship side of work. "I"s will recognize the need for motivation and maintaining team morale. "I"s can temper the tendency of "D"s to drive people to exhaustion and burn out the team.

Finally, if you want to ensure quality and high standards, you'll definitely need your "C"s on the team. Without them, the "D"s could rush to judgment and boldly charge where angels fear to tread with little attention to the details needed for long-term sustained success.

Focus on Strengths, Not Limitations

If each of us is truly honest with ourselves we will admit that along with our skills and competencies we probably have an equal number of areas that we lack. Leaders may recognize this about themselves but apply a different standard to the people in their organization. As we pointed out in our discussions of the Johari Window, people tend to have double standards without even being aware of it; we tend to judge others by their actions while we generally judge ourselves by our intentions. If you want to maximize the effectiveness of your organization and create a culture of inclusion, begin by focusing on people's strengths, not their limitations. For instance, if the individual has a temperament weighted toward "S," they may need a little more time to accept and adapt to change. If weighted toward a "D" temperament they may lack sufficient empathy and people skills to effectively engage others. The effective manager understands these limitations and helps others recognize and accept them as well. When done effectively, the manager builds a team that provides mutual support, shoring up each member of the Team helping to ensure mutual success through mutual respect.

EXAMPLE: One of the best examples of providing mutual support between contrasting temperaments occurred with a colleague whose temperament lay primarily within the "conscientious" quadrant. The power company he worked for frequently utilized the idea generation methodology of brainstorming. On project after project he would be in a meeting among a room full of people shouting out ideas and hurriedly capturing every thought in rapid succession on flip charts. As you can now appreciate, the "D"s and the "I"s in the room excelled within this free flow of ideas. Greg dreaded each one. He would sit back and watch the others madly dash around like ants on a sugar pile—feeling frustrated that he was unable to contribute like the others. After one meeting, his manager took him aside, "Greg, I don't think you are much of a team player. You don't speak up in meetings and don't interact well with others. If you don't start working more like the others, I'm not sure I'll be able to give you a very good rating on your performance review." Greg was hurt, more frustrated, and now he was worried about his future. Greg spent the evening processing the situation. The next morning he stopped by the manager's office.

"I've thought about what you've said and I worked on it last night. Here is a list of my ideas and additions to what the team worked on yesterday." Greg handed her an outlined list of ideas that built upon and expanded greatly what the team had thrown up the day before.

"This is great; you have a lot of ideas that are in an entirely different vein. The team didn't even consider many of these. This is more like it."

"If you want this type of work, then you have to give me time to process. The way I think, I like to turn things over in my head. But I have to take the time to chew on them. I'd like to propose a different approach. If you need instantaneous answers, than I'm not the one to call on. But, if you'd like more in-depth analysis and expansion of ideas, than I think I'll be able to help. I'll attend meetings, participate where I add value, and then give you ideas after I've had some time to think about them. Will that work for you?"

Table 2.15   Strengths of Each DISC Temperament within a Change Initiative

Strengths a "D" Brings to a Team	*Strengths an "I" Brings to a Team*
Leadership, drive, decision making, courage, desire to make things better	Enthusiasm, fun, motivation, influence, team communications, marketing and selling the team's ideas
Strengths a "C" Brings to a Team	*Strengths an "S" Brings to a Team*
Accuracy, quality, attention to detail, patience, playing "devil's advocate," weighing the pros and cons	Balance, historical perspective, good team players, concern for harmonious relations, arbitration between different points of view

"We can work with that. I appreciate you taking the time to work up your thoughts. Why don't you present these to the team at next week's staff meeting?"

Greg recognized his own limitations and had the maturity and courage to be able to help his manager understand how he could best contribute to the team's success.

Table 2.15 illustrates the strengths that each DISC temperament brings to the team.

Forming Element 6: Leaders Set the Tone for Effective, Open, and Inclusive Communication

When considering the Framework for Team Success, introduced earlier and shown again in Figure 2.19, we see how effective communications among the team members is essential to facilitate forming a group into a high-performing team. If the organizational climate is not built on trust (as discussed in Forming Element 4), communications will be impaired. If members don't value and act inclusively toward others with differing temperaments and styles communications will also languish. To create such a climate of trust and build a culture of inclusion requires leadership to set the proper tone for communications and model appropriate behaviors. During the Forming Stage, new members will be watching and assessing whether it is safe to communicate freely and openly. If the words, tone, and reactions

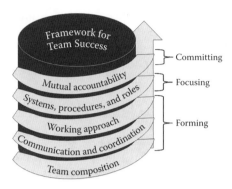

Figure 2.19 Framework for team success.

of the leader aren't congruent with the message, trust will not thrive and communication will be limited. The timeframe to set an appropriate tone begins before the first meeting is even held. Here are a few factors to consider when setting the appropriate tone:

- How were the communications sent out?
- How were people notified?
- Were any expectations set?
- Do people have preconceived ideas based on past projects?

People begin forming their impressions from the very beginning; I tell clients that they are dealing with rapidly hardening organizational climate concrete. If the form is not set early and there is an expectation that things will just form naturally as they flow out—you may not end up with the well formed foundation you were hoping for—more likely you will have a big amorphous blob with crumbling edges and unstable voids that won't bear any stress. To set the foundation, the leader must remain aware of the forming climate and actively work to establish an open and inclusive atmosphere in which the free flow of information establishes a clear vision, sets clear expectation, and helps include as many team members as possible.

There is always ambiguity during the Forming Stage; the degree of ambiguity will vary depending upon the nature of the change initiative and the experience levels of the leadership and team members. As information flows and that which is unknown, hidden, or within a blind spot becomes known, the leader will need to adapt the message and fill in the gaps to build a healthy communication environment. If the gaps aren't filled by sound communication, they will be filled with assumptions, rumors, and speculation.

Hidden Agendas

Sometimes the creation of an open, inclusive, and healthy communications environment is not of concern to the managers and leaders. You may have worked with leaders who have intentionally blocked or limited communication within the group. Their Johari Window is slanted toward a huge hidden agenda. Leaders with hidden agendas create silos among individuals and groups to obscure the "big picture" in attempts to maintain or increase their own power and control. The limited flow of communication stems from the leader's belief that knowledge is power. In their attempts to maintain power and control, they provide minimal information; just the bare minimum they feel is required for people to carry out the tasks that they are assigned, but, not the reasons behind the tasks or how the tasks accomplish the broader mission. In its most malignant form, leaders play one member against another to intentionally create a climate of mistrust. If this is the case, there is little hope of ever creating an open and inclusive communications environment. In such situations more drastic leadership interventions from higher authority are the only recourse.

Assuming it's not intentional and malignant, counterproductive behaviors not borne out of malicious intent may be due to the leader not being communicative by nature—perhaps a DISC style of "C" or an "S." "C"s are particularly prone to struggle with poor communications. They may have very detailed plans and good intents, but, they can fail to fully inform the team because it is so clear to themselves, they simply assume that everyone knows the plan and their part in it. The fact that it is not intentional is of some conciliation but it won't change the fact that the group will never achieve optimal performance.

EXAMPLE: Steve was an extremely introverted manager whose DISC temperament was predominantly "C." Steve rarely provided details, goals, or feedback. Out of frustration, team members attempted to take initiative in various uncoordinated ways to increase productivity and resolve problems. When they didn't guess correctly, if their actions weren't aligned with Steve's unspoken vision, he would provide "feedback" infused with sarcasm and condescension. At other times Steve would straight out berate members for not waiting for direction and calling them incompetent. After a few months of false starts and rising discord in the team, I approached Steve on the team's behalf. In my typical "D" fashion, I didn't think about how I would approach him or what I was going to say; I just dove right in and over my head.

"Steve," I said, "We need a plan."

"I have a plan," he said, indignant that I was even questioning him.

"I'm sure you do, but, we all need to know what it is so we can all get on board with it. Can I see the plan?"

"It's in my head."

"Should I crack it open so we can all see it?"

Clearly not my finest moment for these were the days when my mouth regularly engaged before my brain did—even more frequently than it does today. Needless to say, my feedback was not well received. But, you get the point; people need to know the plan and where they fit in.

Regardless of the leader's DISC temperament, it is crucial that the leader be aware of their communications process and effectiveness. Effective leaders adapt the depth and frequency of communications to match the needs of the group and the needs of the individual team members. This adaptive leadership style also varies with the situation, the task, as well as the abilities, motivation, and the confidence of the team member. As you lead your organization, be aware of the needs of the individuals and the needs of the group and then adapt your approach to the situation accordingly. This is the basis of situational approaches to leadership that have proven extremely effective.

Situational Approaches to Leadership

NOTE: Like personality temperament, the study of leadership is a very broad topic that fills entire volumes. As a practitioner, I have found that employing the situational approach to leadership explained in The Leader's Window© by John Beck and Neil Yeager yields the most consistent results. The brief explanation given below is not intended to be all encompassing, just to provide some background on the view of leadership included throughout this book and to establish a common language that will enhance the understanding of each organizational stage.

If your assessed score for Element 6 in the Forming Assessment Table indicates that a deeper understanding of leadership would be beneficial, I'd recommend contacting the Charter Oak Consulting Group at www .cocg.com.

There are many theories of leadership, including three situational approaches, the first of which is the Situational Leadership Theory (SLT) that was introduced in 1969 by Paul Hersey and Ken Blanchard (Hersey, P. and Blanchard, K. H. 1969. Life cycle theory of leadership. Training and *Development Journal*, 23 (5), 26–34; Blanchard, Kenneth H., Patricia Zigarmi, and Drea Zigarmi. Leadership and the One Minute Manager: Increasing Effectiveness through Situational Leadership. New York: Morrow, 1985). The second is Situational Leadership 2 (SL2), developed by Ken Blanchard in 1985. The third is The Leader's Window, developed by John Beck and Neil Yeager in 1994 with revisions in 2001. All of these situational approaches to leadership utilize slightly different terminology—but they are all based upon the following tenets:

1. There are four basic leadership styles. Each leadership style is classified according to the relative amounts of directive as compared to supportive behaviors demonstrated by the leader.

   If you are the type of leader who gives detailed explanations and gets deeply involved with the day-to-day operations of the work, you would be considered high in directive behavior. If you are not actively involved in the day-to-day details and are comfortable leaving the details to those closest to the job, you would be considered low in directive behavior.

   A leader who demonstrates highly supportive behaviors routinely interacts with his/her subordinates. If you spend a large portion of your time in face-to-face interactions with your people, problem solving, coaching, mentoring, or collaborating you would be considered high in supportive behavior. If you don't frequently interact with your people in this manner, then you would be considered low in supportive behavior.

   Based upon the relative degree of each of these behaviors Beck and Yeager refer to each of the four styles as
   - Style 1 (S1)—Directing (High Direction)
   - Style 2 (S2)—Problem Solving (High Direction and High Support)
   - Style 3 (S3)—Developing (High Support)
   - Style 4 (S4)—Delegating (Low Direction and Low Support)

2. No single leadership style is inherently better than any other—each can be applied effectively or ineffectively. And, according to Beck and Yeager, the effectiveness of each leadership style will vary according to
   - ◼ The situation and what the individual needs to do—the deliverables
   - ◼ The capabilities of the individual relative to those deliverables—the person's performance potential

Understanding the Leadership Styles

Like DISC, the four leadership styles are represented in four quadrants. There is a correlation between directive behavior and task-focused behaviors. Likewise, supportive behavior has a strong correlation with relationship behaviors. Since there is a strong correlation between the elements of the DISC model and the elements of The Leader Window, you will notice some general correlation between an individual's DISC temperament and the leadership style toward which they gravitate. An individual who tends to have a dominant personality style (D) can also tend toward a high direction style of leadership (S1). However, these correlations shouldn't be taken too far. Your personality temperament relates to natural tendencies and preferences, whereas your leadership reflects your working style. Your leadership style is a function of your involvement in the operations and the degree of interaction with your employees that you exhibit as a leader. It's been my experience that leadership is a learned behavior that anyone, regardless of DISC style, can improve with practice and constructive feedback.

Leadership Determinants

According to Beck and Yeager, in addition to the degree of directive and supportive behaviors, your leadership style—how you are perceived by those you are leading—is determined by these three elements:

1. Communication (your use of influencing skills and listening skills)
2. Decision making (how you make decisions)
3. Recognition (what you appreciate people for)

Tables 2.16 through 2.19 summarize each leadership style and the communication, decision-making, and recognition behaviors associated with each style.

Table 2.16 Elements of S1—Directing

Style	S1—Directing
1. Directive versus supportive behaviors	High degree of direction—what to do and when to do it with little interaction of a supportive or mentoring nature. The relationship is one of telling and doing with little or no explanation of why.
2. Communications	Active influencing with limited listening
3. Decision-making process	The leader decides without consideration of input from others.
4. Traits or Behaviors valued or appreciated	The leader values and shows appreciation of individuals who efficiently follow directions.

Table 2.17 Elements of S2—Problem Solving

Style	S2—Problem Solving
1. Directive versus supportive behaviors	High degree of direction combined with supportive feedback to the individual on their progress and areas of improvement. Frequent interaction involving the individual giving input and details and the leader providing explanations of decisions and feedback on the individual's progress and quality of work.
2. Communications	Significant explanation of the rationale for decisions to enable the individual to understand why the chosen course of action is the best given the current problem and surrounding conditions.
3. Decision-making process	The leader solicits input from others and then makes the decision based upon the input received.
4. Traits or Behaviors valued or appreciated	The leader values and appreciates individuals who provide input and who are open to coaching and feedback.

Table 2.18 Elements of S3—Developing

Style	S3—Developing
1. Directive versus supportive behaviors	Low direction. Collaborative discussions center on mutual discovery and involvement. High degree of supportive interaction in which the leader and the individual discuss the situations and weigh the pros and cons of various courses of action.
2. Communications	The degree of explanation is high, but it is not related as much around the details of the task as it is around problem-solving methods and the decision-making process.
3. Decision-making process	The leader collaborates with the individual and then supports the individual's decision.
4. Traits or Behaviors valued or appreciated	The leader values and shows appreciation of individuals who work collaboratively with the team, who accept input and feedback, who engage in constructive dialogue, and who support the team.

Table 2.19 Elements of S4—Delegating

Style	S4—Delegating
1. Directive versus supportive behaviors	Little or no direction provided from the leader. It is left up to the individual to decide how the task should be accomplished. Interactions are limited to reporting out progress and outcomes and occasional requests from the individual for resources.
2. Communications	The leader gives little or no explanation of why or how the task should be accomplished. Explanations, if any, are given to the significance of the task and any parameters that the individual must take into consideration such as time limits or budgetary constraints.
3. Decision-making process	The individual decides without input from the leader and the leader supports that decision.
4. Traits or Behaviors valued or appreciated	The leader values and shows appreciation of individuals who act autonomously to make decisions and act to achieve the organization's goals and outcomes.

Effective and Ineffective Demonstration of Leadership Styles

Like DISC temperaments, there are four leadership styles. And, just as there are no "right" or "wrong" DISC temperament types, there are no right or wrong leadership styles. And just like the temperaments, there are strengths and weaknesses of each leadership style. As the old adage says, "Any strength taken to excess can become a weakness." As such, there are situations when each leadership style can be effective and appropriate and there are times when a particular style would yield better outcomes than another. If you have a certain leadership style that you utilize with every individual and in every situation, there will be times that you are effective and times when things go horribly awry!

To acknowledge this, Beck and Yeager label the four styles differently depending upon whether the style has been shown to be effective or ineffective for a given situation.

S1
  Effective = Directing
  Ineffective = Dominating
S2
  Effective = Problem Solving
  Ineffective = Over involving
S3
  Effective = Developing
  Ineffective = Over accommodating
S4
  Effective = Delegating
  Ineffective = Abdicating

Figure 2.20 pairs the effective and ineffective styles.

When demonstrating S1 consistently regardless of the situation, at times, you may be seen as an effective director, and other times, you will be perceived as dominating and overcontrolling.

If you utilize S2 most of the time, you might be seen as an effective problem solver or you may be overinvolving yourself such that your crew avoids taking ownership and accountability; when you make all the decisions for them, you take all the responsibility and give them deniability for anything that goes wrong.

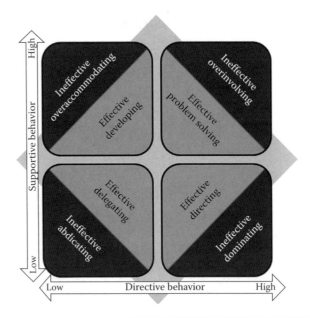

Figure 2.20 Effective versus ineffective leadership styles.

When spending your time supporting your team, effectively mentoring them to make decisions and assume more responsibility, you are applying S3 effectively. However, if you are always listening to problems, trying to be everyone's friend and make everyone happy, you may be well liked but ineffective and not respected as a leader.

Should you release control and send your crew off to accomplish the tasks at hand when they have the experience and a firm grasp of the big picture, you will be perceived as an effective S4 delegator. However, if your crew doesn't have the competencies, authority, confidence, and adequate resources to accomplish the task resulting in missed deadlines or low quality, you have abdicated your responsibility as the leader and set your crew up for failure.

So which style sound most like you?

Quick and Dirty Leadership Self-Assessment

With the four determinants of leadership style in mind, consider what percentage of your time you spend directing? Problem solving? Developing? Delegating? Take a few minutes to fill in Figure 2.21a with the estimated percentage of the time that you demonstrate each of the four leadership styles.

Figure 2.21b shows how I rated my demonstrated leadership styles. I tend to exhibit high supportive behavior (using S2 and S3 70% of the time).

Figure 2.21 **(a) Leadership self-assessment. (b) Manion's leadership self-assessment.**

I can be directing when I need to be (15% S1). Notice that I ranked delegating as my lowest style (only 10%). I know it's not my strongest suit because I become very uncomfortable when I don't know what's going on. I have also learned that I need to do more delegating than my natural instincts would lead me to do otherwise.

What does your self-assessment of your leadership style look like? Are there one or two styles that you use more than the others? Are there styles you need to use more often? Or styles that you'd like to use more effectively? Can you think of times that if you had demonstrated a different style the outcomes may have been better?

How You See Yourself as Compared to How You Are Seen by Others

This quick and dirty leadership assessment is based upon your own perception of your leadership while you're in a low stress, imaginary environment—and it may or may not reflect how you actually act in any given situation. Multiple variables, including stress levels, your perceptions, and your assumptions about the situation, will affect the leadership behaviors you actually exhibit. Your rough assessment also doesn't begin to reflect how your employees perceive you. Think back to the Johari Window—are blind spots obscuring how your leadership style is perceived by others?

If you're not sure and you'd like to get some feedback, ask a few people who work with you to assess you. Compare how they see you with how you see yourself. You can ask them to do the same quick and dirty assessment you just did.

> NOTE: Depending upon your relationship with them and their level of trust, the feedback you receive may not be completely accurate. You may need an objective third party opinion. If you'd like a more in-depth assessment, you could take the L4 Self-Leadership Style Assessment and ask your team members to complete the L4 Other about you—both of which are available from the Charter Oak Consulting Group (www.cocg .com).

Adapting Leadership Styles to Individual Needs

At this point you should have a good general understanding of the four leadership styles and how each can be effective or ineffective; but how do you know when to use each to maximize your effectiveness? I stated earlier that, as a practitioner, the most effective situational approach to leadership I've encountered is *The Leader's Window* by John Beck and Neil Yeager. The reason I like Beck and Yeager's situational approach is that they have developed a pattern for using the leadership styles that is appropriate for almost every leadership situation you will encounter with an individual. The pattern is 1-4-3-2—directing, then delegating, support as needed, and then problem solving only if it's necessary.

Whatever the task and whatever the situation, you need to give clear directions. Begin by telling your crew what the goal is and when it needs to be accomplished (Directing—S1). The amount of detail and degree of specificity you include in the initial assignment will vary depending on the experience, skills, and motivation of each crew member. If the individual is experienced and has performed consistently well in the past, just telling them when it needs to be completed is usually enough. The amount of initial information necessary will vary inversely to the level of experience of the individual; the less experienced, the more specificity will be needed.

After you assign the goal and timeframe, address any questions they may have then let them get to work. Let them work on it for a while (Delegating—S4). After they've had some time to get into the project, stop by and ask them, "How's it going?" The amount of time you leave them alone to work on the project will also be proportional to experience, competence, and motivation. Don't leave a person with very little experience alone to struggle; conversely, don't hover around a seasoned professional.

Giving them time to work on the project will allow them to assess the situation more and may generate questions they hadn't thought to ask when you first assigned the work. When they have questions, work collaboratively with them to explore answers. Even if you know the answer right off the top of your head, don't just jump to S2 and tell them what to do, that may frustrate them and will not develop critical thinking skills. Try asking probing questions that help think through the problem.

- What is the problem?
- What do you think is the cause?
- What have you tried thus far?
- Do you need additional information or resources?
- What options are you thinking about?

Again, the time you spend utilizing style 3 will be proportional to the level of experience. Inexperienced people may not have sufficient insight and understanding of the situation to explore it collaboratively, and asking a battery of questions could make them feel inferior and that you are just testing them. On the other hand, experienced people who hit a snag will usually find it helpful to think out loud without having you take over.

Regardless of the person's capability, if you've spent an appropriate amount of time discussing the situation and the individual is still unsure about the next course of action or unable to make the decision, summarize what you've heard from him or her and offer a solution or make the decision yourself. By following the 1-4-3-2 pattern, the questions you ask to help people develop their own problem-solving skills also enable you to solicit and consider their input before you solve the problem (S2).

Leadership by Default

Even if you are familiar with leadership styles and types, you probably don't think through every situation and analyze exactly how you should respond. Your natural temperament comes through and guides your reactions. As pressure increases due to conflict, timelines, or any one of the other hundreds of pressures that affect you from day to day, you will be more reactive than prescriptive. It's during these times that you may not be able to respond as you would have otherwise wished you had. But, the more you learn about yourself and how you tend to respond, you'll find that you are increasing your effectiveness.

DISC Temperament Effects on Leadership Tendencies

Earlier I stated that every person, regardless of natural DISC temperament, can be an effective leader; but there was a caveat—leadership is a learned behavior. Leaders who aren't self-aware and lack empathy and understanding of the needs of others will tend to react according to their natural tendencies and not adapt their leadership style to affect the most productive outcome. In general when not mitigated by training and experience, the natural leadership styles of the four DISC temperaments tend to be as follows:

"D": Dominating/Directing

As you can imagine, a person who has a naturally dominant personality will tend to exhibit a directing style (S1) of leadership. They make quick decisions and have no problem telling people what to do and when to do it. When at their best, "D"s can be very inspirational leaders who instill confidence in their crew with their courageous and bold leadership. Taken to excess, they can be seen as dominating and even to the point of dictating. Being low on relationship behavior may prevent them from understanding the developmental needs of their crews and thus fail to develop them. Instead, they may define good team behavior as "doing what I tell them." "D"s need to be careful not to dominate their crews so completely that they end up with a passive group of "Yes" people who tell their leader whatever they think he or she wants to hear.

"I": Influencing/Problem Solving

People whose temperament tends toward influencing exhibit both high task and high relationship behavior—high task and high relationship correlate to high direction and high support; they tend to have a problem-solving style (S2) of leadership. At their best, "I"s can be great mentors and teachers. However, if they rely solely on that behavior, they can overplay the part and enable their crews to never take control or to make decisions on their own.

"S": Sustaining/Developing

Sustaining temperament types tend to be high on relationships and low on task behavior leading them to be more developing leaders (S3). They like working within the team and enjoy sharing the camaraderie of team accomplishments. Two areas where an "S" can struggle as a leader are as follows:

1. Setting a vision for the future: Because "S"s tend to enjoy stability and minimal change, their leadership may be more about keeping things running predictably as compared to reshaping the organization to optimal conditions. They may be slow to change when things are going smoothly or they may resist change even when faced with an obvious need.
2. "S"s can also tend to struggle with making hard decisions. Because of their desire to maintain harmonious relations, they tend to be conflict averse. Leadership sometimes requires hard decisions that cause the upheaval that "S"s would rather avoid. They sometimes let problems fester too long and react only when the problem has become a crisis that can no longer avoid being addressed. If predisposed to their natural behaviors, "S"s may be well liked but not well respected and not overly effective as leaders.

"C": Conscientious

Of each of the four DISC styles, "C"s tend to have to work the hardest to adapt their leadership styles. Depending upon the degree, "C"s can tend toward being introverted and noncommunicative. All effective leadership is contingent upon the leader's ability to communicate the vision and the time-frames. Like the story of "Steve" related above, individuals who are heavily weighted toward "C" may have very detailed plans in their heads but may not effectively share their visions with others. Without communicating their visions clearly, "C"s can tend to abdicate when they fail to give adequate direction and feedback.

Another aspect that "C"s struggle with is effective delegation. Remember, "C"s value quality and attention to detail. Because of their own personal high standards "C"s have a tendency not to trust the data unless they've worked through it themselves. "C"s can be very critical of the work of others that fails to comply with their well defined but unspoken standards. To achieve a level of comfort, "C"s may feel the need to go back through the details provided by others until they are completely satisfied to its accuracy and detail. This behavior can be seen as micromanaging that frustrates crew members.

Finally, their need for data, analysis, and detail may cause "C"s to delay making critical decisions as they delay action to gather more data. As the analysis continues, critical windows of opportunity may close and the organization may miss valuable opportunities due to "paralysis by analysis."

Clearly abdication, micromanagement, and failure to make timely decisions are not effective leadership traits. This is why I've stated that of all the DISC temperaments, "C"s have to work a little harder to be effective leaders. When they take the time to clearly share their vision in detail (S1) others will see the strength of the plan and the details that "C"s are capable of developing. "C"s can also improve their leadership effectiveness by developing clear standards and systems that ensure consistency and accuracy.

The four generalities regarding leadership tendencies of each DISC temperament are just that—generalities. No one is strictly "D," "I," "S," or "C." Each has a DISC space as was discussed in Forming Element 5. The key to being more effective as a leader is self-awareness. Being cognizant of your own tendencies allows you to act more deliberative in your leadership approach. As you consciously work to apply the appropriate leadership style to various situations, you will build your leadership muscles and effectively stretch your DISC space. And, correlating with the observation of Supreme

Court Justice Oliver Wendell Holmes Jr. paraphrasing his father's wisdom, "Man's mind, once stretched by a new idea, never regains its original dimensions," the more you try on your new leadership styles, the more comfortable you will become using each at its appropriate time.

Regardless of natural dominant DISC temperament, anyone can improve their leadership effectiveness by adapting their style to the needs of the individuals being led. As such, just as your awareness of your DISC temperament helps you understand your leadership tendencies; understanding of others' DISC temperaments helps you provide the leadership style appropriate to the individual's temperament. When communicating with a "C," open the S1 window a little more because "C"s thrive on details. Use more S2 with "S"s because they feel valued when asked for their input. Use a bit more S3 with "I"s so they know their boss is supporting their problem solving and because they value the collaboration. With "D"s, open your S4 window because they like being in control.

Remain aware of your own tendencies and remain open to feedback that indicates the needs of the team. If the demands placed upon you are affecting your leadership, be willing to make a course correction.

Hijacked Leadership and Best Intentions

Despite our best intentions, in today's business environment of downsizing, global competition, and instantaneous results, you may find that you just don't have the time to coach or collaborate even if that is your natural tendency. If your schedule is so packed that you are running constantly from meeting to meeting endlessly all day, if competing priorities completely hijack your time and leave you scrambling just to meet the most pressing needs, if you struggle daily to balance the needs of your crew, the needs of your superiors, the needs of your family, and whatever time is left for your own needs, something has got to give. Like most people running at this pace, you probably end up leaving your crew alone more often than you'd prefer. They end up making more of the decisions and carrying more of the load in your absence. Be aware of these times and how your crew perceives your leadership style (or lack thereof). If they have to take the initiative to get the job done, don't play "Monday morning quarterback." Recognize that you bear some, if not most, of the responsibility. You, as the leader, are ultimately responsible.

I know this is a tough standard and most of us rationalize our situations because we all have double standards—I've said this before but it is worth repeating—we tend to judge others by their actions yet judge ourselves by our intentions. "I meant to stop by and talk to her about the project; I wanted to take a bit more time to explain his new assignment; I haven't had time to get the new guy up to speed; I know she wanted to work on the report but it was faster just to do it myself, etc." Although we excuse our failings because we are overwhelmed with all that the modern economy imposes on us, it doesn't change the fact that we are not providing the leadership needed. We are abdicating by default.

Leadership Styles and Rewards

In Tables 2.16 through 2.19, each leadership style had an aspect of the behaviors that were rewarded. In reality, what you reward will be the largest determinant of how your leadership style is perceived. No matter what you say, how you present or perceive yourself, or your best intentions, others will gauge your leadership style by what you reward. For example,

1. You may imagine yourself to be a delegating leader, but you have the compelling need to know every detail and second-guess decisions; you are anything but delegating. More likely you are seen as a micromanager—maybe even a tyrant.
2. You may present yourself as a mentoring leader with an "open door" policy, but when people come to your office, you are too busy multitasking, answering phones, and texting; when your answers are terse, perfunctory responses that come off condescending and patronizing, your claims to the contrary won't convince them that you are anything but a self-absorbed dictator or an unconcerned abdicator.

You get what you reward—and sometimes the only reward is the failure to be punished.

"Today was a good day; I didn't get my ass chewed!"
"It has been so great since the boss has been out of town—we've been very productive."

If your crew only receives feedback when there is a problem, there is a good bet that there is a problem with your leadership.

Avoid Being a Bottom Feeder

Again, just like DISC temperaments, there is no *best style*—just as there is no "best" golf club—each style can be effective or ineffective depending on how and when it is applied, the needs of the situation, and the needs of the crew. If the only club you ever use is your driver, you will surely not be an effective golfer. And if you only use one style, your leadership effectiveness will suffer.

Although there is no best style, there are styles that consistently associated with the worst bosses. If you think about it, the worst bosses you have had typically fall into one of three categories:

1. Dictators—the person who is constantly giving directions, barking orders, chastising the work of others, never coaching, never collaborating, and never delegating.
2. Abdicators—the boss who is never out where the work is happening. They are either sequestered in their offices or flying high schmoozing in the offices of their superiors. They don't give good direction; they don't develop a common shared vision; they don't communicate what is happening in all those closed door meetings—and yet they give low marks at the end of the year for people whom they said should have been more productive.
3. Seagulls—John Beck shared with me an analogy of a seagull to describe the style of manager that exhibits a combination of traits from the above two. Imagine you are spending a nice day at the beach. The sun is warm, and a gentle breeze carries with it a pleasant salty aroma. Suddenly and without warning, a mangy looking shadow swoops out of the azure blue sky shattering the tranquility with its frenetic flapping and squawking. The seagull swoops dangerously close, snatches some snacks from your tray, and leaves a nasty yellowish pile in the middle of your forehead. Just as suddenly, the intruder is gone. You are left humiliated, angry, and impotent to retaliate. If you hardly ever see your manager except when she storms into the office or out onto the production floor, barks a bunch of commands regardless if she is fully aware of the details, berates a few of your coworkers, and then storms off to wreak havoc somewhere else—you have a seagull manager. *Don't be a seagull.*

All three of these approaches are characterized by being low in relationship behavior. It is the relationship that forms between leaders and their crews that makes them effective. Remember the four questions posed earlier that every leader must answer before attracting willing followers:

1. Can I trust you?
2. Do you care about me?
3. Are you committed to excellence?
4. Are you going somewhere I want to go?

These questions are only answered in the minds of the crew when a relationship exists. It doesn't have to be a relationship outside of work (and for most situations, I strongly advise against unduly familiar relationships outside of work). But, there does need to be communication, consistency in word as well as in deed, and an investment must be made in the development of each crew member before they will fully engage and commit to you as a leader.

FOUNDATIONAL PRINCIPLE: On any given day, you may be on your game and respond effectively. On other days, you won't. Count on it. The important aspect to remember is the same as was pointed out when discussing DISC temperament—*connection, not perfection.* By remaining open and trying to give your crew what they need when they need it, you will establish a rapport with them that will give you some credits. When you are off your game, they'll recognize it and cut you some slack.

REFERENCE: If your Forming Assessment Table indicates that a deeper understanding of leadership would be beneficial, or if you'd just like to learn more about situational approaches to leadership, your style, and how to increase your effectiveness, refer to Beck and Yeager's work (Beck, J., and Yeager, N. 2001. *The Leader's Window: Mastering the Four Styles of Leadership to Build High-Performing Teams.* Palo Alto, CA: Davies-Black). You can also refer to the Charter Oak Consulting Group website at www.cocg.com.

Individual Emotional Responses to Change

One final note about leadership: As you think about individual personality temperament and the leadership response choices you make, you will also need to keep in mind each individual's emotional response to change. Within your organization you will probably have a mix of members with varying attitudes toward change that fall on a continuum from change ready to change resistant. Some will be eager to make improvements and work proactively with you to affect the change; others will be more hesitant; some may fall even farther on the spectrum and be change resistant. Where each individual falls will be based upon their perspective of the benefits versus the costs and their individual level of trust. Where people fall on the change readiness continuum may not be readily apparent during the Forming Stage. People may be taking a wait and see approach; others don't know enough to have formed an opinion; and still others are laying back to see if the initiative actually begins to gain traction before they voice any opposition to it. The latter of these may have seen many previous change initiatives sprout and wither on the vine; they hold back their comments and concerns waiting for the initiative to fail on its own, thereby sparing their energy and avoiding the risk of looking bad politically. If there are going to be conflicts based upon individual emotional responses to change, they will surface during the later parts of the Forming Stage and within the Focusing Stage, when the plans become more concrete. Accordingly, we will discuss the emotional responses to change as we look at the Elements of Focusing.

Forming Element 7: Communications Are Planned, Deliberate, and Broad Reaching

When analyzing why organizations struggle to achieve optimal performance, failures of communication are among the most frequently reported. According to the Society for Human Resource Management's (SHRM) (http://www.shrm.org/Research/SurveyFindings/Documents/2007%20Change%20Management%20Survey%20Report.pdf) 2007 Change Management Survey Report, the top two obstacles to change are

1. Communication breakdown
2. Employee resistance

We'll talk more about employee resistance when we discuss Focusing Element 10. Right now, let's explore communication breakdown. The failure to communicate stems from three root causes:

- Failure to craft the message to the audience
- Failure to prepare the messengers
- A communications distribution network that is either too limited or used too infrequently

While serving in the Navy, I heard an adage repeated over and over like a mantra, "Failure to plan is planning to fail." This applies to communications in spades. Unless the communications are planned, deliberate, and broad reaching invariably they will become haphazard and indirect. People not present in meetings won't receive the information in a timely manner.

When people don't have the correct information they won't be able to support the change initiative. How can you support what you know nothing about? Lack of understanding and support leads to false starts and limited organizational engagement. At its worst, partial information, misinformation, or completely false information can circulate through the "rumor mill," potentially fueling dissent and giving rise to a climate of fear or mistrust. Within such an organizational climate, the change initiative can stall or derail completely before it ever gets a chance to take root.

Effective communications can limit these ill effects by limiting misinformation and through the alignment of change activities. To be most effective, communications should align and coordinate the activities of individuals and departments through a sequential series of linked messages that cascades down through all levels and areas. Figure 2.22 represents how organizations can be aligned through cascading communication. The top of the organizational pyramid represents the top executive and her or his direct reports.

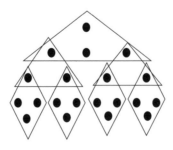

Figure 2.22   Aligning the organization with cascading communication.

This team becomes fully aligned behind the value proposition, vision, mission, and priorities. When they decide upon a course of action, each member of the team has the ability and motivation to carry that message out to their organizational area. In turn, each of that team's members aligns and commits to carry the message to their areas of responsibility thereby aligning the entire organization toward the mission. Cascading communication creates a direct "line of sight" between the activities of the individual departments and subteams to the overarching organizational mission and strategies. Each manager and supervisor down the chain acts as a link in the chain of communications.

EXAMPLE: NOT KEEPING AN EYE ON THE BIG PICTURE: I had a striking example of a manager who did not have a clear line of sight early in my career when employed by a company to implement training and qualifications processes that supported both operations and maintenance. To justify the expense and gauge the effectiveness of our efforts, I felt it was important to understand the metrics that would be utilized to measure the effectiveness of the training initiatives. A senior manager informed me that I didn't need to know any metrics; he alone would be the ultimate gauge of success. I didn't want to argue with him, but I really wanted something a little more accurate since my "manager happiness meter" was still in the calibration shop (I will admit that I was not known for my tact back then—or even now for that matter). I pressed him further to clarify the goals. After several tense minutes of discussion, it became apparent that I wasn't going to get an answer because he didn't really have any effective measures himself. Red faced, with a big blue temple vein pulsing angrily, he sputtered in frustration, "I'm not here to make money; I'm here to make paper!" I paused, but not long enough, "Really, and have you told this to our stockholders?"

In addition to not being known for my tact, I was also known to be a bit sarcastic.

The moral of the story is that every person, from top to bottom, needs to understand the goals and needs to have a direct "line of sight" to that goal. When line of sight is lacking in an organization, infighting and inefficiencies will occur. You may not need to explain every detail to every person (that's not necessary), but everyone needs to know where they fit in. Otherwise,

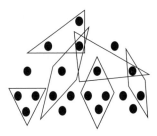

Figure 2.23   Misaligned organizations lacking cascading communication.

they may just be checking a box—going through the motions without engaged critical thinking regarding how their activities help achieve the ultimate mission and vision.

Unless there is a deliberate and structured approach to the organization's communications plans, the organization's alignment can look more like the organization represented in Figure 2.23. The top executive team isn't fully aligned around the strategy and mission. Different leaders focus on their individual priorities to which they work to align their portions of the organization. Some portions of the organization work toward the common agenda while others focus their activities in other directions. This disparate alignment wastes resources and frustrates team members.

NECESSARY BUT INSUFFICIENT: Effective communications is essential, but insufficient in and of itself to create optimal organizational alignment. There are many factors that contribute to an organization being misaligned; poor communications is just one of the factors. Throughout this book we will outline the other factors. We begin with communications because it is essential to all other activities that will create alignment and is one of the most cited causes of frustration, low productivity, and poor morale.

Principles of Communication

Before we outline an organizational communication plan, let's level set our terminology around communications with a quick review of the principles of communication summarized in Table 2.20.

Table 2.20   Summary of Communications Terms

Term	Definition
Sender	The individual or entity that initiates the communication by crafting and sending a message. The sender is ultimately responsible for ensuring that the message is received as intended.
Objective	The intended outcome of the message. The objective can be answered by asking "What do you want the audience to do with the message?" Typical objectives include to entertain, to inform, to elicit support, to change perceptions or belief, and to take action or refrain from acting. These objectives are listed in order of difficulty of achievement. It is far easier to inform than to actually compel action.
Message	The elements assembled for the communication that are intended to accomplish the objective of the communication. The elements of the message could be assembled from a myriad of choices, all of which will affect the impact of the message and whether it will have the intended effect on the audience.
Receiver	The target audience of the message. The receiver may be one person or it could be an entire population. Keep in mind that there is often more than one audience. The primary audience is the direct recipient of the message; the secondary audience may be on the periphery of the message but may still be impacted by the message. Think of unintended consequences. Who is not included may send a clearer message than that sent to those actually included.
Media	The element that carries the message. Media formats include verbal face to face, body language, tone, mass media (radio, television, film), electronic, Web based, telecommunications, art, physical, etc. Stringing together multiple means of communications into a line of communication (LOC) is usually more effective in ensuring that the message is received as intended, e.g., verbal communication with written, Web postings, and signage is more impactful, repeatable, and retainable than verbal alone.
Feedback	The corresponding return message that provides information to the sender whether the receiver has received the message as intended and whether it was effective in achieving the objective. Messages are considered one way or two way depending upon whether feedback is present. One way communications have no feedback mechanisms.
Filters	Impediments to communication. Filters can be physical (loud noises, static, poor connections, distractions, etc.), situational (context, antecedents, etc.), cultural (language, beliefs, etc.), or mental (emotional state, perceptions, preconceptions, prejudices, etc.).

(continued)

Table 2.20   Summary of Communications Terms (Continued)

Term	Definition
Frequency	The number and timing of the communications. The more frequently and more often a message is heard, the more likely it will be received as intended.

Communications Process

Communications should be thought of as a cyclical process more so than an event. It is helpful to think of the communications process as having six or seven steps depending upon whether agreement is initially reached or the need for further discussions are warranted (see Figure 2.24).

1. Preparation
2. Framing the discussion
3. Clarification of positions and interests
4. Involved discussion
5. Reaching agreement
6. Exploring area of disagreement
7. Setting follow-up

Step 1: Preparation: When crafting your communications strategy and message, begin with the end in mind. If it is important for the communication to be effective, then it is important to prepare beforehand. Again,

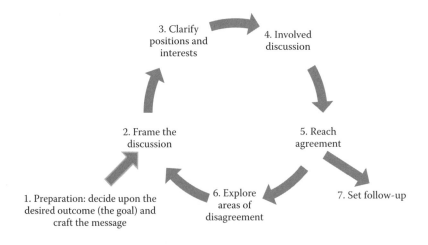

Figure 2.24   Cyclical communications process.

failure to plan is planning to fail. Start the process with what you desire as the intended outcome of the communications. What do you want from your audience? Is your desire to merely inform or do you want them to take action? The format and frequency of your message will be shaped by your intended outcome. Once you've determined the outcome, analyze your audience. What do they already know about the subject? What do they feel? Believe? What are the barriers? Craft your message based upon your analysis. Based upon your desired outcome and your understanding of the audience, consider the possibility that your message may not be received as intended. Be prepared to adapt as necessary.

Part of your preparation should include choosing the location, selecting the timing, setting the tone, providing prior preparatory information, etc. Prior preparation is essential for effective communications. If you begin poorly, you may never be able to successfully navigate the communications process.

ANOTHER GREAT NAVY AXIOM: Prior planning precludes a poor performance!

Step 2: Frame the Discussion: Frame the discussion by clarifying and outlining what you'd like to accomplish during the communication process. Spell out what your intentions are to limit or broaden the scope of communications as necessary to meet your objective.

Step 3: Clarify Positions and Interests: Your position is where you stand on the subject; your interest is the underlying goal behind your position. A person may be arguing for a position when there may be other alternatives to achieving his or her interests. It is important to work to get to the heart of the matter, which may mean moving beyond the surface to much deeper values and objectives.

Step 4: Involved Discussion: Interactions involving a true discussion is the key to effective communications. Many leaders, particularly heavily weighted toward "D" or "C" temperaments, begin quickly and immediately want to jump to closing. Limiting interaction limits the level of commitment. Be open to feedback, both verbal and nonverbal, to continuously gauge the effectiveness of the communication interaction.

Steps 5 and 6: Reach Agreement Explore Areas of Disagreement: Based upon the interaction, work to reach agreement. If you cannot reach agreement, you'll need to circle back and explore the areas of disagreement. It may be necessary to reframe the discussion by outlining the purpose and scope again. Cycle through this process as often as necessary to reach agreement.

Step 7: Set Follow-Up: Once you reach agreement, close out the communications process by setting follow-up. Summarize the areas of agreement, and define what and when each party will act. Set the timing for the next interaction.

This basic communication process will be referred to many times as we discuss execution strategies and tactics of organizational development. Whether giving directions, teaching, or resolving conflict, the same basic process cycle will be utilized.

Developing a Strategic Communications Plan

With the basic communications process cycle in mind, you are now ready to develop the structures for an organizational communications plan. An effective communications plan will encompass verbal, written, visual, and sometimes tactile communication pathways along with corresponding feedback mechanisms. Without a broad reaching strategy, communications rarely cascade effectively throughout the organization in a timely manner.

Craft key messages to include both talking points and frequently asked questions. This will prepare managers and leaders at every level to effectively deliver the message consistently and with adequate detail. During the Forming Stage, some of the key messages that organizations frequently need to address with their communications plans include

1. Communication of the value proposition, organizational mission and vision
2. Compelling reason for change
3. Expected outcomes
4. Realistic costs and benefits of project/change initiative
5. Organizational impact including how it will affect roles, responsibilities, and staffing
6. Assess feedback and address concerns
7. Establish schedules for regular ongoing communications

Table 2.21 is an example of a strategic communications template. Filling out each of the blocks in the table will walk you through the process of

Table 2.21 Strategic Communications Plan Template

Communications Plan		
Message Title:		
Situation:		
Target Audience (Receivers)		
Understanding the Audience	**Primary:**	**Secondary:**
What is the desired communication outcome? Inform—Call to action—Gain their support—Address a concern		
What do they currently know about the topic?		
What do they believe?		
What is their general mood?		
What are their major concerns?		
What is the benefit to them?		
What is the most effective means of communications?		
What do you want them to do with the message?		
Who are the key influencers?		
Any barriers to communications?		
How will feedback be solicited and received?		
Objectives		

Develop effective lines of communication so that these channels can be utilized regularly to ensure a continuous two-way flow of information, thereby facilitating the following outcomes:
  1.
  2.
  3.		

(continued)

Table 2.21 Strategic Communications Plan Template (Continued)

Communications Plan							
Objectives							
4. 5.							
Key Messages							
Strategies							
Tactics							
Line of Communication	**Face to Face**	**Print**	**Web Based**	**Broadcast**	**Local Signage**	**Bulletin Boards**	**Other**
Who develops							
Who delivers							
How frequently							
Feedback							

crafting the message, analyzing the audience, and designing the deliver process.

NOTE: This template is contained on the CD that accompanies this book.

The latter portion of the strategic communications plan translates the strategy into tactics. The strategy is the broad reaching organizational plan; the tactics are the specific actions to employ executing the strategy. Table 2.22 provides another example of a tactical communications template.

Table 2.22   Tactical Communications Templates

Activity	
Audience	
Owner	
Desired outcome	
Resources	
Tools	
Timing	

Each element in the strategic plan should have a number of corresponding tactics that specify exactly who, what, when, and where the activities will be executed to effectively implement the strategic communications plan.

NOTE: An in-depth discussion differentiating strategy from tactics is contained in the Focusing Stage section.

Communications and Feedback: More Is Better

In the case of communications, frequency cannot be overemphasized. A rule of thumb in marketing stipulates that a person has to hear the message seven times before it is readily recalled. There is a popular headache remedy whose initial marketing campaign revolved around repeating the name of the product and where to apply it—annoying, but very effective at ensuring that the intended audience, the potential consumers, remember both the name of the product and its intended use.

The fact is, the more often the audience hears the message, the better chance they will understand and believe the message. Too often, initiatives are launched with a major initial push of communications involving top management talking about the new vision and all the benefits that will result, and then…nothing. To execute the communications plan at the required frequency requires enlisting every member in a leadership, management, and supervisory position throughout the entire affected organization. Hearing the message once at a large organizational meeting won't have a significant impact. But, hearing the message daily in team meetings, shift changes, and shop floor discussions helps infuse the language of change into the organizational vernacular.

Provide Regular Updates on Organizational Progress

To effectively support change initiatives, communications need to be targeted, consistent, frequent, and provide regular updates on organizational progress. It is also important to celebrate wins along the way—publicize the major milestones the organization achieves. These positive messages help sustain the organizational energy to continue moving forward. Think of it like taking a long road trip. If you are going to travel from Los Angeles to Orlando, you're not going to see a sign that says, "Orlando, 2510 miles." Instead, you'll see I-10 East Riverside, followed by AZ, NM, TX, etc. These markers reassure you that you are making progress in the right direction and inspire you to continue the long journey. Communicating organizational mile markers provides the same encouragement and inspiration. The problem comes when the work, the problems, the frustration, and the distractions cause you to lose focus on communicating the message. This is why it is so important to develop a strategic communications plan during the Forming Stage and continue to execute the plan as part of the overall project management methodology.

Sneaking the Camel in under the Tent

In addition to the frequency, it is important that the message be believable. Unless the organization is staffed with young workers freshly minted into the world of work, it is likely that the crews have been through multiple organizational change initiatives. They've seen them come and they've seen them go. When one more change comes down the pike their eyes roll as if to say, "Here we go again." As a practitioner, I've found it to be far better to soft launch initiatives. Don't overexaggerate and don't sell it as a "new!" and "revolutionary!" panacea. As much as practical, anchor the change in the foundations of the past. When affecting change, link the initiative to relevant current and past initiatives. Explain that the organization, in its quest for continuous improvement, is seeking to build upon what has worked well in the past. This will provide a sense of continuity to the organization and validate the work done before. Very frequently, the audience you are talking to will have had some ties to the past initiatives and may have felt significant ownership in them. When those initiatives failed to bear the desired fruit, they probably felt a sense of loss and frustration. Minimizing their efforts by implying "This is a new day—out with the old and in with the new," may very well alienate a significant portion of your audience at the beginning of the imitative. You will have opened poorly.

Keeping It Consistent versus Keeping It Fresh

Much of the discussion on communications thus far is commonly accepted among best practices. Where I diverge from many communications and marketing theorists lies in the balance between consistency and freshness. Every year marketing and communications specialists come up with new logos, new branding initiatives, and new campaigns. Since it is their bread and butter, this only makes sense from their perspective. But, if you really want to make sustainable changes, you may want to think twice before you follow their advice. Change takes time for people to assimilate. If you change the message too frequently you will be wiping out the gains you've made and starting over from ground zero. Consider the experience of a major transportation company.

The company had wanted to increase the professionalism and degree of engagement of their operations and maintenance staff. They started a "professional mechanic" communications campaign complete with slogans, logos, patches, and stickers. The initiative was met with skepticism and very little buy-in. Eventually, after a few years, the mechanics began embracing the idea—slowly, quietly, and with very little fanfare, the slogans and logos began showing up on crew procedures, reports, and other documents. A few of the mechanics incorporated the logos into hardhat stickers and embroidered jackets. The initiative that had lain dormant so long was finally taking root and beginning to bear fruit. Mechanics were showing a growing sense of ownership. Unfortunately, the corporate communications department had already moved on. They had formulated another campaign with the same objective but new slogans, logos, and branding. An edict went out from corporate that the mechanics were to cease using the old logos and slogans and begin to use the new ones. As you can imagine, this didn't sit well with the intended audience. They had no buy-in to the new message. The well intentioned mandate sent from on high did nothing but fuel the alienation, frustration, and anger of the audience—the opposite of the desired outcome.

Believability

One last note about communication—it has to be believable.

The initial believability of a message will very often be determined by the credibility of the messenger. As you roll out the message, think about who will be delivering it. Work with the individuals who are well respected by the audience. If the most influential members are on board, there is a far better chance that the message will be resonate and have the desired impact.

Regardless of initial impact, the message won't be believed for long if it isn't true. People know when something is true and represents the heart of the matter. Some companies I've worked with have spent more effort spinning messages rather than improving the quality of their products or services. One corporation retained 24 members, including a senior vice president and several directors in their communications department funded by a multimillion dollar budget, yet only employed two people in their training department. Considering this ratio, was the company more concerned about what they were or what they looked like? No matter how well crafted, messages contrary to actual outcomes won't be believed for long.

Forming Element 8: Clear Behavioral Norms Are Established and Broadly Observed

Every group has behavioral norms that govern how the members interact—these are all part of the third plank in the Framework for Team Success: the working approach (shown again in Figure 2.25). These norms are frequently unspoken and assumed to be universally accepted—after all, "everyone

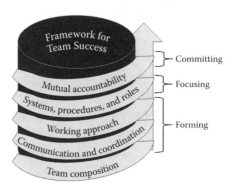

Figure 2.25   Framework for team success.

knows how to behave, don't they?" This is not always a valid assumption. Taking the time to develop group norms and behavioral expectation in the form of team ground rules helps facilitate the forming process.

Team Ground Rules

Ground rules are the stated expectations that team members agree to adhere to when interacting with each other. Just as it is beneficial to develop a team charter, taking time to explicitly define, develop, and state these norms and behavioral expectation during the Forming Stage contributes to a solid foundation upon which organizational success can be built. Writing them down and having the team members sign off on them makes a powerful statement. The activity will also help empower members to hold each other accountable when tensions start running high in subsequent stages of organizational development.

Going through the process of brainstorming, recording, and agreeing to ground rules will also help identify some unspoken fears, anxieties, and concerns crew members may have based upon past group experiences.

NOTE: If you are not familiar with the process of brainstorming, refer to Focusing Element 8 for an explanation of the brainstorming process.

This simple, "obvious" and almost mundane, process may be the single factor that helps you navigate through the rocky times that come with almost every major change initiative.

NOTE: The actual content and wording of the team's ground rules is less important than the fact that they are shared and widely adhered to. I've seen ground rules that are lengthy and formal and I've seen short whimsical lists. As long as they foster a cohesive environment with the underlying objective of "mutual success through mutual respect," the form is far less critical than the function.

Enforcing the Ground Rules

Developing ground rules is important; enforcing them is critical. Developing ground rules that are not utilized is more destructive than if they were never written down. Having ground rules from which the leader and select other people are exempt sends a powerfully negative message through the organization. I've seen many groups where a double standard is routinely observed. Behavioral expectations are enforced for the rank and file, but the behavior of supervisors and managers is overlooked. This applies to their being on time, how they interact, and how they participate.

A very common example of this is attendance at training. The discussion on the Forming Stage thus far has spent the majority of time talking about leadership styles and interpersonal skills—that's because these foundational elements are critical to building a healthy organization. However, nine times out of ten when I have conducted classes on these subjects, the managers and executives don't attend. And almost invariably in these classes the participants ask, "Have you taught these things to our managers?" If the managers say it's important enough for team members to attend, then they should participate as well. Even if they are knowledgeable, their presence in the class creates a shared experience that accelerates the forming process. Conversely, their absence sends a powerful statement that overrides any words they might say to the contrary—especially when they don't know the common language nor do they demonstrate the skills accepted as appropriate group norms.

NEGATIVE CLIMATE IS A DIRECT REFLECTION OF POOR LEADERSHIP: If the culture and organizational climate are negative such that group norms are not adhered to, diversity of personality temperament is not valued, and interactive adaptive leadership styles are not effectively demonstrated, poor leadership is responsible. Leaders are either directly responsible by modeling the behaviors or they are indirectly responsible by failing to address unconstructive behaviors in an open and timely manner. Perpetrating and propagating a negative climate erodes the cohesiveness and effectiveness of the group.

Forming Element 9: Meetings Are Well Planned, and Prior Notice Is Provided

BACK TO THE BASICS: Senior leadership frequently scoffs when I suggest that they should attend training on effective meetings. They see such training as too elementary and "beneath" them. Just as frequently,

I have experienced some of the most ineffective meetings held by that same leadership. Just because someone is in a senior position does not make their meetings effective.

Analogous to how in 2007 college football unranked Appalachian State upset no. 5-ranked Michigan, mastery of the fundamentals combined with hard work, attention to detail, and conditioning can overcome some incredible odds. Mastery of the basics of communications, including holding effective meetings goes a long way in forming effective organizations.

It ain't fancy or glamorous—but it works!

Meetings are essential to the success of an organization; meetings are huge wastes of time. These diametrically opposite views are almost universally expressed in every organization I've worked with—and both views are equally valid. Despite the critical need for meetings, I've attended far more that fell into the time wasting category than those that added value. The differentiators between an effective meeting and a huge resource sucking black hole can be broken down into three categories of before, during, and after:

1. Failure to plan and prepare for meetings
2. Failure to effectively facilitate
3. Failure to follow up

NOTE: Forming Element 9 addresses planning and preparation; Forming Element 10 addresses facilitation. Follow-up is embedded throughout the process and will be dealt with topic by topic. Planning, preparation, facilitation, and follow-up are all key elements in the team's working approach.

Planning for a Meeting

Failing to plan a meeting is the same as failing to plan anything else—it is planning to fail. Meetings are a form of communications. As such, the cyclical communications process we outlined in Forming Element 7 applies:

Preparation → Framing → Clarification → Discussion
→ Agreement → Set Follow-up

Like other communications, begin with the end in mind. Too often the one calling the meeting is unprepared. They've done no planning, preparation, assigned no prework, and have given limited notification—they just wing it. People show up to the meeting unprepared to participate. The first portion of the meeting involves getting participants up to speed on the purpose of the meeting and answering questions that could have been handled with a prior agenda and information packet. Eventually, as time is running out, the leader hurriedly tries to salvage some productivity out of the remaining time or the meeting runs over its allotted time, thereby encroaching on other scheduled events and priorities.

To avoid this common pattern, it is better to have already worked out what you want to accomplish during the meeting before the meeting. Which of the following five outcomes are you driving toward?

1. To inform
2. To solicit input
3. To solve problems
4. To make decisions
5. To take action

Keeping the purpose in mind, send out prior information that prepares attendees. Inform them of the meeting purpose. Provide pertinent background information. Make preassignments and expect people to come prepared to participate. Prior preparation will make the actual meetings much more productive. I find it useful to prepare and send out the agenda at least a week in advance if possible. Table 2.23 shows a sample agenda template prepared using Microsoft® Excel that is also available on the companion CD.

Recognize that the purpose of meetings changes as the organization or project team matures. In the early phases of the Forming Stage, meeting contents will initially require a bit more of S1—Directing leadership. You'll need to tell people what they don't know. As the group grows and the organization moves through forming and begins to focus, the purpose of the meetings should adapt to move the organization to higher levels of performance; correspondingly, your leadership style should adapt as well.

However, be conscientious that your directing style isn't perceived as dictating. Remember, S1—Directing is characterized by the leader providing the majority of the information. Certainly, in the initial phases of the Forming Stage, this is required—you need to give information to share the

Table 2.23   Meeting Agendas

Meeting Agenda				
Date:		**Place:**		
Start Time:		**Stop Time:**		
Ground rules:				
(1) Mutual success through mutual respect				
(2) Come prepared				
(3) Begin and end on time (staying on time to accomplish tasks)				
(4) Flexible to adapt as needs of group dictate				
(5) Have fun				
Team Members and Other Attendees:			*Meeting Assignments:*	
			Meeting Facilitator:	
			Note Taker and Timekeeper:	
Start Time	**Stop Time**	**Topics**	**Agenda Topics:**	**Presenter**
Meeting Notes				
Future Topics				*Presenter*

vision and mission with the team. However, how you provide direction will determine whether or not your style is seen as dictating. When you dictate, you stifle communications and create barriers to team cohesion and effective performance.

Allow for input—but be clear what aspects of the mission or vision are open for discussion and which aspects have already been set. There is nothing wrong with having some predefined limits. In fact, people appreciate them. Where people can become frustrated is when they thought they had input when they don't. By setting the topic, tone, purpose, and limits up front, people can come prepared to engage. We'll discuss this fine distinction in more detail within Forming Element 10.

Forming Element 10: Meetings Are Well Run, Structured, and Productive

I once asked a manager why she didn't take charge of a particularly frustrating and unproductive meeting. "I didn't want people to feel like I was telling them what to do. I wanted the group to decide what we should do." What she didn't recognize—or accept—is that her failure to lead was actually more frustrating to the team than if she had been more direct. This aversion to being direct stems from the misconception that direction is not as valid a leadership style as collaboration is. All four leadership styles discussed in Forming Element 6 are necessary for team success. If you are the one calling the meeting, you had better be prepared to lead it.

The simple fact is that effective meetings don't just happen. In order for meetings to be effective they require key group roles to be performed. Within each meeting the following roles are required: facilitator, timekeeper, participants, and scribe.

NOTE: Robert's Rules of Order are rarely invoked outside of government committee meetings. Less formal meetings can encourage involvement and free discussion. However, chaos rarely yields productive outcomes. Establishing and respecting defined meeting roles and responsibility is a proven effective compromise between the stringent rules governing committees and meeting anarchy.

Required Roles for Effective Meetings

Facilitator: Each meeting needs a designated facilitator. The facilitator ensures that the meeting does the following:

1. Starts on time
2. Sticks to the agenda (unless variation is required to advance the team's mission at that time and the topic cannot be tabled for a future meeting)
3. Engages all participants to solicit input and ensure that one or two people don't dominate the conversation
4. Limits unproductive discussions
5. Facilitates group decision making process
6. Ends on time

Another key element is to develop facilitation skills within multiple members within the organization. Should the designated facilitator be unable to attend, a designated alternate should be able to step forward to facilitate the meeting ensuring forward progress of the group. This can only be accomplished if the participants received an agenda and premeeting materials sufficiently early enough to give them adequate time to prepare.

Timekeeper: To stay on track, someone needs to be keeping track of the time. Often, the facilitator can play this role. However, the facilitator may get so caught up in the process of the meeting that they lose track of time. That is why it is often helpful to designate someone specifically to be a timekeeper and empower them to intervene as needed if the group veers excessively from the agreed upon agenda.

NOTE: A frequent problem with meetings is overpacking the agenda. The person planning the meeting can be too ambitious/optimistic about what can be accomplished in the meeting. Be realistic, the more complex or controversial the issue and the more people involved—the more time it will take to facilitate through the process.

Participants: Following the ground rules outlined in Forming Element 8, meeting participant should each feel comfortable contributing in meetings. In addition, members should feel empowered to intervene in meetings as needed to help keep them on track. I have found that participants can be empowered to intervene by using interjecting "process checks." When a participant invokes a process check, the phrase cues the group that the individual raising the concern is working within the established guidelines to keep the team moving forward productively.

Scribe: The scribe is a designated recorder. Its role is to document the key outcomes of the meeting. For every meeting held, the results need to be shared with all interested parties, including decisions made, action needed, who is responsible, and projected completion dates. To be effective, each member needs to be clear about who will do what and by when at the conclusion of the meeting. During meetings, I find it helpful to project the same agenda spreadsheet sent out before the meeting onto a wall or screen to be

Table 2.24   Meeting Notes and Assignments

Meeting Minutes					
Team					
Meeting Date:					
Meeting Objective:					
Action Item		*Owner*	*Resources Needed*	*Due Date*	*Status*
Decisions Made					
Parking Lot					

used during the meeting. Typing notes directly into the spreadsheet keeps everyone on track and understanding what has been decided and what is next.

In addition to the meeting agenda, I finish out meetings by completing the meeting minutes template shown in Table 2.24. This template summarizes assigned action items, decisions made, and any topics reserved for future discussion by placing them on the "parking lot." Seeing the consensus of the group in writing eliminates much of the frustration caused by post-meeting confusion.

Conducting Meetings Following the Cyclical Communications Process

Preparation for the meeting and working through the agenda is an effective start to conducting effective meetings—but, the pure mechanics of the process should never take priority over achieving the desired outcome. It's impossible to know, let alone outline, all the multiple permutations and variations a meeting could take. Accordingly, it is much more important to work through the process in such a way that you and your team arrive at a mutually satisfactory conclusion. To achieve these conclusions, follow through on the communications cycle:

Preparation → Framing → Clarification → Discussion
→ Agreement → Set Follow-up

Preparing an agenda for the meeting and notifying all the participants ahead of time, as well as providing any needed background materials, inform the participants of your desired outcome. They are much more likely to attend ready to help you accomplish the objective of the meeting. Prior preparation also provides more time during the meeting to interact and reach agreement. You will have to spend less time getting participants up to speed on background and details. They will be able to interact in a meaningful way.

As the discussion ebbs and flows, continue to move the group toward the desired outcome through effective facilitation.

During the course of the discussion, you may have to go around the loop several times, reframing the discussion and interacting until you reach the desired outcome. This doesn't mean that you drive for a foregone conclusion decided in advance. If the decision has already been made, then notify the attendees that the meeting will be to notify them of the decisions that have already been made. This is a critical aspect of framing the discussion. By explaining which variables are in play and the limitation to the group's authority, you will be much less likely to have unproductive conflicts. Conflicts arise and people disengage when they think that it was their decision to make and then find out that their input wasn't valued. Being clear up front removes these miscommunications and allows the team to focus their energies on the elements that are within their span of control.

EXAMPLE: I was working with a Midwestern manufacturing firm that had experienced a rapid increase in demand for their product. To meet the need, the management team wanted to move from two shifts per day/5 days per week to a 24 × 7 operation. The plant manager commissioned a team of operators to research and make recommendations on the type of 24-hour shifts they'd like to implement. Hesitant at first, the team began to research all the variation of shift schedules. They explored 8- and 12-hour shifts, rotating and fixed shifts, four on–four off, and seven-day sliding schedules. They even researched the long-term medical effects of various shifts on sleep patterns and safety. They took their research to the crews and solicited 100% participation from the operations and maintenance teams. By the time they had reached a conclusion, there was a large degree of ownership and a commensurate amount of pride in the work the team had accomplished. The team practiced their presentation in preparation for the big day. When that day came, they stood before the management team with their presentation printed out and the research piled at the ready to answer any questions that might arise. After making a very professional presentation explaining the decision they reached and the process they used, they waited expectantly for feedback. The plant manager picked up the teams' selected schedule, tilted his head to one side like a confused puppy, crumpled up the paper and threw it behind him. "That's all well and good, now here is the schedule we're going to implement."

The team spirit was crushed. The news spread like wildfire through the plant. The operators were incensed; plant morale plummeted. That was also the last time that the plant was able to get that level of participation from the crews.

There is a lesson to be learned from this demonstration of dictatorial leadership; don't set expectations of involvement and solicit input if it doesn't matter. If the plant manager had just stated the new shift schedule at the very beginning, there would never have been a problem. The crews had never expected to have input to their schedules; they had never had any input before. It was the plant manager that had assembled the team and sent them off on the assignment. Remember, whenever you raise expectations and subsequently fail to deliver, you are worse off than you would have been if you had never started.

Once the team has reached a mutually agreed upon decision, summarize the decisions made and tasks assigned on the meeting minutes template and set the follow-up dates necessary to keep the team moving ahead on the project plan.

Key Takeaways: Forming—Preparing for the Voyage

Forming occurs when the individuals first come together as a group and begin to transition from a group of individuals into a team. Leading this transformation requires both leadership and management responses to address both organizational and individual needs. Like most organic processes, there is no clear transition or line of demarcation between one stage and the next—just as there are no clear markers indicating when babies become infants, toddlers become adolescents, adolescents become preteens, etc. The stages blend and flow. You may think that you've addressed the needs of a stage when an event that uncovers one of those hidden areas we explored discussing the Johari Window occurs, making you realize that there is an element you have to go back to and address in order to continue moving forward. Just keep in mind the indicators that define the needs of forming and remain flexible in your approach. Table 2.25 outlines the indicators, organizational and individual needs, and some effective leadership and management responses, tools, and techniques that will serve as milestones marking your progress through the Forming Stage of organizational development.

Table 2.25 Key Takeaways: Forming

	Focus	Commit	Sustained Performance	Renewal
Form	Stumble	Fragment	Variable Performance	Level

Forming: Occurs after individuals first come together as a group and begin to transition from a group of individuals into a nascent team

Team Needs: Individuals joining a new team need
- Orientation
- A sense of purpose
- Building trust

Indicators of Effective Navigation	Indicators of Ineffective Navigation
• Shared purpose and identity • Widespread understanding of the team's mission • Growing excitement	• Lack of understanding • Mistrust guarded communication • Anxiety and apprehension

Effective Leadership Responses: Initial focus on providing direction
- Set a clear vision and mission
- Communicate organizations mission and vision

Effective Management Responses:
- Apply a holistic approach organizational development
- Define the strategies that will accomplish the mission and vision
- Coordinate resources with timing and needs
- Facilitate effective meetings that focus and engage

Tools and Techniques:
- Orientation meetings
- Mission and vision
- Basic skills training
  - o DISC
  - o Situational approaches to leadership
  - o Communications
  - o Effective meetings
- Communications plans (strategic and tactical)
- Meeting facilitation
  - o Meeting notification and prework agendas
  - o Meeting minutes and assignments

Forming Project Plan

Table 2.26 provides a quick synopsis of the elements of a project plan to build upon during the Forming Stage.

Table 2.26 Forming Project Plan—Preparing the Organization and Initial Design

Project Step	Responsibility	Date Planned	Date Complete
1. Designate project sponsors and team leaders, taking into consideration process improvement and ongoing current operations. • Outline leadership responsibilities and expectations • Conduct adaptive leadership training as appropriate to prepare leaders to lead			
2. Define the value proposition in terms of internal and/or external customers and stakeholders. Develop the project charter document.			
3. Develop the project staffing plan, staffing both Team "P" (present ongoing operations) and Team "F" (future process improvements)			
4. Develop strategic and tactical communications plans: • Communicate organization mission and vision • Compelling reason for change • Expected outcomes • Realistic costs and benefits of project • Organizational impact including how it will affect roles, responsibilities, and staffing • Assess feedback and address concerns • Establish schedules for regular ongoing communications			

(continued)

Table 2.26 Forming Project Plan—Preparing the Organization and Initial Design (Continued)

Project Step	Responsibility	Date Planned	Date Complete
5. Conduct orientation sessions: • Orientation for all organizational members • Orientation for project members			
6. Review project charter with teams • Modify as appropriate to promote involvement and commitment among teams			
7. Conduct team and process improvement skills training for project team members • DISC temperament • Effective meeting skills • Process improvement technical skills • Group decision-making and problem-solving techniques			
8. Teams define their team's working approaches • Team charters • Team ground rules			
9. Refine the vision and mission, working collaboratively with key stakeholders and organizational influencers to ensure broad acceptance.			
10. Team report out sessions and process check • Value proposition • Team initial project plans and team working approach • Team charters and ground rules • Next steps to move toward focusing			

Chapter 3

Stage 2—Focusing: Establishing the Ship's Routine

Overview and Assessment: Moving from Forming to Focusing

Focusing begins once there is a widespread clear understanding and acceptance of the organizational vision among the entire team. To transform this understanding of the vision into effective execution of the mission now requires the development of systems, assignment of roles and responsibilities among the crew, and the development of objectives and goals through the establishing of detailed action plans. Figure 3.1 graphically represents the building of the Organizational Development logic model showing the transition from Forming to Focusing. You will know that the organization is focusing well when you see a rising tide of optimism and individuals begin taking accountability for their roles and responsibilities. In contrast, if you observe confusion, reluctance, cynicism, or anger leading to conflicts and pushing back, the organization is not focusing—it is stumbling. The crew hasn't formed well. What is lacking must be addressed in order to gain their commitment and move toward a higher level of group commitment and performance. Table 3.1 summarizes the indicators of focusing well as compared to stumbling if the change initiative is faltering.

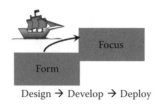

Figure 3.1   Moving from Forming toward Focusing.

Table 3.1   Summary of Indicators: Focusing versus Stumbling

	Focus	*Commit*	*Sustained Performance*	*Renewal*
Form	*Stumble*	*Fragment*	*Variable Performance*	*Level*

Focusing: Occurs when the team becomes aligned around the vision and mission. Systems and procedures begin to form and there is goal and role clarification

Team Needs:
- Understanding of how the mission and vision are to be accomplished
- Inclusion and involvement
- Initial training
- Assignment of roles and responsibilities
- Development of processes and procedures

Indicators of Effective Navigation	**Indicators of Ineffective Navigation**
• Growing optimism and commitment	• Fear, anger, cynicism
• Understanding and acceptance of individual roles and responsibilities	• Conflicts and confusion
	• Unproductive challenging

Focusing Assessment

Complete the Focusing Assessment Table (Table 3.2) to determine how well systems, procedures, objectives, and goals focus the organization's efforts toward achievement of its vision and mission. The more effectively the organization is focused, the more efficiently resources will be deployed and utilized and the fewer organizational conflicts will arise.

Once you've completed the Focusing Assessment Table, transfer your scores into the Focusing Scoring Matrix contained in Table 3.3.

Table 3.2 Focusing Assessment

For each of the paired statements or groups of statement below, decide which statement most accurately describes your experiences in the day-to-day work activities within your organization. For the statement that is chosen, check to what degree you believe the statement is either Most or Somewhat like your routine experience within your organization's work activities.

Check only one statement per paired question.

Assessment (Select One)			Choose the Statement that Best Describes Your Organization
1	+4	Most Like Us	The vision, mission, and values of the organization are clearly defined and articulated. The strategic goals and initiatives of the organization are clearly stated, widely understood, and aligned with achieving the vision and mission such that there is a clear line of sight between initiatives and organizational success.
	+2	Somewhat Like Us	
	−2	Somewhat Like Us	The overall direction of the organization is unclear. The group's strategy and overarching goals are either ambiguous or poorly communicated. Area goals are not aligned between departments creating operational or functional silos.
	−4	Most Like Us	
2	+4	Most Like Us	Systems are well designed and function to increase productivity. Process flowcharts are utilized to understand system functions and system interconnectivity.
	+2	Somewhat Like Us	
	−2	Somewhat Like Us	Systems are ineffective, misaligned, and/or overly complex such that they must be overcome to accomplish work rather than aiding in efficient execution of work. Systems are not documented and/or not well understood. If documentation does exist, it is out of date.
	−4	Most Like Us	
3	+4	Most Like Us	Those responsible for executing the work have significant input and involvement developing the mission, systems, processes, and procedures such that they feel a growing sense of engagement and ownership.
	+2	Somewhat Like Us	
	−2	Somewhat Like Us	The leader (or leadership team) develops the mission with little input from those closest to the work. Fully formed goals are broadcast from on high with the expectation that the organization will embrace and comply with directions. If input is solicited, it is either after the fact when decisions have been made and there is little chance of meaningful engagement, or it is seen simply as a cynical attempt to create a facade of engagement.
	−4	Most Like Us	

(continued)

Table 3.2 Focusing Assessment (Continued)

Assessment (Select One)			Choose the Statement that Best Describes Your Organization
4	+4	Most Like Us	There is a well-defined organizational structure for the group that equitably parses out the work necessary for mission accomplishment. Members at all levels of the organization work at the appropriate strategic or tactical level within the organization ensuring that important activities are not neglected by continuous "firefighting."
	+2	Somewhat Like Us	
	–2	Somewhat Like Us	Reporting relationships and structures are unclear and not aligned to accomplish the organization's mission. Members don't work at the appropriate strategic level spending much of their time checking on other organizational members or scrambling to avert crisis.
	–4	Most Like Us	
			There are too many "leaders" and not enough leadership.
			Roles are poorly defined resulting in overlaps and gaps where tasks fall through the cracks with no clear attribution of responsibility.
5	+4	Most Like Us	Team members understand the mission and are gaining commitment to it. Goals and priorities are understood by all members and resources are allocated consistent with the organization's priorities.
	+2	Somewhat Like Us	
			Individual goal-setting is integrated, aligned with, and directly support the organization's mission.
			Team members are involved in setting goals, objectives, and in making critical decisions.
			Each member has a clear understanding of what is expected of them within the organization, their own roles and responsibilities, and the roles and responsibilities of others.
	–2	Somewhat Like Us	The overall direction and ultimate mission of the organization is not shared, understood, or is not used as a guide for individual actions.
	–4	Most Like Us	
			Individual goals and plans are set in isolation or simply carried over from year to year with no line of sight to accomplishment of the organization's mission.
			Goals are assigned from above and the leader does not involve the team in critical decision making.

(continued)

Table 3.2 Focusing Assessment (Continued)

Assessment (Select One)			Choose the Statement that Best Describes Your Organization
			Responsibilities and accountabilities are ambiguous, not understood by all members, confusing, and or disregarded. Members do their own thing without attention to team objectives.
6	+4	Most Like Us	Goals convert the team's mission into concrete action plans with measurable success criteria, milestones, and key performance indicators (KPIs).
	+2	Somewhat Like Us	
			Goals are consistent and build consecutively toward accomplishment of the mission—the goals evolve as the mission evolves situations provide a compelling case for altering goals and priorities.
	–2	Somewhat Like Us	Plans are not effective and there are no clear metrics gauging the effectiveness of the plan's execution.
	–4	Most Like Us	Goals are unclear and not integrated with the team's mission.
			Goals frequently change with little warning or understanding of the change in priorities and/or the organization's direction.
7	+4	Most Like Us	The leader is effective at focusing the team for decision making and continuous improvement to solve problems.
	+2	Somewhat Like Us	
	–2	Somewhat Like Us	The leader is not effective, does not engage the team in problem solving, ignores problems, or resists making improvements.
	–4	Most Like Us	
8	+4	Most Like Us	The organization has a well-established approach to solving problems and uses effective techniques for exploring the possible causes of a problem and the driving and restraining forces that contribute to the problem.
	+2	Somewhat Like Us	
	–2	Somewhat Like Us	The organization does not always analyze problems by identifying drivers and causes before seeking solutions.
	–4	Most Like Us	Techniques like brainstorming are not used to explore multiple potential solutions before selecting a final solution.

(continued)

Table 3.2 Focusing Assessment (Continued)

Assessment (Select One)			Choose the Statement that Best Describes Your Organization
9	+4	Most Like Us	The organization members listen to one another, often restating another team member's point of view to be sure it has been understood.
	+2	Somewhat Like Us	
			The organization members give each other constructive feedback on how their behavior is affecting others.
	−2	Somewhat Like Us	Members ignore each other often speaking over the top of one another in order to be heard. Less assertive members of the group remain in the background to avoid being involved in conflict.
	−4	Most Like Us	
			Team members do not share responsibilities for problems and prefer playing behind the scenes politics. When one team member has a problem with another they do not address the conflict directly but brood about it or talk to others rather than addressing the individual with whom they have the conflict.
10	+4	Most Like Us	Individuals treat differences of opinion as strengths such that sharing different viewpoints can produce better decisions. When there is a difference of opinion among organization members, a solution is sought that can be supported by everyone. Voting is only used to decide routine administrative matters.
	+2	Somewhat Like Us	
			There is a healthy attitude about conflict with an emphasis on seeking resolutions that move the organizations together toward achieving the mission rather than placing blame. Organization members deal with conflict openly and honestly in an effort to resolve it.
	−2	Somewhat Like Us	Conflict is not constructive and is frequently more about member egos rather than achievement of the organization's mission. Conflicts are often hidden and addressed through indirect back channels creating a climate of mistrust, redirecting resources away from achieving the goal.
	−4	Most Like Us	
			When members disagree with a proposed course of action for the organization, they feel pressured by the other team members to simply conform and accept the majority viewpoint. The tyranny of the majority is frequently imposed.

Table 3.3 Focusing Scoring Matrix

No.	Score	Element of Focusing	Effective Leadership	Effective Management	Tools and Techniques
1		The vision, mission, and values of the organization are clearly defined and articulated	Development of strategy	Disaggregation of strategy into tactical plans	Strategy maps Sustainability engine Framework for Organizational Success
2		Well-defined and functioning systems	Prioritization of projects and resources	Process analysis and systems design	Flowcharting, process improvement and optimization
3		Significant involvement of the crew	Authority, delegation, empowerment, and engagement	Strategic planning, team building and engagement	Levels of engagement matrix
4		Well-defined organizational structure	Inclusion and empowerment	Organizational design	Roles and accountabilities matrix
5		Gaining commitment and alignment of individual tasks and goals	Authority, delegation, empowerment, and engagement, staffing, roles, responsibilities, accountability, and authority	Goal development and alignment Performance management	Action planning and goal worksheets

(continued)

Table 3.3 Focusing Scoring Matrix

No.	Score	Element of Focusing	Effective Leadership	Effective Management	Tools and Techniques
6		Development of goals, action plans, and KPIs	Prioritization and alignment with organizational mission	Planning and goal setting Project management	Action planning, KPIs, mission scorecard Organizational roles, responsibilities, and accountabilities
7		Effective leadership toward problem solving	Inspiring creativity Adaptive leadership	Systemic problem solving, effective meeting facilitation	Situationally based approach to leadership
8		Organizational problem solving	Decision making and problem solving	Effective meetings and managing the groups interactions	Structured approach to problem solving
9		Tactical interpersonal communication and feedback	Modeling effective communications	Interpersonal skills and feedback	Cyclical communications process
10		Healthy attitude about conflict	Culture of inclusion Valuing diversity of thought and style	Decision making and problem solving	Conflict resolution model Emotional responses to change (change ready as compared to change resistant)
_____	Cumulative Focusing Score				

Analysis: Focusing versus Stumbling

During the Forming Stage, the organization's value proposition was defined. The vision and mission were communicated in meetings and broadly cascaded across and throughout the organization to bring everyone onboard and into alignment. Having the organization aligned toward a common goal is a significant step in achieving sustainable high performance. However, as stated in the second cardinal sin of change leadership, "saying isn't doing"; articulating the vision won't make it a reality. The vision must be broken down into strategies and the strategies divided into tactics; the tactics become objectives that are then broken down into goals with measureable outcomes and well-defined metrics. To take it to the individual level, the measurable outcomes must be further broken down into observable behavioral expectations, roles, and responsibilities. Let's take each of these steps in order to explore the leadership and management techniques and the tools and templates that can be employed to successfully transform the vision into a reality. From a practitioner's standpoint, I have found the six-step project structure illustrated by Figure 3.2 helpful in successfully focusing teams, resulting in building strong commitment and leading toward sustained performance. Analogous to building the hull of the ship, this plan forms the Framework for Organizational Success.

1. Define the organization's value proposition and establish its mission and vision
2. Disaggregate strategies and goals into clearly defined behavioral expectations, roles, and responsibilities
3. Create the structures, systems, and metrics that define and reinforce expectations
4. Conduct targeted functional and professional training
5. Reinforce with LSS, 5S, and visual management
6. Continuous improvement and organizational development

The foundation of the framework organizational success was laid down during the Forming Stage when the value proposition was defined along with the vision and mission. Like the foundation of the ship, the keel, the value proposition, vision and mission will determine how true the organization will sail and how sturdy it will be navigating the waters of change.

Figure 3.2   Framework for Organizational Success.

We will discuss tiers two and three as we explore focusing. Tiers four, five, and six will be addressed during the discussions of Committing, Sustaining, and Renewal, respectively.

Notice along the right side of the pyramid the project phases of Design and Develop are listed. These phases really overlap each other as do the stages of organizational design. And let me reiterate, just as there is not clear demarcation growing up (when does an infant become a newborn?), there really aren't clear separations between each organizational development stage; one flows into another seamlessly. This is because the growth of an organization is also an organic process. And analogous with the growth of a child into a healthy productive adult, proper care and supervision enables your organization to grow and mature as well.

Focusing Element 1: The Vision, Mission, and Values of the Organization Are Clearly Defined and Articulated

The first assessment element for focusing begins by asking you to evaluate how well the vision, mission, and values of the organization have been clearly defined and articulated. This condition is a direct outcome achieved by successfully navigating the forming process. If you haven't formed well, you won't be effective at focusing the organization. The

Figure 3.3   Creating line of sight through clear goals.

assessment then goes on to evaluate whether or not "the strategic goals and initiatives of the organization are clearly stated, widely understood, and aligned with achieving the vision and mission such that there is a clear line of sight between initiatives and organizational success." This second part is the bridge between Forming and Focusing. To bridge the gap between visions and reality the mission must be disaggregated into strategic goals and initiatives such that they are aligned with achieving the vision and mission. Systematically breaking down the vision and mission creates a clear line of sight between initiatives, including individuals' activities, and the achievement of organizational success. Figure 3.3 represents the hierarchy of functional managerial elements that help create the line of sight between establishing individual tactical goals up to achieving the organizations vision and strategic mission according to its core values. Before we delve deeper, let's first differentiate between strategies and tactics.

Strategies Compared to Tactics

The terms strategies and tactics widely used in business originated from military doctrine. In general, strategies are endeavors that span large geographical spaces and involve longer spans of time whereas tactics involve more immediate execution of activities within more narrowly defined geographical spaces. Strategies relate to planned outcomes more so than the execution of details. Strategies relate to winning a war while tactics usually involve "boots

Table 3.4   Strategy versus Tactics

	Strategy	*Tactics*
Meaning (Military)	Strategy is the application of long-term plans and policies concerning a nation's military force and diplomacy, to ensure security during times of peace or victory during times of war.	Tactics are actions employed to achieve objectives defined within the overall strategy. Tactics are typically related to the deployment and direction of individual troops, aircraft, or ships against an enemy combatant.
Meaning (Business)	A business strategy is enterprise-wide utilization of planning, development, and execution to delivering on the business's value proposition to profitably satisfy customer and stakeholders requirements.	Tactics are the shorter-term, measureable, activities and techniques employed to affect the local subcomponent of the overall business strategy. Different tactics may be deployed as part of a single strategy.
Scope	Large scale; enterprise wide	Small scale; local or regional
Time frame	Long range	Shorter term
Plan	Broad plan	Narrow plan
Measure	Measured as cumulative progression	Measured through achievement of objectives
Action type	Intangible generic action	Tangible specific action
Example	A strategy to gain market share could be "brand building."	Tactics employed as part of a company's "brand building" strategy may be to implement online advertising or utilize celebrity endorsements.

on the ground" performance in battle. Table 3.4 compares and contrasts the differences between strategy and tactics.

As an enlisted member of the armed forces, my general focus was to execute tactics; when I became an officer, I began to focus more on strategic objectives—especially as I became more senior. In business, tactics are executed by the day-to-day operations personnel; strategies are defined and implemented by the executive leadership team.

Strategy Maps and Logic Models

> NOTE: There are many excellent resources available that give detailed instructions for creating strategy maps; our discussion is designed to simply give a broad understanding as to the importance of these tools in focusing the organization.

Strategy maps are graphical representations of how an organization accomplishes its mission. Having a visual display of how the organization accomplishes its mission is an effective way of aligning the organization. If they can see it, they can understand it. Just communicating with words and text leaves a lot of room for various interpretations and misunderstandings. Strategy maps generally fall into one of two broad categories: outcome driven and process driven.

Outcome-Driven Strategy Maps

Outcome-driven strategy maps outline the elements that combine to produce a given outcome. For instance, if I want to increase my profit for each unit I

> NOTE: This is a partial example showing only a portion of the flushed out strategy. The complete strategy map is made up of a series of diagrams flushing out each element in further detail.

sell I can either increase the price of the product or reduce the cost to make and deliver it. Outcome strategy maps help understand broad business concepts involved in achieving business objectives such as increasing profit or increasing market share.

Figure 3.4 shows an example of an outcome-based strategy map for the American Paper Company.

Crowning the figure is the ultimate objective of improving company profit and loss—known as the P&L. To achieve improved P&L, American Paper could increase sales or reduce costs. To reduce costs, they could reduce fixed or variable costs. To reduce variable costs, they could increase operating efficiencies or reduce their raw material costs. To improve operating efficiencies, American Paper had three levers they could pull: equipment

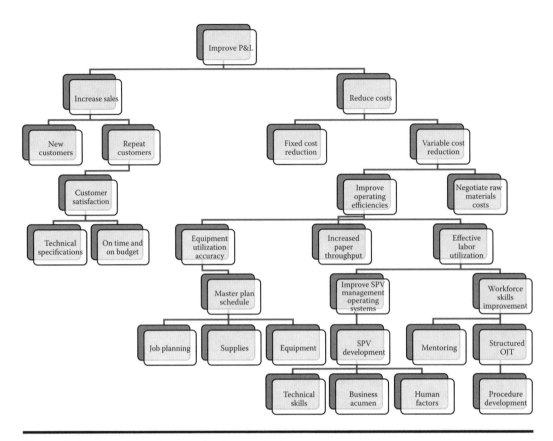

Figure 3.4   American Paper—business strategy.

utilization, mill throughput, or labor utilization. To improve mill throughput, a separate strategy map was developed (Figure 3.5). Four operational areas each having associated losses were analyzed: paper machine (makes the paper), supercalendar (compresses and polishes the paper), winder (cuts the giant paper rolls into customer size rolls), and slab losses (waste caused by cutting paper off the top of rolls between each stage of paper production).

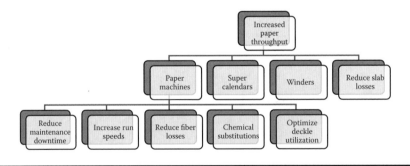

Figure 3.5   American Paper operations throughput improvements.

To increase output from the paper machine or lower the cost, they could improve one of the following:

1. Reduce maintenance downtime
2. Increase the machine's run speed
3. Reduce fiber losses (raw material)
4. Chemical substitutions (reduce chemical costs)
5. Deckle utilization ("deckle" is the width of paper manufactured—improving utilization means selling more of what you make)

It's not important for our purposes to go into the specifics of each of these strategies. The idea is that the American Paper Company analyzed its business and determined the strategies that would help it achieve its objective of improving the bottom line profit of its operations. I also wanted to show that strategy maps may need to cascade to more and more granular levels of detail through a succession of interrelated strategy maps.

NOTE: Before embarking on a specific process improvement initiative, American Paper needed to quantify the total value each loss contributed to its overall P&L as well as the potential impact and probability of success within each category of loss. Discussions of this nature are beyond the scope of our discussion but should be considered when selecting process improvement plans.

Process-Driven Strategy Maps (Logic Models)

Process-driven strategy maps, often referred to as logic models, represent how process functions interact to achieve the vision. Process-driven strategy maps outline how activities or agencies tie together such as a supply chain. Figure 3.6 shows a process map for developing a regional workforce development system (courtesy of the City of Richmond, VA).

Participants enter into the process through the intake points where they're needs and levels of workforce readiness are assessed. Based upon the assessment, they may need to have essential services or life skills developed. These essentials are barriers to gaining fulltime employment. With the essentials satisfied, the participants need to gain common work readiness skills such as time management, communications skills, conflict resolution, etc. These are the skills common to any employer in any field. Next,

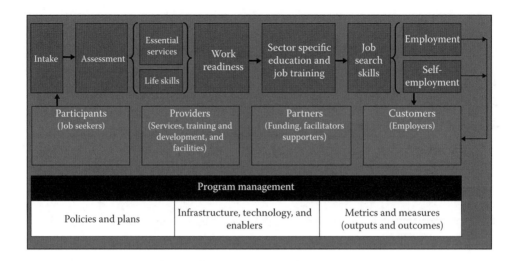

Figure 3.6   Workforce development.

participants gain skills in the specific industry sector such as healthcare or manufacturing. With these skills, participants are ready to look for jobs. They will either find work with an existing company or, for some who have the desire and aptitude, they can become self employed.

This logic model is set up with businesses as the customers. Partners are people who fund or facilitate the system processes. Providers are those who provide products or services to the participants within the greater workforce system such as training providers, childcare services, etc. Undergirding the entire system are policies, technology infrastructures, and the metrics and measures that gauge the overall effectiveness of the system.

Logic models like this are especially good at outlining the processes, services, and systems that often cut across multiple agencies and organizations.

Disaggregating the Mission and Vision into Strategy and Tactics

Think about the myriad of strategies and tactics that actually affect the ability of your organization to achieve its mission and deliver value consistently; behind each one of those blocks on your strategy map, there are initiatives, projects, resources, staffing, scheduling, communications, goals, rewards, and managing poor performance if all doesn't go according to plan. It can all become a bit overwhelming. To help bring order to the process it helps to place all of these elements into one of three categories I refer to the as the "performance triangle" (Figure 3.7).

Figure 3.7   Performance triangle.

Just as three legs of the fire triangle are needed to start a flame (fuel, air, and heat), an organization needs three legs of the performance triangle to start the fire of engagement of their workforce: systems and technologies, business acumen, and human factors. Leadership sits at the heart of the performance triangle. Leadership is required to align all the elements, light the spark, and fuel the flame. However, as we've said before, leadership alone is not sufficient to achieve sustainable superior performance. Leadership can light the flame but without effective management the team may burn out to the point the flame withers and dies. Management is required to build the systems that channel the energy and efficiently sustains high performance. But on the other side, in the midst of all these details, managers can get so caught up in the *how* that they lose sight of the *why*. To achieve this sustainable balance between the how and the why, both leadership and management are required to assemble all of the essential elements together into a Vessel of Organizational Success©.

Building a Vessel of Organizational Success

The Vessel of Organizational Success helps create alignment of all the functional and structural elements of the performance triangle. Alignment of each element orients the entire organization toward one common goal. Without alignment, inefficiencies will constantly arise, wasting valuable resources and limiting an organization's effectiveness.

To begin to build a Vessel of Organizational Success, we must first begin with the end in mind—the organization's value proposition. We've discussed that when the value proposition becomes a shared vision it is the common outcome that everyone and everything focuses on.

NOTE: If your area or department isn't focused on the business as a whole, what is it that your area is contributing toward that greater value proposition? Areas and departments that haven't clearly defined their value proposition by defining how their outcomes directly benefit the greater organization find it very difficult to create alignment. Instead, each area will be defining what they think is most important and discord will arise as we showed when organizations weren't aligned with cascading communications disseminated throughout the organization by engaged leaders acting as critical links in the communications chain.

The value proposition is the vision—visions without action remain castles in the air. Building a Vessel of Organizational Success translates the vision of the value proposition into the tangible results essential to consistently achieving the vision.

Look again at the three legs of the performance triangle: business acumen, systems and technologies, and human factors; each is an essential element to the creation of sustainable engagement within your organization. Let's outline the blueprint for assembling these timbers into a worthy craft.

In ships, the solid foundation of a seaworthy vessel is the keel. Without a well-formed keel, a ship will never sail true and won't withstand the storms that will be encountered on the voyage. Just so, a durable organization is built around solid business acumen. Figure 3.8 shows how the three major

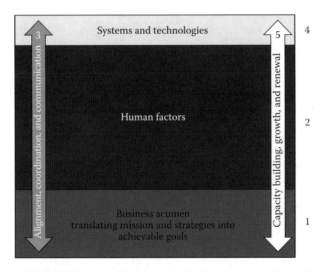

Figure 3.8 Stacking the performance elements.

organizational performance elements stack onto the solid foundation of business acumen.

Business acumen is the knowledge and ability to make sound decisions that are likely to lead to good outcomes. Another way of thinking about business acumen is business wisdom combined with business expertise. It takes business acumen to break down the value proposition into strategies and tactics. The timbers that form the keel of business acumen are laid bare (Figure 3.9), revealing how the strategies necessary to realize the value proposition are developed. Depending upon which level of responsibilities you have within your organization, there will be multiple sets of strategy maps nested within one another as we discussed earlier. There will be enterprise wide strategy maps that address the business as a whole and there will be strategy maps for each region, location, and department. Each of these elements will have goals each area will be accountable to accomplish for the overall organization to achieve its mission. Accomplishment of each of these goals will require the use of people, processes, and systems effectively transforming your resources into outcomes applying technologies and tactics.

Notice too on the left side of Figure 3.9 that resting on the value proposition foundation and rising the entire height of the organizational structure are the frameworks and planks of communication. Both the foundation and the frameworks are built into the organizational architecture during the Forming Stage. The value proposition forms the solid base and the strong framework of communication strengthens, aligns, and binds the entire organization together.

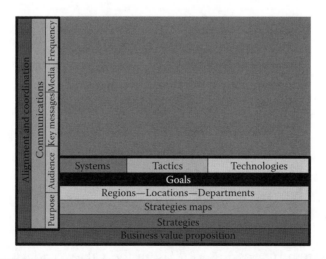

Figure 3.9   Business acumen, the foundation of the Vessel of Organizational Success.

Focusing Element 2: Well-Defined and Functioning Systems

The transformation of resources into outcomes is most efficiently accomplished through the design and ongoing utilization of systems. Whether your organization is focused on manufacturing a product or delivering services, the use of systems will improve your outcomes.

Introductions to Systems Thinking

APPLICABILITY OF SYSTEMS THINKING: Often clients whose organizations are strictly service based and involve only limited technologies and hardware question whether systems thinking is relevant to them. Absolutely! Systems thinking is applicable to every facet of human behavior regardless of whether you are running a small hot-dog stand or a multinational manufacturing firm. The complexity of the systems may vary, but regardless of complexity, systems thinking is an effective tool to help understand and optimize every organization. Don't think of systems in physical terms; think of them in terms of functionality.

A system is a group of interrelated and interconnected elements that accomplish a given outcome. All systems consist of

- Inputs
- Activities/Processes
- Outputs

These elements interact to accomplish a given outcome. It has been said that every system is perfectly designed to achieve the outcomes it gets; if you don't like the outcomes, the problem lies within one of these three elements of the system.

For illustration, let's water the lawn using a simple lawn sprinkler system, shown in Figure 3.10. We'll need a water source (Input), a hose, and a sprinkler (Activity—water flowing to a desired location). Hook up the hose from the faucet to the sprinkler, turn it on and "Walla!" wet grass (Output). We can alter the system by opening or closing the valve to adjust the amount of water (Inputs) or adjusting the sprinkler to control the arc (Activities).

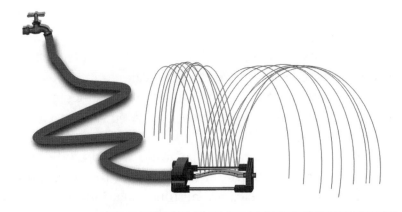

Figure 3.10   A simple lawn sprinkler system.

Usually, just having wet grass isn't the desired outcome; the desired outcome is a green, healthy lawn. The wet grass is an output from the system that contributes to the desired outcome of a healthy lawn. This reminds us of the difference between outputs and outcomes—recall the fourth cardinal sin of change leadership: rearranging deck chairs on the Titanic—majoring on the minors. Proper watering is necessary for a healthy lawn, but by itself, it is insufficient to guarantee a healthy lawn. The lawn also needs sunlight, fertilizer, and protection from lawn destroying pests. When we consider what it takes to make a healthy organization, thinking systematically helps us differentiate between outputs and outcomes. Organizations utilize inputs, activities/processes, and outputs to effect given outcomes. Process improvement and change management is all about modifying the inputs, activities or processes to alter the outputs to maximize the quality and value of outcomes.

The inputs to organizations can be grouped into three major categories: technological, functional, and social as shown in Figure 3.11. Combined the

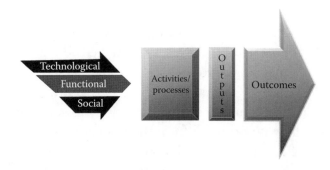

Figure 3.11   Organizational inputs to systems.

inputs can also be considered as resources. These resources feed into activities and processes to yield outputs.

Technological inputs are anything that has to do with technologies, hardware, software, electronics, electrical, mechanical, etc.

Social inputs are anything to do with the human elements of operations—people, talents, time in terms of person hours to accomplish the task, etc.

Functional inputs are anything that has to do with the other resources necessary for operations that don't fall into either of the other two categories. So raw materials, energy, etc., are all functional inputs.

Manual versus Automatic Systems

The sprinkler is a simple system that requires manual control to start, stop, and adjust. It's not automatic. Whether the system is manual or automatic it is beneficial to understand the basic aspects of system process control. The basic principles of all process controls are the same and entail three elements: sensing, interpreting, and responding. The complexity of the control strategy doesn't matter; these three elements will always be involved. Let's take another simple analogy, driving, to illustrate how the three elements of process control work.

Imagine you are driving a car. You notice your speed and decide that you are going too fast for the posted speed limit. You let up on the gas pedal to slow the car down. In a few brief moments, all three elements of process control were used. Your eyes *sensed* the position of the needle of the speedometer. Your brain *interpreted* the visual input of the position of the needle to correspond to speed of the car. Your brain sent out the signal for your foot to *respond* and let up on the gas. The car analogy is simple, but contains the principles needed to control even our most complex systems. The speedometer indicates a variable—speed. We call this variable a process variable (PV). The posted speed limit might be considered a set point (SP). The driver functioned as a control system to make the PV match the SP.

When a system is manual, it requires the operator to monitor (sense), interpret, and manually respond to control the system to get the desired outputs. When you automate a system you install technology to sense, interpret, and respond automatically with no input from the operator. Once the operator has entered a set point, the system will continue to respond as necessary to maintain the process variable at the desired value. The desired value is called the parameter. A parameter is any measurable item. Flow rate, level, pressure, temperature, speed, and amperage are all examples of parameters. Sales volume, customer satisfaction, profit and loss are also all parameters that are monitored.

An example of an automatic system you use every day it the thermostat on the wall. You enter a desired set point of a temperature. The thermostat *senses* the room temperature. If it *interprets* that the room is too cold, the system *responds* automatically by turning on the heat without you having to take any further action. Cruise control on your car is another common example of an automatic control system. It *senses* actual car speed, *interprets* whether it is too fast or too slow, and automatically *responds*. Sense, interpret, and respond—no matter what the system, these three elements of process control will always be present.

Since the focus of this book is leadership and management and not horticulture, driving, or how comfortable your room is, let's discuss a specific type of system that is essential to management: the management operating system.

Management Operating Systems

Management operating systems use the principles of systems thinking to affect human performance. A management operating system uses the elements of system control (sense, interpret, and respond) to ensure consistent results from the nontechnological inputs—the human resources. Thus, we can define a management operating system as an interconnected set of elements composed of inputs, activities, and process that work in concert with each other to deliver an output.

If we were to apply our systems thinking to a strictly human process—customer service in a small grocery store—then the interaction may be something like this:

1. Input—a customer enters the store
2. Sensing—the sales clerk is alert and immediately greets the customer with a friendly smile and a standard greeting, "Good afternoon. Welcome to Manion's Market. Can I help you?"
3. Process variable—the customer says, "I'm looking for eggs, milk, and motor oil."
4. Interpret—the customer can find two of the three desired items here, but not the third.
5. Respond—"I'd be happy to show you to the dairy section where you will find fresh milk and eggs just delivered today. I'm sorry, we don't

carry motor oil, but I'm happy to give you directions to the automotive supply store just down the street."
6. Feedback—"Thanks, that will be great."

The customer comes to the front of the store to check out having found what he needed available in the store and with directions to obtain his other needed item. The customer leaves satisfied that he received excellent customer service.

To make this experience the norm, you, as the manager, set the parameters for how the employees will continuously be alert for customers. You've trained them on appropriate levels of service, product locations, as well as other useful information customers may require. To maintain an eye on your system, you occasionally survey customers to get their feedback.

Maintaining the quality of inputs (the employees, the material condition of the store, the physical inventory on the shelves, the cash register, etc.) combined with managing the processes and activities of the operational systems (employee training, the inventory control and tracking systems, check out process and technology, etc.) determines the quality of outputs which, when appropriately combined and controlled determine the quality of outcomes your organization experiences every day.

Every system is designed to give the outputs it produces. It doesn't matter if the systems evolved organically or through focused thought—the fact is systems exist. This doesn't mean that the systems are consistent either. Every single employee may have their own way of doing things, their own systems. Thus, you get varying levels of satisfaction depending upon which customer service representative you draw in the luck of your shopping experience. If you want different results than those being produced through your current activities, you must alter the systems.

Principles of Systems Design

Basically, systems consist of inputs flowing into processes/activities leading to outputs. The systems are controlled through sensing, interpreting, and responding to the parameters in line with limits set by the operators. Each in their own way, 5S, Lean, and Six Sigma methodologies all focus on systems design and improvement; it is not our primary focus to discuss these elements in depth since there are many excellent resources and references that explain these principles extremely well. What I do want to share is a practitioner's quick and easy method for systems design, after which we will continue exploring the human factors as they relate to system operations.

> NOTE: Sustaining Element 8 will discuss the utilization of lean concepts, 5s, and visual management in slightly deeper levels, but to really understand and implement these concepts, requires information well beyond the scope of this book.

Flowcharting Systems Made Easy

Every process that consumes resources and impacts the organization's value proposition must be thoroughly understood before it can be optimized. The simplest methodology I know of to help understand an operation and its associated human interface is by flowcharting the system. I haven't found an operation that hasn't benefited from flowcharting, and yet, most organization's I have worked with that struggle with their effectiveness haven't taken the time to flowchart their processes. One reason that some organizations don't flowchart their operations is because they don't think their processes lend themselves to diagramming because their processes are too complex with too many variables. The simple answer to this is if you're going to manage something, you have to understand it; if you can't explain it, you don't understand it; and if you don't understand it, you can't manage it. The more common reason operations don't flowchart their processes is that they are way too busy fighting fires to figure out how to prevent the fires from starting in the first place. And perhaps, they have a point considering that I've seen some really complex flowcharting methods with multiple signals that take a long time to develop and end up looking like hieroglyphics requiring an advanced degree to interpret. Honestly, I find these methods less than helpful. So let's lay all this to rest and show you a simple efficient way to flowchart—the fabulous Yellow Sticky Note methodology.

Like all other forms of communication, flowcharting is only effective if people understand it, so keep it simple. In creating a flowchart, I find it most helpful to use a big white board with a handful of dry erase markers and a couple of pads of sticky notes. They don't have to be yellow; they can be any color you want. If the process involves multiple persons, positions, pieces of equipment, or departmental interfaces, it can be helpful to use a

NOTE: There are some very good flowcharting software programs out there, but I find that it is much more effective to design the flowchart on the whiteboard first—when you are satisfied with it, take a picture of it and replicate the flowchart with the software for printing, distribution, and incorporation into procedures and job aids.

different color for each. Before you start, mark a legend on the bottom of the board defining your color choices.

You only need two symbols to effectively flowchart; a square and a diamond—both of these can be represented by a square sticky note: the square with the note stuck parallel to the floor and the diamond created by rotating the sticky 45 degrees so that a corner points toward the floor. The square represents an action or process step the diamond represents a decision point or interchange (see Figure 3.12).

Assemble a team of subject matter experts into a room with a large white board. I've found it helpful to get operators, supervisors, suppliers, customers, and any other stakeholder who has a good working knowledge of the process together to work out the details together. You'll find the process really binds them together and clarifies many misconceptions.

Working on the white board, write a process step on a sticky note. Stick the note on the white board. Write the next step and stick it on the board. Connect the two with a line drawn on the board. Keep writing and sticking

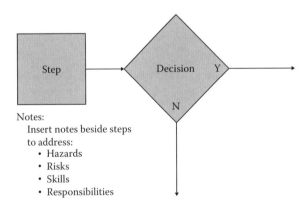

Figure 3.12   Flowcharting symbols.

one step per sticky note. As you come to decisions points, tilt the sticky note and write the decision question. Stick it on the board. Write "Yes," "No," or any other decision criteria you may need. Draw arrows to the next step or back to a previous step as necessary. Change sticky note colors as desired to represent changes in responsibility, location, equipment, etc. As you create, you will find you may have missed steps; move the notes around as necessary to insert, delete, combine, reword, or make more room as required until you and your team of assembled experts all agree with the process. Photograph it so it can be referred to easily while recreating it in a flowchart program. Once redrawn, disseminate it widely for review and approval.

If you have multiple processes to work through, sketch it out on a piece of paper or photograph it so it can be recreated in electronic format later. Once you've captured it, you can remove the sticky notes, erase the lines and decision words, and start flowcharting the next process. Figure 3.13 shows an example of a flowcharted process involving three operating positions: the case packer, the operator, and the warehouse fork truck driver. Each is represented by its own color code to differentiate each one's responsibilities in the process. This flowchart is just one of many done for a manufacturing plant that greatly improved their quality, consistency, and their productivity.

SIDE NOTE: In addition to their quality, consistency, and their productivity, developing this particular flowchart also eliminated ongoing conflicts the plant was experiencing across shifts. Before developing the color coded process flowcharts, each crew performed each task a little different. When an operator from one crew would fill in on a different shift, conflicts invariably arose. "We don't' do it that way on my shift." "That's not my job," etc., etc., blah, blah, blah. After developing this flowchart, laminating it, and sticking it on the wall above where they picked up their blank case labels and load sheets, almost overnight every shift started doing it the same way and there was no more petty bickering about "whose job is it anyway?" The diagram answered it definitively once and for all; every person on every shift could see for themselves, and every new person hired into the department learned it the same way—case closed.

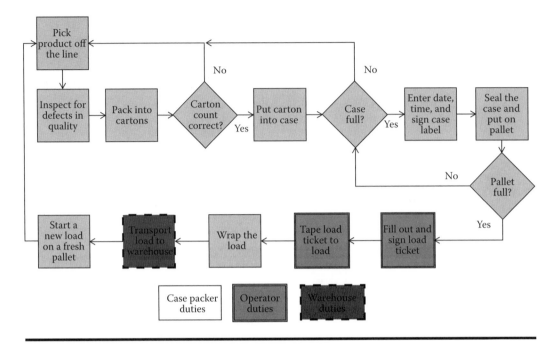

Figure 3.13   Flowcharting case packing.

From Strategy Maps to Process Steps: Peeling Back the Layers of Systems

To truly gain a full understanding of geography, it helps to have a world map. However, a globe is hardly useful trying to locate that specialty deli on the other side of town. For that you'll need a city map. So depending upon your needs, you may have to shift from a world map, to a country map, to a state map, and to a city map. The same is true of flowcharts. Within your organization you probably have multiple departments each of which has multiple systems. Trying to understand the big picture then drilling down to individual process steps would become a confusing mess if you stuck all of that onto a single diagram. That is why it is almost always required to create a series of flowcharts that interrelate to each other like a set of coordinated maps. Start with your organization's strategy map. Then break that strategy out to the tactics. Divide the tactics into systems to accomplish the tactics and then flowchart out the systems. For particularly complex steps in the process, you may need to even create flowcharts covering a single block of a larger scale flowchart. Creating these interconnected process maps will guide you while navigating through each of the stages of organizational design and development.

Figure 3.14 shows how the elements of systems are integrated into the Vessel of Organizational Success. The system concepts of inputs, activities

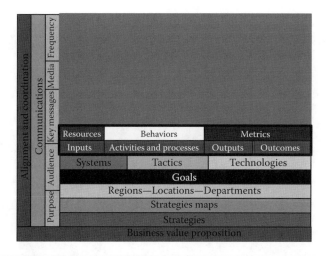

Figure 3.14   Integration of systems elements into the Vessel of Organization Success.

and processes, outputs and outcomes are paired with their physical counterparts of resources, behaviors, and metrics. These two timbers represent what human factors engineers refer to as the man–machine interface. Together they represent how people interact with systems to transform inputs into outputs. The efficiency and effectiveness of these interfaces will greatly determine the quality of the outcomes.

Installing the Process Sustainability Engine into the Vessel of Organizational Success

The hull is necessary, but alone it is insufficient to build a ship—you need a propulsion system—an engine. To propel organizations let's conceptually integrate all the concepts introduced thus far to integrate systems thinking into the sustainability engine introduced during the discussion of Forming Element 1. As shown in Figure 3.15, we extend the systems into the sustainability engine as the means through which initiatives actually yield value-added outcomes. The initiatives convert the inputs into outputs through the processes and activities that make up the systems. The outputs yield the outcomes that were integral in the basic organizational sustainability cycle. Budgets and planning are essential managerial tools that govern the processes and systems.

An essential element of any effective system is the ability to monitor the system's operation as close to real time as possible. If we compare the management operating system to our thermostat example discussed earlier, how effective would your heating and cooling system be if it only monitored

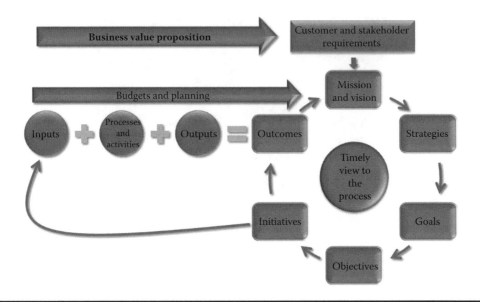

Figure 3.15   Building systems into the sustainability engine.

average room temperature and reported it back in a color coded spreadsheet a month later?

Manager: "I see the temperature of the building was maintained at a steady average of 68 degrees throughout the entire month, great work!"
Employee: "Yes, but one room remained around 38 degrees and the other was 98."
Manager: "Yes, but statistically speaking, you were all very comfortable."

A timely view to the process lies at the core of any effective sustainability cycle. Keeping an eye on the values of key parameters (like temperature, expenses, sales, etc.) integrated with a solid understanding of how the inputs, activities, and processes combine to generate the required outputs will enable you to more effectively create plans and budgets that support your organizational initiatives. Without such a deep level of understanding, budgets and plans will very likely be SWAGs (silly wild-ass guesses) with little validity.

Focusing Element 3: Significant Involvement of the Crew

When analyzing and diagramming the systems and processes to develop flow-charts it was recommended that you assemble a team of subject matter experts. The purpose of these activities is not only to utilize the experience and knowledge of those most involved with the process to design the most effective systems possible, but just as importantly, involving them gains their buy in.

Two Parables of Engagement

Humans are storytellers. Some of our most powerful life lessons are told to us in fables, fairytales, and legends. People will remember parables much longer than they will a lecture. To help understand the lessons of engagement, let's look at two parables.

The Chicken Is Involved…

An Ol' Boy from L.A. (Lower Alabama) once told me, "When it comes to a breakfast of eggs and bacon, the chicken is involved but the pig is committed." I like the story, but neither the chicken nor the pig had a choice. If you want your employees to be committed, first, you shouldn't kill them and serve them with grits. Second, commitment is a choice. I can hire your hands, but you have to give me your head and your heart. If you want employees to be truly committed, you need to get them involved. Let's look at another parable.

River of Commitment

Imagine that you and I are walking together beside an icy river just after spring thaw. I happen to fall in. How involved am I? Very! There is probably nothing else on my mind. I can assure you that I am not thinking about that hallway closet I've been meaning to organize. I am 100% involved and, therefore, 100% committed to my solution. With me in the icy river, how involved are you? Well, you're not as involved as me, but you're more involved than our friend who is vacationing in St. Thomas working on his tan and his third piña colada. Let's say you are 50% involved. You are thinking, "Gee, I'd like to save him…but that water is cold. I wonder if there is a stick I can throw him?" At the same time you are weighing your rescue options, our well-tanned friend in St. Thomas is frustrated that they don't seem to make the little drink umbrellas as colorful as he remembers them. He is 0% involved in my problem. Meanwhile, I am flailing among the ice flow. To help you decide whether or not to brave the icy waters and rescue me, you take a moment to sketch out a little graph depicting our personal relative degrees of commitment against our respective levels of involvement (Figure 3.16). While studying your sketch, you have a stroke of insight as I'm going down for the third time; you discover the first rule of engagement.

> Rule of Engagement No. 1:   There is a direct correlation between involvement and commitment.

Imagine if the scenario were a little bit different. Suppose you and I had been handcuffed together. How committed would you be to helping me find a way out of the river (or at least finding a sharp object to sever my hand from my wrist, thereby unencumbering yourself from me)?

EXAMPLE: As a supervisor I was frustrated with having system variations across multiple shifts. I scheduled the lead operators off of the four different crews and stuck them in a room and told them to work together until they had come up with a single process they all four agreed to perform consistently. After several hours, two pizzas, and a jug of sweet tea, they arrived at a mutually agreeable solution. They were all involved and they were all committed to the solution they had worked out. This was a good example of adaptive leadership. I used a directing style (Style 1) to setting the expectations and parameters: "You will all agree to one way to perform this task." Then I applied delegation (Style 4). When I had stopped by to check on them, they had a few questions, I collaborated with them for a bit (Style 3); when they presented their solution, I took their input and set their plan as policy (Style 2). I rewarded their efforts with pizza and encouragement. As a result, we had a process that satisfied each of the shifts and satisfied me by having a single consistent method.

Lesson of the parable: If someone is not involved, they won't have any commitment. Remember this the next time you roll out to your crew the newly minted and brightly polished transformation plan that will finally take your organization to the apex of performance (unlike the other 27 previous programs outlined in the past three years).

FAMOUS QUOTE: "This time for sure!"

Bullwinkle Moose
Fictional Adventurer, Poet, and Philosopher

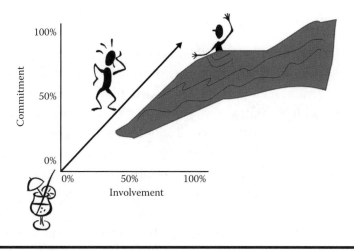

Figure 3.16   Involvement versus commitment.

Focusing Element 4: Well-Defined Organizational Structure

Now that the team is moving deeper into focusing and you have engaged key players in the work of designing or redesigning systems, you have begun to explore who will be doing what in the operation of the systems. As you become deeply involved in the details of the design remember to lift your head up regularly to think strategically about the long-term consequences of your designs. The tasks need to support the strategic plans that deliver on the value proposition. The objective is to extend the strength of the value proposition and strategies into a framework of goals that are then transformed plank by plank into a solid structure of roles and responsibilities, as shown in Figure 3.17.

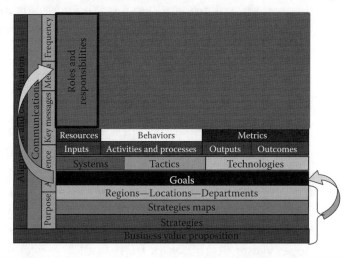

Figure 3.17   Converting goals into roles and responsibilities.

Disaggregation of Strategies into Goals and Roles

The first step of translating strategies into tactics involves disaggregating the strategies into goals and clearly defined behavioral objectives, roles, and responsibilities. This forces you to clearly articulate what must happen to translate our vision into reality. Only by articulating the strategy through disaggregation into roles and responsibilities can it be clearly communicated. In addition, the process of disaggregation forces you to fully understand the strategy and all that it will entail to accomplish it. Don't worry if you discover that you don't have all the answers—I haven't met anyone yet who did. The process helps you discover what you didn't know or hadn't even thought of yet. The process helps frame the questions and helps define the answers.

The disaggregation will usually need to be done in stages and involve different individuals and teams. Involving others helps facilitate the communications process and increases commitment through involvement.

I find that this is the juncture that many organization's get so busy going about the business of the business that they lose sight of the linkages and fall back into business as usual (for existing organizations) or let the roles and responsibilities grow organically instead of thoughtfully aligned (for new organizations). When you are developing a new organization or reforming an old one, you are dealing with rapidly hardening cultural concrete. If you don't take the time to set the forms early and manage the process, you'll have the functional and cultural equivalent of pouring concrete from the truck directly onto the ground in front of your house hoping it will form itself into a perfectly smooth, square, and level driveway; odds are it isn't going to happen without the work of a skilled mason. As you craft your new organization, work to define an organizational structure that equitably parses out the work necessary for mission accomplishment. The objective of well-defined roles and responsibilities is to ensure that all of the tasks essential for mission accomplishment are being done and to ensure that members at all levels of the organization work at the appropriate strategic or tactical level within the organization. Working at appropriate strategic and tactical levels helps ensure that important activities are not neglected because the organization's time is too consumed by continuous "firefighting."

What I find frequently in organizations is that members at all levels are not working at their appropriate level. Managers do the work that supervisors should and supervisors do the work that should be accomplished by line operators. It is not uncommon to survey an organization and find individual spending 50%–75% of their time working on tasks that should be accomplished by individuals who report to them.

Primary Reasons Organization's Work below Their Strategic Optimum

In my experience there are two main reasons why individuals spend so much time working below their level: trust and training. Often, managers and supervisors become so involved in the day-to-day details because they have a need to feel confident that the job is being performed to their exact specifications. Just as frequently, I find that those specifications are unclear, ill defined, or ever shifting. Because the manager hasn't set clear expectations, the individuals doing the work don't have an effective standard by which to gauge their performance outcomes; thus, they complete the work as they see fit.

The second reason goes along with the first in much the same manner as the old conundrum, "Which came first, the chicken or the egg?" Because expectations aren't well defined, training is ill defined so the manager has every reason to be concerned about quality—the crew isn't adequately trained. We'll talk more about performance improvement and training during the Committing Stage.

DISC Impacts on Delegation and Trust

When you think about the four personality temperaments, there is no single style that holds a monopoly on poor expectation setting and poor development of their employees.

"D"s don't always pay attention to the details so they may bark out orders expecting things to happen without setting clear expectations. In addition, they may be moving at such a pace that they don't take the time to develop their people. The vicious cycle of "You didn't do it the way I wanted, I'll do it myself!" and "You didn't tell me what you wanted so I couldn't do it the way you wanted!" breeds mutual frustration among "D" managers and their employees.

"I"s aren't always great about attention to details either. They are more social and collaborative, but they may not take the time to develop their crew because they themselves haven't focused on the detailed tasks required to accomplish the goal. This generates a similar cycle of frustration.

"S"s may know the task well as they have done it for years. But "S"s fall into the trap of enabling others' nonperformance, preferring instead to just do it themselves. Because of this tendency, "S"s can become overloaded as they try to take on more work to please others, frequently frustrating all involved.

"C"s are very task oriented but not always communicative. In addition, "C"s don't easily trust the data given to them by others unless they validate it for themselves. As such, "C"s end up doing the work to assuage their own levels of anxiety and concern by completely submersing themselves in the details of the matter. This equally frustrates and disenfranchises the crew.

As you can see, every temperament type can struggle with delegation and empowerment. To help you establish the most appropriate levels of delegation and prioritization of strategic versus tactical behaviors, think first about the time horizon of the work. Once the time horizon is established, then the prioritization of the tasks can be set and the investment in clearly defined standards and training will become clearly justified.

The Time Horizon—Keeping It between the Two Ditches

Deciding what tasks should be performed at various organizational levels is best explained using the concept of a "time horizon." As each of us is painfully aware, we only have a finite amount of time in which we can accomplish our tasks. In that limited timeframe, we must do the immediate pressing items that are considered "urgent," and we must take time to perform the important long-term work such as strategic planning, creating systems, organization and streamlining of work process and work spaces, documentation of policies and procedures, and, to go along with documentation, training and development of others. The urgent eclipses the important, and we spend all our days scrambling from crisis to crisis, continuously firefighting. If the important work is to get done, it is performed during nights and weekends, thus eroding the quality of our lives and leaving us worn out, frustrated, and with short fuses that erupt in tension and conflict.

To parse the work into categories of tasks between strategic and tactical, it helps to think of the day-to-day operations as "running the business"; the long-term important work can be classified as "leading the business." The time horizon associated with running the business usually spans periods of weeks to hours. The time horizon required for leading usually runs from months into years. When our days are consumed with urgent tasks running the business, we have no time for such activities as developing new strategies, expanding the business, making contingency plans, and working on improvements that will sustain the business. Our businesses end up running us instead of the other way around. As a result, we spend our days running in place with no forward progress. And as Will Roger's said, "Even if you're on the right track, you'll get run over if you just sit there." So if an organization is caught up in the continuous firestorm of "The Crisis Du Jour," they are at real risk of losing any competitive advantage they may have as other more strategic and innovative thinkers overtake them and drive them out of business. We'll call this one of our ditches.

The other ditch in which an organization's leadership team can get stuck occurs when the leadership team consumes precious time and resources developing strategies and plans but never executes. I've spent far more time than I'd like to admit working with organizations to develop process improvement plans and business strategies that never go any further than a lovely three-ring binder with a cool sounding project title collecting dust on a shelf. Each of these projects was aspirational in design but ineffectual in reality. You know the drill: you assemble a project team, and then you have a grand kick-off meeting with inspirational speeches, banners, slogans, and all the sundry accoutrements designed to inspire, empower, and engage. The project team gets jackets and hats, and they spend their days developing plans, presentations, and policies that then fill up the binders that then collect dust. I call this "management by whitepaper." Unfortunately, I see it over and over again within some businesses, and it is rampant in government operations.

The Lasting Impact of Failed Change Initiatives

It is bad enough that these activities consume time, capital, human, and other resources, what's worse is that these "bridges to nowhere" consume hope and organizational capacity to change. Every person has a limited amount of discretionary effort just like they have a limited amount of discretionary income. They could spend it on this or they could spend it on that, but there is not an infinite supply. When someone vests their time and effort into a project, they become engaged; their hopes are raised, and they begin to imagine how the world will be when they achieve the aim of their invested activities. When these dreams fail to materialize, they're disappointed; a piece of them is lost, and they feel betrayed. They are that much closer to death with nothing to show for it—in fact, they can think back on all the things they missed putting in that extraordinary effort to develop the plans. They've missed family events; they've missed nights and weekends pursuing hobbies and personal interests; and some have even missed promotional opportunities. I've known several managers who were placed on special projects where they traveled and sacrificed only to find that in their absence, someone else was promoted to the position that they would have been slated to fill if they had stayed and focused on the day-to-day matters instead of building castles in the air. This doesn't sound fair and it's not, but unfortunately, when someone is assigned to a special project that is ill conceived, underfunded, undersupported, understaffed, or under-whatever such that it is doomed from the outset, they can be tainted by that failure. The powers-that-be distance themselves from a "stinker" of a project and don't take any responsibility, so when it goes horribly awry, they won't get any on themselves. Or, even worse, they take credit for success early on when the project is in the "honeymoon" stage—get promoted, and leave a wake of disasters in their progression up the ladder of success. Like the old song says, they got the goldmine, you got the shaft.

These less than optimal experiences make employees wary of change and reticent to dive right in with both feet when they see another "program of the month" coming down the pike. They'd prefer to spend what discretionary time on activities they find rewarding—coaching little league, spending time with children and grandchildren, reading, traveling, or doing anything that rewards their efforts more rather than spending good effort on bad programs that they don't believe will have any impact. We'll talk more about resistance to change when we talk about Focusing Element 10.

Example: Defining Roles, Time Horizons, and Responsibilities

Thinking of the extreme ends of the spectrum that mark the boundaries between the two ditches is a helpful concept as far as theory goes, but as I said in the beginning of the book, if it's not applicable to the real world, it's not to be found within the covers of this book. So to make it worthwhile, let's see an example of how the theory has been applied in the real world.

A small Midwestern manufacturing plant was deep into the crisis-to-crisis ditch and wanted to hook onto a strategic tow truck. We began the analysis process by defining where along the strategic/tactical spectrum each level of the organization could ideally perform. We wanted to move away from lofty nebulous terms like "run" versus "lead" toward more specific terms, but we didn't want to get lost in the minutia that could have derailed any substantive discussions. We brought the discussion from the 40,000-foot level down to about 10,000 feet by defining the roles and responsibilities of each organizational level in more actionable terms. Table 3.5 shows the breakdown of roles, time horizons, and responsibilities.

Table 3.5 Manufacturing Plant Breakdown of Roles, Time Horizons, and Responsibilities

Plant manager	Role	• Preparing for what is to come—macrostrategies
	Time horizon	• One to three years
	Responsibilities	• Establish and validate strategy • Strategic customer focus partnering with Sales and Operations • Mentor converting manager to become plant manager • Continuously grow business leadership and ensure development at all levels
Converting manager	Role	• Develop operational strategies to deliver on value proposition
	Time horizon	• Month to year
	Responsibilities	• Production operation optimization • Structure and staffing • Consistency across plant • Mentor process leaders • Prepare to become plant manager
Process leaders	Role	• Translating strategy into tactics
	Time horizon	• Weeks to months and seasonality
	Responsibilities	• Long-term operations tactical planning • Setting expectations • Managing costs • Mentor supervisors • Prepare to become converting managers
Supervisors	Role	• Execution of tactics
	Time horizon	• Today to weeks
	Responsibilities	• Manage the exceptions (absenteeism, scheduling changes, material or process disruptions) • Care and feeding of operators (reward and discipline) • Mentor Op-Techs and ensure crews are self-mentoring • Prepare to become process leaders

(continued)

Table 3.5 Manufacturing Plant Breakdown of Roles, Time Horizons, and Responsibilities (Continued)

Operations technicians	Role	• Operate and verification that processes are in control
	Time horizon	• Hours and shifts
	Responsibilities	• Lead daily operations
		• Mentor other Op-Techs
		• Conduct routine maintenance
		• Empowered to perform all tasks and make all decisions necessary to convert raw materials into high-quality finished goods
		• Continue to grow skills and knowledge

This strategic organizational chart became the guiding vision to form the plant around. Since a picture is worth a thousand words, we developed Figure 3.18 to help communicate the concept in such a way that it could be cascaded down throughout the plant.

Consider the overlap between run the business and lead the business within the midpoint of the pyramid. This is the point in which strategies are

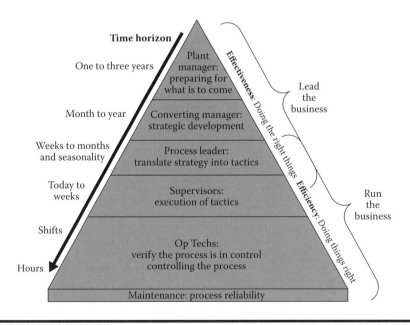

Figure 3.18 Ideal plant time horizon.

transformed into tactics. The management team felt that with this structure, they would be able to efficiently execute their business and still have time for continuous improvement.

"To Be" as Compared to "As Is"

After defining the "ideal" level of organizational performance, the next step is to determine the actual so that the two states can be compared and the "gap" can be measured. Only by understanding the nature and magnitude of the gap can a realistic project plan be created to guide the organizational change initiative. The actual becomes the baseline from which progress can be measured.

At the same Midwestern facility we surveyed the management team to determine the percentage of their time spent doing tasks associated with a time horizon they assessed to be at a tactical level below ideal. Table 3.6 shows a partial analysis of the plant's gap analysis.

Based upon the gap analysis, a second pyramid graphic was made showing the time horizon of the tasks being performed within the facility (Figure 3.19).

With the time horizon gap determined, the plant leadership team was staged to break down the roles and responsibilities into individual tasks and goals.

Focusing Element 5: Gaining Commitment and Alignment of Individual Tasks and Goals

With a clearly defined mission and vision, well-defined systems, involvement of the crew, and a well-defined organizational structure you will notice growing levels of excitement and commitment. Initially, there may not have been much input from the crew because they may not have known enough to ask any questions. But as their understanding grows they begin to see where the organization is heading and become more empowered to contribute ideas. This is desirable but, if improperly managed and channeled, could lead to confusion and conflict. You want to keep the ideas coming, but you want to align them such that they build systemically and sustainably.

Table 3.6   Manufacturing Plant Gap Analysis

Production Ops (Hourly)	
(48% of Time Working below Level)	
Current	*Desired*
• Execute tasks without full understanding of consequences • Lack of engagement/ownership for quality of finished goods • Development of crew skills not ingrained in culture • Entitlement vs. Accountability	• Empowered to perform all tasks and make all decisions necessary to convert raw materials into high-quality finished goods • Perform routine maintenance on the line • Continue to grow skills and knowledge
Supervisors	
(46% of Time Working below Level)	
• Supervisors responsible for directly managing the shifts • Supervisors make the decisions regarding running the processes • Firefighting to the exclusion of developing the crews	• Manage the exceptions (absenteeism, scheduling changes, material or process disruptions) • Care and feeding of operators (reward and discipline) • Mentor Op-Techs and ensure crew is self-mentored • Prepare to become process leaders
Process Leader	
(71% of Time Working below Level)	
• Integrally involved in running the daily operations • Executes the plan compared to developing strategy • Lack a view to strategic alignment of location to the business • Lack real time view to the health of the business	• Align department to the business and ensure development of all • Establish and validate departmental strategy • Strategic customer focus • Mentor supervisors • Prepare to become converting managers

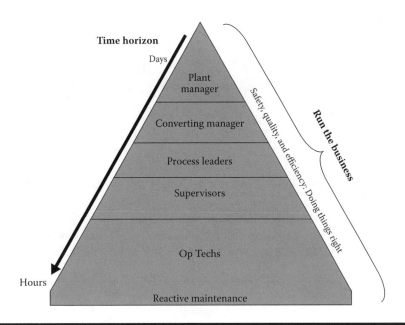

Figure 3.19 Actual plant time horizon.

To define the roles in terms of tasks and individual goals, utilize the flowcharts you developed when designing the systems (Focusing Element 2). Think about who will do the work and label each step. As you label the steps with who is performing them, you'll begin to discover efficiencies and conflicts. If this person is doing "X" at this location, they won't be available to do "Y." It also helps to think beyond just the day-to-day operation of the systems. It's usually not during routine operations that things really snowball out of control—it's during the unexpected times. As such, think about process upsets.

To help determine optimal staffing, assign timeframes to the tasks and add up the time per shift period. Based upon the sum of timeframes you will be able to approximate the number of individuals needed to do the work. Ensure that you have added time for breaks and about a 10%–15% flex to account for variations.

Example of Defining Individual Roles and Responsibilities

Let's refer back to the example of the Midwestern Manufacturing Company who had defined the roles, responsibilities, and time horizons. They broke down each role into tasks by systems and assigned specific responsibilities for each operations position.

For each system, they categorized tasks as operations, maintenance, safety, or housekeeping. The systems were listed down the first column and the five operating positions were listed across the first row. For each system the required tasks were then filled into the matrix under each operator's position. Table 3.7 shows a portion of the tasks matrix showing only the raw

Table 3.7   Tasks Matrix—Raw Material/Set-Up Tech's Responsibilities

Raw Material/Set-Up Op-Tech		
This is a general list of duties that will need to be completed each day but is not an all inclusive list. Each operator is expected to perform other duties as required and as assigned.		
Raw materials and supplies	**Operations**	Monitor supplies, restock and prep as necessary
	Maintenance	Conduct preventive maintenance inspections as planned
	Safety	Follow all safety guidelines
	Housekeeping	Empty trash hoppers 1× per shift
Winder	**Operations**	Prep and load all parent roll on the winder
	Maintenance	Conduct preventive maintenance Inspections as planned
	Safety	Follow all safety guidelines
	Housekeeping	Daily blow down—night shift
Ink kitchen	**Operations**	Monitor Ink Operation
	Maintenance	N/A
	Safety	Follow all safety guidelines
	Housekeeping	Daily blow down/ wash up—night shift
Product quality		Quality checks and other normal SOPs
Production flow		Keep product flowing
Troubleshooting		Assist in "trouble" spots as needed to keep product flow going

(continued)

Table 3.7   Tasks Matrix—Raw Material/Set-Up Tech's Responsibilities (Continued)

Raw Material/Set-Up Op-Tech		
General housekeeping	Empty broke hopper/carts 3× per shift into the baler	
	Empty trash hopper on the line 1× per shift	
	General housekeeping on the line and around the perimeter	
Mutual team support	Safety	Support and hold each other accountable to follow safety guidelines and policies
	Assist each other with machine operation	
	Relieve each other for breaks	
	Monitor the production schedule for changes and assist with change-overs	

material/set-up tech's responsibilities. In addition to the systems, the bottom of Table 3.7 contains other expectations that are more global in nature:

■ Product quality
■ Production flow
■ Troubleshooting
■ General housekeeping
■ Mutual team support

The completed matrix containing the other four positions gave a very good overview of the entire manufacturing plant's operational requirements and how each individual operator was tasked to support the systems and support each other. Implementing the matrix set very clear expectations for every operator on every shift.

Framework of Effective Individual Success (Steps 1–5)

Even though I recommend defining the tasks which are involved in each role to my clients, many managers still don't take the time to do it. I believe this occurs partly because it can seem overwhelming; other times, managers think they don't need to get into the details; others say that the exercise is simply administrative in nature and isn't required for operations. To counter these commonly held perceptions, let me explain why I advocate so strongly the clear delineation of tasks into behavioral based expectations.

Breaking down the roles into tasks not only helps clarify how the strategy is to be achieved, it helps create the line of sight between individual tasks and the overall strategies. It is an essential step to creating and sustaining effective performance. Recall from the beginning how we defined the seven cardinal sins of change leadership; now let's explore the seven structural timbers that form effective individual performance enumerated below and shown graphically in Figure 3.20.

1. Define acceptable performance
2. Set clear expectations
3. Provide timely feedback
4. Provide adequate resources
5. Set performance conditions
6. Define gaps and train as appropriate
7. Sustain with management systems

The first plank, defining acceptable performance, aligns with the first step of effective leadership (Style 1). It lets the employee know what has to be done by defining the goal to be achieved.

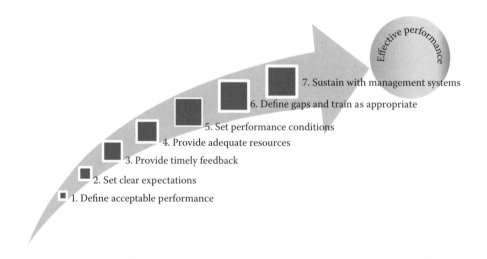

Figure 3.20 Framework for individual success.

The second plank specifies the standards of how much, how high, how often, how well, etc. Too often managers give vague directions and expectations assuming that the crew already knows it. Remember, the degree of specificity will be inversely proportional to the level of experience, ability, and motivation of the individual being assigned.

The third plank, provide timely feedback, is one that is frequently lacking. A majority of employees I've interviewed in low-performing organizations receive performance feedback only annually, and frequently, that feedback is not specific enough to be actionable, and it is definitely not timely enough. All they know is that they will not be getting the raise they wanted or the promotion they thought they were in line for because of inadequate performance. Imagine you were trying to improve your golf swing. You are blindfolded and told to hit the ball. Six months later I tell you that you didn't make the cut because you sliced hard into the woods. The example may be extreme, but I can give numerous examples where individuals have had quality defects in their work and were only informed after the product had been rejected by the customer—and depending upon the time period required for inventory turn, those complaints can be months after the work was completed. And if the company doesn't have a sophisticated enough system to trace back the production to the date and operator, the complaints may become aggregated into a large pool and the individual responsible never gets specific feedback as to how their performance affected the organization's delivery on its value proposition. To be effective, feedback needs to be specific, actionable, and timely.

The fourth plank, provide adequate resources, is a key component driving effective performance. If you want the employees to produce quality products, they need quality materials. If you want them to wear the proper safety equipment, you need to provide it for them. If you want them to complete a task, you need to give them the time to perform the task well. Very frequently organizations give "unfunded mandates." They want the outcome, but don't provide sufficient resources to accomplish the task.

ANONYMOUS QUOTE: "We, the unwilling, led by the unknowing, are doing the impossible for the ungrateful. We have done so much, for so long, with so little, we are now qualified to do anything with nothing."

Anonymous quote falsely attributed to Mother Theresa (but still a great quote)

The fifth plank, setting performance conditions, requires management to provide the appropriate balance between rewards and consequences. We will talk more about this during the Committing and Sustaining Stages of organizational development. For now, suffice it to say that very frequently organizations reward the wrong behaviors. Their incentives don't align with their directives.

We began the discussion of the sixth plank, define gaps and train as appropriate when we talked about Focusing Element 4 and we will continue the discussion in greater depth when we talk about the Committing Stage of organizational development when we talk about the principles of adult learning and systems based training.

The final plank, sustain with management operating systems will be an ongoing process of designing and developing and refining your systems. Consistent systems thinking is essential to building sustainable high-performance organizations. Regardless of your level of experience with systems thinking, two elements seem to be continuously reoccurring themes: fall points and communications.

Fall Points and Communications

When exploring the causes of low organizational performance you need to be able to adjust the focal point of your lens from macro to micro, from organizational systemic causes to individual idiosyncrasies, and to switch between your management and your leadership hats. To help bring the picture into focus, look to your multiple scales of process and system maps discussed in Focusing Element 2:

- Organizational strategy maps
- Departmental strategy maps
- Systems flowcharts
- Process steps

If you've been using the multiple color sticky method, you'll be able to graphically see the interconnections that link department to department and individual to individual. It is at these junctures that process handoffs occur, and like geographical fault lines where earthquakes are born, it is at these junctures where multiple defects and conflicts arise. You've heard this story before.

Employee 1: "I gave it to you."
Employee 2: "I never received it."

Employee 1: "I left it on your desk."
Employee 2: "Have you seen my desk?"

These junctures are known as "fall points" because it is the systematic and process seams where one system comes up against another that things "fall" through the organizational cracks. If you pay close attention to these points you'll identify many connections and transfers that are root causes of organizational problems. If you standardize and simplify, you'll eliminate the problems. To help you standardize and simplify, let's define in general terms what happens at the fall points.

Behavioral Responses Essential to Eliminating Fall Points

Comparable to a relay race in track where one runner passes the baton to the next team member, at the juncture between two systems there is an expectation of a transfer. It could be a transfer of physical product, a transfer of knowledge, or a transfer of responsibility. One must pick up where the other left off. To facilitate the smooth transition requires a series of four events:

1. Trigger
2. Response
3. Timing
4. Feedback

Figure 3.21 reveals the next planks laid into the Vessel of Organizational Success.

NOTE: "Response" is not shown. This is intentional because there are multiple elements that govern response, which will be uncovered as our exploration continues.

Trigger: The trigger is the signal that the transfer is occurring. It's what alerts the next step in the process or the next person in the chain that a response is required on their part. In business the trigger might be an email, a phone call, or a yellow sticky sitting on the seat of your chair. The more standardized and simplified the trigger, the more likely that the transition will occur and not fall into the gap.

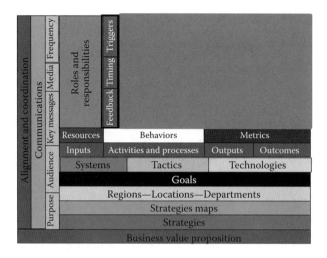

Figure 3.21   Behavioral response.

One of the most common root causes of fall points is communication. If the communication isn't received as intended or isn't received at all, the appropriate and timely response won't be triggered. When one shift relieves another, incomplete information is transferred. When one person goes on vacation, others don't know the status of projects and deadlines—things fall through the cracks.

THE INADEQUACY OF EMAILS AS A TRIGGER: If your organization is like most, there is an overabundance of email and too many managers who manage remotely by email. When you get hundreds of emails every week, one more ping of your computer doesn't cause you to jump up and say, "OOO, an email!—It must be important requiring my immediate response." I don't know how many times I've been asked, "Didn't you get my email?"

EXAMPLE: Susan sat in the office immediately next to Doris. Doris wasn't particularly sociable or ambitious. Instead of expending any energy on speaking, Doris sent emails. The little electronic messages had to run through the cable, down through the server in the basement, and back up, "PING," it would pop up on Susan's screen. Over time, Susan became so frustrated by this antisocial behavior that she began to block Doris's emails. After a time, when Doris didn't get any response, she had to look up from her terminal and actually speak to her coworker.

Don't be a "Doris"—take the time to actually speak to your coworkers—it will eliminate a lot of frustration and improve your communications.

FOOTNOTE: My apologies to all you Doris's out there who are sociable and ambitious—this example is not indicative of, nor meant to impugn any "Doris" who is not like the "Doris" in this example. But to that one specific "Doris," please stop being a "Doris."

The story of Doris and Susan is a humorous (and true) example of how "newer" isn't always "better." Honestly, face to face is a better form of communication. If not face to face, pick up a phone and go voice to voice. Naturally you shouldn't abandon email—it is extremely useful and also creates a great paper trail (not always desired but sometimes essential). Just be careful and recognize the limitations of the media you choose. Managing by email more often than not is abdication.

Response: And like a relay race, there is an expectation of a response after the transfer in order to keep the process flowing. You're not likely to win many track meets if your teammate just stands there when you pass off the baton. The expected behavior after the trigger is called the response and there are many variables that govern the effectiveness of behavior. We'll explore behavioral drivers in greater depth when we discuss training and performance management. For now, for purposes of this discussion it's important to recognize that a holistic, system's based approach is necessary to understand individual behaviors and overall organizational performance. Behavior is the result of the complex interaction between four groups of performance drivers, as shown in Figure 3.22:

- What: systems, equipment, and technologies
- Who: individual competencies and motivation
- How: policies and procedures
- Why: leadership and management

Combined correctly, you get to the "Wow!" of outstanding organizational performance. Single-focus solutions rarely yield optimal results. The organization must employ the right tools, techniques, and training necessary to improve all the factors that affect performance.

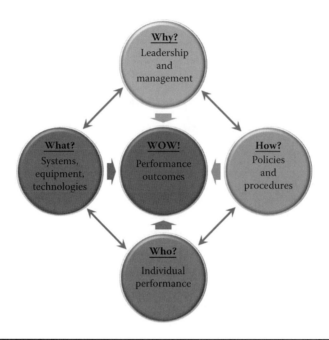

Figure 3.22 Organizational performance drivers.

Timing: Timing has to do with both the trigger and the response. If the trigger is delayed, so will be the response. Even if the trigger is timely, the response may not be. Therefore, it is essential to set the timing for both triggers and responses to close the gaps and eliminate fall points. Policies and procedures are often developed to address timing. Some operating systems incorporate physical and visual cues to facilitate timing—for example, an alarm that won't stop until the operator responds. There are many other examples of ways organizations address timing. Table 3.8 shows how the Midwestern Manufacturing Facility formalized the expectation of the frequency which they wanted communication to flow within their organization.

The plant manager spoke with the converting manager daily, the process leaders weekly at the production meeting. He only met with the supervisors during a monthly meeting and with the Op Techs directly during the quarterly update meetings where he reviewed the prior period's performance, challenges, customer feedback, and the plant's financial results.

Feedback: Feedback is the assurance that the handoff occurred successfully. If it is important that the transfer occurs smoothly, it is important for each handoff to build in feedback. However, too much of a good thing is not a good thing. Some folks have the autoreceipt feature turned on with every email. This is an intrusive use of technology to micro manage and is

Table 3.8 Communications Frequency Matrix

	Plant Manager	*Converting Manager*	*Process Leaders*	*Supervisors*	*Op Techs*
Plant Manager	N/A	Daily	Weekly	Monthly	Quarterly
Converting Manager	Daily	N/A	Daily	Weekly	Monthly
Process Leaders	Weekly	Daily	Process dependent	Daily	Weekly
Supervisors	Monthly	Weekly	Daily	Shift to shift	Daily
Op Techs	Quarterly	Monthly	Weekly	Daily	Process dependent

ultimately ineffective. In addition, it automatically doubles your volume of email (as if we didn't have enough already). If every email requires a return receipt it minimizes the significance of the feature. The psychological term for learning to ignore routine stimuli is acclimation.

We can become acclimated to almost anything that we are overexposed to. Another example of acclimation is seen in some systems with multiple built in redundant alarms and alerts—when an alarm is always going off, people tend to tune them out over time. And if every event causes an alert, how do you differentiate between routine, urgent, and critical. The same is true for people who send every email with an URGENT flag. Over time, they all become meaningless. Use the features to signify what is truly urgent and classify the rest accordingly.

Detailed Analysis of Fall Points

Understanding in general what happens at a fall point is a starting point; if you are actually going to improve your own processes in a tangible manner, you'll need to examine the seams between your systems and processes in much greater detail. When you do, utilize the system flowcharts you developed earlier.

Similar to the process you utilized to develop the flowcharts, bring together the subject matter experts, customers, and suppliers who touch or are impacted by the process failures. At each juncture list the ways that the process fails. Figure 3.23 shows the a few of the process fall points a hospital identified that affect the ability of a patient to schedule a follow-up appointment.

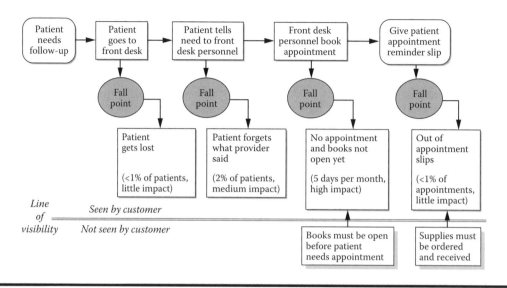

Figure 3.23 Fall points of patient follow-up.

For each fall point they quantified how often the failure occurred. Based upon the frequency of the event, the team prioritized which fall points they should develop formalized responses to build into the system. Detailed analysis and prioritization will also help you determine where to expend your time and resources. We'll talk more about methods to address fall points when we explore behavioral drivers.

Focusing Element 6: Develop Goals, Action Plans, and KPIs

With systems developed, roles and tasks articulated such that individuals are interacting with the systems and each other effectively, paying particular attention to the seams where fall points occur, you are now ready to set goals and develop detailed action plans. Properly set goals convert the team's mission into concrete action plans with measurable success criteria, milestones, and KPIs.

Famed management guru and pioneer Peter Drucker observed, "If you can't measure it, then you can't manage it." Without the ability to accurately measure your organization's performance you won't be able to determine if your systems are effective, if you are delivering on your value proposition, or be able to accurately calculate the overall return on your investment. Despite this obvious truth, many organizations don't have effective performance indicators. This is particularly true for service based organizations. It is easier to measure machine speeds and production rates, scrap, and overall output than it is to determine the effectiveness of a training class. Despite the challenges, it is important to implement some form of metrics from which you will be able to gauge the effectiveness of your operations. This concept is integral to systems thinking.

As you develop your action plans to implement your organizational changes you will want to develop cumulative metrics that act as guideposts along your journey. The current terminology for these metrics is key performance indicators (KPIs). KPIs are the parameters that most accurately indicate whether the organization is making progress toward its overall mission of achieving its value proposition. Throughout this book, every section and every heading is built around indicators of effective organizational formation. When you see growing trust and a clear understanding of the mission you can feel confident that your forming process is on track thus far. When you see growing alignment between individuals and department's activities, rest assured that the organization is becoming focused. In the same way, identify the indicators that will indicate your organization is accomplishing its primary objectives to deliver on its value proposition.

As you outline your milestones, be sure to include short-term as well as long-term indicators. Reaching these short-term objectives will help continue to fuel the change initiative and keep people motivated toward the vision. Insufficient attention to short-term results may allow people to become so caught up in the big dreams that they don't effectively manage the current realities. Only by generating short-term gains can credibility be gained to sustain the efforts for the long haul. Plan for short-term successes.

In Forming Element 7 (communications are planned, deliberate, and broad reaching), we discussed how communicating frequent milestones is critical. Let's consider the same roadtrip analogy but this time we'll drive from New York to Orlando (you may have guessed that I like Orlando). Leaving New York you don't see any signs in the city that say, "Orlando 1100 miles." Instead, you'll see signs along the way that say "95S," "Welcome to New Jersey," etc. These signposts provide assurance that you and your organization are heading in the right direction and that, if you stay the course, you will reach your destination. To maintain overall effectiveness and maximize engagement at all levels of the organization, the signposts must be relavent and visible to every single person in the organization. Otherwise, they won't maintain their line of sight to the overall mission objective.

SMART Goals

There are five standard elements commonly used throughout business, industry, and some governmental sectors for developing effective goal statements. These standard elements are often stated with the aid of a mnemonic, SMART. Effective goals are **s**pecific, **m**easurable, **a**chievable, **r**elevant, and **t**ime bound.

Specific: State exactly what will be accomplished

Measurable: State how goal achievement will be measured including the baseline and the target

Achievable: The goal should stretch the current capabilities but not be so lofty and esoteric that it will never be accomplished

Relevant: The goal should directly relate to the organization's value proposition such that it establishes a line of sight from individual activities to overall mission and vision

Time bound: The goal should have a timeframe within which it will be achieved

Defining goals using the SMART criterion helps clarify expectations as well as further define roles and responsibilities.

Cumulative Goal Development

Like mile markers, goals should build consecutively on each other toward accomplishment of the mission. The goals must also be consistent between areas. Too often separate departments and areas within an organization set goals in isolation without regards to the goals of other departments or areas. For instance, the operations department may have the goal to increase production while the maintenance department has the goal of reducing maintenance costs. The maintenance department could achieve their goal of controlling costs by not doing the essential maintenance needed to keep the equipment operational. The maintenance department would have the best year ever spending no money, but the equipment didn't run and the company made no product and went out of business—but the maintenance department made their goal! This example is obviously extreme, but it makes the point. A far better goal might be controlling maintenance costs through a proactive approach that maximizes operational reliability—they reduced costs by not having the machine break down. By having both operations and maintenance working toward the common goal of maximizing productivity, they align their activities and resources.

This is where the strategy maps you developed earlier really become vital tools to the ongoing operation of the organization. Aligning goals to the common strategy points out the "disconnects" between various individuals and departments. From an organizational perspective, I'm a strong proponent of having maintenance and all other support organizations report to operations and not exist as stand-alone entities.

To maintain ongoing improvements in efficiency and productivity, support departments must always remain focused and relevant to the operational mission of the organization. Too often I've seen the tail wag the dog as operational departments are hampered in achieving their missions by limitations placed on them by "support" departments. Two of the most commonly cited departments that hamper operations are Information Technology departments and Human Resources. In dozens of organizations I've worked with, I've witnessed Information Technology departments impose "solutions" on operations that don't improve productivity.

WHEN THE GOAL IS CONSISTENCY: A manufacturing facility had developed multiple procedures and wanted the operators to access the latest version before performing any critical evolution. The procedures were accessed through a shared drive. Launched through MS WORD™, the operators printed the procedure prior to each use. The operators were frustrated by waiting for WORD to launch each time on the slow network. In addition to the time to launch, accessing the document in WORD allowed operators to modify the procedures without prior reviews or quality checks. This led to confusion and created the potential for serious injury or equipment damage if an incorrectly modified procedure was used. Seeking a solution, the supervisory team wanted to save the files as PDFs. This was possible with a download from the manufacturer but the IT Department disapproved of the request because it would have required the nonstandard download. The group contacted the supplier's help desk and learned about a program called, "WORD VIEWER." This was 100% compatible, 100% secure, utilized less bandwidth, it launched almost instantaneously, and it was free. When the case was made to remove the full version of WORD from floor computers and utilize WORD VIEWER, that request was also denied. This time the group appealed to the IT Standards group. They made their case for security, speed, reliability, and it was free. Again, the operations team was denied. The IT review panel continued to explain how the operations team, "Just didn't understand the features of WORD." They suggested that the operations group put passwords on every file and lock down the drives. The operations team explained that passwords wouldn't prevent operators from doing a "Save As" and still modify the files. Even if they couldn't save the files, they could still print them out. And their solution wouldn't address the speed of access issue. The work around being suggested was unnecessarily confusing, created more work, and there was a much better solution. The IT panel became belligerent and stated, "Your time is up, we've told you that you can't use WORD VIEWER and that's the final answer. Frustrated, the operations leader stated, "So you're telling us that although we have a better solution, that is faster, more secure, and absolutely free, we can't do it because it is 'not standard'?" The VP of IT curtly replied, "Now you understand." CLICK, he hung up, ending the conference call with the frustrated operations team.

The little drama between operations and IT is not uncommon; I've seen it in for-profit companies, government agencies, and military commands. This internal goal misalignment is indicative of a common complaint about support departments and staff. Although support departments invariably think they are relevant and adding value, they often become tied down by their own "administrivia," majoring on the minors. They lose sight of the greater organization's mission and value proposition. They become part of the problem—added cost with insufficient added ROI. If yours is like most organizations, you have experienced support departments that are seen as just one more impediment to mission accomplishment while justifying their actions and their budgets with lofty terms like *strategic HR, business solutions engineering, IT solutions teams*, etc. Truly, there are many exceptional service organizations that do align their mission to the overall value proposition; however, when a support organization seems to be out of alignment yet holds unwarranted power and influence, the organizational leadership must stop and apply the logic test: "Are our customers willing to pay more for the services that this department provides?" If not, then it is a support department and not an operational department. As such, it needs to support cost effective delivery of the main value proposition through efficient achievement of the mission—not impede or derail the mission. Granted, these organizations may be essential to provide oversight, governance, or compliance to laws and regulations, but keeping them aligned to the mission helps them maintain their relevance without imposing any undue burdens.

While in the military, after serving in both operational and support commands, I developed MANION'S DOG THEORY OF ORGANIZATIONS: "On a dog, the further away from the teeth you are, the more crap comes out." The more removed the organization is from day-to-day operations, the more political games, bureaucracy, and pointless administrivia they generate that the "war fighters" have to endure and overcome to accomplish their missions.

Goal Consistency

In addition to having aligned goals that build consecutively on each other, it is equally important to have goal consistency. Refer back to the sixth cardinal sin of change leadership: "failure to stay the course: are we there yet?' When goals frequently change, progress is impeded, and people become discouraged and frustrated. It is important to maintain a consistent trajectory toward goals. Like our trip to Orlando, if we stop along the way and reverse directions, we won't ever arrive at our destination. It's not only in governmental agencies that organizations find themselves responding to political whims instead of strategic priorities. Remember that between 100 mph forward and 100 mph in reverse is dead stop. Select a strategic direction and continue to move toward it. You may have to make course corrections along the way, but if the organization maintains a clear line of site toward the value proposition, it will be readily apparent to everyone involved that the course corrections are either bringing the organization more in line with their objectives or enabling the organization to avoid an obstruction that was blocking progress.

Focusing Element 7: Effective Leadership toward Problem Solving

NOTE: Focusing Element 7 and Focusing Element 8 are integral to each other; they are discussed separately because they speak to the two separate concepts of leadership and management.

As the organization forms systems and aligns individual roles, the work of accomplishing the mission coalesces from a nebulous concept into tangible activities. It is during this focusing period when the disparities between "theory" and "practice," between "aspiration" and "execution," and between "as designed" and "as built" become apparent. Problems arise that require effective leadership to tackle and sound management to solve. Effective leadership takes a conscientious and deliberate approach to solving problems.

Adaptive Leadership and Problem Solving

To lead organizational change, use of all four leadership styles is essential. Remember, each style can be used effectively and each can be ineffective. Let's explore both for each style.

Directing: As the organization is forming, it needs direction to clearly outline the vision of the organization. Forming requires direction to align the organization *toward* a common path—thus the term "direction." However, if the leader stays grounded in a directing style, there will be limited crew involvement thus limited commitment toward the mission. If a directing style is used excessively communications will flow from the leader with limited input from the crew. Individuals won't have developed the level of trust that gives them the confidence to point out potential problems for fear of being seen as wrong, fear of reprisal, or the erroneous assumption that the leader is "all knowing" and has the situation well in hand. Maintaining a purely directive style of leadership will also limit the leaders awareness of evolving situations and conditions that might facilitate or impede achievement of goals. Leadership decisions will not be as effective because of the limited free flow of information.

Delegating: As the crew forms and moves into focusing, the leader needs to shift styles from directing if the crew is to become engaged. Delegate to the teams to go and begin designing systems. Set boundaries, give clear expectations, and then delegate. If the leader doesn't, the crew members may not engage in critical thinking and continue to look solely to the leaders for the solutions. However, if delegation becomes the predominant style in the early phases of the Focusing Stage and if the leader remains disengaged or altogether absent from the process, a lot of time and energy can be lost in developing systems that don't align and don't efficiently move the organization toward the achievement of its goals.

Developing: After the members have had a chance to work out some of the details on their own, reengage—check in on the process. Inappropriate intervention by the leader after a long period of absence may be seen as "Monday morning quarterbacking" and could discourage further engagement

by the crew. To navigate these multiple variables in a rapidly shifting organizational landscape requires the leader to "hold on loosely." Ask them what
they have developed thus far, what problems they are encountering, and
what they think the possible solutions could be. If the solutions proposed
by the crew are sound, be sure to congratulate them and reinforce their
initiative.

Problem solving: If there are gaps in the crew's experience or awareness of all the variables or requirements, shift more toward a coaching/
problem-solving mode. Draw out additional details and help them think
through the problems. Reinforce the systems thinking model. What are
the inputs? Are they sufficient? Do current activities and processes produce
acceptable outputs? Do those outputs yield the desirable outcomes?

Based upon their input and building upon their ideas, make any decisions
that are needed to support the development of comprehensive and effective systems. Provide any resources and additional information that the team
may need. Once you've made any required decisions, provided resources,
and validated the work of the team, ask them what they think the next steps
should be. Discuss their ideas and provide any clarification needed. Ask if
any additional resources are required and what support they need. Based
upon this discussion, agree to the next steps to be taken and the required
timing. Then close, let them go, and work some more on the next steps.

And the process is repeated. Consistent repetition of this pattern of
interactive adaptive leadership engages the crew into the problem-solving
process and develops their critical thinking skills without spending excessive time in unproductive activities that don't ultimately lead to workable
solutions. Consistent application of this methodology builds a "solutions-
oriented" organizational climate that focuses on solutions through engagement and systems thinking.

Focusing Element 8: Organizational Problem Solving

Focusing Element 7 outlined how utilization of an interactive adaptive style
of leadership to focus the team's problem-solving efforts creates a "solutions-
oriented" organizational climate. However, leadership alone is insufficient
to solve organizational problems. As explored in the discussion of cardinal
change sin no. 5, organizational behavior is complex with multiple drivers.
To understand and solve complex organizational issues, the problem-solving approach must be holistic, encompassing technologies, human factors,

leadership and management, operating procedures and systems. To effectively recognize, analyze and solve systemic organizational problems the organization needs a methodical approach to solving problems that explores both driving and restraining forces that contribute to the problem.

> NOTE: It is not the intent of this section to provide a complete analysis of problem solving. There are many excellent texts on that subject. Our intent is to understand the need for a systematic approach to problem solving, the basic structure of all problem-solving methodologies, and a few of the major pitfalls to be avoided.

Driving and Restraining Organizational Forces

Within every system, there are also always forces of change at work; some forces are at work contributing value while others are at work reducing value. The first cardinal sin of change leadership states that the status quo exists to serve the status quo. There are reasons why things are as they are—there are people who are benefitting from the current situation and there are systems in place that perpetuate it. These elements inhibit the organization's ability to improve—these forces are restraining progress (change restraints). At the same time, there are forces seeking to improve the organization's operations and add value. These could include improvement initiatives, new technologies, or just a team of dedicated professionals working hard to do the best job they can every day. As they do, they gain experience and insight that enables them to do things a little better each time. These are change drivers.

There is a constant tension between these two sets of forces—change drivers and change restraints. Like a tug-of-war game, if the forces driving change are greater than the forces restraining change, the organization will advance toward a higher state of performance and value generation. If the forces restraining the organization are greater, performance will falter and the organization will move further away from achieving its goals. The status quo exists where these forces hold each other in equilibrium. And where are you in all this organizational tension of pushing and pulling, driving and restraining? You're caught smack dab in the middle trying to juggle the day-to-day activities, get your job done, fight the fires that continuously spring up all around you, and trying to have a life outside of work on occasion (Figure 3.24).

Figure 3.24   Organizational tensions.

Think of these two sets of forces as a taunt elastic band held between your finger and thumb. The size and oval shape of the band are maintained at the point where the expanding pressure of your fingers exactly matches the contracting pressure of the elastic. If the expanding pressure were greater, the oval would enlarge; if the contracting pressure were greater, the oval would contract.

What are the driving forces seeking to improve our organization's operations? Are there economic imperatives—cut costs, improve productivity? Are there enabling technologies? What forces impede your organization's ability to change? Are there resource constraints? Outdated technology? Bureaucratic systems? Organizational apathy? Self serving management? Wherever your organization is at right now, you can be sure that those two sets of opposing forces are in equilibrium maintaining the current state in a dynamic balance of two sets of opposing forces. If there were fewer restraints or if there were more or stronger forces of change, the organization would move ahead. If the pressure to improve slacks off, the restraining forces move the organization back to its previous state.

When the organization does advance, the tension to return back to equilibrium increases—like stretching an elastic band further. Sometimes, a single person can be the driver of change. Think of a manager you've worked with in the past that really worked to change the organization. She came in with a passion, a vision, and a plan. She inspired others to align behind her vision and she led them to a place of higher performance. Then she left—promoted, transferred, or was fired. Not too long after her departure, things drifted back to the way they were. Bit by bit, everything seemed to just fall back into place. Like a rock stirring the surface of a still pond, she passed through, made waves for while, then was covered over as if she had never been. Just like the elastic band when you release the pressure applied by your finger and thumb, without constant effort expended to resist contraction, the elastic springs back to its previous size.

Avoiding Being Martyred for the Cause by Ignoring the "Sacred Cows" and 800-lb "Gorillas"

As you read the last description of the forces that impede progress, you may have taken a little guilty pleasure thinking, "Yeah, the real reason we can't improve the operation is… (fill in the blank!) Right, like that will ever change!?" Let's be real; there are some things within almost every organization that are limiting progress, but no one talks about let alone does anything about. There are the sacred cows—the pet projects, the "politically correct," and the legacy systems that will not be addressed in a change initiative—to do so would be career limiting. And there are the 800-lb gorillas that everyone knows are in the room that are untouchable; maybe it's the tenured employee, the "Teflon" manager, or the dinosaur CEO. Taking on these topics would not just be career limiting, it would be downright career suicide. So they continue on, impeding progress, utilizing resources, and feeding the status quo by undermining progress through benign neglect, subtle sabotage, malicious compliance, or all-out war. This is reality, and as Jack Welch so famously said, "Face reality as it is, not as it was or as you wish it to be." When you think about the many organizational barriers sustaining the operation, identify the snakes, classify them according to their degree of deadliness, and then tread lightly. Remember the difference between leaders and martyrs; chief among the difference is that leaders are alive and martyrs are dead. As you try to make a difference, getting yourself fired won't improve your effectiveness. Identify what is within your ability to change and what is not—your span of control and your span of influence. This is where the Serenity Prayer comes in handy: "Lord, grant me the serenity to accept the things I cannot change, the courage to change the things I can, and the wisdom to know the difference."

I'm not saying that you shouldn't try to improve organizational performance; after all, that's been my life's work, and it's the purpose for this entire book. What I am saying is that there are usually multiple forces acting to restrain progress, not just the one or two cows and gorillas. When you begin to change initiatives, the naysayers and would-be saboteurs are likely to hang back and let things percolate. Only when they see that their little corner of "status quodom" is threatened will they seek to intervene. When they do, it might be to stop progress or to take full credit for it. It's at this point that you will need to decide how to act. Focusing Element 10 deals more with conflict. For now, take a lesson from statistical analysis. When you plot all the points on a scatter diagram and they're all over the place, it's hard to see what's out

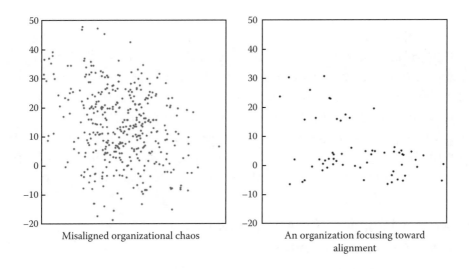

Misaligned organizational chaos

An organization focusing toward alignment

Figure 3.25   Organizational scatter plots.

and what's in—everything is hidden in the blur (Figure 3.25). As the organization focuses and moves toward alignment, it becomes easier and easier to see the real outliers. The more the organization moves toward a common goal and improves performance, the more likely that those outside the norm will either find a way to leave the organization to continue their behaviors in an organizational environment conducive to their behavior or begin to move more into alignment. Being seen too far out of the norm exposes them for what they are. For their own survival, they'll shift such that they can continue to hide in the light—not being too light or too dark, floating as a gray blob camouflaged within a sea of gray. Whether they leave the organization or alter their behavior to align to the new organizational direction doesn't matter; either way, the problem of their disruptive behavior is solved.

POLITICAL SURVIVAL HINT: Sometimes you may find yourself in a complete nest of vipers feeling like a stranger in a strange land. When you do, remember, snakes don't live in the arctic. Snakes live in environments conducive to snakes. If there is a significant majority of political intrigue, backstabbing, and ineffective activities that only give the illusion of activity without actually changing anything, you are working within an organization where management promotes and fosters these behaviors. There may be little hope of you actually making a difference because to do so would mean exposing the seat of power that's breeding the snakes. My advice to you is, unless you are a snake, or are willing to become one, the best thing you can do is carefully and quietly plot your exit strategy as expeditiously and painlessly as possible. That way you can leave on your terms without having to be rushed to the "career emergency room" or even worse the "morgue." One final word of advice to remember, *your career can die from terminal candor!* So be careful when living in a den of political intrigue, your attempts to point out the flaws may not be received well and could hasten your departure.

Choosing a Vehicle: The All Purpose Tool— Using the Crescent Hammer

So, assuming you are not dealing with a completely political situation in which you will not be able to affect true change, you will need to utilize a methodical and systematic problem-solving approach. But which approach should you use? The answer depends upon what the basis of the problem is. There are more than enough "solutions" out there—it really becomes a matter of choosing the correct tool. If you're not familiar with your options, you'll attempt to fix the problem with whatever tool you have in your toolbox. A crescent wrench can be used as a hammer and to a hammer, everything looks like a nail—or put another way, "The solution to any problem is the one I happen to know."

There are multiple problem analysis tools—each with its own terminology, acronyms, and tools, and each with a varying degree of complexity. Here are some of the more common problem-solving techniques listed in the degrees of relative complexity:

1. Systematic troubleshooting (scientific method)
2. Statistic process control
3. Total quality management—The Demming Cycle (Plan Do Check Act; PDCA)
4. Six Sigma (DMAIC)

If you've been working in the business world for any length of time you have seen these management trends come and go, become in vogue and then fade away like last year's fashions when replaced by the next greatest thing. You watched as Motorola improved upon the total quality concept by adding a structured toolkit and methodology all housed under the Six Sigma umbrella. The DMAIC (Define, Measure, Analyze, Improve, and Control) method added some more structure to the PDCA methodology of total quality management. PDCA was itself a variation of the scientific methodology outlined in the 1600s by Francis Bacon and further clarified by René Descartes. Bacon, Descartes and their contemporaries were further clarifying concepts outlined by the ancient civilizations of the Greeks and the Egyptians.

Regardless of the problem-solving methodology you use, all of them boil down to the basics of the scientific method.

1. Problem recognition
2. Problem definition
   a. Research the problem
   b. Develop a hypothesis
3. Test the solution and
4. Analyze the results
5. Ensure repeatability and state the conclusion

These general steps of the scientific method lie at the heart of all problem-solving techniques. To ingrain systematic problem solving into day-to-day operations, I developed a simple acronym that helped my maintenance crews remember the process: PARTS.

1. **P**roblem recognition and definition
2. **A**nalysis
3. **R**epair
4. **T**esting the repair
5. **S**topping future occurrences of the problem

NOTE: It is not my intent to advocate for one problem-solving methodology for you to adopt over any other. If you have a methodology that is systematic, effective and works well, continue to use it. The point of this discussion is to stress the importance of a methodical approach to problem solving. If you don't have a strategy, feel free to use this one.

Problem Recognition and Definition

The first step is to solving the problem is to first recognize that there is a problem. This sounds simple and simplistic, but failure to recognize the problem and/or failure to act on it in a timely manner is extremely common. Too often problems go unaddressed because managers don't want to make waves—it's no big deal. They excuse behaviors, "That's just the way he is." Or they have been so long in the midst of the situation that abnormal is the new normal. As they say, fish are the last to discover water. Remember, there is a point in the life of every problem where it is big enough to recognize but small enough to manage without having to go in and blow it up. Like medical problems, the trick is early detection and intervention.

Seeing that there is a problem may be challenging, but defining exactly what the problem is can be even more difficult. This is where the work you did in Focusing Element 6 (develop goals, action plans, and KPIs) can be really crucial. When you defined specific, measurable, and actionable goals along with their associated KPIs you'll have a solid foundation to identify a problem because you know you're not achieving your goals. But (there is always a "but") it's not always that simple—you can have a very specific goal, but not fully understand why you're not achieving it. So, when you begin your problem definition, try and describe exactly what is or is not happening. Just saying vague generalities won't help you understand the problem nor will they help you resolve them. If the problem is operational, describe what is not happening, who is not performing, and how it should be performed including when and to what degree.

When defining the problem look at all the factors that may be contributing to the problem. List each of these as either a change driver or a change restraint and chart them. I've found that use of fishbone diagrams is very effective in understanding the elements contributing to a problem (Figure 3.26). Methodically listing the drivers of the problem under categories helps you fully think through all the contributing factors.

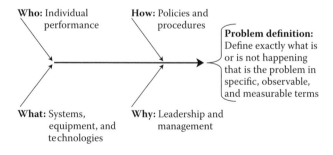

Figure 3.26   Use of a fishbone diagram for identifying possible causes.

Analysis

Once a problem is recognized and the causes have been identified and prioritized, organizations may flounder by applying resources that treat the symptoms not the causes. Even when treating causes, if your analysis is not in depth you won't get to the root causes. For instance, imagine your power goes out. You look for the cause: a breaker has tripped. You reset the breaker. Power goes back on. The problem is solved—or is it? Why did the breaker trip in the first place? Breakers are vital safety switches that trip when there is a potentially dangerous electrical condition drawing excessive current. Simply resetting the breaker doesn't solve the problem of why it tripped. You need to drill down and find the reason, the root cause, of why the safety feature was activated.

The root cause is the very substance of why a problem occurred. For each of the elements listed during your definition of the problem that are driving and sustaining the problem, ask yourself "why" multiple times until you can no longer ask it. A simple example of root cause analysis is shown in Figure 3.27.

Problem: The boiler tripped off line
    Why? The fan pump tripped out.
    Why? The motor overheated.
    Why? The bearing went bad.
    Why? There was no lubrication.
    Why? The bearing wasn't greased.
    Why? The bearing is not on the lubrication schedule.
Solution: Add the bearing to the lubrication schedule.

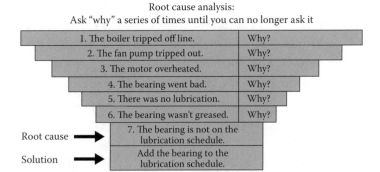

Figure 3.27　Root cause analysis.

In this example, once you've asked why for the sixth time, you realize why the bearing wasn't lubricated. This is the *root cause*. Once you have the root cause, you can take the actions needed to stop the problem from occurring in the future. Solution: Add the bearing to the lubrication schedule.

The seven steps listed above are as far as you need to go to understand the mechanical aspects of what went wrong. To take the analysis further, turn the crank one more time and drill down one more level: Why wasn't the bearing on the lubrication schedule? Someone didn't add it. If this were an ongoing problem where the maintenance planner consistently failed to develop effective preventive maintenance plans, you may need to get to the human factors and systems that caused the problem.

As part of the deeper problem-solving process, it's necessary to understand and address the human factors tied to business processes if you want to affect lasting positive change. It is ultimately the human factors that will determine the success or failure of any change initiative.

When planning for the implementation of a change initiative, remember that behavior is the result of complex relationship of multiple factors driving, repressing, and sustaining behaviors. Some of these factors are extrinsic, and some are intrinsic; some are real and tangible, and some are perceived. It's never as simple as "We just need to motivate them" or "They're just not holding people accountable." We'll talk more about individual performance when we analyze Committing Element 4.

Use of Brainstorming

Once you've defined the problem, brainstorming will help your group explore the multitude of causes and drivers. Brainstorming is a technique used to generate ideas drawing on the collective insight and creativity of a group. The technique is based upon the psychological principle of word association—each word and each idea might spawn others, building one upon another or spinning off into new tangents and ideas. The process encourages everyone to contribute as many ideas as possible in a free flow of thought. Basic ground rules for brainstorming usually include the following:

1. Everyone contributes.
2. Be nonjudgmental; don't critique ideas; every idea is listed.
3. Quantity is the goal; generate as many ideas as possible.

After I've introduced the ideas of drivers and restrainers, fishbone diagrams, and brainstorming, I break a large group into smaller teams of six or less. Small groups are more conducive to full participation than a single large one. Once in groups, list the categories of the fishbone diagram:

- Who: Individual performance
- What: Systems, equipment, and technologies
- How: Policies and procedures
- Why: Leadership and management

More ideas are consistently generated when you brainstorm in categories. The process also improves the quantity, quality, and breadth of ideas generated, thus reducing the tendency to drift into group thinking. I also find that groups are more successful when the brainstorming process is done in four phases:

1. Individual idea generation
2. Small group idea generation
3. Large group idea generation
4. Idea antithesis and synthesis

In the smaller subgroups, have each person think along each category and list as many ideas as possible. Next, have the small group blend their ideas followed by coming together as a large group to generate a master list. New ideas that occur during any phase are added whenever they come up. Finally, ask to think through the opposites of each idea. Asking the group to think about the opposites of each will spark even more creativity in generating more ideas. This delves into the concepts of drivers and restrainers of organizational change.

This process is rather long, and after you've been through the four steps, everyone will feel like their minds have been wrung out like damp rags. Because of the long process, I don't recommend that you use this in-depth brainstorming process for every problem every time. Overuse minimizes the impact, and people will eventually get to the point where they are just mechanically going through the motions. Instead, use this process for the high-priority problems, the ones that will really move the dial.

IS IT WORTH PURSUING? To help you prioritize, before you seek to find a solution to a problem, ask yourself, "Is it worth it?" I've found some managers spend an inordinate amount of time on issues and problems that are really more a matter of style than substance. Raymond used to say, "Got it" all the time. Whenever his supervisor would give Raymond a task, he would say, "Got it." The supervisor felt that Raymond was mocking him. When the problem was brought to me I asked the following series of questions:

Is Raymond a good worker? "Yes, he always gets his work done."

Does he do what you ask him to? "Yes, after he says, 'Got it' and gives me an annoying little salute."

Does he badmouth you or get others to not do what they are supposed to do? "Never, he'd be ideal if he just didn't do that annoying thing he does."

"My advice: Get over it. So what if he says a goofy phrase and gives an annoying little salute?" We all have our own little foibles and idiosyncrasies. Raymond said "Got it" but got his work done. The problem was the supervisor's, not Raymond's.

FOOTNOTE: Once the supervisor moved past his single-minded focus, he was able to be more productive not allowing the minor distraction from diverting his focus from the real work at hand.

Decision Analysis Criteria

If a solution is worth pursuing and you've brainstormed multiple solutions, determining which path forward is the most appropriate may not be straightforward. When confronted with multiple possible paths, it helps to make the best possible decision by considering aspects of decision quality through a process of decision analysis.

Decision analysis is a structured process that breaks down the decision into elements and criteria in a way that allows you to weigh the various attributes, pros and cons, as well as prioritization of each. When selecting a solution to a problem, consider the objective that you hope to reach. Clearly state the decision that needs to be made. Develop a list of decision criteria that will help you make your decision. Classify the criteria as either essential (musts) or supplemental (wants). Prioritize the useful criteria from most important to least. Table 3.9 shows an example of a decision analysis

Table 3.9 Example of a Decision Analysis Matrix

	Features/Description	Option 1	Option 2	Option 3
Overall Cost	**Base Cost**			
	Supplemental Costs (etc.)			
Overall Impact vs. Feasibility	**Feasibility (Hi–Med–Lo)**			
	Impact (Hi–Med–Lo)			
	ESSENTIAL CRITERIA/ATTRIBUTE: List each of the Essential Decision Criteria that, without which the option is not viable. For each of these elements, list whether that option satisfies it completely, partially, or not at all. Any option that does not satisfy an essential criterion will not be considered for adoption.	*Option 1*	*Option 2*	*Option 3*
Essential Criteria/ Attribute				

(continued)

Table 3.9 Example of a Decision Analysis Matrix (Continued)

Features/Description	Option 1	Option 2	Option 3
Overall Evaluation of how well the decision option satisfies all the essential criteria: Fully, Partially, or Not at all:			
SUPPLEMENTAL DECISION CRITERIA: List each of the supplemental features or benefits the option has that enhance the decision. Not having one of these items is not a "deal breaker"; however, each feature would be desirable if available. For each feature, you will list the scale by which option is rated for the criteria or attribute. Then you will list the relative weight of the criteria or attribute (the same weight for each option). For each option, you will rate how well each option satisfies the Rating and then multiply that by the Ranking to get a desirability score for each supplemental criteria.			

	Description	Description Desirable Rating	Criterion Relative Ranking Scale	Option 1		Option 2		Option 3	
				Rating	Rating X Ranking	Rating	Rating X Ranking	Rating	Rating X Ranking
Supplemental Criteria/ Attribute									
Overall Score:									

matrix that will help you compare and contrast the possible option you are considering.

> NOTE: An Excel version of the decision analysis matrix is available on the CD.

Next consider alternatives. Brainstorm a list of alternatives by identifying choices available to you. Amongst your alternatives, always consider the option of doing nothing at all. There are times that taking no action may be the appropriate action.

Evaluate each of the alternatives against the list of criteria you have developed. Any alternative that does not have all of the essential criteria can be immediately ruled out. Rank those remaining alternatives according to the useful criteria you have established.

Finally, make your conclusion. Validate your decision by checking any risks and ways to minimize them. Once you have brainstormed, analyzed, priority ranked, and considered the risks, you should have a clear indication of the best decision to act upon.

Leadership and Problem Solving

One final note about systematic problem solving, remember to adapt your style to guide the problem-solving approach. If you utilize too much direction, you will hamper brainstorming and creative problem solving. If you aren't engaged enough, people may simply apply the first fix that comes to mind and not drill down to the root cause. If you continuously collaborate, the process may take too long and the problem may not be fixed in a timely manner. If you strictly use the problem-solving approach, you may not encourage engagement nor have deep buy in to the solution. Adapt your leadership style to keep between the two ditches of over and under management.

> A MODERN TWIST ON AN ANCIENT CONCEPT: The idea of keeping it between two ditches is a parable to help visualize and remember. The roots of the concept date to antiquity. It was Aristotle who advocated for the golden mean: moderation in all things. Maintain the desirable middle between two extremes—something we see little of in today's leadership and even less in politics.

The Second Difference Separating Leaders and Martyrs

When we started the discussion we mentioned a major difference between leaders and martyrs: alive versus dead. There is a second difference to keep in mind between martyrs and leaders; leaders are one step ahead of their people whereas martyrs are about two. When you are running fast you may get too far out ahead. As you're fixing problems and implementing changes, your crew may lose sight of what you're trying to accomplish; they'll become nervous, may get lost along the way, stop following you, or start following someone else who they feel will lead them to that better place their dreaming of. You will then become irrelevant as a leader. Irrelevance is a synonym for expendable in the business world. To stay connected as you move ahead, check back frequently to ensure that people are still tracking with you and you are addressing both their needs and their concerns. Utilizing those lines of communication you established during the initial forming period to facilitate clear communications and receive timely feedback will be essential to your successful navigation of the Focusing Stage.

Focusing Element 9: Tactical Interpersonal Communication and Feedback

As you get deeper into the focusing process, developing systems, defining roles and responsibilities, and setting goals, your communications will shift frequently between group and individual communications. At the same time you're communicating one on one, the process of cascading communication will be occurring almost continuously. As the organization is building momentum, there is a virtual explosion of communication—everyone is talking with everyone. Keeping consistency and clarity of the message as it is promulgated is key.

It is during this stage that the integrity of your organizational vessel will begin to be tested. Miscommunications will arise between individuals. Individuals may ignore each other, often speaking over the top of one another in order to be heard. Less assertive members of the group will tend to remain in the background to avoid being involved in conflict.

It's at this point that you'll really appreciate having spent the time up front forming the team. It will be helpful to pull out the team charter and ground rules you established. Remember to follow the guidelines you set forth for effective meetings. During this crucial time, you, as the leader, must model the way; everyone is watching. Listen attentively to the individuals in the team and insist that others do the same. If you fail to address dysfunctional behaviors as they arise, they can lead to ongoing conflicts, ill feeling, and ultimately sow the seeds of failure. Frustration and cynicism may derail the change initiative.

Use the cyclical communications process introduced during the Forming Stage and shown again in Figure 3.28. Encourage the members to listen to one another. Demonstrate restating different points of view to ensure understanding. Give constructive feedback and encourage others to communicate how specific behaviors affect each other in both constructive and destructive ways.

Encourage the team members to address problems collaboratively, to share responsibilities for problems. When one team member has a problem with another, insist that they address the conflict directly; do not enable bypassing of the chain of command. Moderate discussions if necessary but ensure that the individuals have tried the established channels before you intervene. If you allow conflicts to go unaddressed, members will brood unproductively; they'll gossip and snipe rather than addressing the individual with whom they have the conflict. Left unchecked, these behaviors will propagate and solidify into communications patterns that feed behind the scenes politics. Before you know it, you will have nursed your own brood of vipers.

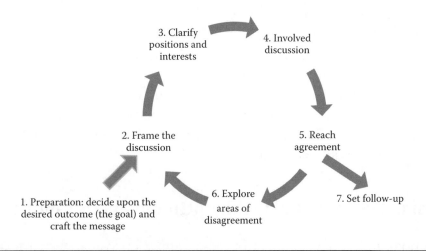

Figure 3.28   Cyclical communications process.

Rules of Engagement in Support of Team Ground Rules

During the forming process, along with the team charter, the team's ground rules were developed; they must not be abandoned when conflicts begin to surface. Leaders and individual team members must insist upon their adherence. As the rules are used, they will be tested. During these trying times, how the rules are used is equally important. It's like your mom told you when you were little, "It's not what you said, but how you said it!"

Speak for Yourself and Speak of What You Know to Be Fact

When giving feedback own your statement. Don't refer to absent or anonymous people. Don't say, "Everybody is saying…" nor say, "I heard this about…" If you feel strongly enough to address a behavior, speak for yourself. State your concerns clearly and concisely with the intent of reaching a resolution, not just placing blame. Avoid absolutes like, "You always" or "You Never."

Restrict your feedback to things you know for certain. Separate what you "know" from what you "think" and from what you "feel." Don't present your opinions as facts. If you don't know the facts, seek them in an open and nonaccusatory manner. Utilize the communications cycle and remember that communications is a process.

To help set the tone, avoid "You" statements. Speak for yourself. A helpful methodology is to use the following sentence template:

I feel (or felt) _____ when you _____ because _____.

For instance: "I feel frustrated when you interrupt me in the middle of my sentences because I lose my train of thought and I can't completely develop the point I'm trying to make."

Starting out the statement with "You" immediately puts the other individual on the defensive and will begin to shut down the communications process before it even begins. When tensions are running high, it may be quite difficult to calmly work through the communications process. When you consistently utilize the ground rules, they become the rules of engagement, the communications process will flow much easier and it will continue to become easier with each time it is practiced.

Focusing Element 10: Healthy Attitude about Conflict

At this point in the development of the organization you and your team have formed and are moving well into focusing such that

- You have a well-stated value proposition that has been disaggregated into strategies
- Systems have been designed and are being implemented to execute the strategies
- Well-formed communications plans are being well executed
- Roles, responsibilities, and goals set clear expectations
- Established key performance indicators (KPIs) are tracking the organization's accelerating progress toward achieving its objectives
- The team charter and ground rules continue to be referred to and guide interactions

As you develop the organization, differences of opinions, miscommunications, and varied approaches and strategies will likely lead to friction among team members. Understanding of different temperaments and leadership styles aided by the utilization of ground rules and charters will help the team work effectively through these discussions. As effective as these proven tools and techniques are, there is a strong possibility that the organizational growing pains will lead to deeper tensions and possibly erupt into conflicts. After forming, it is not uncommon for organizations to stumble on their journey toward higher performance (Figure 3.29).

The point of placing the *stumbling* block off the path toward *sustained performance* is to indicate that a state of confusion, chaos, and frustration diverts the organization from reaching the desired end state. When conflicts arise the question becomes whether the conflicts will serve as catalysts that reveal opportunities for improved efficiencies and alignment that propel the organization forward toward achieving the mission and adding greater value, or will they splinter the planks of the organizational vessel being built?

Conflicts should not just be ignored hoping that they'll work themselves out and the team will naturally progress toward greater cohesiveness. Left unaddressed, the negative emotions of animosity and resentment that are byproducts of conflict could harden into dysfunctional behavioral norms

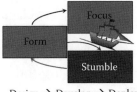

Design → Develop → Deploy

Figure 3.29   Stumbling on the journey.

with lasting repercussion. Navigation of these tempestuous waters requires both leadership and managerial acumen along with a solid understanding about the sources of conflict, options for responding to conflict including the pros and cons of each, and an effective approach to reaching conflict resolution.

Building Bridges before the Flood—Laying the Foundation Conducive to Managing Conflict

Waiting until conflict occurs to manage it is about as effective as waiting to have a heart attack before you decide to take care of yourself. The work you do up front will help you avoid many conflicts, minimize those that do occur, and help the organization survive after them. Effective conflict management depends upon four elements:

1. Climate—fostering a healthy, mutually supportive environment will set the stage for effective management of conflicts before they occur. A healthy climate conducive to managing conflict demonstrates
   a. Empathy for individual views
   b. Recognition that conflicts will occur and are a part of dynamic relationships
   c. A bias toward cooperation rather than competition
      Much of this work needs to have been done during the Forming Stage; otherwise, it will be too little too late when the Focusing Stage reveals organizational rifts.
2. Effective leadership—How the leader responds to conflict will have lasting impacts on the organization's climate and its ability to manage future conflicts. When a manager is seen as impartial, fair, and focused on achieving the best possible solution for all concerned a healthy climate is promoted. If the manager shows favoritism, involves themselves in petty political games and gossip, or dictates capriciously there is little chance of establishing a healthy climate.
3. Communications—Skilled use of the cyclical communications process is essential to managing conflict. Without effective communications managing conflict becomes almost impossible.
4. Problem-solving techniques—Working through a systematic problem-solving approach that utilizes effective techniques to explore the root causes of problems and relies on facts rather than assumptions is essential to managing conflict effectively.

Understanding the Sources of Conflict

When you seek to change an organization, you embark on a complex and multifaceted journey. At the heart of organizational change is the desire to change behaviors. People will need to act and think differently if the organization is expected to produce different results. Changing behavior often results in "unintended consequences" as we described earlier in cardinal change sin no. 5. Coupling unintended consequences with the challenges of changing behavior often breeds conflicts. After all, most people have a hard enough time changing their own behavior, let alone changing an entire organization.

Even if someone desires to change, they may be limited in their ability to change because of limited resources. How many times have you wanted to make a change but didn't really have sufficient resources to implement the ideal solution? You may have needed additional support but weren't able to hire additional staff. Or, your design called for a computer application upgrade, but your budget wasn't able to afford the customization that was required. Consequently, you implemented off-the-shelf software and then forced your systems to accommodate the program instead of the program facilitating simpler operations.

To understand the sources of conflict, we'll explore the tensions that arise from changing behavior and the conflicts that arise from goal disparity and limited resources.

Conflict Arising from Change

Do people resist change? According to the Society for Human Resource Management's (SHRM) 2007 Change Management Survey Report, the top two obstacles to change are communication breakdown and employee resistance. So it certainly appears that people do resist change. When we explored DISC profiles, it was seen that some temperaments are change resistant—conversely, there are personality temperaments that are constantly seeking to change. But let's be honest here; many of those individuals seek to change others but not themselves. So, are people resistant to all changes? If you won a large lottery, would it change your life? Would you turn it down to resist that change? Compare these scenarios:

■ You win the lottery and quit your job. OR You are fired.
■ You sell your car. OR Your car is stolen.

■ You buy a new top of the line computer. OR Your company changes computer systems.
■ You move to a new state for a better job. OR Your company forces you to relocate to keep a job.

Each of these scenarios has two differentiating factors:

1. One is your choice; the other is someone else's choice forced upon you
2. One has a clear and immediate benefit for you; the other does not

As shown in Figure 3.30, people resist change when

A. They are not involved in making the change decision
B. The change does not seem to readily benefit them

Figure 3.30 also shows where people will fall on the willingness spectrum between "change resistant" and "eager." If there is a clear benefit and you choose to make the change because you anticipate a net gain, you'll probably be eager for the change to happen. If you see a benefit but it really wasn't your choice, you may be willing. If you choose to make a change but there is no clear benefit, then perhaps you're doing it to accommodate someone else, which may then make you reluctant to make the change. However, if it's not your choice and you see no benefit and see the change actually resulting in a net loss, you will probably resist the change.

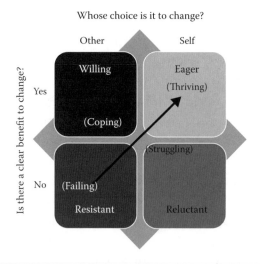

Figure 3.30   Factors affecting change response.

Also shown in the figure are behavioral responses to change, spanning the following range:

Failing → Struggling → Coping → Thriving.

These terms help you think through the emotional phases of change that you will need to help the members of your crew traverse along your organizational change journey. Depending upon whether the person sees the coming change as a gain or a loss will determine in part their emotional response.

Emotional Responses to Change

When change is seen as a loss people will tend to grieve the loss. The amount of loss will obviously impact the degree of grief experienced. Dr. Kübler-Ross mapped out the stages of grief in her groundbreaking study (Kübler-Ross, E. 1969. *On Death and Dying.* London: Routledge). These five stages are commonly known as the stages of grief:

1. Denial
2. Anger
3. Bargaining
4. Depression
5. Acceptance

When you implement changes, those that are change resistant will exhibit many or all of these symptoms. It is good to keep in mind as you help your organization move through the transformation that the order of the stages may vary and people can slide in and out and back and forth between stages as they work through the process. Remain focused on the outcome and you will be able to help people through the process.

Not as well recognized but every bit as important is the understanding that even when people see the change as a net gain, they too will go through an emotional roller coaster. However, theirs takes a slightly different trajectory. Don Kelley and Darryl Conner charted "The Emotional Cycle of Change" (Kelley, D., and Conner, D.R. 1979. The emotional cycle of change. In: Jones, J.E., and Pfeiffer, J.W., eds. *The 1979 Annual Handbook for Group Facilitators.* San Diego: University Associates) for desired change.

1. Uninformed optimism—Incomplete understanding combined with near certainty of success—"This is going to be a 'slam dunk'!"
2. Informed pessimism—Optimism turns to pessimism as it becomes clearer what is involved and the amount of effort required—"What have we gotten ourselves into?"
3. Hopeful realism—Overcoming some obstacles and seeing a path forward brings hope that success may be possible—"You know, we might be able to pull this off."
4. Informed optimism—Building momentum begins to solidify the belief that the goal will be achieved, many of the naysayers begin to come on board—"We are definitely going to make it!"
5. Rewarding completion—The problems have been worked out and the project was a success. "As built" doesn't necessarily reflect "as designed" but the project is a resounding success—"Was there ever any doubt?"

Within your organization you will probably have individuals from both the "change resistant" and the "change ready" points of view. Be aware of where your people fall on the spectrum and be prepared to provide the leadership they need to guide them along the path to success.

Based upon my observations, I've combined these two stage approaches into the stages of organizational development model, as shown in Table 3.10.

During the Forming Stage, people who are ready for the change will experience anticipation looking forward to the wonderful world of what will be. Those who view the change as a loss may be in denial, "I've seen plenty of changes in the past—this one won't amount to anything either." Or, they

Table 3.10   The Change Readiness versus Response Continuum

		Focus	*Commit*	*Sustained Performance*	*Renewal*
	Form	*Stumble*	*Fragment*	*Variable Performance*	*Level*
Change Readiness vs. Response Continuum					
Change Ready	Anticipation	Excitement	Collaboration	Optimism	Celebration
Change Resistant	Denial or Anxiety	Anger	Compromise	Skepticism	Acceptance

may have feelings of anxiety and trepidation as they worry about how the change may affect them.

As the change initiative begins to take hold, those who wanted the change will feel growing excitement, others will become angry since there is no more denying the changes and the possibility of experiencing the loss they fear moves one step closer to becoming a reality.

As the organization moves into the Committing Stage, those opposed to the changes will bargain to minimize their losses, and those in favor of change will collaborate with the others to try and win them over and get them aligned with the change initiative.

Even when the change is implemented and the organization is operating differently in the Performance Stage, there will be differing views between those that believe it will continue to improve and those who are skeptical that the changes will last.

Finally, as that change which was new becomes the new status quo the levels of acceptance will range between satisfaction and grudging compliance. The organization will seek to renew itself or level in its performance.

Since you will likely have both camps within your organization you will continuously have to balance and moderate between the two. If not done effectively, having opposing views further sets the stage for ongoing conflicts.

If the forming and focusing process doesn't proceed as planned, the organization will stumble. I refer to this as stumbling instead of storming because not every organization or change initiative results in a full-fledged storm. After all, there's a big difference between a summer shower and a category 5 hurricane. So, if an organization stumbles they may just stub their toe or they may break their neck. How severe the stumble will be determined by the leader's ability to manage and the manager's ability to lead. As we have discussed in Focusing Element 8, the difference will be early recognition and intervention.

Factors Affecting the Difficulty of Change

One of the factors that will determine if conflicts arise and how severe they become will be the nature of the change itself. After all, not all changes are equal. Consider changes within yourself. Even if you believe that a change will be beneficial, making the change can still be difficult. Are there any changes you've tried to make that were unsuccessful? New Year's resolutions? We all can think of changes we had the best intentions of making, but, for whatever reason, the change just didn't work out. What does it take for an individual to change? What would it take for you to change?

- Your shirt?
- How you act?
- What you believe?

Obviously, it's harder to change something you believe in as compared to your shirt (which I hope you change fairly frequently). Figure 3.31 illustrates four levels of individual change:

1. Superficial changes
2. Conscientious behaviors
3. Habits
4. Values, core beliefs, emotional responses, and addictions

Each subsequent level makes it harder and harder to affect a change and then to sustain the change. Organizations have similar depths of change, as shown in Figure 3.32:

1. Individual tasks
2. Procedure and process changes
3. Cross-departmental changes
4. Cultural changes

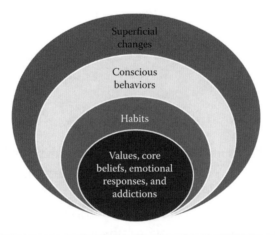

Figure 3.31   Levels of individual change.

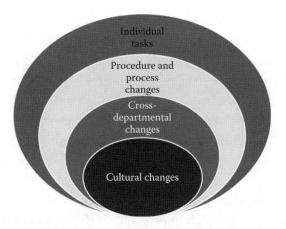

Figure 3.32   Levels of organizational change.

It is easier to change how one individual performs a single task than it is to change an entire organization. Depth of change is one of five factors affecting the difficulty of organizational change. Figure 3.33 shows all five:

1. Depth
2. Span
3. Drivers
4. Duration
5. Degree of ambiguity

As we have just discussed, the depth of organizational change ranges from superficial to core changes. The span is based upon whether you are trying to change an individual or an entire organization. Obviously, changing one is easier and faster than changing thousands. The drivers relates to whether the organization desires the change or not. Getting an organization

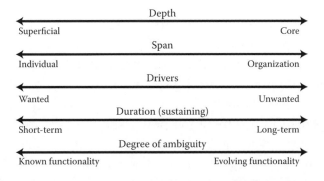

Figure 3.33   Factors affecting the ease of organizational change.

to want to change is why John Kotter of Harvard Business School advocates the identification of a "burning platform" (Kotter, J. 1996. *Leading Change*. Boston: Harvard Business School Press). It's easier to get an organization to change when they see that there is a compelling reason to do so. Just as it is easier to change when you want to, it is easier to change for a short time as compared to a permanent change. Almost anyone can change for a brief span of time; the difficulty comes in making the change stick. Just as Mark Twain pointed out, "It's easy to quit smoking; I've done it hundreds of times."

The final factor that determines the difficulty in affecting change lies within the very nature of the change itself: Is the outcome concrete or ambiguous? If what is desired is a well-defined outcome with known parameters, it's easier to affect as compared to trying to hit a moving target. In today's rapidly evolving technological landscape, managers don't fully know the organizational impact of implementing a new technology, nor do they fully understand the range of possible unintended consequences that may spring out of making such a change. Companies have experienced this when they've tried to implement open architecture communication tools and other adaptive software. The technology itself may have wide-reaching ramifications well outside the organization. In addition, people may find new and creative ways of applying the technologies that the designers never intended let alone anticipated by the purchasing manager. As a result, designing a change management approach to move toward a future you can't imagine adds an entirely new and complex level of difficulty. More difficulty and more ambiguity breed more conflict.

THE IMBALANCED SCORECARD: A southeastern services company's leadership team wanted to implement a Balanced Scorecard goal setting and metrics tracking methodology. As they started down the road, they took the advice of the articles they had read and involved the subject matter experts (SMEs) to develop the goals and metrics. The SMEs all worked on the project in tandem, with their regular roles and responsibilities requiring most of the work to be performed after regular working hours. Over the course of months, the teams spent long hours developing plans to implement the new method of setting priorities and managing the organization. As they did, the SMEs became more and more vested in the process. Their level of commitment increased along with their level of understanding of the organization's mission, vision, systems, and processes. After more than six months in the design phase, the plans were presented just in time for input into the annual budget.

Although the teams had been integral in the development of the plan, they were not permitted to be involved with the budget process. They became frustrated with being excluded but tried to keep faith that all the extra hours of work they had poured into the process would weigh significantly on the executive decision process. They were wrong. When it was all said and done, the plans and recommendations had little impact on how the organization prioritized its scarce resources. As a result, the levels of cynicism and frustration increased dramatically, and the organization drifted further away from the originally stated goal of engagement and increased efficiency.

Conflict Arising from Goal Disparity and Limited Resources

Change entails both choices and losses—choices on how to proceed, which priority is resourced, and how systems will be designed and staffed. As we have just discussed, the more difficult the change, the more rife the situation is for out and out conflict. Even when the change is minor and the resources are adequate, conflicts can still arise.

The simplest explanation of why conflicts arise is that a situation exists where two individuals or groups have differing goals with limited resources. The goals could be external or internal, real or perceived. The limitation of resources could also be tangible and quantifiable involving finances, materials, manpower, time, etc., or intangible involving egos, self-esteem, and power. If we had unlimited resources, unlimited time, unlimited funding, talent, recognition, glory, and strokes to delicate egos, then we might never have any conflicts—you could always get everything you wanted and I would always get everything I wanted and everyone would always feel valued, honored, and respected. Clearly, this is not the case. Even when we have sufficient tangible resources, conflicts will arise from differences of opinion, perceptions, styles, and approaches along with conflicts of ego.

The exploration of intangible resources delves into the emotional roots of conflict—emotional, perceptions, ego, or perceived imbalances of power, etc. It is often easier to recognize the root causes and seek resolutions to conflicts involving tangible goals than those stemming from differences in approach, power, or ego. It is far easier to address how we spend limited funds on our respective goals than it is for us to address my resentment of something you said or did. Not only are the conflicts regarding the emotional factors harder to resolve, they are the ones whose effects linger far after the physical conflict has ended. "I may forget exactly what you said or did, but I will always remember the how you made me feel!"

Responses to Conflict—Reactionary versus Deliberate

Conflict is a part of life and conflicts can have permanent consequences. We learn at an early age that events will not always go our way. As we encounter obstacles that impede our progress and impair us from achieving our desires, we learn to fight for what we want. As we get older, we alter our approaches by adding negotiation, guilt, and manipulation to our arsenal of conflict resolution tools. Over time, friction between our natural temperaments rubbing up against our experiences shapes our responses and our conflict resolution styles becomes ingrained and habituated. Consequently, our reactions to conflict can be much more reactionary than deliberate. The fact that there are differing approaches to address a conflict implies that it is possible to choose how you respond which, in turn, will influence which path the conflict takes and how events will unfold as well as the lingering effects after the conflict is thought to be resolved. Will the outcome yield a better solution, clear the air, and edify the team, or will the conflict escalate to an emotional maelstrom that consumes the team and inexorably alters both the interpersonal dynamics and the effective functionality of the group? The answer lies in how well you are able to handle both your emotional and cognitive responses to conflict.

The Emotional Response—A Tale of Two Roses

To understand our responses to conflict, first, let's imagine a situation that, on the surface, should yield anything but conflict: a simple act of kindness. A man leaves his office for home after another long stressful day in an even longer string of stressful months. Walking toward his car he encounters a street vendor selling roses on the corner. On a whim, he buys two perfect little roses to take home to his wife, one yellow and one lavender, the same as their wedding colors. It wasn't their anniversary, her birthday, or any other occasion requiring flowers; it was just another ordinary Tuesday. The thought of the smile that would surely spread across her face immediately lightened his mood. She'd been working hard, and the preceding months had taken their toll on her as well. He drove home anticipating the unexpected joy he was delivering. He ebulliently arrived home, quietly slipped into the house without being heard until he called out, "Surprise!" She turns to be greeted by her smiling husband and the sweet aroma of the flowers he is holding out to her…and her response is?

a. Honey! They're beautiful! Thank you!
b. Huh?
c. You forgot to pick up eggs didn't you?
d. What the hell is this? Did you wreck the car?
e. She doesn't say a word and the tears begin to flow.
f. <FILL IN YOUR OWN RESPONSE>!

One simple act could result in two, three, or even more differing responses, only one of which was intended. The reaction from the surprised wife will depend upon multiple factors, some of which include the following:

1. Her present emotional state—Did she have a bad day? Has she been brooding about his long hours? Is she worried about their marriage? Other? When emotions are already raw, our responses might vary dramatically.
2. Her temperament—trusting and accepting or cynical and skeptical.
3. Her perception of intent—example: if I like you I can take almost anything you say the "right way." "Geez, Jamison, you look like crud today." "Thanks, I feel like crud. And I appreciate your concern." If I don't like you, I can take anything you say the "wrong way." "You look nice today." "What? Don't I look nice every day? What are you insinuating? You're such a jerk!" If the wife interprets his motives to be anything other than pure, her reaction will be predicated upon her perception rather than his actions.
4. History—Has he ever brought her roses before? If so, why? Apology, bribery, guilt, or purely out of love? Something else? This will also feed her perception of intent.
5. Expectations of the future—events not going according to the planned script. She may jump to the conclusion that the roses are an indication that he has different plans for the evening that will necessitate her changing her own plans to spend an evening with her friends.

If a simple act of kindness can cause so many emotional reactions, how much more can vitriolic confrontations sparring over scarce resources that will impact your ability to a accomplish your objectives and achieve your desired goals?

Emotional, Cognitive, and Physiological Behavioral Drivers

The principles of communications were introduced as part of Forming Element 7; we expanded upon this discussion in Focusing Element 2 with the introduction of management operating systems and system fall points. Now we will expand the concept further by looking at the interaction between various behavioral determinants and physical chain of events that drive behavioral responses:

$$\text{Trigger} \rightarrow \text{Response} \rightarrow \text{Timing} \rightarrow \text{Feedback.}$$

With mechanical or electrical systems, the response to triggering events is usually straightforward and predictable; when we throw in the human element, the responses can be much more unpredictable. A particular trigger today may trigger a different response tomorrow. As Figure 3.34 helps illustrate, the variability of human responses arises from the interplay between the triggering events, filters that obscure or alter the awareness of the triggering event, and internal emotional, cogitative, and physiological processes. By overlaying these variables onto the systems process control model that we introduced during the discussion of Focusing Element 2, we construct a model that helps us explain, but not always understand, why people may respond in unexpected ways.

Running vertically along the left side of Figure 3.34 are the process control elements of

$$\text{Sense} \rightarrow \text{Interpret} \rightarrow \text{React}$$

A triggering event, condition, or fact will initiate a chain reaction that will culminate into a response based upon the interaction of multiple variables. The trigger in our example happens to be "roses." The multiple determinants that shape the response to the trigger are subdivided into four categories:

1. Physical reality
2. Emotional processes
3. Cognitive processes
4. Physiological processes

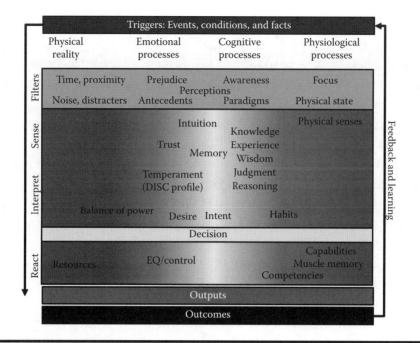

Figure 3.34 Behavioral determinants.

Each of these determinant categories interacts with the control elements:

$$\text{Sense} \rightarrow \text{Interpret} \rightarrow \text{React}$$

The chain reaction begins with sensing—the individual must become aware of the triggering event. How or even if the event is sensed will be affected by filters.

Filters: Filters limit or screen out certain elements. In the communications, filters can be physical, emotional, cognitive, or physiological.

Physical filters could include time—wasn't there when it happened, proximity—wasn't close enough to clearly see or hear what happened, noise—didn't hear what happened, or other distractions—my dog was talking to me so I missed what you said.

Emotional filters could include prejudices—preconceived notions about the person, place, or thing, or antecedents—the emotional state of the individual prior to the triggering event occurring can play a significant role in determining the resulting behavioral outcome. A normally calm individual may react quite strongly if they were previously upset, worried, or otherwise predisposed.

Perceptions are filters that span the gap between the emotional and cognitive realms.

Cognitive filters can be a matter of temporary awareness—you may not have been aware of an annoying background noise until someone pointed it out to you and now you can't ignore it—or more permanent such as mental models and paradigms—fish are the last to discover water.

Physiological filters, like cognitive filters, can be a temporary focus or physical condition (i.e., tired) or of a more permanent nature—physical limitations such as degrees of blindness or loss of hearing.

Assuming that the triggering event makes it through the various filters, it can be intact, accurately representing reality, or distorted—altering our perceptions of reality.

Having become aware of the trigger, our response will be predicated upon our interpretation of the scope and significance of the triggering event. Significant to understanding human behavior is the recognition that although it is our five senses that inform us of what's happening in our world, it is frequently our emotions and not our intellect that assign meaning to those events. The predominance of emotion over intellect varies according to temperament, but it is a factor for everyone regardless of temperament due to the speed of emotional reaction as compared to the processing of rational thought. Just how fast is an emotion? Depending upon the trigger, some people can go from zero to pissed in nothing flat!

Any surprising/unexpected event can cause both a physiological and an emotional reaction initiated through the hormone adrenaline. Adrenaline acts as a neurotransmitter triggering our sympathetic nervous system with a chemical jolt that increases heart rate, constricts blood vessels, and dilates the air passages. This is the body's fight or flight response, which lasts about 90 seconds—after that short span of time, the chemical boost dissipates. Beyond the autonomic reaction our continued response to the triggering event will be predicated by our cognitive and emotional processes. Will emotions drive the situation or intellect? It will all depend upon what emerges from the "stasis cloud" of our emotional and cognitive processes—those complex interactions that continuously seek equilibrium between our intuition, knowledge, sense of trust, memory, experience, temperament, wisdom, judgment, and reasoning skewed by our desires and our intents, tempered by our perceptions of the balance of power, and coupled to our habituated responses. If it all sounds a bit complex, it is.

Habituated Responses

The brain is amazingly efficient. It continuously monitors thousands of stimuli and sorts and categorizes them as to whether an event is deserving of our attention and, if so, what the appropriate degree of response is. If the event is one that we have encountered before, the efficient brain will apply a past response to the present. The more frequently you encounter the event, the more automatic the response will be. Think of driving home. Have you ever arrived home and said, "Wow, I'm here already." You were so caught up in your thoughts that you scarcely remember driving there. You had to have turned into the neighborhood, stopped at the sign, avoided the annoying dog that lives on the corner, etc. You must have done each but don't remember any. During the missing periods of time, your highly efficient brain was using its short-term memory circuits to perform discrete "routine" transactions, subroutines, that enabled you to focus on whatever was preoccupying your mind. (NOTE: This is not an endorsement of inattentive driving—simply an observation of reality).

The same process that allows you to drive on "autopilot" can also govern your responses to conflict. Have you ever been just sitting, unperturbed and perfectly content, then look up to see someone approaching and immediately become angry? You feel the tension in your chest, your heartbeat accelerates, your breathing becomes a little faster, your pupils dilate, and you feel the knot in your stomach and some tightness in your throat. These are the physiological results of the adrenaline boost. At that moment the person hasn't done anything to you, but the last time you interacted was tense conflict. Perhaps many of the times you have interacted resulted in conflict. You anticipate the coming interaction—you prepare for fight or flight. In your mind you may be anticipating the coming storm. You'll say this, they'll say that, you'll respond by saying "X" and they'll retort with "Y." You don't want it to go that way, but it always seems to. You feel like an actor assigned to play a part that you would prefer altered—but you don't think it will. You may experience this particularly often with teenagers and other rebellious headstrong types. The more frequently the brain processes the transaction, the more ingrained the autonomic response becomes. In fact, neurons physically grow new synapses that literally hardwire the response. Your emotions become set, and each time you experience the event by seeing the person, hearing the noise, smelling the fragrance, etc., the emotion is triggered. As a result, you develop habituated responses that can continue to influence all future interactions. The past shapes the future.

QUOTE: "The soul becomes dyed with the color of its thoughts."

Marcus Aurelius Antonius
Roman Emperor (188–217)

Scripting

Even if you don't experience a habituated response to an event, the physiological reaction can still kick in when life doesn't follow our anticipated scripts. The entire time the husband was driving home, he was scripting out in his mind how he expected his wife to respond. He imagined how she would act in the supporting role he had cast for her. "Oh, Honey, they're beautiful. I love them! And I love you so much. How thoughtful. Let me show you how grateful I am, etc." If she doesn't say her lines and act according to the script he has assigned for her, he will be disappointed, hurt, and frustrated. Disappointment and frustration can escalate into anger, and the situation could descend into an argument. How often have you been hurt and angry when others didn't stick to the script you've assigned them?

Your habituated responses can become the patterns within which you cast the forms of your interpersonal relations. This is particularly true during the stressful conditions surrounding conflict—the more stressful the situation, the more you rely upon your autonomic responses. You may perceive that there is no time to think—only time to react. Before you can alter your reactions, you must first recognize that you have other options. You have choices. You can improve your interpersonal effectiveness and reduce the frequency and duration of stressful conflict situations by being more thoughtful and strategic in your responses to affect better outcomes.

Five Response Options to Conflict

When a conflict arises, how do you know when you should demand your way or acquiesce to another's desires? Assuming that your reaction is not strictly a habituated response or one where emotions govern the course of events, you can make a conscious decision about how you will respond to any potential conflict by beginning with the end in mind. What is the best possible outcome that could come out of the conflict? What is best for the organization?

- Should you argue vehemently for your point?
- Should you acquiesce to the other person's desires?

- Should you seek a mutually agreeable outcome through collaboration?
- Could you partially achieve your goal through compromise?
- Should you avoid the situation and put off the discussion by agreeing to disagree?

Contrary to popular belief, collaboration is not always the best approach to every problem. Each conflict position has both advantages and disadvantages. The one you choose will depend upon the situation, the cause, relative power, available resources, and available time.

Multiple models have been used to understand the various approaches to conflict. Most of these stem from the work of Robert Blake and Jane Mouton (Blake, R., and Mouton, J. 1964. *The Managerial Grid: The Key to Leadership Excellence.* Houston: Gulf Publishing Co). Blake and Mouton utilized the two factors that form the basis of Marston's DISC model, concern for task compared to concern for relationship, and paired them on a high and low scale. Their Managerial Grid became the basis for explaining and evaluating conflict modes built upon by Kenneth W. Thomas and Ralph H. Kilmann (Thomas, K.W., and Kilmann, R.H. 1974. *Thomas–Kilmann Conflict Mode Instrument.* Tuxedo, NY: Xicom) and Dr. Ronald S. Kraybill in his "Kraybill Conflict Style Inventory" developed in the 1980s (Kraybill, R. 2005. *Style Matters: Kraybill Conflict Style Inventory.* Harrisonburg, VA: Riverhouse Press).

For the purposes of our discussion, we'll use the "concern for task/desire to please self" compared to the "concern for relationship/desire to please the other" to explore the five major approaches to conflict. Figure 3.35 shows

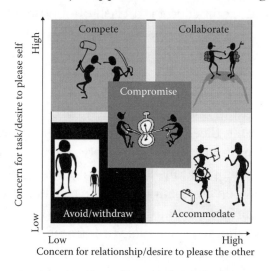

Figure 3.35   Conflict positions.

the possible conflict positions that can be taken depending upon the relative strength of these two opposing desires and will be referred to during the discussion of strategic conflict choices.

Strategic Conflict Choices

QUOTE: "You've got to know when to hold 'em, know when to fold 'em, know when to walk away, and know when to run."

Kenny Rogers
American Singer and Song Writer (1938–Present)

When a conflict arises, how do you know when you should demand your way or acquiesce to another's desires? Ultimately, your choice will be determined by how ardent you are to complete the task and satisfy your own desires or needs or subsume your desires and needs for the sake of the relationship by allowing the others to achieve their desires utilizing their methods.

Compete—Desire to Please Self Stronger than the Desire to Please the Other

If my desire to accomplish the task and/or satisfy my own desires is stronger than my desire to satisfy yours and I feel I have the power to invoke my will, I will compete with you. Competition is a clash of opposing forces with the outcome determining winners and losers. I will approach the conflict assertively in order to achieve my objective; I must make you lose so I can win. The impact on the relationship is of secondary concern. It is less important how you feel after the competition than it is for me to achieve a clear victory over you.

In life, we are taught to compete. It is the quickest way to reach a decision—flip a coin, roll the dice, arm wrestle, shout the loudest—whatever the method of competition it will almost always be quicker than taking the time to fully explore opposing positions and ensuring that your position is fully understood as well. When competing, it doesn't matter if you understand my position—just like your parents said, "Because I said so, that's why!"

Voting, the democratic way, is actually a form of competing. When members disagree with a proposed course of action, they sometimes feel pressured by the other team members to simply conform and accept the majority viewpoint. Voting can impose the tyranny of the majority.

DON'S DILEMMA: I had the honor of working with a team of senior operators who all got along well with each other. We were working out a strategy for implementing a new training program. The conversation was winding down to what looked like a unanimous decision. Just as we were ready to conclude, I noticed Don looking pensive. Don was naturally quiet, somewhat shy, and had a temperament that leaned heavily toward "C." "Don, it looks like you have some concerns." "No, it's OK. They're not important." "Really, Don, I'd like to hear what you're thinking." After a long meeting, the others weren't nearly as open to rehashing the past discussions and tried to stem off any further discussions with comments like, "Don, you're always nervous." "Come on, Don, we're all in agreement here." We could have easily voted at that point and would have moved on expeditiously. However, something in me told me to dig deeper." "Guys, let's give Don a chance. What are your concerns?" Don was visibly flustered and was uncomfortable belaboring the point. "Don, why don't you go to the board and work out your thoughts, we'll all sit here and be quiet while you do." Reluctantly, Don went to the board. With his back to the group he began making notations and diagrams. Bit by bit, he was able to give form to his ideas. As he did, the light of understanding broke on everyone in the room. Don was absolutely right and the rest of us were wrong. If we had voted and moved ahead with our plan we would have implemented an unworkable solution. This was a valuable lesson to me that sometimes the wisdom of crowds is foolishness.

Voting should only be used to decide routine administrative matters. If the decision is one of any consequence or impact, you should seek the best solution, not just the most expeditious.

Because of the emotional cost, competition should never be the dominate position if it is important to maintain an ongoing relationship. If every time you interact with me you feel like you are walking away a loser, over time your self-esteem will suffer and you will seek to avoid the relationship. Like a directing style of leadership, competition is useful when a quick decision is needed. It is also the right approach when there is a clear right or moral imperative. We will not compromise or collaborate with our enemies. There are clearly times when we must compete, be aware of the potential costs and only compete when appropriate—not as a default conflict position.

Accommodate—Desire to Please Other Stronger than the Desire to Please Self

If my desire to please you is stronger than my desire to satisfy my own objective, I won't compete with you; I'll concede the point and allow you to win. Accommodation is not the same as losing—if you compete and you lost, you still competed. Accommodation is choosing not to engage in a conflict so that the others can have their way, thus sustaining the relationship and avoiding the conflict. This is done for the sake of the relationship or because I don't feel I have sufficient power to overcome you to achieve my desires.

Accommodation is an appropriate conflict mode if I don't really have a strong conviction for my position. If it just doesn't matter that much to me, then let the other person have his or her way. "Where do you want to eat?" "It doesn't matter to me, you choose."

Often accommodation can be used in a quid-pro-quo relationship, "OK, I'll go along with your plan this time, but next time you owe me."

Accommodation should not be used if you feel strongly about the goal nor should it be used if you are going to carry a grudge and harbor resentment toward the other because you acquiesced. Very often you will see an ongoing dynamic between accommodators and competitors. Their relationship is sustained by the ongoing accommodation of one toward the other—a marriage of one continuously seeking to please the other in order to maintain the relationship. That's why it has been said, "The person who cares the least controls the relationship." Over time in such a relationship a slow-burning anger and resentment can build up to the point where the one who has accommodated a thousand times before won't do it again. As Popeye the Sailor said, "Enough is enough and I can't stands no more!" At that point the normally passive individual explodes in rage. "I'm not going to order a cheeseburger, I'm having a hotdog!" When this occurs and the usually combative one will often back off and accommodate the atypical demand. After which, the relationship may return to its past pattern now that the typically passive individual feels they have one in their column.

The point is, be conscientious of your decision to accommodate. If you are doing it and then feeling resentment and seething anger, your position is not beneficial.

QUOTE: "Resentment is a poison you take every day and hope the other person dies."

Anonymous

Collaborate—Strong Desire to Please Self and Equal Desire to Please the Other

Collaboration can be a beautiful thing when it is possible. Collaboration occurs when we work together to overcome limited resources and barriers to achieve what appeared to be mutually exclusive goals. You get everything you need and so do I. Collaboration requires strong communication skills and the willingness to engage productively to fully explore mutual goals and all the various factors involved in achieving them. It invariably requires more time to achieve collaboration, but when possible, it yields mutually beneficial outcomes—win–win.

Collaboration is not always possible—there are some goals that are mutually exclusive. Collaboration is also not appropriate when a quick decision is needed. Collaboration is the appropriate response when you have time to explore the various drivers and sustainers of the situation as well as the needs and motivations of the other. It requires a high degree of mutual trust. Also, collaboration won't be possible if the individuals are arguing from a position of scarcity. Like underfed dogs, they don't see enough resources to go around, so they have to fight for whatever scraps they can get. However, if time is available, better decisions can be made when conflicts are used as opportunities to explore creative alternatives and seek resolutions that are supported by everyone. Find a way to make a bigger pie instead of everyone scrambling for crumbs from a small one.

Avoid/Withdraw—Low Desire to Please Other and Unwillingness to Engage for Self

When you don't see any chance to achieve the goal and don't have the desire to engage in debate or the drama of competition you may choose to not even show up. Your absence may be physical, mental, or emotional; either way, you pull back from interacting with the other and avoid the competition. They won, you didn't play. Withdrawing is not the same as accommodating. When you accommodate you are still involved; when withdrawing, you purposely remain uninvolved.

Avoiding is a perfectly valid conflict mode when strong emotions would cause the conflict to escalate to a point that regrettable things are said or done. Avoiding may allow enough time for tempers to cool such that a productive discussion can occur. Avoiding is also appropriate when time will reveal information essential to reaching a resolution. Arguing today about an announcement you expect to hear next week is unproductive. Just wait till next week and there is no need to argue.

Like accommodation, avoiding should also be a strategic choice. Avoiding making a decision that must be made because you don't feel comfortable making it is clearly abdicating your responsibilities. Failing to make a decision is a decision.

AMICABLE OR AMIABLE: When my wife and I were first married we had a heated argument about the definition of a word. We were driving through the Southern Idaho dessert and she used the word amicable. I corrected her and said, "You mean amiable." The argument heated up, amicable, amiable, amicable, amiable, etc., ad nauseam. Sparks continued to fly until we reached a convenience store (this was before the days of smart phones and the Internet—oh how many fights those marriage-saving tools have avoided). With dictionary in hand, I stomped back to the car. When we looked up the meaning, we were both basically right. We were violently agreeing with each other. The irony was not lost on us. We managed to remain married and still use that book as our official Scrabble® dictionary.

Clearly this is a case when avoiding an argument would have been better or, wiser still, accommodating would have won me some much valued "husband points."

Compromise—Willingness to Accept Less for the Sake of the Relationship or to Move Forward

I may not get everything I want and you may not get everything you want, but we compromised and split the resources. It wasn't everything we wanted, but both got something out of the deal.

Compromise is a way to move the organization forward when it appears to be unable to find a collaborative resolution and neither party is willing to accommodate. However, this isn't always possible nor always desirable. Sometimes, compromise is a recipe for mediocrity. There are times that an autocratic response of "this is the way it is" will be required; however, these times should be the exception, not the rule, lest you create a closed culture with limited communication, involvement, and engagement. Each time you stand intransigent, you spend emotional capital—spend too much, and your credibility will become bankrupt with your team.

CONFLICT IN THE MILL: When I first became a supervisor at a paper mill, I had two senior employees who despised each other. They would not cooperate on work assignments and would often attempt to subtly sabotage each other whenever they could—even at the risk of production. Seeking advice from others, I learned that these two had been best friends over 20 years ago. Yet, neither could give me any single specific source of their long-standing feud. Each would simply give me a laundry list of petty complaints. Something said was taken wrong and through a series of "tit for tat," snipe and countersnipe that spanned decades the two had built up a wall of hatred between each other, invisible to the naked eye but physically palpable whenever the two were anywhere near each other.

Having neither the time nor the negotiation skills to arbitrate their issues, the best I could do was separate their animosity for each other from the workplace. I stated explicitly that, regardless of their feelings for each other, production was not a weapon they could continue to use against each other. There would be performance consequences for whoever played that card again.

Fortunately, the work space was large enough that a compromise could be reached; each could work in different areas and not have to see each other during the course of the shift. One would park in the front of the mill and the other parked in the back. Their paths never crossed.

This solution is different than avoiding because the two parties involved were able to arbitrate a solution that each could live with. They had just been avoiding each other and seething about it, the compromise laid out clear areas each could live with.

To the best of my knowledge, the issues they had against each other have never been resolved, but at least the efficiency and safety of production were no longer affected.

Temperament, Desire to Please Self versus Desire to Please Others

Like DISC, the analysis of conflict modes pairs the natural tendency toward task as compared to relationships. Accordingly, you can see that if you don't make a conscious choice about your approach to conflict your natural temperament can sway your behavior toward habituated responses. Figure 3.36 lays the DISC patterns over the conflict modes to show the strong natural correlations.

People that lean more strongly toward having dominant "D" temperaments are more likely to argue for their positions than people more prone to exhibit an "S" temperament. If you tend toward a dominant temperament, you may tend to approach conflicts by aggressively attacking. If you are a natural people pleaser, you may tend to accommodate. Remember, "S"s value harmony and will be more likely to try and smooth over a conflict than escalate it. "C"s tend to withdraw and avoid conflicts while "I"s like to collaborate. When pushed far enough and feeling like they are backed into a corner with little options, both "C"s and "S"s will engage in conflict but not directly. "S"s tend to draw upon their social network and invoke the power of someone who sits in a position of authority. They will solicit the support of others through back channels and private meetings to build a coalition against the other with whom they are having the conflict. "C"s can tend to be just as indirect, but they can become quite passive–aggressive in their response to conflict, withholding information, not fully engaging, and displaying other behaviors that will keep them out of a direct face-to-face

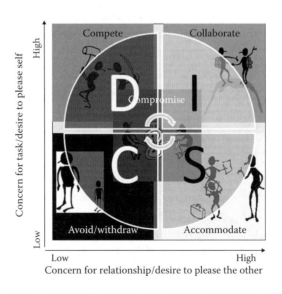

Figure 3.36 DISC conflict tendencies.

conflict. Since it is not straightforward, these types of conflict behaviors are harder to recognize and address. They tend to go on for longer periods of time before they are recognized. As such, they can be tremendously damaging to the cohesion of the focusing team, boring holes into the hull of the organizational vessel. And when confronted, these behaviors are almost always coated with a layer of "plausible deniability," so they can be very difficult to address and to resolve.

Conflicts and the Balance of Power

Regardless of your natural temperament, there are times when you feel so strongly about a particular point of view or cause that you are compelled to speak your mind. Even in such times of strong conviction, when faced with a large imbalance of personal power you will probably choose your words a little more carefully than you might otherwise if you were in a room of your peers or your subordinates. Even a naturally aggressive individual will tend to alter his or her approach when confronted with a strong imbalance of power. There are times that the most ardent "D" will avoid conflict when faced with an overwhelming imbalance of power. Imagine you are sitting in room with your boss, the CEO, and the board of directors. Will you be more or less likely to point out that you are right and they are wrong?

The imbalance of power doesn't have to be based upon formal hierarchal positions—it is often based upon the relative desire to sustain a relationship. Think back to your first awesome emersion into the warm pool of love. What did you do to nurture the relationship? Did you argue for this restaurant versus that one? Or it didn't matter as long as you were together. Even if it's not love, the desire to maintain the friendship or even the amicability of an acquaintance can cause us to alter our demands for the sake of harmony.

However, there are some lines that each of us will not cross even for the sake of a relationship. When you or I feel so strongly about a situation, an objective or goal, a guiding personal principle, or a core value, we will not bend and we will not yield—consequences be damned. The relationship may suffer, but we will not compromise our integrity.

QUOTE: "I would do anything for love, but I won't do that."

Meatloaf
American Singer and Songwriter (1947–Present)

We can see how our perception of the situation, the balance of power, and the ardor with which we are pursuing our objective combine to govern our ongoing conflict response. Much of this will depend upon how we perceive our relative power in the situation. However, the overarching factor in this equation is our relationship with the other individual with whom we are in conflict. The effect the relationship will have is dependent upon the degree to which we desire to please ourselves as compared to the degree to which we desire to please the other person with whom we are in conflict.

TERMINAL CANDOR: When compelled by strong emotion you may speak your mind even when it would be more prudent not to. I refer you again to these words of wisdom: Your career can die from terminal candor.

Thoughtful Reactions to Conflict

Conflicts in life are unavoidable. Sooner or later you will all bump up against one another. When there is a healthy attitude about conflict the organization can focus on seeking resolutions that align with the mission and help deliver on the value proposition. It is paramount that managers and team members deal with conflict openly and honestly to resolve the conflicts rather than avoiding the issues, stroking egos, or placing blame. Allowing conflicts to remain hidden and addressed through indirect back channels, gossip, and political gamesmanship creates a climate of mistrust, wastes significant amount of time in nonproductive activities, and draws resources away from achieving the goal. Only when you courageously face conflict and promote healthy solutions oriented approach will conflicts be constructive.

Effective conflict resolution is an ongoing communications process that follows the same cycle discussed earlier. Review Figure 3.37 as we walk through the communications cycle to show an effective technique for addressing conflict.

1. Preparation
2. Framing the discussion
3. Clarification of positions and interests
4. Involved discussion
5. Reaching agreement

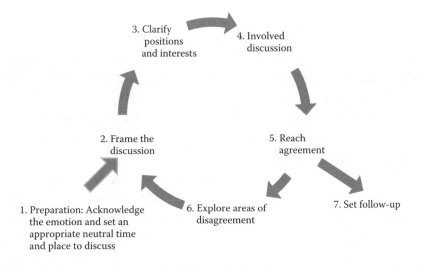

Figure 3.37   Communications process applied to conflict resolution.

6. Exploring area of disagreement
7. Setting follow-up

Step 1: Preparation: When conflicts arise, you may be drawn into the fight suddenly without warning. Caught up in the emotion of the adrenaline rush you may naturally gravitate toward competing or accommodating depending upon your temperament, your relationship, and the relative power position. It is important to acknowledge the influences emotions are having, recognize that you may not be in the best state of mind to navigate the process. Your natural instinct when we are attacked may to launch an immediate counter attack. Just as two cars hitting head-on at 35 miles per hour is equivalent to hitting a brick wall at 70 mph, when force meets force, the magnitude of each is amplified. A more effective technique to minimize the conflict may be to avoid the head-on collision. A very effective technique for dialing back the pitch of the conflict is not to begin by defending yourself or counterattacking but first *acknowledge the emotion.* Acknowledging the emotion is not admitting fault or agreeing that the other person is right. It is simply recognizing the other's emotional state. Statements like, "I can see you're really upset" or "You obviously feel very strongly about this" often have an immediate calming effect. If you try to ignore or minimize the other's emotions they may continue to escalate in order to be heard. Once the other feels their emotions have been validated, they can begin to focus on the issues.

After acknowledging the emotion, you may not want to just jump into the conversation. Initially, your best option is *avoidance*, even for five minutes to allow yourself to collect your thoughts and take the discussion to an appropriately neutral location. When choosing a location, avoid overly public settings that will showcase the conflict on a stage. A completely private setting may not be a much better choice if you are concerned about misunderstandings escalating or a "he said–she said" scenario. You may want to have an unbiased third party present.

Unlike the first time we went through the communications cycle, in conflict communications, don't begin with the end in mind. If you start the conversation with the mindset that you're right and the other is wrong or that you are going to accommodate or any of the other five modes, you will probably not be fully open to the other person's concerns and points of view. Deciding up front how you're going to respond often sets you on the path of scripting the argument; "I'll say this, they'll probably say that, to which I'll respond…" This rehearsing of your arguments will act as a filter closing your mind to the root causes of the problems and will also minimize the options you see to successfully navigate the conflict. You'll be so busy trying to remember your lines or looking for openings to use this point or that one that you won't see areas of agreement that can lead to the best possible solution. You've probably experienced this when you were in "violent agreement" with another. After time had passed, you both came to realize that you were both basically saying the same thing.

Step 2: Frame the discussion: With emotions dialed back and situated in an appropriate location with sufficient time to explore the conflict you are now ready to frame the discussion. When framing a conflict identify what the concerns are and what are the roots of the conflict. Outline the conversation to set an appropriate tone that focuses on the problem not personal attacks. At these times, the value of the team's ground rules becomes even more apparent. Reviewing the team's charter is also helpful when framing the discussion so that both parties are reminded of the overall objectives and the priorities of the team. Remember that conflicts arise when disparity of goals combine with limited resources. The charter will help clarify the goals and establish the priorities such that decisions regarding resources can be more easily made.

Step 3: Clarify positions and interests: With the ground rules as a foundation and the charter defining your common goals, clarify the position of each party along with interests. Remember that your position is where you stand on the subject whereas your interests are the underlying goals behind your position. As was pointed out earlier, the other may be arguing for a position ("That's his job, not mine!") when there may be other alternatives to achieving their interests ("I believe there is an inequitable distribution of work and I'm overloaded."). It is important to work to get to the heart of the matter, which may mean moving beyond the surface to much deeper values and objectives.

Step 4: Involved discussion: With the positions and interests clarified, you can now delve into the discussion. Conflicts revolving around processes and systems can almost always be resolved utilizing a systematic problem-solving approach such as that discussed in Focusing Element 8. Working through a collaborative problem-solving approach often reveals the most practical and effective solution to these types of problems. Using this process routinely avoids many conflicts. However, not all conflicts stem from the process or even the mission. Conflicts with their roots in approach, perception, and power are more common and much more difficult to resolve, requiring more skill and deeper trust to discuss.

Discussing the situation that raised the conflict will be dynamic and often flows down unexpected avenues. Recall the Johari Windows that opened revealing blind spots, hidden agendas, and areas unknown. It is important to keep the discussion focused on the issue and not digress down unrelated or unproductive paths unless that path reveals the root cause of the argument that may not have been even related to the current situation. The event that occurred last week may have been the catalyst that triggered the reaction today.

The path an argument takes usually begins with attempts to convince the other person of the validity of their position as compared to the opposing one. This usually involves efforts to persuade. If the individual is committed to achieving their goal regardless of the strength of their argument, they may take alternative approaches to compel the other to accept their position.

Compelling Behavior through Persuasion or through Manipulation

Techniques used to compel behavior fall along a continuum that spans the spectrum between persuasion and manipulation, as shown in Figure 3.38. Where you place your stake in the ground along that spectrum will depend upon three factors:

1. The ardor with which an individual desires the other to acquiesce
2. The *degree of clarity* of the argument—benefits weighed against costs
3. Relative *balance of power* of the opposing parties—equal or unequal

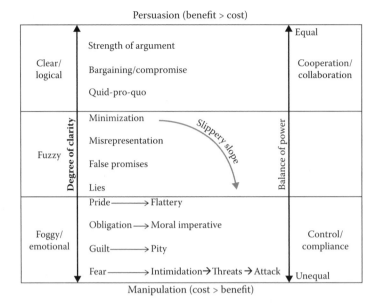

Figure 3.38 Compelling behavior.

The lengths that someone will go to compel another's behavior will depend upon how strongly they are entrenched within their own position coupled with their natural temperament—assertive or passive. Temperament aside, the degree of clarity of argument and the relative balance of power govern the interactions between two opposing viewpoints.

The vertical axis shown on the left side of Figure 3.38 represents the "degree of clarity" of the argument. When the benefits of a position or course of action greatly outweigh the costs, it is much easier to make a compelling case for action. It can be shown clearly and logically that the course of action is superior based upon its own merits, and the other will be willing to act to satisfy their own interests. However, as the costs relative to benefits continue to rise, it becomes more and more difficult to make a compelling argument on the face of the matter. Without a compelling argument, one can attempt to compel action either by making an emotional plea or through force.

The vertical axis shown on the right side of Figure 3.38 represents the relative "balance of power" that exists between the two opposing parties involved. If one party holds substantial power over another, the strength of the argument won't matter. The one with more power can simply force the other to comply.

When the costs relative to the benefits are not balanced the techniques employed to compel another to act shift from persuasion toward manipulation and possibly into intimidation depending upon the relative balance of power. Figure 3.38 ranks the methods employed along the spectrum sliding down from persuasion toward intimidation depending upon the clarity of argument and the balance of power:

Strength of argument: When two parties are in parity such that neither holds power over the other only when they both clearly see the benefits of the course of action will they reach agreement through cooperation and mutual commitment. The strength of the argument is sound. "This is a good deal for both of us; let's do it!"

Bargaining/Compromise: If the benefits are not equal, an agreement may have to be reached through bargaining and compromise. "OK, I'll go along with the plan because I can see the relative strengths and it will get us to where we want to be."

Quid-pro-quo: Barring a compromise, one may agree on the condition that in the future, the other will return something of equal value—this for that—quid pro quo. "I'll go along with you, but you owe me big time."

Minimization: Minimization is a technique that one party may use to convince another that the costs are not nearly as high as they think thus making the benefit appear more in line. "Look, it will only take a minute of your time. It's no big deal."

Misrepresentation: Whereas minimization is lessoning the cost, misrepresentation obscures the cost or inflates the benefit. An example of obscuring the cost may occur when someone doesn't tell you the full scope of what is involved knowing that once you are in it, you will be publically committed and have to see it through. Misrepresentation can also reflect over inflation of the benefit. "This project has a lot of visibility; the big bosses are supportive, and this will be a real feather in your cap."

False promises: Minimization and misrepresentation obscure or gloss over the costs, false promises fabricate a benefit. "Look, I know you've been burning the midnight oil on this project, but you can be sure that success will land you that promotion."

Lies: False promises are lies but they maintain a veneer of "plausible deniability." "Believe me, I wanted to give you that promotion, but it was taken out of my hands." Lies are out and out false, no "ifs," "ands," or "buts" about it. Figure 3.38 shows a downward arching arrow spanning the distance between minimization, misrepresentation, false promises, and lies—this represents the *slippery slope*. When you start with misrepresentation you can quickly slide into lies as you strive harder and harder to compel the other's acquiescence to your position.

Pride → Flattery: Appealing to ones pride through flattery is a classic manipulation technique. "Look, we need you on this team; nobody knows the project like you." These types of compliments may be sincere, but if they are used as a means of trying to compel acceptance, they cross the line into manipulation.

Obligation → Moral imperative: Barring none of the previous techniques were effective, obligation can be used to compel someone to action. "Come on, you owe me this." This is a danger of entering into a quid-pro-quo arrangement in the past. The other may call you on their past acquiescence to compel your involvement in something you don't feel is in your best interests. Short of a debt you owe, the other could still try and compel your with a moral obligation. "Come on, I know you've worked every weekend, but you've got to do this for the team. You know how much is riding on it."

Guilt → Pity: If they can't obligate you, they may try to guilt-trip you: "Come on, you know how much this means to the others. You wouldn't want to disappoint them." If guilt doesn't work, pity might: "If you don't help me deliver on this project, it could cost me my job." They may also combine the two: "You wouldn't want me to lose my job, would you?'

Fear, intimidation, threats, and attacks: The bottom rung of the persuasion/manipulation ladder plays on baser, more primal emotions. Seeing all previous efforts have been unsuccessful compelling you to agree, the other may become even more aggressive, raising their voice and take a dominant posture in an effort to intimidate you. Threats could follow, "You know, I can make things very tough for you around here." Out and out physical attack is rare but not unheard of. More likely, the attack could come in the form of retaliation, slander, and other behaviors that create a hostile work environment. When this occurs, it is imperative that you document the events and get support from higher authority. As a manager, you need to be aware of the interactions occurring within your team since you are ultimately accountable. You can be held personally liable for a hostile work environment you foster or allow to fester if you fail to address the situation.

REFERRAL: If you want to learn more about how to become more effective at resolving conflicts I recommend *The Power of a Positive No* by William Ury (Ury, W. 2007. *The Power of a Positive No: How to Say No and Still Get to Yes.* New York: Bantam Books).

All of the techniques listed above are not necessary if the balance of power is such that one could just order the other to comply. There is no need to discuss; just tell them that they have to do it. Many times this is more palatable and has less negative impact than feeling like you are being lied to or manipulated. It's more honest. "I'm the boss, and I said so." It's autocratic, but it's honest.

Steps 5 and 6: Reach agreement or explore areas of disagreement: As the conversation evolves take note of areas of agreement. These areas of agreement can form the basis of a bridge between the parties in conflict. By listing out those areas that are agreed upon differences become more focused. The areas of agreement may also be enough to point toward a mutually agreeable solution; for instance, you may be able to agree to one point, acquiesce to another, compromise on one, and collaborate on the most important element. If the differences still merit resolution, cycle through again reframing the discussion to those items still in contention. Doing so will continue to auger in. You may need to clarify positions and interests relative to the more narrow points; these may be significantly different than were originally stated or understood. The communications process helps you reveal blind spots, hidden agendas, and flush out what is not known, thereby opening the Johari Window area of free activity such that the items in contention can be discussed and dealt with in a healthy and productive manner.

Step 7: Set follow-up: After the conflict has been resolved and a course of action has been agreed upon, summarize the agreement. You have probably covered a lot of ground and may be feeling completely drained at this point. It is important to document what was agreed upon and what each party is responsible for to move forward. Without documentation, the conflict can resurface at a later time.

Ground Rules to Consider that Promote a Healthy Approach to Conflict

Conflicts are bound to occur. The outcomes of those conflicts will be determined by how the organization addresses the conflicts. Better solutions can occur when the organization treats differences of opinion as strengths and when the cyclical communications process is consistently used to explore and resolve conflicts as compared to allowing conflicts to go unaddressed or to be resolved through power struggles or manipulation. To help set the stage, consider adopting the following guidelines when addressing conflict:

1. Utilize an agreed upon approach to solving problems and work through the cyclical communications process
2. Assume "positive intent"
   a. When we have a confrontation with someone we often feel they are attacking us personally. If we try to give the person the benefit of the doubt that they are interested in doing what is best for the organization, then we start out on a better footing. Naturally, if it is shown that the person is arguing for an ulterior motive or mal-intent, then we should address these behaviors separately and act accordingly
   b. Remember, conflict frequently has roots in the fear of loss. If someone approached you and said "I'm hurting" would you respond the same as if they said "You've made me angry"? The emotion of anger is often the child of pain and loss. If someone is angry, there is a good chance that they are anticipating or experiencing a loss.
3. Attack the problem, not each other
   a. Keep the discussion on the issues and don't make it personal
4. Separate what you know, from what you think, and from what you feel
   a. We often act on our assumptions—work from the facts
   b. Don't confuse what you think with what you know. There is a difference.
5. Document the agreements and ensure both parties continue to fulfill their obligations

Leadership Necessary to Create a Healthy Organizational Climate

All behaviors are rewarding on some level. If there is a climate of mistrust and conflict, then it is rewarding some behavior. When Sally runs to Mom and says, "Johnny is being mean," she is rewarded when Mom intervenes on her behalf. Leaders who allow or even encourage similar behavior in organizations promote divisiveness.

To be effective, leaders need to be detached enough to observe the forest for the trees. If they consistently choose sides or play favorites, the balance of power will be shifted in favor of their pets. Others will acquiesce to the "most favored child" to avoid a conflict with the boss. This can give rise to little tyrants who "speak for the boss" and use it as a trump card to compel behavior even when they don't have a compelling argument. This tends to further personal agendas much more than organizational excellence and goal achievement.

In the same manner, emotional tyrants can control a conflict-averse boss. "I don't want to have a bunch of drama, just try and get along with her to keep peace." Emotional tyranny fosters a climate of fear that impedes creativity and initiative.

The most effective role a leader can assume is one that fosters a meritocracy. The decisions made are based upon the strength of the argument—not the ardor of the emotion. As such, when one employee complains to the manager about another, the first question out of the manager's mouth should be, "Did you try and work it out with him?" If the answer is, "no," send the person back to attempt to resolve the issue in a mature and professional manner. If they are unable to resolve it, then the manager should appoint an unbiased third party of equal status to be the arbitrator. Too often and too quickly the manager steps in as the arbitrator. When they do they immediately shift the balance of power and disempower the team. They are rewarding the wrong behaviors.

PLAYING THE POLITICAL TRUMP CARD: In our twenty-first century society certain individuals have become adept at achieving their ends without the benefit of a strong compelling argument for their positions. If they are unable to get their way based upon the merit of their proposition, they play a trump card—he offended me, she "disrespected" me—etc. To create a true climate of organizational excellence, these methods of compelling behaviors need to be minimized to the greatest degree possible. Managers need to foster a climate of mutual success through mutual respect and that does not include an imbalance of power based upon factors that are otherwise not germane to the issue. We will discuss this in greater detail in Sustaining Element 10 (balance of challenge and support through rewards, opportunities, and consequences).

Another vital role an effective leader should fulfill to create a productive climate with minimal conflict is that of a "filter." Often, those outside the immediate team but with greater organizational power dilute the effectiveness of the department by directly tasking members who do not directly report to them. The leader should shelter his or her team such that, as long as they are working on the tasks assigned by the leader, they are protected from direct conflict from outsiders. The most effective managers filter out the drama and miscellaneous administrivia and side projects, allowing their people to focus on the priorities. This maximizes efficiencies and minimizes conflicts. Leaders who lack the courage to defend their people are not respected and are not in control of the organizational climate. We will discuss this in greater detail in Committing Element 6 (strong leadership and appropriate delegation of authority).

When to Revisit Forming

Given all the moving parts of systems, drivers, competing resources, and shifting priorities in play as your organization moves forward it is understandable that there is some friction that periodically erupts into full conflicts. However, if conflicts regularly flair up impeding progress and diverting significant time and resources away from progress, then you can be assured that some timbers are missing within the organizational vessel you are building. Are people still unclear about the vision or mission? Do they not understand how the tasks they are assigned and the systems they operate accomplish the strategy? Is there role confusion? Are systems and resources not aligned and not sufficient? Is there still a lack of trust? Whatever the seeds of conflict are, you'll need to circle back and address them by refocusing. You may even need to return to address issues that ideally would have been resolved during the initial Forming Stage (Figure 3.39).

As was discussed in the Overview of Focusing, it is important to keep in mind that there is no clear demarcation between organizational stages of development. Figure 3.40 helps illustrate the concept of the ebbing and

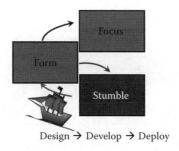

Design → Develop → Deploy

Figure 3.39   Return to Forming.

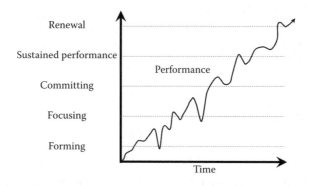

Figure 3.40   Ebb and flow between stages of organization development.

flowing that occurs between stages as the organization develops. You may feel that your organization has moved out of Forming and into Focusing when something that was unknown is revealed as another Johari Window opens. Once revealed, the organization may need to backtrack for a time to clarify roles, reestablish trust, improve communications, or address any of the other frameworks being built into the organizational vessel. This is also why it is critical that leadership is able to adapt their styles to the needs of the situation and the individuals.

Key Takeaways: Focusing versus Stumbling

The Focusing Stage is one of true transforming. You are literally fashioning the tools that transform your ideas into reality. Initially, dark clouds of pessimism may begin to obscure the sunny optimism that was fueling the

Table 3.11 Key Takeaways: Focusing versus Stumbling

	Focus	Commit	Sustained Performance	Renewal
Form	Stumble	Fragment	Variable Performance	Level

Focusing: Occurs when the team becomes aligned around the vision and mission. Systems and procedures begin to form and there is goal and role clarification

Team Needs:

- Understanding of how the mission and vision are to be accomplished
- Inclusion and involvement
- Initial training
- Assignment of roles and responsibilities
- Development of processes and procedures

The Change "Readiness vs. Response" Continuum	
Change Ready:	Excitement
Change Resistant:	Anger

Indicators of Effective Navigation	Indicators of Ineffective Navigation
• Growing optimism and commitment • Understanding and acceptance of individual roles and responsibilities	• Fear, anger, cynicism • Conflicts and Confusion • Unproductive Challenging

Effective Leadership Responses:

- Mutual regard and inclusion
- Cascading organizational mission to individuals
- Problem solving
- Conflict resolution

Effective Management Responses:

- Meeting facilitation that maintains the crews focus on the tasks at hand and minimizing tangents that distract from the focusing process
- Development of systems and processes
- Assignment of roles, responsibilities, and goals
- Allocation of resources
- Scheduling and coordination of work

(continued)

Table 3.11   Key Takeaways: Focusing versus Stumbling (Continued)

	Focus	*Commit*	*Sustained Performance*	*Renewal*
Form	*Stumble*	*Fragment*	*Variable Performance*	*Level*

Tools and Techniques:

- Systems thinking around organizational and systems design
- Flowcharting and analysis of fall points
- Roles and responsibilities matrix incorporating strategic and tactical time horizons
- Development of key performance indicators (KPIs)
- Group decision making, decision criteria and decision analysis tools
- Problem solving
- Conflict resolution

enthusiasm and involvement during the initial phases of the Forming Stage; the honeymoon is over, and the organization has to undertake the hard work of creating systems, clarifying roles, and building skills and competence. It is important that your leadership maintains the focus and that you don't allow your own feelings of pessimism and frustration to fan the flames of others' emotions. To lead, you must be the one to inspire the organization to strive onward until the organization's mission comes into focus. When it does you'll feel the excitement building and see the light of cautious hope growing brighter. Those who had a hard time visualizing how things could be any different are beginning to see tangible operations that further clarify the direction the organization is heading. Table 3.11 summarizes the key indicators that are road markers along your journey through focusing and lists the appropriate managerial and leadership responses along with the tools and techniques that will help you construct your organizational vessel of success.

Focusing Project Plan

Table 3.12 provides a quick synopsis of the elements of a project plan to build upon during the Focusing Stage.

Table 3.12   Focusing Project Plan—Finalizing Designs and the Start of Systems Development and Deployment

Project Step	Responsibility	Date Planned	Date Complete
1. Develop organizational strategy maps that define the elements that accomplish the mission			
2. Disaggregate the mission and vision into strategy and tactics by developing subsequent strategy and process maps			
3. Select and implement management action teams (MAT) that cooperate to execute the communication plan, roll out strategy, develop leaders and align the organization			
4. Utilizing SMEs, design and begin development of systems that transform the strategies into day-to-day operational tactics			
5. Utilizing the process maps created for systems, identify the roles and responsibilities including the associated time horizons for each organizational layer and position, develop metrics and behavioral anchors aligned to the strategy map(s)			
6. Begin the deployment of systems			
a. Conduct initial training of operations			
b. Explain the roles and responsibilities for each position including interrelations of systems and the obligations to upstream processes and downstream customers			
c. Ensure that each system has measurement devices and/or methods capable of accurately monitoring and recording each essential parameter			

(*continued*)

Table 3.12 Focusing Project Plan—Finalizing Designs and the Start of Systems Development and Deployment (Continued)

Project Step	Responsibility	Date Planned	Date Complete
d. Ensure systems response feedback loops are sufficient to allow operators a timely view to each process			
7. Develop initial goals for each position			
a. Based upon the initial parameters set for each system, develop KPIs			
8. Set up focus sessions to receive feedback to the effectiveness of each newly deployed system			
a. Pay particular attention to the "seams" between processes that can be fall points where outputs from one system don't feed the downstream system in a timely manner			
9. Use a systematic problem solving approach to adapt your systems as required and appropriate based upon the functionality and effectiveness of the system			
a. Adjust the goals as necessary based upon system modifications			
10. Ensure project teams and SMEs document system and procedural changes to capture "as designed" as compared to "as built/implemented"			

Chapter 4

Stage 3—Committing: Building Speed

Overview and Assessment: Committing versus Fragmenting

With major organizational design decisions made and being implemented with systems that are transforming inputs into outputs, the organization is beginning to see results. This is the stage where people begin to commit. If we look again at the Framework for Organizational Success (Figure 4.1), we see that the organizational stage of Committing (shown on the left) aligns with the project management stage of Deploy. To deploy the systems across the organization, targeted functional and professional training will need to be conducted. Functional training is considered technical training focused on operational principles, tasks, and procedures, etc. Professional training focuses on giving people the other skills and competencies essential to the success of their position.

As individuals see the first fruits of their collective labor, they generally begin embracing the mission as their own and committing to team success, becoming even more engaged. They were involved before this point, but now they are really taking ownership and becoming committed (Figure 4.2). Their understanding is deeper as is their growing pride and optimism. The organization has moved beyond the informed pessimism stage, and once again, hope is in bloom. If you don't see these indicators at this point, then the work of focusing is not complete, and possibly, elements of forming are still missing. Table 4.1 provides a summary of

Figure 4.1   Framework for organizational success.

indicators associated with the organizational stage of Committing along with the needs of the team.

Organizations without widespread commitment are fragmented. Multiple factions exist and individuals and cliques pursue their own agendas with little concern and less commitment to the overall stated mission of the organization. Other, less assertive individuals may feel apathetic toward the goals of the organization and are simply putting in their time trying to survive until something better comes along and they can affect their escape.

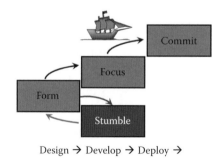

Figure 4.2   Moving beyond focusing into commitment.

Table 4.1 Summary of Indicators: Committing versus Fragmenting

	Focus	Commit	Sustained Performance	Renewal
Form	Stumble	Fragment	Variable Performance	Level

Committing: Occurs when team members embrace the team's mission as their own, become more engaged and commit to team success

Team Needs: • Inclusion • Training • Opportunities to practice—growing mastery • Timely feedback

The Change "Readiness vs. Response" Continuum	
Change Ready:	Collaboration
Change Resistant:	Compromise

Indicators of Effective Navigation	**Indicators of Ineffective Navigation**
• Growing skills • Clear integrated goals • Culture of inclusion • Building Esprit de Corps	• Apathy • Internal competition and political gamesmanship • Blocked team communication • Lack of accountability

To assess where your organization falls along the spectrum between committing and fragmenting complete the Committing Assessment contained in Table 4.2. This will help you determine how well individuals are engaged in the organization's mission along with the factors that have an ongoing impact on the overall level of organizational engagement.

Once you've completed the Committing Assessment, transfer your scores into the Committing Scoring Matrix contained in Table 4.3.

Table 4.2 Committing Assessment

For each of the paired statements or groups of statement below, decide which statement most accurately describes your experiences in the day-to-day work activities within your organization. For the statement that is chosen, check to what degree you believe the statement is either Most or Somewhat like your routine experience within your organization's work activities.
Check only one statement per paired question.

Assessment (Select One)			Choose the Statement that Best Describes Your Organization
1	+4	Most Like Us	Members are committed to the vision, mission, and values that drive the organization. There is a high degree of congruence between individual values and drive and the organization's values and degree of control
	+2	Somewhat Like Us	
	–2	Somewhat Like Us	Members do not identify with the organization or its mission. People do their time—punching in and punching out. Those who are considered engaged are often furthering personal agendas. Many others feel stifled by the lack of alignment with the organization's values and degree of control
	–4	Most Like Us	
2	+4	Most Like Us	Team members have the skills required to accomplish the team's objectives. Necessary competencies have been determined for each position. There is a structured approach to qualifications based upon observable behavioral based outcomes that promote a proactive culture of ownership, action, and responsibility. Individual abilities are assessed and individual development plans are implemented. Records are kept documenting education, training, skills, and experience
	+2	Somewhat Like Us	
	–2	Somewhat Like Us	The team is missing certain skill sets needed for achieving its goals. Members are often assigned with little or no orientation or training. Most training is through informal, unstructured on-the-job (OJT) training. A person is considered qualified when a supervisor or manager proclaims they are not against any objective standard. Any formal training programs are "one size fits all" regardless of individual needs, background, experience, aptitude, or aspirations
	–4	Most Like Us	

(continued)

Table 4.2   Committing Assessment (Continued)

Assessment (Select One)			Choose the Statement that Best Describes Your Organization
3	+4	Most Like Us	Team members have confidence in the team's ability to get the job done and trust others to deliver on their obligations
	+2	Somewhat Like Us	
	−2	Somewhat Like Us	Team members doubt the team's ability to achieve the mission. Members don't trust others to do their part, relying instead upon their own individual abilities
	−4	Most Like Us	
4	+4	Most Like Us	Performance feedback is appropriate and timely helping team members achieve success. There is frequent and specific feedback to individuals regarding their performance and contributions as well as opportunities for growth and improvement
	+2	Somewhat Like Us	
	−2	Somewhat Like Us	Performance monitoring is ineffective. Either cursory, not timely, or may feel intrusive and judgmental rather than constructive
	−4	Most Like Us	
5	+4	Most Like Us	Leaders are appropriately engaged and available to support team members as appropriate and needed. Leaders act as mentors and sponsors providing opportunities for members to advance their skills and their careers as they grow their span of control and authority
	+2	Somewhat Like Us	
	−2	Somewhat Like Us	Leaders are not engaged and frequently absent from day-to-day operations inaccessible to support members' efforts. Because of their lack of timely engagement, situations frequently erupt that require crisis management, decisions based upon partial information, and extraordinary efforts of the crew. This reactionary environment leaves little opportunities for individual learning and growth
	−4	Most Like Us	
6	+4	Most Like Us	Leadership is strong but is shared when appropriate. The organizational span of control is clearly defined and decision criteria are broadly understood such that those closest to the work with the greatest awareness of condition have the authority to quickly make quality decisions. They are also well aware of which decisions should be escalated to higher authority. Based on the situation, decisions can be made by the leader, delegated to a member, or made by consensus as appropriate to ensure maximum decision quality
	+2	Somewhat Like Us	

Table 4.2 Committing Assessment (Continued)

Assessment (Select One)			Choose the Statement that Best Describes Your Organization
	−2	Somewhat Like Us	The leadership falls on the extreme edges of the spectrum—either dominating or abdicating. Members frequently have accountability but not authority. Permission to act must be obtained from others before those most involved in the processes and activities can move forward. The group's decision making approach is limited: (1) either the leaders decides all the time, or (2) a select few opinion leaders steer the organization's course, or (3) no decisions are made until there is a large enough consensus such that everyone is covered by plausible deniability
	−4	Most Like Us	
7	+4	Most Like Us	Members understand, act upon, and hold themselves accountable for the quality of the product and services they provide. People are motivated and empowered to take on meaningful responsibilities and authority. Calculated risks are encouraged and supported. If a decision turns out poorly, lessons learned are captured and shared to foster a learning organization
	+2	Somewhat Like Us	
	−2	Somewhat Like Us	Members are guarded, defensive, and afraid to take risks. Team members avoid responsibility and accountability and try to "pass the buck." Risks are not tolerated—an air of fear and caution pervades the culture. It is better to seek the shelter of unanimity around a mediocre approach upon which everyone can agree rather than risk appearing weak or stepping out and being wrong
	−4	Most Like Us	
8	+4	Most Like Us	Organization members usually work together collaboratively as a team because they are secure enough in their own abilities and have the motivation for collaborative team efforts. People support each other as well as respecting the boundaries of each other's authority and accountability. Members are concerned with both getting the task done and getting each other involved and motivated
	+2	Somewhat Like Us	

(*continued*)

Table 4.2 Committing Assessment (Continued)

Assessment (Select One)			Choose the Statement that Best Describes Your Organization
	−2	Somewhat Like Us	Individuals lack the experience or commitment for collaboration. There is a general feeling of imbalance in the amount of effort and degree of involvement from some members of the group as compared to others. Some members are seen as "free riders" who do not pull their fair share of the load. Some members engage in power plays for authority and control while others try to cope by "flying below the radar screen"
	−4	Most Like Us	
9	+4	Most Like Us	The organization lives its values such that there is a high degree of integrity and employees trust what management says
	+2	Somewhat Like Us	
	−2	Somewhat Like Us	There is a widespread perception that the organization's true values are not aligned with its espoused values: leadership is viewed with cynicism and thought of as hypocrites—do as I say, not as I dohypocrites - do as I say, not as I do
	−4	Most Like Us	
10	+4	Most Like Us	There is a well-defined group identity, esprit de corps, and pride in being a part of the organization. People have a "can-do" attitude with individuals identifying with the organization's mission and the value they personally bring to the organization
	+2	Somewhat Like Us	
	−2	Somewhat Like Us	Members work from differing sets of values from each other and from the organization as a whole resulting in fundamental conflicts due to the incongruence of values and working approaches
	−4	Most Like Us	

Table 4.3   Committing Scoring Matrix

No.	Score	Element of Committing	Effective Leadership	Effective Management	Tools and Techniques
1		High degree of congruence between individual and organizational values and working approach	Continuity with degree of engagement: effective delegation and empowerment	Continuity with degree of engagement: support through resources	Degree of engagement matrix Workforce Engagement Equation
2		Structured approach to training and qualifications	Setting clear expectations, mentoring, and modeling the way	Provide opportunities to train, reinforcement through feedback	DACUM training checklists, structured training process
3		Team members have and keep faith with their teams	Modeling the way—integrity	Frequent communications	Network of formal and informal communications
4		Performance feedback is appropriate and timely	Courage to address violations of organizational norms and integrity	Clear and timely feedback. Development of metrics and KPIs	View to the process leading indicators feedback sessions
5		Leaders are engaged and act as mentors	Ongoing involvement, sponsoring, and mentoring	Remaining aware through regular engagement with the process and operators	Management tours and listening sessions

#					
6	Strong leadership and appropriate delegation of authority	Appropriate delegation and sponsoring and supporting team by flying cover and not allowing bypassing up or down the chain of command	Ensuring equitable division of labor, establishing and enforcing limits of authority, and ensuring accountability	Chain of command and reporting, defined limits of authority and reporting requirements	
7	Individuals and teams hold themselves accountable	Courageous leadership that doesn't settle for the sake of harmony	Establishing a climate of logical consequences	Balanced and logical consequences	
8	Individual and intraorganizational alignment and collaboration	Courageous leadership that confronts non-team players and free riders	Assessing progress and team formation	Establishing incentives and disincentives	
9	Organization lives its values with integrity	Walk the talk—courageously address those that don't	Assess culture and incentives, address inconsistencies	Differentiation of market norms from social norms	
10	Well defined group identity and esprit de corps	Encourage the team to build up their pride and team spirit	Recognize and reward excellence	Symbols of achievement and group identity	
	Cumulative Committing Score				

Analysis: Committing versus Fragmenting

In these times of global competition, downsized workforces, and continuous change, companies derive their competitive advantages from their people. When companies can buy comparable equipment and technologies, it's the human factor that differentiates those that adapt and thrive from those companies overwhelmed by competitive pressures. In those organizations where members are committed to the vision, mission, and values that drive the organization, they find a way to overcome obstacles and continuously achieve the mission they see as their own. Compare this to the organization's whose members don't identify with the organization or its mission. People do their time—clocking in and clocking out. Those who are considered engaged are often furthering personal agendas. The majority of the rank and file members feel stifled by the organization's culture and not aligned with the organization's true values.

To tap into the human potential, companies implement initiatives to stimulate engagement; unfortunately, many of these initiatives fail to produce the intended result—often seen as insincere attempts at manipulation, ineffective "dog and pony shows," or disappointing projects that further disillusion the workforce by raising expectations and once again failing to deliver. What many managers fail to recognize is that engagement can't be artificially stimulated; like all living things, it only grows and thrives when the environmental conditions are right.

> QUOTE: "The beatings will continue until morale improves!"
>
> **Unknown**

Six essential elements must be present to create the right conditions; three of the elements address fundamental human satisfiers, and the other three address the alignment between the individual and the organization. Together, these six elements form the Workforce Engagement Equation. Before we talk about the 10 elements of organizational commitment, let's explore the three fundamental human satisfiers: hope, control, and equity. We talk about these apart from the 10 elements of commitment because these fundamental human satisfiers have deep roots that extend throughout the organization. Just as Mahatma Gandhi observed that "one man cannot do right in one department of life whilst he is occupied in doing wrong in any other departments"—organizations are one indivisible whole. Where there are activities that are counter to the espoused values of an organization, the effect of those activities will be felt in other areas of the organization.

> SALIENT QUOTE: "One man cannot do right in one department of life whilst he is occupied in doing wrong in any other departments."
>
> **Mahatma Gandhi**
> *Leader for Indian Independence (1869–1948)*

Hope, Control, and Equity

Hope, control, and equity are the three fundamental satisfiers upon which human dreams are built.

$$\text{Hope} + \text{Control} + \text{Equity} \rightarrow \text{Individual Satisfaction}$$

When denied, their absence sows the seeds of revolution as eloquently stated by Thomas Jefferson in the preamble of America's Declaration of Independence: "We hold these truths to be self-evident, that all men are created equal, that they are endowed by their Creator with certain inalienable rights, that among these are life, liberty, and the pursuit of happiness." Hope is embodied in the "pursuit of happiness; control is the essence of "liberty"—the freedom to act and to chart one's own destiny; and equity is plainly seen in the "self-evident truth that all men are created equal." Abraham Lincoln understood that the defense of these same three pillars was sufficient justification for the terrible cost of a civil war; on the blood-soaked battlefield of Gettysburg, he invoked them to strengthen the country's resolve to continue to pay the price until the war had been won: "Four score and seven years ago our fathers brought forth on this continent, a new nation, conceived in liberty, and dedicated to the proposition that all men are created equal." Hope is freshly minted in that which is new; control only exists where there is liberty to act; and again equity is plainly stated in "the proposition that all men are created equal." The South fought for the same three principles, as they believed that autonomy of individual states was the best way to secure their own hope, control, and equity. One might propose that the institution of Southern slavery nullifies this argument since there is no equity in slavery, but it was not the slaves who waged the war against the North. Remember, many a slave rebelled in the pursuit of hope, control, and equity. The power of hope, control, and equity is not unique to the United States—it is universal to mankind. They are woven throughout the tapestry of human history—in the stone tablets of the Ten Commandments, the Code of Hammurabi, the justice of the Magna Carta, in the flames of the French Revolution, in the words of Mahatma Gandhi, and Martin Luther King Jr.'s letter from a Birmingham jail. In our time, the world is struggling to recover from the greatest economic downturn since the Great Depression; millions are out of work and face the very real possibility that, despite their best efforts, their conditions may not improve for years to come. They are losing hope, have little control, and are well aware of the inequity of their situations; a pall has been cast across the worldwide workforce that affects all those directly concerned as well as those still fortunate enough to have employment. Fear of losing their jobs and losing their benefits infuses insecurity that undermines control and erodes hope. Since everyone knows someone affected, they too feel the inequity.

Inclusion, Purpose, and Congruence

When a company seeks to create workforce engagement under such severe economic conditions, they need to closely review their policies, practices, and their culture to ensure that the three fundamental human satisfiers of hope, control, and equity are cultivated. Do the opportunities for advancement or promotion foster hope? Are opportunities directly linked to the actions and contributions of the individual such that they clearly understand what is within their control? Are the opportunities and rewards determined equitably? We will talk in much greater depth about the policies and practices that foster hope, control, and equity, but before that, let's look at the second set of factors—the ones that build organizational commitment.

Inclusion + Purpose + Congruence → Organizational Commitment

We discussed the correlation between involvement and commitment earlier in Focusing Element 3. For someone to be committed to an organization, they need inclusion. They need to feel a sense of belonging and alignment with the others with whom they are working. Without this inclusion, they may be present, but they will be as if they are on the outside looking in and not truly a part of the organization—alone in a crowd.

The second factor in this equation is "purpose." If a person does not identify with the purpose of the organization, they won't be committed to its success.

Can a committed pacifist thrive within an organization dedicated to building weapons? Could a devote atheist work for an evangelical mission? Even if the individual is afforded the three fundamental human satisfiers, hope, control, and equity, if they don't identify with the purpose for which the organization stands, they won't be truly committed to its success. Since alignment of purpose has more to do with selection and hiring, we don't include that in the 10 elements of building commitment. If it's not there, you won't be able to build it in. The third factor in the Organizational Commitment equation is the first of 10 committing elements: organizational congruence.

Committing Element 1: High Degree of Congruence between Individual and Organizational Values and Working Approach

Whereas inclusion is an ongoing activity and purpose lies at the very heart of the organization's mission, congruence is a controllable factor that forms the foundation of an organizational culture that either bolsters or erodes individual commitment to an organization.

Congruence refers to the degree of alignment or correspondence between two items or elements. In my work with organizational culture, I've found that there are two major areas that need to be aligned between an individual's style and an organization's culture for the member to feel ongoing commitment to that organization: congruence of values, and congruence of degree of freedom to act. The Venn diagram shown in Figure 4.3 illustrates the alignment of these elements to create organizational congruence.

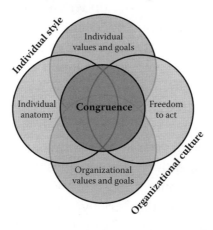

Figure 4.3   Individual congruence with organizational environment.

Alignment between Individual and Organizational Values and Goals

Everyone and every organization acts according to their true values. This is a fundamental truth—they may not act in accordance with their "espoused values," but rest assured, they act in accordance with their values. Frequently, espoused values don't align with demonstrated values. For instance, if I say that I value the poor but the only act of charity I demonstrate is once per year at Christmas when I throw some loose change into the red bucket to assuage my guilt when confronted with the incessant ringing of the hand bell outside the department store, do I really value the poor? If an organization says it values "risk taking and innovation" but imposes stringent controls and only acts after interminable study, committee discussions, and attainment of widespread group consensus such that no single person could ever be held accountable for the decision while competitors have seized the emerging opportunities, do they really value risk?

Given that there is no inherent superiority of one school of thought over another, problems arise when there is a mismatch between what is stated or implied and what is actually desired or rewarded (even if that reward is failure to punish). For a person to develop strong commitment, their values must align with those of the organization.

I separate out the values and goals from the purpose because they are not the same. I could be very committed to the organization's purpose, to eradicate disease for instance, but my values don't align with the methods and practices of how the organization works to accomplish that mission— animal testing or stem cell research. The purpose is the explicit mission of the organization—its values are the underlying motivational drivers that affect prioritization and behavioral expectations.

Even if my values align with the overall organizational values, I can still feel disconnected from the greater organization because of the leadership values of my direct management team. There is an inverse relationship between your position in an organization and the number of people that can screw up your day. When you are in an entry-level position, you are affected by your team leader, your supervisor, your manager, your director etc., etc., etc. Anyone up the chain who decides to dump on you has the ability to impact you unless one of those in the chain has the courage to act as a filter and your organization strictly respects the reporting chain of authority. But more often than not, "crap rolls downhill." When an organization respects the hierarchy, managers can act as filters for their areas and shelter their people from outside elements, insulate their teams and allowing them to stay focused and remain productive.

> **REMEMBER:** People join organizations, but they leave poor managers. Beware the manager who "kisses up" but "craps down."

Freedom to Act—Be Careful What You Wish for: Do You Really Want Engagement?

The second major area of alignment necessary for an individual to commit to an organization is the congruence of the freedom to act with their own degree of autonomy. When a person is fully autonomous, they have full authority along with freedom to act within their scope of responsibility and span of control. What's the right amount of freedom and control? The answer is, "it depends." It really depends upon the nature of the work being performed.

To help clients define their appropriate level, I draw the degree of autonomy along a spectrum that ranges from little autonomy (hired hands) to full autonomy (skilled professional). There are some instances where companies don't want employees making creative decisions and modifying procedures; it is essential that they perform each task in a highly standardized and structured manner following explicit instructions. You never want your medical lab technician just "winging it" with your medical tests. There are other areas and businesses where companies need employees to have full authority and autonomy to act with little direction and little structure. The creativity of artists would be constrained if they were limited to a single style and confined to a single pallet of muted colors.

Some individuals desire autonomy and have a strong internal drive to act independently. Others are quite content following routines and performing their tasks according to prescribed standards. They do not have the desire to stray from the routine and are most satisfied working within very structured expectations. If the organization's freedom to act is aligned with an individual's desire of autonomy then these factors are in congruence.

Whether the work is highly structured or nebulous you want your employees to be fully engaged in the work such that they are paying close attention to detail and focusing on quality and productivity. To create engagement appropriate to the type of work, the organization must create a conducive climate. Engagement doesn't exist in a vacuum. Interplay of multiple factors coalesces to create a culture of engagement. This spectrum of employee engagement, ranging from hired hand to trained professional, must be aligned with five other factors, as shown in Figure 4.4:

1. Behaviors
2. The role of supervision
3. The structures and rewards
4. Access to information and decision authority
5. Accountability for organizational results

Lack of alignment of these factors invariably generates confusion, conflicts, and fails to create sustainable engagement. If you want someone to independently take action, you need to ensure they have sufficient access to timely, relevant information and the appropriate level of authority. Table 4.4 expands upon these areas listing within the matrix the degrees of engagement and the major factors that must align to ignite the fire of engagement in your workforces.

Once you determine the degree of autonomy you desire to foster in your workforce, that decision will affect every other decision, interaction, and management structure to foster the appropriate climate. It will also affect all hiring, training, and promotion decisions. If you ultimately desire your operators to act in the capacity of partners fully engaged in business, the criterion you use for hiring will be far different than those you use to screen applicants if what you truly desire is a group of individuals quite content to do exactly what you tell them when you tell them for as long as you tell

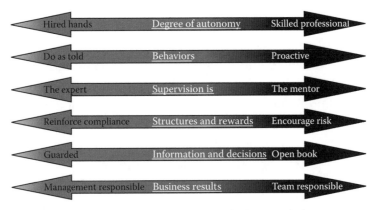

Multiple factors coalesce to determine the degree to which
employees demonstrate initiative and engagement

Figure 4.4   The spectrum of employee engagement.

Table 4.4 Degree of Engagement Matrix

	Little Autonomy	*Full Autonomy*
Role of employee	• Hired hand	• Skilled professional
Employee behaviors	• Compliance • Reactive • Willingly does as told • Alerts supervision when a problem arises	• Process owner • Proactive • Actively engaged and involved • Works to solve problems and informs supervision of decisions made
Role of supervision	• Technical experts who correct problems	• Mentors who continue to develop empowered professionals
Structures and rewards	• Compliance is reinforced	• Risks are encouraged
Communications and information sharing	• Guarded • Strictly on a need to know basis	• Open book • Only information of a strictly confidential or proprietary nature is not shared freely
Decision authority	• Decisions are made only within the narrow scope of the approved process • Independent decisions are the exception—not the rule	• A wide latitude is provided for employees to make decisions • Only a narrow set of extraordinary conditions require supervisor decisions
Trust	• Employees are trusted to follow the rules as directed	• Employees are trusted members of the business who actively drive toward the common vision
Business results	• Management is entirely responsible for the results the business achieves	• The entire team takes responsibility for and shares in the rewards of business results

them. Incongruent activities or messages will be seen as hypocritical and will undermine the degree of trust and engagement within your organization. As you can see, *this is a big deal!*

Does that mean that one degree of autonomy is better or worse than any other? Absolutely not! There is no right and no wrong in this. It all depends

upon the nature of the business and the type of workforce you believe
will be most beneficial to help you achieve your goals. Not every company
should have complete autonomy of their workforce—not every organization
can. The important thing is that there is congruence between all the factors so that you can be as efficient and effective as possible. To illustrate the
point, let's look at an organization that effectively maintains alignment of all
these factors, the U.S. Military.

The Engagement Model of the United States Military

The military uses the terms "fog" and "friction" to describe two phenomena that
occur in battle. The "fog of war" refers to the confusion and chaos that occurs
when fighting a battle. Information is in short supply and invariably runs behind
the events in the field. Because of the speed of events, the geographical disper-
sion of individuals, and the sheer number of people involved, it is just not possible for top leadership to know everything that is going on at every moment—a
fog obscures their view. Friction refers to the fact that things seldom occur
as fast as the commander would like. Events unfold in unexpected ways. To
execute all of the "major muscle movements" of combat forces, logistics, communications, and intelligence effectively, military doctrine states that the ultimate
objective should be clearly defined before any plan is executed.

The business world has adapted this concept in the form of mission statements. The mission is broken down into objectives which are assigned to
various groups. These groups employ tactics for which they've been well
trained to fulfill their roles as they carry out their responsibilities. Every
member of the team knows the objective and what they need to do for mission success. Each group trusts their counterpart to fulfill their objectives.
And if everything goes according to plan, the mission is accomplished. But it
must be pointed out that things rarely go according to plan.

Nowhere is this as true as in the military. Military doctrine is predicated
on the concept that plans are only accurate until the day of battle arrives."
That is why every member of the team needs to knows the final objective.

When conditions change in the field, and the team sees a chance to
secure the objective and accomplish the mission, they are empowered to act
accordingly. The motto "Adapt and overcome!" inspires engagement and creativity. When a postaction analysis of a mission is performed, if a leader has
been found to obstruct or preclude a member of their squad who was acting
within the mission guidelines from taking actions that could have resulted in
success, the leader is frequently reprimanded.

As you can see, the U.S. Military has aligned its roles, responsibilities, communications, and rewards to create a culture of engagement and accountability. The reality is quite different from the stereotypical view that the military is a strict "command and control" organization. The armed services have adapted to the lessons learned in Vietnam, the Soviet occupation of Afghanistan, and the ongoing wars in the Middle East. I have worked with far more civilian organizations with cultures steeped in autocratic command and control than I encountered in 20 years of military service.

Environmental Incongruence: "Planting Seeds in Bleach"

Whether you want to have a nimble reactive workforce or a compliant workforce is a matter of individual management style and business necessity. Having a creative worker who decides to add a little dash of this and a little pinch of that probably isn't as beneficial for a concrete manufacturing business as it is in an interior design firm. The workforce you develop needs to be aligned with the demands of the work. Furthermore, the freedom to act should be clearly defined to prevent misunderstandings—otherwise, problems arise when employees think they are empowered to act or decide and the manager sees it differently.

Whenever people's expectations of empowerment are thwarted, disappointment and frustration occur and their sense of engagement ebbs. The behaviors you want to incent must be congruent with the organizational values and culture; otherwise, it will be as effective as "planting seeds in bleach." Whatever tender sprouts of desired behavior grow will quickly wither and die in the wrong environment. When a lack of congruence exists within an organization, there will be indications at both the individual and the organizational level depending upon the degree of incongruence and how widespread it is.

Individual Indicators of Incongruence

An individual can only act incongruently with their core temperament and values for limited periods of time. Continuing exposure to an incongruent environment will lead to displays of progressively maladaptive behaviors:

- Emotional flare-ups
- Malicious compliance
- Learned helplessness
- Emotional collapse

EXAMPLE FROM AN ENGINEERING DEPARTMENT: I was asked to provide performance consulting for a "problem employee" in the engineering department of a manufacturing facility. Lisa, a project engineer, was being put on a performance plan as a last chance agreement. When I was first consulted by the manager, I was told that Lisa had a bad attitude and poor performance. She was technically brilliant and personable and got along well with all the crews and other managers, but she was an ineffective project engineer.

When I met with her, I found Lisa to be energetic, funny, and as brilliant as they said. However, she was miserable in her job as a project engineer and was ready to resign. She really wanted to be a production engineer. However, her manager had structured the progression in the department to require every engineer to start out as a project engineer, and when the manager felt they were ready, they could then be promoted to become a production engineer.

The jobs of project engineers and production engineers are very different. Project engineers need to have great project management skills, strong attention to detail, and the ability to stay focused for long, long periods of time—slow and steady wins the race. This is not the case for production engineers; chaos is their daily norm. When a machine goes down they have to rush in, find and fix the problems as quickly as possible, and get the machine up and running—time is money! A production engineer never knows what they are getting into on any given day. By definition, well-managed projects should never be in chaos.

The two different jobs demand two different temperaments—the accounting office versus the emergency room. If someone really enjoyed the steady flow of project management, they may not like the hectic world of production. Lisa loved activity and liked to be continuously challenged. She didn't like the tedious monotony and endless attention to detail required by managing projects. It made perfect sense to me that she would be better suited as a production engineer than a project engineer. Her manager didn't see it that way—everyone must be a project engineer before they become a production engineer. That's the way I've always done it at every place I've worked.

I acknowledged his view and then offered a counter perspective. We discussed the differences in temperaments and job requirements. After a time, he nodded, "We do have several production engineers who were much better at project management. If she finds someone willing to switch from being a production engineer back to project engineer, we'll give it a try."

As you can imagine, it wasn't hard to find someone willing to go back to the strictly day-shift routine of project management. The two swapped and Lisa went from "zero to hero!" She thrived as a production engineer. Whereas before she was going through the motions and punching the clock, now she was engaged and motivated. It was not uncommon to see Lisa stay over extra shifts to keep working on problems.

Lisa's was a clear case where alignment between the individual and the job made all the difference in the world. Lisa kept her job and the organization gained its best production engineer ever.

Organizational Indicators

Incongruence is often a case of misaligned individual temperaments compared with the requirements of the job. There are also short-term conditions where the entire organization experiences a period of disruption to the culture that temporarily affects everyone's outlook and attitude. However, in some organizations widespread, long-term inconsistencies persist between what is said and what is done to the point that the ongoing cultural climate is chronic if not terminal. In such organizations, the following performance indicators will be observed:

■ Low employee morale
■ Impacted productivity
■ High employee turnover

To address such a malignant organizational climate requires management to do much more than apply quick fix projects to improve morale. Morale and climate are symptoms; they are outcomes arising from multiple drivers and conditions, not root causes in themselves. To cure what ails an organization in such crisis requires fundamental changes that address each element of the Workforce Engagement Equation.

Balancing the Workforce Engagement Equation

We began the discussion of commitment with the three fundamental human satisfiers, and we added three factors affecting that which governs an individual's commitment to an organization. When these six elements are effectively combined, you have the complete equation for workforce engagement:

$$\text{Hope} + \text{Control} + \text{Equity} \rightarrow \underline{\text{Individual Satisfaction}}$$

$$+$$

$$\text{Inclusion} + \text{Purpose} + \text{Congruence} \rightarrow \underline{\text{Organizational Commitment}}$$

Yields:

<u>Impactful Outcomes</u>

Resulting in:

<u>An Engaged Workforce</u>

Achievement of these results requires aligning individual values and goals with those of the organization as well as aligning shared expectations with the conditions needed by individuals to act at the appropriate level of autonomy. Supporting the desired degree of autonomy, each of the five operational conditions fostering autonomy must also be appropriately aligned:

1. Behaviors (Do as Told → Proactive)
2. The role of supervision (The Expert → The Mentor)
3. The structures and rewards (Reinforce Compliance → Encourage Risk)
4. Access to information and decision authority (Guarded → Open Book)
5. Accountability for organizational results (Management Responsible → Team Responsible)

It is more effective to set clear expectations at the very beginning specifying the level of individual autonomy rather than to pay lip service to the degree of empowerment that can be expected within the organization. Too often organizations make claims that sound empowering that raise employees' expectations only to subsequently disempower employees when one or more of the essential elements are not aligned to the degree purported.

Committing Element 2: Structured Approach to Training and Qualifications

With a firm understanding of the desired degree of empowerment combined with the systems and processes designed during your Focusing Stage you

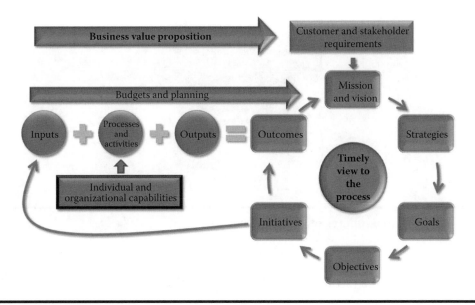

Figure 4.5 Sustainability engine—building capabilities.

are no prepared to train the crew on their tasks, roles, and responsibilities. Training the crew builds the individuals capabilities which both impacts and enables the overall organization's capacity to achieve its mission. It only stands to reason that the organization will not function well if its individual members lack the knowledge and competencies essential to mission accomplishment. Figure 4.5 builds on the sustainability engine logic model by adding the block of capabilities that forms the foundation of every process and activity.

Both functional as well as professional training will need to be commensurate with the degree of empowerment desired in the workforce. Strictly training on the functional aspects of the tasks involved is rarely as successful as when some degree of professional training is combined. To help you think through the types of training that will be required, consider the five spheres of competence.

The Five Spheres of Individual Competence

An old adage observed that anyone who desires to manage others must first be able to manage themselves. Growth in managerial competence requires the cultivation of skills and knowledge within five areas of competency as shown in Figure 4.6. Both personal and professional growth requires

Figure 4.6 The five spheres of competence.

mastery of elements contained within each of the five spheres as described below:

1. Individual: Management of self
   a. Work habits
   b. Time management
   c. Attention to detail
   d. Emotional control
   e. Judgment
   f. Continuous learning
   g. Financial management
2. Professional and technical skills of an individual contributor
   a. Basic skills
   b. Computer skills
   c. Technical professional skills
3. Social and team skills: Ability to work with others
   a. Communications
   b. Giving and receiving feedback
   c. Emotional intelligence
   d. Interpersonal styles and temperaments
   e. Team skills
   f. Conflict resolution
4. Management skills: Ability to manage people and processes, plan, and execute work
   a. Effective meetings
   b. Planning

    c. Structuring of roles and responsibilities
    d. Delegation
    e. Business acumen
    f. Development of systems and metrics
    g. Performance management
    h. Organizational and lean concepts
    i. Legal considerations
5. Leadership skills: Ability to craft a vision and inspire others
    a. Principles of leadership
    b. Crafting a vision
    c. Leading individuals, inspiring of others, and building commitment
    d. Developing, coaching, and empowering
    e. Climate creation
    f. Change management

As an individual develops greater areas of expertise, the competencies gained in one sphere enhance others. For example, a manager who is adept at planning will improve her effectiveness when she can inspire others and craft a shared vision.

Principles of Training Every Manager Should Know

COMMON FALLACY: Too frequently I've seen managers fall into a logic trap in which they believe because they can do something they are qualified to teach it. There is more to training than simply telling. Managers that value effective training ultimately create more sustainable organizations that are less prone to crisis management.

Though it's not the intent of this book to delve excessively deep into the details of training design, delivery, and the principles of adult learning, because training is so critical to process improvement and organizational development it is essential for every manager to have some basic understanding of what constitutes effective training. Three criteria form the strategic foundation managers should know about training:

1. Training is not the goal of "training"
2. Setting clear expectation through the use of training checklists
3. Systems thinking and the principles of learning/memory

Training Is Not the Goal of "Training"

When I tell clients that training is not the goal of the training department they look at me as if I've lost my mind. Training adds costs that directly impact the bottom line, and, in and of itself, training does not inherently add value to the product or service. Having well trained competent employees certainly does add value, but the reality is if organizations could find perfectly trained and qualified individuals there would never be a need for training. We have seen this with the high unemployment rate resulting from the Great Recession. Organizations have cut costs by hiring the qualified employees who come to them pretrained and ready to work, thereby reducing indirect costs. But this condition will not last forever, and even if someone has experience in the field, they won't be familiar with your organization's specific processes and procedures; therefore, some level of training is required. Even still, training is still not the goal of the training department.

When organizations are truly honest with themselves, they recognize that the desired outcome of training is not the transfer of knowledge but the modification of behaviors. Because when you really stop to think about it, it doesn't matter that someone possesses knowledge if they don't apply it; how many of us know that we'd be better off if we ate less and exercised more? How many of us do it? Similarly, there is still a portion of the population that doesn't wear seatbelts even though there is strong evidence that the simple act of buckling up dramatically increases their chances of surviving an accident. Obviously, knowledge alone is insufficient in changing behaviors. If training alone changed behaviors, it wouldn't be one of the first things cut out of organizational budgets when times get tough and money gets tight. If training modified behaviors, it would be the first thing that companies would invest in when they need improved efficiencies. Training professionals who recognize this try to understand the myriad of factors that govern why people behave the way they do and work diligently to add multiple tools to their behavior-altering toolkit. Yet, traditional training remains the primary approach to behavior modification, and the truth is that it's just not that effective.

The traditional training methodology is evangelical in its approach. Leaders stand before their congregations and read from books of wisdom in the hopes that the audience will heed all that is being said and change their behaviors accordingly. This approach has limited behavioral impact since only a small percentage of people successfully alter their behaviors based solely upon the acquisition of knowledge. Just because someone has the knowledge or even the skill to perform doesn't mean they have the will. When looking for improved performance, keep this in mind: Is it a matter of skill or will? Obviously, if the person has never been trained, they need to be. But if they've been trained and still don't perform, the problem lies in the area of will rather than skill.

Will versus Skill

If you have a fever, taking an aspirin can reduce it; however, taking aspirin to reduce the fever does nothing to treat the underlying infection that caused the fever. You're treating the symptoms, not the cause. In the same manner, managers often apply insufficient fixes to behavioral issues. This is particularly true when a manager is conflict averse. As a result, the solutions applied don't address the real issues, or, they are addressed in an ineffectual manner by applying a training solution to a management problem.

TIME MANAGEMENT 101: A manager once tasked me with developing a time management course for one of his employees. When I asked why the course was needed, the manager said, "He's always late." Desiring to solve the problem, not just treat the symptom I asked, "I see in his record that he went to a time management course last year."

"It didn't help; he's still late all the time."

"Is it an issue of will or a skill?"

"What does it matter?"

"Does he have a watch?"

"Yes."

"Does it work?"

"I suppose it does."

"If his life depended on it, could he show up on time?"

"Sure he could?"

"Then what would you like me to train him on? The theory of time? The history of time? The importance of time? (Fortunately, I was friends with the manager and knew he had a good sense of humor.) The point I was trying to make was that sending the employee to another time management course when he'd already been trained wouldn't change the behavior. Either the employee had too many items that were a priority or didn't feel that being on time was a critical component of his performance.

The main point to keep in mind is that behavior is complex and knowledge is only one component that, in and of itself, is nececssary but insufficient to ensure desired behavioral outcomes.

Setting Clear Expectation through the Use of Training Checklists

If traditional training isn't the answer, what is? Recall the seven structural timbers of effective individual performance introduced during the Focusing Stage and shown again in Figure 4.7:

1. Define acceptable performance
2. Set clear expectations
3. Provide timely feedback
4. Provide adequate resources
5. Set performance conditions
6. Define gaps and train as appropriate
7. Sustain with management systems

As you were designing the systems and communicating the roles and responsibilities during the Focusing Stage, you were laying down the first two planks: defining acceptable performance and setting clear expectations. Those guidelines that set forth the criteria and expectations of acceptable performance enable you to clearly define the performance gaps within the five spheres of competence and train as appropriate. As a resource to help

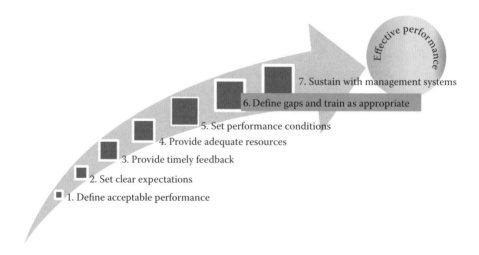

Figure 4.7 Framework for individual success.

you set clear expectations, I recommend the utilization of competency-based training checklists.

Training Checklists

A training checklist, sometimes referred to as a task list, is a summary of the competencies, knowledge, and skills required by a particular job or position. These checklists are not to be confused with procedures or job aids; they are broader in scope addressing the elements required within the five spheres of competencies needed to be successful in a position. Training checklists are not as detailed as procedures or other training documents and job aids; they don't list step-by-step actions required to accomplish the tasks. Training checklists inventory what needs to be done, not how to do it. Table 4.5 shows a sample of a training checklist developed for a construction client.

The training checklist is used to define the gap in an employee's knowledge and skill sets and track the individual's developmental progress toward

Table 4.5   Training Checklist for Construction Laborer—Site Clearing Essential Skills

Tasks	Date Demonstrated	Validated By
1. Overview of duties and responsibilities of construction helper		
2. Basics of construction math		
3. OSHA 30 and other safety training (including certification card)		
3.1.1. Personal protective equipment (PPE)—purpose, requirements, uses		
3.1.2. Compressed air hazards and proper use		
3.1.3. Basic first aid		
3.1.4. Fire protection		
3.1.5. Confined space safety requirements		
4. Construction communications—signaling (hand and flag)		
5. Proper installation and inspection of silt fences and other best management practices (BMPs)		

(continued)

Table 4.5 Training Checklist for Construction Laborer—Site Clearing Essential Skills (Continued)

Tasks	Date Demonstrated	Validated By
6. Material identification, handling, and storage		
6.1.1. Lumber and wood products		
6.1.2. Metal handling and storage—rod (rebar) and sheet metal		
7. Safe use of hand tools and fasteners		
8. Safe use of digging and trenching tools		
9. Safe use of power tools		
9.1.1. Use of electrical tools		
9.1.2. Use of pneumatic tools		
9.1.3. Use of small engine powered tools		
9.1.4. Safe use of powder-actuated tools		
10. Safe rigging and lifting basics		

closing identified knowledge or skill gaps. As part of a structured OJT process, each employee works with a senior qualified employee. As the employee gains experience, understanding, and demonstrates their knowledge and skills, the senior member validates the performance and signs off the appropriate item. Line item by line item the training gaps are closed.

The DACUM Process

The process of developing a training checklist is referred to by training professionals as "developing a curriculum," or DACUM for short. The DACUM process is a structured approach to identifying the competencies and tasks that enables the planning, prioritization, and tracking the development of a comprehensive body of training documentation.

A shortcoming I have found among some training approaches is once the DACUM is used for the documentation planning process, it is never used again. It is treated as a means to an end rather than incorporating this comprehensive inventory into the ongoing structured OJT process. As a practitioner, I have found that using the DACUM as a training checklist incorporated into the structured OJT process greatly improves the effectiveness and impact of OJT. In fact, given the choice of utilizing training checklists or developing reams of procedures, manuals, and other documentation, I'd implement the use of training checklists because they alone form the basis of a sustainable training process thereby minimizing generational competency decay.

Minimizing Generational Competency Decay

I cannot overstate the value of utilizing training checklists as part of your organization's developmental strategy. Don't underestimate their value because they appear so simple. Even if you never develop any other manuals, procedures, or other specific job related training materials, the training checklist will provide you with 70% or more of the value needed in training. I can confidently make this statement based upon years of field experience; allow me to explain.

In a stable operation, most, if not all of the information required to safely perform the job is available within the corporate knowledge of the seasoned employees currently doing the job—it's just not readily accessible. To train new employees almost all of the organizations I've worked with outside of the nuclear industry rely on unstructured OJT as their primary method of developing employees. A new employee is assigned to work with another employee to train them; I call this "following Fred around." Over time, the trainee picks up bits and pieces of knowledge, skill, and experience as opportunity and the ability of the trainer to effectively train allows. This process can be limited by the trainer's level of interest in training the new employee as well as the trainee's initiative and inquisitiveness within the context of the trainee/trainer relationship. After a period of time, the senior employee makes a determination of whether the new member has learned enough. Fred may ask, "Got any questions?" The trainee feels comfortable with everything he's seen Fred do and says, "Nope, none that I can think of." Fred pronounces the trainee to be qualified just in time for Fred to go on vacation (I'm certain the timing of the vacation had nothing to do with proclaiming his replacement trained). Fred heads out of town and out of touch and the new employee is left alone to mind the shop. Unexpected things occur that didn't come up while following Fred around that he never mentioned. Suddenly, the new employee has lots of questions to ask Fred if he were around!

The problem with unstructured OJT is that it is not consistent; if a particular situation doesn't arise or the seasoned employee forgets to talk about one aspect or another of the job, gaps are left in the individual's development. When the one partially trained individual trains the next, more gaps form and generation after generation the depth and breadth of job knowledge decays. Just think of the hole that would be left in your operation if your most trusted senior employee suddenly left. Figure 4.8 shows a hypothetical situation in which one employee generation successfully transfers 80% of their knowledge to the next and each subsequent generation transfers 80% to the next; soon, the level of knowledge in the workforce is reduced to a point of overall ineffectiveness. Granted, this is a simplistic illustration and discounts individual employees taking the initiative to learn on their own and continue to gain experience, but the point is still valid. I've seen it played out within organizations time and time again. I've even seen employees with less than one week of experience left unsupervised to train the newly hired.

Utilization of a comprehensive training checklist ensures a minimum level of familiarity with all the essential elements of the position thus minimizing competency decay. Like a grocery list, checklists remind trainers of the essential elements to train the next generation; although there is no substitute for experience, consistent utilization of training checklists prevents the organizational competency level from falling below a minimum threshold. In addition, the checklist informs the employee in training what is expected of them. Consider how much faster you could have learned life's lessons if you knew the questions to ask? Having implemented the use of training checklists in dozens of locations, I've seen the time to qualify reduced by half to two-thirds. And where the process has been institutionalized, supported by managers, and owned by employees, it has been consistently sustained year after year.

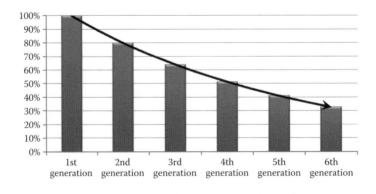

Figure 4.8 Generational decay of organizational competence.

EXAMPLE: A senior vice president of human resources shared with me the ongoing success of their use of training checklists implemented in a paper manufacturing facility in western Oregon. Prior to the implementation of checklists, millions of dollars had been spent in several training initiatives. Training consultants had been hired to develop training manuals and procedures. The materials were used sporadically to train the first generations. This method was doubly expensive because, in addition to the developmental costs, there were the costs of conducting the training on overtime. Due to the burdensome costs, none of the previous training initiatives had ever been sustained. The manuals weren't utilized outside of classrooms; they weren't kept up to date with modifications made to equipment and procedures—they became very expensive dust collectors. The first generation of trained employees still had some of the old manuals in lockers, garages at home, or thrown in the trunks of their cars. Every previous training initiative died, crushed by unsustainable administrative burdens and excessive costs.

In 1995, I began working with a team of operators and engineers to develop and implement the use of training checklists for each position. Utilizing the operators to develop the checklists created a strong sense of ownership in the program as compared to bringing in outside technical writers to develop the manuals as had been previously done. After the checklists were introduced, the consistency of training improved and the time required to qualify was reduced by half. What's more important, the qualifications methodology continues to be utilized as of the date of writing this book. In addition, by developing the checklists, the senior operators learned more about the process and became better operators themselves. If you really want to learn about something, try teaching it to someone else.

The low-cost, simple solution succeeded and has been sustained where millions of dollars and thousands of man-hours spent previously failed.

NOTE: When developing training checklists it is beneficial to utilize the work done by the Department of Labor and others who have uploaded their work onto the DOL website. These competency models identify the core competencies for most sectors and industries within the

U.S. economy. These resources provide an excellent start from which you can build upon and customize according to the specific roles and responsibilities defined for your organization. These resources are free of charge and are part of the public domain not protected by any copyrights. Refer to the Career One Stop website at: http://www.careerone stop.org/competencymodel/. By selecting your sector and industry, you will see a competency pyramid (Figure 4.9 shows the competency pyramid I accessed to build the entry level construction laborer training checklist contained in Table 4.5). You will need to drill down on the various links and export the data for your own use, but I have found this resource to be a good foundation upon which to build. You can also customize your competency maps and career ladders on the website. If you choose, you can also share what you've created with others through the website so that others may build upon what you have created.

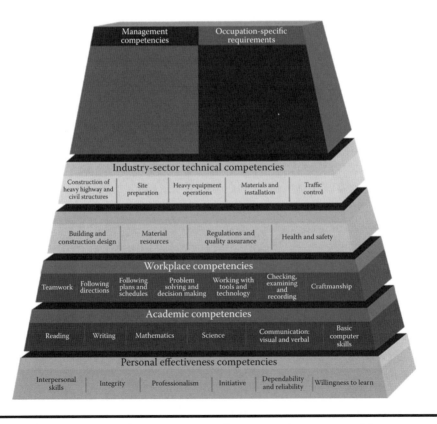

Figure 4.9   Career one-stop heavy construction competency pyramid.

Principles of Learning: Systems Thinking

The third essential element in implementing effective training and developmental processes is to structure the process around systems. We discussed the need for a systematic approach to problem solving during the Focusing Stage. But having a systematic approach doesn't help if the employees don't have any systems.

EXAMPLE—THE LIGHT PUMP: I was tasked with developing operating procedures for the auxiliary systems of a manufacturing plant in West Virginia. One of the systems assigned was the elevator sump pump. During rainy seasons water seeped into the elevator shaft and eventually an alarm would sound when the level rose to the set point. When the alarm sounded, the on-shift operator flipped a switch on the wall near the elevator. After a period of time, the water level would lower and the alarm would go out. The facility was over one hundred years old and no manuals were still in existence for the original systems. To develop the materials I interviewed operators and physically traced out each system.

"What kind of pump is it?"

"I don't know, but it's wicked slow. Sometimes it takes hours for the alarm to clear."

"Does the pump have a suction strainer that is clogged? Perhaps that's why it's so slow."

"I don't know, I've never gone down and looked at it."

"Well, let's lock it out and I'll go down and check it out."

After I locked out the elevator, I went down into the shaft. I found a small, corroded centrifugal pump half submerged in mud and water covering the motor and pump casing with both its inlet and outlet pipes cut off. Obviously, this was not the pump; it hadn't pumped anything for years. "OK, turn on the switch." Moments later, the bright light shone from an incandescent light installed just above the mud-covered floor. It was ancient—large and bulbous—probably handcrafted by Thomas Edison himself. "Is that the same switch?"

"Yep, that's the one."

"No wonder the pump is so slow—it's not a pump; it's a light bulb!"

The lesson of this true story is that many employees operate equipment and systems without full understanding of what they are actually operating. For some unknown long period of time, the standard operating procedure for the facility was to turn on a light when the water level got too high. The heat from the bulb would cause the water to evaporate and the alarm would eventually clear. Generation after generation of operators were taught that they were operating a pump that no one ever verified, inspected, or performed any preventive maintenance on. Good thing it had never burned out, it would be very hard to replace!

As extreme and humorous as this example is, it's not unique. In most locations I've worked with, I've encountered operators who go through the motions they've memorized by rote with little understanding. Some organizations have more some have less but almost all have at least one. Another example of operations without understanding I worked with was a chemical facility in the Southeast that utilized an advanced computer interface to control systems remotely. Through the course of our discussions, it became apparent that the operator hadn't really made the mental connection that when he operated the computer, he was actually operating valves, switches, and pumps in the plant. To him it was more like playing a video game.

To develop a higher quality of operator capable of critical thinking and problem solving the training process needs to be holistic and systems based. To help illustrate the depth of understanding I'm describing, imagine you're going to train a team to be the world's greatest automotive engineers. You want the team to design and build the safest, fastest, most reliable vehicles on the market. There's just one problem: they've never seen a car before and have no concept of what one is. How would you propose training them?

First, you would probably show them a car; give them an overview of what it is. You may have to teach them principles of internal combustion engines, hydraulics, or whatever is needed to fill the gaps in their understanding. Second, you would then teach them systems—how the drive train connects to the engine, how the brakes work, etc. Then you would teach them controls and logic. Controls and logic explains how all the systems interface with each other to fulfill their given functions. For instance, the clutch must be pushed in before the engine is started, etc. Next, you could teach them how to operate the vehicle. With their solid understanding of the principles, systems, and controls, they could become extremely proficient operators. Once trained to this level, you could teach them to troubleshoot and maintain the vehicle. Understanding all the systems and controls helps them quickly diagnose abnormal operations. Finally, with a solid understanding of operations and maintenance, you could teach them to design a better vehicle. They know the needs of the operators and they understand what it takes to maintain the vehicle. They will have the foundation necessary to be great engineers. Figure 4.10 represents the technical hierarchy of systems training.

Compare this ideal example with what typically happens in operations throughout the country. We hire operators into the facility and teach them to operate without giving them any foundational training in principles, systems, and controls and logic. This explains why we have operators running facilities without understanding the implications of their actions or the repercussions of symptoms they observe such as an operator in northern mill who opened a drain valve in the basement for a tank that was supposed to be empty and then went back to sit with his friends in the control room upstairs. Hours later, the supervisor discovered over three feet of flooding in the basement. When the operator was asked why he just walked away when he saw water flowing out of the valve. "I thought it was supposed to do that." There are also maintenance personnel who don't understand the operations so they treat symptoms rather than fix root causes and engineers who, having never operated or maintained the systems, are asked to design better ones. That's why we have systems that are difficult to operate by putting controls in inaccessible places and harder to maintain such as installing filters with only three inches of clearance so that they can't be cleaned.

Operators trained with a systems mindset should think about the expected system response before they perform an action and then observe the actual response during and after they act. If the actual deviates from the expected, the operator should stop and investigate.

Even though I've used a mechanical systems example, the same concepts can be applied to office procedures, call centers, or any other operation or business. Think of the insurance claims adjuster who mechanically enters a code that reports the client deceased when they are clearly alive and talking

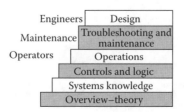

Figure 4.10 Technical hierarchy for systems training.

on the phone or the bank loan processor who places a foreclosure on a home that has been paid off for years—mindless operations are clearly not limited to manufacturing and manufacturing facilities.

Principles of Learning: Memory

In addition to helping employees think critically to effectively operate the systems, the systems approach also helps them learn the systems easier and remember the correct way to maximize the outcomes of those systems.

The human mind, though amazing and highly efficient, is also somewhat erratic and random when left to its own devices. Have you ever seen a face but couldn't remember the name? How about had a memory triggered by a song or a smell? In the first instance, your mind has filed the memory of the face separately from the name; in the latter, you've filed that memory under a sound or a smell. This is certainly not an efficient filing system. Filing things by smell probably won't be too effective unless it's your tuna fish sandwich.

To help add order to chaos, structure the training such that it progresses from simple to complex and from known to unknown. Take something that is complex and break it down into more digestible chunks: Systems are made up of subsystems that are made up of components which are made up of parts (Figure 4.11).

- Systems: complete a function
- Subsystems: multiple components combined to carry out a portion of a function
- Component: assembly of parts that do not function outside the subsystem
- Parts: individual elements that, when assembled, form components

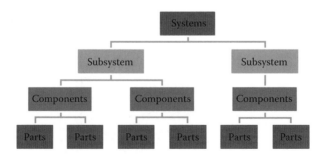

Figure 4.11   Systems structure.

Using these definitions and referring back to the automotive example, an engine is not a system; it is a subsystem. The engine doesn't complete a function; a running engine outside of a drive train only converts gasoline into mechanical rotation and exhaust fumes.

When training checklists are created, structure them by systems. I've seen training professionals structure training by timeframe—daily, weekly, and monthly tasks, and I've seen them structure the training strictly by operations position. Neither of these approaches helps establish a systems understanding. Within the training for each position, include the system elements identified in the technical hierarchy.

- Overview of the function of the systems along with fundamental principles
- Detailed systems training, including the subsystems, components, and essential parts as necessary
- Controls and logic that explain the interworking of systems and the interlocks essential for proper system function
- Operations training, including normal operations, start ups, shut downs, abnormal conditions, and emergency conditions
- Troubleshooting and maintenance that address the routine, preventative, and problem solving and repairs
- Design not being something routinely trained, but the need for designers and engineers to have thorough knowledge of all those elements for which maintenance and operators are trained

These same concepts are transferrable to the service industry when modified as follows:

- Overview—the overall function of the system or process as to the outcomes the system is designed to produce
- Detailed systems training—how the elements of the system interact with each other to accomplish its given outcome
- Controls—interlocks and relationships that govern how the elements work within the system and how the employee must interface with the system
- Operations—the step by step procedural process to utilize the system to accomplish the desired outcome
- Troubleshooting—the types of errors the system can produce and how to correct them
- Design—the methodology to rework the system to improve system function, efficiency, and quality

Applying a holistic systems-based approach yields better outcomes and produces employees who are more adept at operating and maintaining the system who also possess the critical thinking and problem solving skills to keep the operation functioning effectively.

Outcomes of Utilizing a Structured Approach to Training and Qualifications

For the group to be effective and deliver on the value proposition it is essential that each team member has the skills necessary to accomplish the team's objectives. Once the necessary competencies have been determined for each position and incorporated into training checklists the checklists form the basis of individual development plans that are utilized as part of a structured approach to training and qualifications. The training checklists are also effective records that document each member's education, training, skills, and demonstrated competence. This structured approach has been proven and documented as a simple, sustainable, and highly effective method for developing the competencies that will lead to team success.

Committing Element 3: Team Members Have and Keep Faith with Their Teams

One of the key indicators that marked an effective transition through the Forming Stage was the growing trust between team members (Forming Element 4). Trust in the early stages was primarily developed by the actions of management and leaders outlining the path and helping people answer the question for them, "What's in it for me?" Individuals began to have trust in the organization's mission and leadership capabilities of the management team. Trust between individuals was more of a matter of faith than of demonstration. This goes back to the basic tenant that most people are willing to accept others at face value unless the other demonstrates behaviors that undermine their trust. When you first meet someone, you generally don't have reason to doubt them, so you don't. However, by the time the organization has moved through the stages of Forming and Focusing there have been ample opportunities to either validate or negate those initial assumptions. If the team has been working well, people are becoming more engaged, and individuals' skills are growing, the levels of trust will move from a superficial "benefit of the doubt" to a more entrenched feeling of genuine trust based upon demonstrated behaviors. At this point, team members will have more confidence in the team's ability to get the job done and they trust others to deliver on their obligations. Being among others you know and respect builds your sense of commitment to the team. You know they count on you as much as you count on them, and you don't want to let them down. Many members of the armed forces I've had the honor to serve with have told me that they frequently put in the extra time to get the job done because they didn't want to be the one to let the team down. This is a sign of a truly cohesive team.

But what if this is not the case within your organization. What if team members doubt the team's ability to achieve the mission? Members don't trust others within the team to do their part. If this is the case, then they'll either do the jobs themselves or double-check the work of others; either way, you are not harnessing the full potential of the team. The team is only as fast as its individual members. There is no economy of scale through the division of labor. Each of us has had the experience of waiting for another to perform their piece. It could have been within a group assignment in school, a project at work, or even the 11th hour before a community or civic event when someone hasn't delivered on their commitment. These situations are particularly frustrating because they strike at the very core of individual satisfaction: hope, control, and equity. As you wait, you feel like you're losing control. It's not fair that you have done your part and someone else has let you down. The hope you had anticipating the favorable outcome is slipping away as time passes and the other still fails to deliver on their promises. So what can you do?

To Be Trusted, You Must First Be Trustworthy

I've been asked on multiple occasions, "How can I get them to trust me?" The answer is so simple it sounds glib, "Be worthy of their trust." This is particularly true during the initial stages of organizational development when you are pushing back the barriers of the Johari Window. Share as much as you can as soon as you can. If you don't, they'll fill in the gaps of what they don't know with assumptions and suppositions and they may even throw in a wild rumor here and there. Here are three tried and true techniques for growing trust:

1. Timely and complete communications
2. Deliver on commitments
3. Admit mistakes

Timely and Complete Communications

The more you can share, the more confident the group will feel. And when you can't share something, tell them up front that you know the answer, but aren't at liberty to say. People understand this and respect it more than if they suspect you know but just won't say. Some managers have told me that they are reluctant to share information because the situation is changing so fast that they don't want to give out incorrect information. This is a valid concern. But there is a solution. Explain up front that the situation is fluid and dynamic, changing day to day, or sometimes even hour to hour. Then tell them that you are committed to give them as accurate and timely information as possible; however, because of the shifting situation, things may change. So, when you give an update, use the term "today's truth." This actually works very well. I've been through several instances where facilities were facing the possibility of closure. The anxiety and frustration levels in these situations can become almost unbearable. As a result, productivity drops off and safety incidents increase because people are either so concerned about the possibilities of closure that they don't focus on the tasks at hand or they withdraw and emotionally check out as a mechanism for coping. It can almost be a "self-fulfilling prophesy." They are so certain that they will be closed that they give up, productivity drops off and the falling production numbers seals the fate of the organization. By keeping people as informed as practical, they at least know that they have all the information available and that provides some since of control and reinforces that you are being fair and up front. Remember, the certainty of pain is more bearable than the pain of uncertainty.

INTERESTING HISTORICAL FOOTNOTE: In January of 1848 Edgar Allan Poe wrote about the pain of uncertainty to a friend as he described the daily horror of his vigils at the bedside of his ailing wife: "I became insane, with long intervals of horrible sanity. During those fits of absolute unconsciousness, I drank—God only knows how often or how much. As a matter of course, my enemies referred the insanity to the drink rather than the drink to the insanity. I had, indeed, nearly abandoned all hope of a permanent cure, when I found one in the death of my wife. This I can and do endure as becomes a man. It was the horrible never-ending oscillation between hope and despair which I could not longer have endured, without total loss of reason."

Edgar Allan Poe
American Author and Poet (1809–1849)

Deliver on Commitments

The second element of becoming trustworthy is doing what you say you're going to do. Do not make promises that you are not certain you will be able to keep. If it is not within your power to deliver, say so up front. If you commit to going to bat for someone, follow through. Let them know that you did what was possible. In the initial stages of a relationship, when there is not a deep pool of experience from which to make comparison, a few actions or words have a significant impact. Imagine you have an employee who is late for work; if the employee has a long history of reliability and promptness working with you, you would probably be more worried than angry. When the employee does arrive and you find that it was mechanical problems or traffic, you may just give her a good-natured hard time. How would this situation be different if it were her first day on the job? Or arriving for an interview? If you are like most people, there would be a significant difference in your perception and the significance you assign to the event. So, lead by example—say what you will do and then do what you say.

Admit Mistakes

The third key element to building trust is honestly admitting your mistakes. There are some people who make excuses or deny the obvious when they are clearly in the wrong. This only adds dry tinder to the fire. When you make a mistake, say so. Don't cover, don't justify, and don't pass the buck. When you own up to your mistakes, you will build credibility with your team. It will also set the tone for them to own up to their mistakes. Remember, as many politicians have learned, openly addressing minor mistakes is far easier than dealing with the lies perpetrated covering them up.

By setting expectations that everyone will abide by these three simple tenets that you personally demonstrate day in and day out you will lay the foundation of an open and honest workplace that fosters trust in you and among all the members.

Committing Element 4: Performance Feedback Is Appropriate and Timely

Trust is essential, but what should you do when trust is broken? Address it. Managers who are conflict averse may shy away from providing feedback because they don't want to create more problems and escalate the level of tension and conflict within the department; however, failure to address subpar behavior undermines the integrity of the organization and sows the seeds of fragmentation. Too many managers grumble about certain employees while never actually addressing those employees directly. Other members notice. They know who is contributing and who isn't. When they believe that the work is not being divided fairly or that certain individuals consistently fail to deliver on their commitments with seemingly no consequences, they begin to doubt the organization's commitment to its values and to excellence. They'll see the double standard and recognize the inequity. Failure to address situations where members don't fulfill their obligations and commitments only serves to reinforce substandard performance. It is imperative that each individual receive direct, timely, and specific feedback on their behaviors.

Avoid the "But" Sandwich

I've had many managers tell me that they like to give "balanced" feedback. They include positive feedback along with the feedback for improvement. I agree that you should provide both types of feedback. Employees shouldn't feel like the only time they hear from their manager is when there is a problem. Managers should spend as much if not more time pointing out what is going well as they point out the areas for improvement. The problem occurs when the positive feedback is only provided as a precursor to negative feedback. Too many managers serve their employees "but" sandwiches. A "but" sandwich is made up of a "positive," a "but," and a "positive." When the only positive feedback given is sugar coating on the bitter pill to follow, the compliment, no matter how sincere or valid, is not valued. People hear a compliment and wait for the "but" that will surely follow. Other managers I've worked with try to alleviate this by changing the "but" to "and." This doesn't work, and people see through it; an "and" is a "but" by another name when overused. The "but" sandwich has been justified by some who say that, "There is always room for improvement." This is true; it is important to give balanced feedback. When your employees hear compliments only when preceding something they did wrong, they focus on what is to come, thereby negating the praise. People will appreciate hearing that they are doing well and will be more receptive to feedback for improvement when it is given honestly with the specific intent of helping them improve in the spirit of excellence. Remember the four reasons why people follow a leader:

1. They trust the leader
2. The leader cares about them
3. The leader is committed to excellence
4. The leader is headed somewhere they want to go

Providing appropriate feedback reinforces all of these.

The Odometer in the Trunk

Not only is it important that employees receive appropriate feedback, it is equally important that the feedback is timely enough to be acted upon. Scolding the puppy for wetting the carpet last week is not going to change its behaviors. The more the feedback relies strictly on managers or supervisors to deliver it sets up fall points in the system. The more automated and timely the feedback mechanism is the more effective it will be. In sports, no one has to tell you when you swing and miss—it is readily apparent. You know it right away and you can work to correct it.

Focusing Element 2 defined a management operating system as an interconnected set of elements comprised of inputs, activities, and processes that work in concert with each other to deliver an output. An essential element that keeps systems in control is maintaining a timely view to the process. Having a timely view to the process provides feedback that allows employees to make corrections in a manner that maximizes quality with minimal waste. Too often process feedback is delivered in aggregate weeks or months after the fact. Companies often don't know if they had a good month until after period close or even the following quarter. This is the business equivalent of driving a car with no speedometer—having only an odometer in the trunk. When the traffic cop pulls you over and asks, "Do you know how fast you were going?" you answer, "No officer, but I can calculate it." You check the odometer in the trunk, get the number of miles traveled, check your watch and get the time, pull out your calculator and respond, "Officer, I'm happy to report that on average I was travelling 55 mph." Unimpressed, the officer writes you your ticket and tells you your court date. But on average, you weren't breaking the law. The more closely you can monitor your processes, the more readily you'll be able to keep them in control.

Leading versus Lagging Indicators

Feedback after the fact is better than no feedback. Instantaneous feedback is better; better still are indicators that predict the future so that you can address the issues and avoid poor quality and waste altogether. Metrics that have strong correlation with future events are called leading indicators; metrics that report after the fact are called lagging indicators. Lagging indicators inform after the fact whether a system's past outputs or outcomes are within standards. Leading indicators build quality into the process thus eliminating the problem before poor quality is produced. A lagging indicator of heart disease is when you have a heart attack. Far superior is avoiding the heart attack altogether by controlling the leading indicators of high cholesterol, excessive weight, and lack of exercise. In the same manner, taking the time to identify and put in place leading indicators promotes the health and longevity of the organization.

EXAMPLE: The process of making plywood involves shaving the circumference of trees into long thin sheets, gluing the sheets layer upon layer, and pressing the resultant composite board flat under applied pressure until the glue dries and the wood cures. There are literally hundreds of variables that can affect the resultant quality of the finished plywood product. Struggling with inconsistent quality a plywood mill spent significant time researching the dozens of variables involved. Through systematic research, they found that of all the variables involved, only three had significant impact: amount of glue (less is better), amount of pressure applied, and humidity control. Prior to doing the research to determine these three leading quality indicators the firm lost time and generated excessive waste chasing all the variable trying to get their processes in control. Identifying the key three leading indicators allowed them to quit focusing on the distracters and concentrate all of their efforts where they made the greatest difference. Subsequently the firm's quality improved, waste was reduced, and profits were increased.

Committing Element 5: Leaders Are Engaged and Act as Mentors

To build a committed workforce leadership needs to be both fully aligned and fully engaged. Many change initiatives fail because they aren't supported by the entire organization from top to bottom. Some are driven from the top partially down, some grassroots initiatives start and whither from lack of support from above, while others are nothing more than superficial activities that give the illusion of activity without changing the core drivers. As we explored in Focusing Element 1, every leader at every level needs to fully understand, be fully supportive, and be able to effectively communicate the vision within their areas of responsibility to create the cascading communications that facilitates alignment and optimization. Accordingly, if you are truly committed to making organizational transformation, you must be confident of the level of engagement of those responsible for implementing the initiatives and monitor the messages being disseminated at all levels. Otherwise, transformation won't occur in the areas of managers and leaders who are only half-heartedly engaged. The effectiveness of all other organizational areas and functions impacted by those areas will be encumbered as well.

As has been stated before and will be again, the status quo exists to serve the status quo. Change implies loss, and most frequently, the loss is borne by the individuals at the lower levels of the changing organization. Process improvement efforts may cost operators their jobs and teaming initiatives may eliminate levels of management and supervision. Those who may be adversely affected have a vested interest in ensuring that the change fails and their jobs are protected—or so they believe. This line of thinking can result in mired improvements, low productivity, and low profits that result in the entire facility being closed, costing everyone their jobs, including those who wanted things to continue on forever unaltered from the way they had always been.

Even when there is not an imminent threat to one's job, there are some individuals who tend to not share information and not empower their subordinates. They may do this out of a mistaken view that knowledge is power, believing that if they have knowledge that someone else doesn't they will be able to continue to exercise power over them. They may also believe that because of the knowledge they hoard, they are irreplaceable—impervious to downsizing and layoffs. Such was the case of "Jerry and the Coating Machine."

EXAMPLE: JERRY AND THE COATING MACHINE: Jerry was a supervisor who had been promoted from the ranks. He had been at the plant longer than any of the managers and executives and longer than most of the other employees who operated the machine. Jerry didn't believe in training his people. He closely guarded his knowledge like a secret treasure. When he made adjustments to the machine, he would do so with his back to the operations crew. Asked by one operator, "Jerry, what are you doing? Can you show me?" Jerry responded, "Don't ever touch that; if it needs to be adjusted I'll do it." Jerry trained his crew by rote memory—push this, now push this, then push that and turn this. The crew could perform satisfactorily when the machine operated normally. However, when things went awry, Jerry's crew couldn't troubleshoot and fix the problem (refer to the discussion on systems-based training in Committing Element 2). When the machine broke down, production came to a standstill until Jerry arrived to rescue the crew and set the world right again. To compound the problem, Jerry lived an hour away from the factory. As you can imagine, Jerry's crew had low morale, low production, and poor efficiency numbers.

Eventually, the management couldn't ignore the poor production in Jerry's area any longer, so he was fired. Jerry's "knowledge is power" strategy backfired. I was asked to work with the senior operator to develop a training program that would empower the crew. Since I didn't know much about the coater and neither did the operator, we set out to figure it out. With old equipment manufacturer manuals, blueprints, and drawings dug out and dusted off from the engineering library archives in hand, Brandon and I set out to decipher some mysteries. We loaded up some off-quality paper in the backstand and started the coating systems running only water. When it was time to apply the spray to the running paper, I asked Brandon to go through the process methodically so we could document the machine response.

"Now, I push these three buttons in succession, 1, 2, 3." Each button on the control panel was labeled in Jerry's handwriting.

"OK, push number one." Nothing—no system response. "Push number two." Still nothing. "Oh-kay, push number three." The coater head rotated up into the spray position, and a flow of water began coating the running sheet just as it would if it had actually been coating. "Hmm, I wonder what the first two buttons do?"

Brandon shrugged his shoulders. "Don't know, maybe they're interlocks."

The blueprints weren't any help. They hadn't been updated in decades since the original design and installation of the machine. To investigate, we shut the machine back down and crawled around the panels and piping to trace out the leads to see where they went.

To my surprise, and Brandon's dismay, when we crawled behind the panel, we found that both buttons one and two had their wires cut off in the back. They were attached to nothing and, consequently, did nothing. At some point in the past, they probably did something, but hadn't done so for a long, long time. Brandon was clearly embarrassed. "I feel so stupid. I've been pushing those buttons for five years."

"Hey, don't feel bad; you're not stupid; you were doing what you were trained to do. You operated this equipment as Jerry had taught you."

We continued to trace out and document operations, and little by little, the crew's knowledge increased, as did their pride, their ownership, and their commitment along with the machine's efficiencies, production quality, and output.

Though extreme, Jerry isn't the only supervisor out there who trains his crews to operate on "myth and superstition." When I was first trained aboard ship to start up a piping system called air ejectors, the engine room operator told me to "open this valve first, then this valve, and then that valve." "What happens if I open that valve first?" "You don't." "OK, I won't, but what if I did?" "You don't. Here, let me make it simple for you." He took out an ink pen and wrote 1, 2, 3 on the respective valve handwheels, just like Jerry. I really wanted to open them 3-2-1, or 2-1-3, or 1-3-2, but I never did. I just opened them in the order I had been told. Only later, when I traced out the piping systems, did I learn that the first was the 150-psig steam inlet, the second was the steam discharge, and the third was the suction to the condenser. If you opened the suction before the discharge, there was a theoretical chance that the 150-psig steam could flow backward and risk damaging the condenser by overpressurizing a vessel designed to operate at a vacuum. Now it made sense. If you teach the people the "why" they are more likely to understand and comply with the "how."

The Role of Mentor

To execute your strategy, transform your processes, and create a high-performing organization you'll need "all hands on deck"—leaders as well as crew members. When leaders are appropriately engaged and available to support team members they provide opportunities for members to develop their skills and advance in their careers. Paradoxically, the more leaders develop their people to act independently they actually increase their own spans of control and authority. People do the right thing even when no one is watching because they understand why it's the right thing to do and thus they become more committed to the overall success of the organization. Contrast this with the disengaged leader.

When leaders aren't engaged in day-to-day operations, frequently absent in endless meetings or sequestered in their offices, they are inaccessible and provide little if any support. This lack of timely engagement gives rise to situations that erupt, requiring crisis management. In their firefighting mode, decisions are often based on partial information. This lack of sufficient information comes partially from the limited time the crisis affords the manager to assess the situation and partially because crew members may not be willing to offer up much information. The oft-absent manager often lacks credibility with the crew resulting in their unwillingness to offer up support. They won't necessarily lie, but they won't offer up anything additional beyond what is specifically asked. Poor information leads to poor decisions which ignites crisis after crisis. Each new crisis requires extraordinary effort on the part of the crew to react and implement damage control. The order gets filled, and the report gets done, but at a high cost that extracts a toll; after a while, nothing is really a crisis because everything's a crisis. A consistently reactionary environment leaves little opportunities for individual learning and growth. People's skills stagnate; creativity is drained from the exhausted organization—people get burned out. They go through the motions but their hearts aren't really in it.

To turn the tide and engender commitment, all leaders at every level must consistently answer in the affirmative the four critical questions follower's ask of their leaders introduced during Forming:

1. Can I trust you?
2. Do you care about me?
3. Are you committed to excellence?
4. Are you going somewhere I want to go?

The best way to show someone that you care about them and to build trust is to mentor them, help grow their skills, and support their decisions.

Committing Element 6: Strong Leadership and Appropriate Delegation of Authority

Learning to trust your employees, delegate, and let go is one of the hardest competencies for individuals to master as they develop into effective leaders. Delegation doesn't mean uninvolved. As we discussed in Forming Element 6, there is a distinct difference between delegation and abdication. It is critical to organizational success to have strong leadership and it is equally important to share authority and delegate appropriately. It is one of the many paradoxes of leadership; the tighter hold you have, the closer you are to losing control. So how do you strike that fine balance between control and autonomy? It can only be accomplished by defining your span of control and setting clear limits on delegated authority.

Span of Control

Most of us maintain the illusion that we are in control of much more than we actually are; this little coping mechanism helps each of us get out of bed every morning and face the day. However, if we are truly honest with ourselves, the only thing each of us can even hope to control is the person who greets us each morning in the mirror; even then, that level of control is questionable. So, when you consider your own span of control, think of it as concentric circles like ever-widening ripples on a pond—the further away from the center, the more the energy dissipates and the less impact the ripples have. Accordingly, it is important to recognize what's within your control, what's within your influence, and that which you are aware of; everything else remains hidden, waiting to be discovered (Figure 4.12).

In life there are things which you directly control (the frequency which you brush and floss your teeth for instance). There is some broader range of things you influence though you may not directly have control over them (toddlers and pets). There is an even greater sphere of things you are aware of, but have no influence or control over (teenagers come to mind). Beyond that, there is a vast array of things of which you have no knowledge of whatsoever (represented by the unknown space of the Johari Window). To be effective and not frustrated all the time, it helps to keep

Figure 4.12 Span of control and influence.

these differentiations clearly in mind: be conscientious toward and take responsibility for those things you control. Be mindful and diligent of those things you can influence. Be cognizant of what you are aware of and always try to expand your level of awareness. Finally, don't ignore those previously unknown things that pop up on your radar screen. They may have profound impact on your life, and the sooner you understand if they're friend or foe, benign or deadly, the more effective you'll be at maintaining the ship of your life on an even keel and heading on a steady course.

Triggers and Limits of Authority

When we discussed systems design and behavioral drivers, we defined how triggers lead to responses. Essential to efficient operation is the timing. Figure 4.13 shows how triggers, timing, and feedback extend the framework of roles and responsibilities within the Vessel of Organizational Success©.

Within mechanical and electrical systems, the coordination and timing are built in through relays and linkages; this is frequently not the case for management operating systems. One person hands off the task to the next, where it is delayed. The delay may be due to lack of awareness ("Your email went to my junk mail."), competing priorities ("Sorry, I had 17 other things ahead of yours."), or lack of empowerment ("I was waiting for approval from the committee."). These delays are all examples of fall points described in Focusing Element 5.

Essential to organizational effectiveness is defining the span of control including the limits of authority along with the behavioral triggers. It may seem counterintuitive, but clearly defining limits and boundaries is actually empowering. Doing so also minimizes confusion, prevents misunderstanding, and reduces conflicts; even toddlers know how frustrating it is when

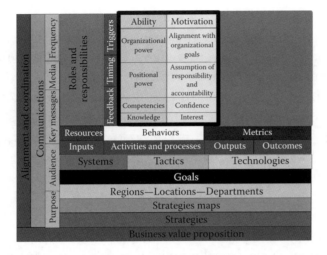

Figure 4.13   The timbers of ability and motivation.

they think something is within their control only to have someone countermand their decisions. When setting up management operating systems and subsequently assigning roles and establishing accountability, spelling out clear limits of authority establishes autonomy within the boundaries of their authority and span of control. It lets people know what authority they have and how broadly that authority extends. This empowers the organization to act while at the same time maintaining a level of comfort for you. For instance, front line supervisors may be fully empowered to make all decisions that relate to employee scheduling and line production as long as the decisions don't impact safety or delay production for more than four hours. Another example of setting limits of authority could be giving department managers signature authority of up to $10,000; higher value purchases require submitting an engineering review along with a business case justification through the purchasing department review board. These examples are not meant to be recommendations; they only serve to illustrate how some firms have set limits of authority and control, thus empowering their employees to act independently within their defined span of control.

By clearly defining the space within which people can freely act empowers creativity. People become liberated to make decisions and act quickly in response to the needs of the process. Uncertainty of the limits of their authority, questions whether their decisions will be countermanded, and concerns for overstepping some unknown boundary that may shift from situation to situation and day-to-day limits engagement. When people feel they are in a potential minefield, fear inhibits them from acting.

One of the key lessons the U.S. Military learned from the Vietnam War is that those closest to the situation usually have the greatest awareness of the actual conditions on the ground and are best suited to make quality decisions; limiting their authority and their ability to make decisions to respond in a timely manner is costly and impedes mission accomplishment. The same is true in virtually every other organization that desires a responsive and empowered workforce. It is critical to empowerment to delegate the authority to those who are accountable. Too often people are given responsibility and accountability without authority; this only sets them up for failure.

Authority must accompany responsibility to be effective. However, delegating authority requires more than just simply stating who is in charge. Saying doesn't necessarily make it so. The outcome may still lie outside the designated leader's span of control because it may not be within their ability to control or they may lack the motivation. Thus, when you empower, you must first consider the individual's ability and their motivation.

Factors Affecting Ability and Motivation

To be truly "in control" requires all the elements and drivers affecting a situation to be maintained under your direct command such that you can execute the task when and how you deem appropriate. This is why your sphere of influence clearly extends well beyond your sphere of absolute control. Understanding the limits of control and influence helps managers explore why performance falls short of expectations. We introduced the performance analysis within Committing Element 2 with the initial discussion of ability and motivation (will vs. skill). We'll dig down deeper into this analysis with a deeper exploration of these two concepts.

The assessment of an employee's ability is often limited to weighing their knowledge and competence to perform a task. In the same manner, the determination of motivation is generally limited to someone's interest in the task. These views are incomplete because someone may have knowledge, competence, and interest for a given task but still be unsuccessful in accomplishing the task as directed. Knowledge, competence, and interest are essential but insufficient to ensuring successful task completion. Several more factors are involved with both ability and motivation. Figure 4.13 uncovers the timbers that combine to build ability and motivation within the Vessel of Organizational Success.

The Four Factors Governing Ability

The ability to perform a task is dependent upon four factors:

1. Knowledge—I need to have an understanding of the principles, concepts, as well as the facts that govern the execution and quality of the task.
2. Competencies—combined with the knowledge, I must be able to apply what I know competently. There are those with a theoretical book knowledge who don't have the competence to execute.
3. and 4. Power to deliver (formal and informal)—just because you are capable of doing something doesn't mean you'll be able to do it. For individual contributors who don't rely on the involvement of others to accomplish a task, knowledge and competence are usually all that is required to perform their roles and deliver on their responsibilities. However, when the task depends upon the cooperation and collaboration of others, knowledge and competence alone are often insufficient. Power is required. When someone has power, they can compel others to act, as was shown again in the diagram in Figure 4.14. Power flows from two sources, one formal and the other informal.

   a. Formal power is generally related to the position within the organizational hierarchy. Positional power exists when one individual is given

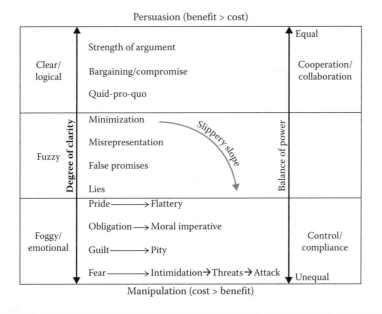

Figure 4.14   Compelling behavior.

defined and explicit control over another. This is widely understood in supervisor–subordinate relationships. This type of power is fairly simple to understand: "That which interests my boss fascinates me." When your boss tells you to do something, you are inclined to do it to avoid any negative consequences that may affect your livelihood.

b. Informal organizational power can be more impactful than formal positional power, but the sources of informal organizational power are more nebulous. Within most organizations, there are those who seem to wield more influence than their formal position or title indicates. Informal organizational power generally stems from one of three sources:

(1) Individual expertise—The power of expertise exists when others recognize someone for their knowledge and skills that are valued by the organization. Their opinion matters because they are recognized experts in the field.

(2) The power of persona—The power of persona surrounds someone who is able to influence others through relationships. Their charisma, drive, or persuasive abilities compel others to follow them. Those with the power of persona are often referred to as "natural leaders."

(3) Relationships to formal power positions—Sometimes people draw their strength not from their own expertise or their natural leadership abilities but rather from who they know. This relationship power is often the most resented and can be frequently abused.

When looking at the graphical representation of the span of control shown in Figure 4.15, formal power can be closely aligned with control while inform organizational power can be correlated with influence. Our purpose for this discussion is not to explore all the sources of power but

Figure 4.15 Power's impact on the span of control and influence.

recognize that, regardless of its source, power is required along with knowledge and competence for someone to have the ability to perform. Without power, someone with knowledge and competence is generally positionally limited to being an individual contributor. This explains why some managers must frequently do things themselves: they are ineffectual at wielding their positional power and lack the power of influence to motivate others to act. We will discuss this more when we talk about performance management during the Sustaining Stage.

One final point to make about power is that the sources of power are additive. A manager with formal positional power is even more powerful when he or she also has informal organizational power based upon expertise and persona. If you add in being related to the president of the company, you have a very powerful person indeed.

If an individual possesses all four ingredients of ability, you can feel confident that they have the skill to perform the delegated task. Whether they actually perform the task as desired will depend upon whether they have the right motivational ingredients.

The Four Factors Determining Motivation

Just as there are four factors governing ability, there are four essential ingredients that determine motivation. Motivation depends upon the following:

1. Interest—I may have all the ability in the world, but if I lack the interest, I may not act, and if I do, it will be hard to sustain the motivation to keep it going. Thus, interest is certainly an essential ingredient for motivation, but interest alone will not always result in effective and impactful activities.
2. Confidence—I may be interested in doing a task, but I may not have the confidence that compels me to act. My fear impedes my action.
3. Willingness to assume responsibility and accountability—There are some who have an interest in doing a task that they are confident they would be good at, but they fail to act because they don't want to be held accountable for the results. They refuse to take responsibility to avoid being accountable.
4. Alignment with organizational goals—Individuals may have interest in a task, be confident in their abilities, and perfectly willing to assume responsibility and willing to be accountable, but their purposes are counter to the organization's mission and vision. Technically speaking,

the individual is motivated, but without alignment to the organization's goals, leaders should be careful how much authority they delegate to the individual. They are willing to lead; you're just not certain which direction they will lead.

Ability and motivation are essential for effective performance. When an individual is imbued with both it is likely they will perform successfully. As a leader, keep this in mind when you delegate: authority must accompany responsibility; otherwise, the foundation for failure is laid.

Despite your best intentions, this may not always be possible because of the very structure of the organization. Some organizational structures are better suited for effective leadership and appropriate delegation of authority.

The Seeds of Confusion Inherent within Matrixed Organizations

Delegation without the empowerment of authority is a condition pervasive within many low-performing organizations. This is particularly true in highly "matrixed" organizations. As organizations work to do more with less, there has been a movement toward "matrix" management. A matrix is an interconnected web where elements are linked to two or more others. Ostensibly, modern organizations adopt matrix organizational formats to promote cooperation and break down silos. An alternate reason for implementing matrix management is to fill voids in leadership left by layoffs, downsizing, and closures. Matrix management is also frequently found in low-performing organizations steeped in entitlement; because there are so many low-performing managers, those with strong leadership capabilities are unduly tasked with multiple projects throughout the organization.

RIDING THE GOOD HORSE: I call the management style whereby a manager consistently relies on the work of a few such that the division of labor is greatly unbalanced "riding the good horse." There may be dozens of horses in a stable but the owner always rides his best, the one or two that are fast, reliable, and don't complain. While the chosen horses are overridden and underrested, the other horses stand idly by, watching from the sidelines. These other horses could be feeling resentful that they're never given an opportunity or they could embrace their entitlement—neither is of concern to the rider nor any comfort to the tired horses. Eventually, a "good horse" succumbs to the unrelenting pace. When this occurs, the rider usually brings in another horse outside the fold rather than bother with those he's written off in the stable.

Where individuals have multiple reporting relations and are assigned to manage projects made up of members from multiple other departments, their efforts are invariably divided among multiple conflicting priorities. In addition, team members assigned to these cross-functional projects have little if any accountability to the project manager. Their success is measured against the priorities of their primary job assignments by the department managers to whom they directly report, not the collateral tasks that fall under "other duties as assigned." Consequently, they have little vested interest in the success of the project. Whether by design or by default, what invariably ends up happening is that individuals are left trying to satisfy multiple managers with conflicting priorities and little accountability. Project outcomes suffer as a result.

Seasoned employees know the track record of these grand schemes referred to as "Program of the Month," "Flavor of the Day," or another equally cynical moniker. Not wanting to be held accountable for something they have little authority to execute, these projects are generally managed by consensus. Because there is strength in numbers and it is easier to hide in a crowd, decisions are delayed until a large enough consensus has been developed such that everyone is covered by plausible deniability; if we all decided together, then no one individual is accountable.

Because of the chaos, confusion, and frequently poor outcomes created within matrixed managed organizations, the most efficient and effective organizations limit this organizational structure in favor of a more structured chain of command.

Importance of the Chain of Command

The concept of a chain of command is traditionally associated with military organizations, and unfortunately, many civilian organizations chafe against formalizing their organizational reporting relations. They think that the concept is counter to creativity and high performance; I completely disagree.

To be very clear up front, utilizing a chain of command is not the same as utilizing a command and control organization. I strongly support the former while strongly rejecting reliance on the latter. Utilizing a situation-based approach to leadership is essential to effective organizations regardless of the

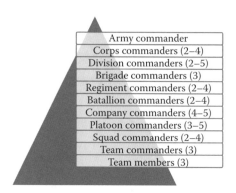

Figure 4.16 Army chain of command.

organizational structure. Establishing a defined chain of command clarifies communication and promotes the distribution and delegation of authority by dividing larger groups into smaller, more manageable teams. Each organizational level has a clearly defined reporting relationship both above and below. In addition to the reporting relationship, dividing the larger group into smaller teams improves the supervisory ratio allowing each leader the opportunity to give ample support to the individuals reporting to them thereby promoting a true mentor/mentee relationship. To illustrate, refer to Figure 4.16 as we discuss a very successful chain of command structure.

United States Army Organizational Structure

The foundation of the United States Army is the individual soldier. Each individual soldier is assigned to a team: team members (three per team) report to the team commander, who reports to the squad commander (three teams per squad), who reports to the platoon commander (two to four squads), who reports to the company commander (three to five platoons), who reports to the battalion commander (four to five companies), who reports to the regiment commander (three to five battalions), then the brigade commander (two to four regiments), then the division commander (three brigades), and then the corps commander (two to five divisions), who reports to an army field commander (two to five corps).

The strength of this organizational structure ensures that each of over 70,000 individuals within the organization have clearly defined, understood, and respected responsibilities and accountabilities. Leadership is developed at every level, and no single individual directly supervises more than five individuals.

Strengths of an Organizational Chain of Command

An effective chain of command provides three key operational features:

1. Effective mentor to mentee ratio
2. Effective cascading communications
3. Effective accountability

Effective Mentor to Mentee Ratio

Compare the leadership ratio of the U.S. Army (1:5) to a supervisor in a paper manufacturing plant (1:60). In a northern mill I worked with, each shift supervisor had responsibility for three paper machines (five operators each), three rereelers (three operators each), four supercalendars (two operators each), four winders (three operators each), a forktruck driver, the color kitchen (two operators), the repulper (two operators), and shift maintenance (two mechanics) as well as two to three extras to support training and to provide vacation relief. Each supervisor was directly responsible for between 55 to 60 individuals, and you can lay odds that not all of those individuals were as carefully selected, rigorously trained, nor nearly as self-disciplined as the members of the United States Army. Granted, each piece of equipment had a senior operator that was expected to lead the others operating the machinery, but because of the union guidelines, hourly operators were allowed to only give directions limited strictly to operating the equipment—they didn't provide holistic support for developing the five spheres of competence within their team members. The crews operated on 12-hour shift schedules, alternating between days and nights. This meant that each crew worked about half the year on shift, approximately 26 weeks. Given that most supervisors had four weeks of vacation, they had 22 weeks a year with their crews. In those 22 weeks, each supervisor was expected to complete targeted developmental plans for 60 individuals providing a minimum of two reviews per year (a midyear and an end of year performance review). How well could you give 110–120 well thought out, individually specific, and meaningful performance reviews in the 22 weeks available? Even if this were their only responsibility, that would mean that every working week, each supervisor would need to give five to six counseling sessions. Between production runs, scheduling changes, maintenance breakdowns, operations problems, etc., it was completely unrealistic to expect that the supervisors were able to give anything more than the most cursory guidance to any individual. Instead, they managed by exception. They spent their time on whatever crisis arose and the rest slid by the wayside.

This inordinately large supervisor to employee ratio is not that uncommon. I've seen ratios as high as 100:1. As businesses work to cut costs they "optimize," "right-size," "smart-size," "down-size," "flatten," and otherwise lower their fixed costs through the reduction of employees, these ratios become more and more the norm. There is no possible way that a person can really know, let alone effectively mentor that many subordinates.

So what is a realistic ratio? Throughout the ages, 1:10 is considered the maximum effective ratio. The Bible tells how Moses was becoming overwhelmed listening to each of the individual issues and concerns of the Hebrew Nation as they wandered through the dessert. To alleviate the overwhelming burden, Jethro, Moses' father-in-law, advised him to delegate his authority to others subdividing the tribe into tens, hundreds (10 groups of 10), and thousands (10 groups of 10 groups of 10) (Exodus 18). The Roman legions were similarly subdivided such that each leader held charge over 5–10 men. So, if Moses couldn't effectively manage more than 10, think carefully before you try to effectively manage dozens or more.

Effective Cascading Communications

The effectiveness of a well-structured chain of command extends beyond effective developmental leadership. The chain of command creates a chain of communications. Each group leader is responsible to ensure that their team fully understands and complies with the directions provided. This division of communication helps to ensure a well-aligned organization. Earlier, the communication process was outlined to show how you may have to go through a cycle multiple times before agreement and alignment are reached. When you are trying to communicate with a multitude of people, in depth communication will not occur. Communication will simply be a "tell" and the level of commitment will be minimal.

Effective Accountability

The third reason for defining an effective chain of command is probably the most important. Without it, there will be little accountability within the organization. To illustrate the point, here's my twist on a humorous old parable of four people: Everybody, Somebody, Nobody, and Anybody.

"Somebody" Will Do It—A Parable for Our Times

The Acme Widget Factory had four employees: Everybody, Somebody, Nobody and Anybody. One day Acme's best customer called in an important unscheduled job that they needed done right away. Everybody assumed that Somebody would do it. When Nobody did it, the customer took the work to Somewhere Else. Everybody became angry and blamed Somebody for not doing what Anybody could have done. If only Everybody hadn't assumed that Somebody would do it, Everybody would still be employed. The moral of the story is that if Everybody's responsible, then Nobody's accountable.

Defining an Effective Chain of Command

You may be shaking your head right now and thinking, "Wow, this guy wants me to double the size of my organization and add all kinds of middle management. There is no way I can afford that." Let me dispel that thought: I am not advocating for adding layer upon inept layer to an organization. What I am advocating for is a direct line of accountability that is clearly understood and effectively utilized. You don't have to have scores of middle-management writing reports and building empires to justify their positions, but you do need to have clear reporting relationships and aligned objectives.

1. Define your reporting relationships with everyone directly accountable to someone; matrix management structures where individuals have multiple accountabilities add confusion and weaken accountability.
2. Utilize the chain of command for effective communications both up and down the chain. A chain of command is only effective if it is respected by every member of the organization (no bypassing up or down the chain). When an organization allows the chain of command to be bypassed, breakdowns in communication, authority, accountability, and efficiency ensue. Let me cite an example.

Problems Created by Bypassing Up the Chain of Command

Each individual should have someone from whom they take their directions and to whom they are directly accountable. Without this, there is miscommunication and inefficient operations. A common example occurs when a senior manager has direct contact with an individual not directly under their supervision.

EXAMPLE: Lyle prided himself as being a maverick; many people suspected him of using drugs based on his aggressive and erratic behavior. He was aggressive toward coworkers and difficult to manage; Lyle knew how to work the system; he had successfully done it for years. He knew the HR policies and labor contract by heart—better than his supervisors or managers who hadn't taken the time to learn. He knew just how far to push the system and how to always maintain "plausible deniability." Many managers had tried to manage Lyle and failed. Invariably, in their impotent frustration, they would transfer Lyle out of their department—never addressing the problem, just shifting it to someone else. Finally, Lyle was transferred off the production line to the shipping department. The shipping manager at the time was determined not to just pass the problem off to someone else. He began the drawn out process of performance management, documenting each interaction and each instance Lyle failed to perform at the required level. Lyle, chaffing at being managed, fired back with an email to the CEO of the company claiming he was being persecuted in a "hostile" work environment.

Now, one would think that if the CEO of a multibillion-dollar corporation received an email from an hourly operator at a plant, he would write back and say, "Did you talk to your management at the mill?" If nothing else, you'd expect a high-powered executive to at least give the management team the benefit of the doubt and assume they were innocent until proven guilty. Nope, that's not what happened. He forwarded the email to the plant manager and the HR manager with a flaming note in all caps, "INVESTIGATE THIS AND TELL ME WHAT YOU ARE DOING ABOUT THIS SUPERVISOR!"

The supervisor was reprimanded for trying to manage a long-standing and ongoing problem. He was directed to "work with the employee and make him feel valued," "empower him," and "validate his emotions." As you can imagine, Lyle's performance didn't get any better. He was emboldened more than ever because he knew there were never going to be any consequences to his actions. He became even more belligerent and even less productive than he had been in the past. And as far as I know, he's still there; multiple managers have come and gone, but Lyle remains.

Respecting the chain of command means that individuals must go through their supervisors with problems or concerns. If there is a concern that the supervisor is the problem creating a hostile environment or that there may be repercussions against the individual, there should be channels where the individual can seek support through local HR or through the supervisor's manager. When something like this happens, appropriate procedures must be followed; however, the process must be nonbiased and nonjudgmental until a complete investigation has been conducted, and the benefit of the doubt should lean toward the supervisor. Otherwise, some employees will utilize the system as Lyle did to avoid accountability.

Unless the problem is one of harassment or creating a hostile work environment, the appropriate response to an individual who bypasses their supervisor is, "Did you speak to your supervisor about this? Once you do, and you still can't come to a solution, then come talk to me with your supervisor." If the organizational reporting structure is not respected up the chain, it is tantamount to when a child tattles on their sibling to get the sibling in trouble. It puts the supervisor on the same level as the subordinate, undermines their authority, and removes their ability to manage. To maintain an effective organization, supervisors and managers must be allowed to, and held accountable for, managing their employees. The same situation occurs in the public sector. When citizens call up politicians and the politicians respond directly without investigating the veracity of the call, the credibility of the caller, or the requirements of the process, then the ability to govern erodes just as rapidly as it does in a for-profit corporation.

The other problem that occurs with this condition is a disproportionate distribution of work. What work Lyle didn't do had to be picked up by all his other coworkers. They took up the slack and resented it; they resented Lyle and the resented management for their inability/unwillingness to manage. Bypassing the chain of command invariably leads to inequities in work.

Problems Created by Bypassing Down the Chain of Command

Far more common than bypassing up the chain is bypassing down—particularly in matrixed organizations. Bypassing down the chain of command occurs when a manager jumps their direct report and works directly with a member further down the chain. Though opposite in direction, bypassing down the chain of command is equally disruptive to efficient operation and equally disempowering to managers and supervisors.

EXAMPLE: Paul was a director. Paul was a micromanager. Paul's temperament as indicated by his DISC space lay predominantly in the "C" quadrant, with a fair amount of overlap into "D" thrown into the mix. Skewed heavily toward being "task focused," the relationships that bound the department together were very weak. He had several managers that worked for him but he didn't trust any of them enough to allow them to manage. Paul insisted on being involved in the day-to-day details at all levels of the department. Daily, Paul would go to the offices of anyone and everyone in the organization to check on their work and make assignments—assignments the department managers knew nothing about. When a manager would attempt to task an employee they would invariably be told, "I'm sorry, Paul has me working on something else." Just as frequently, the manager would ask for the status of an assignment and they'd be told, "I didn't get to that because I was working on something else for Paul." After all, when the boss's boss tells you to do something, it obviously takes precedent over something the boss says.

Paul's micromanagement disempowered the managers from being able to effectively manage their departments. When managers did try and lead, they were frequently rebuffed and told that they must wait until Paul was available. But Paul wasn't available very often. He was so busy trying to directly manage every detail his days were endlessly consumed in meetings. Failing to effectively delegate caused his managers to withdraw and focus strictly within the very narrow confines of their immediate tactical focus; they did the work themselves that should have been delegated to others. This, in turn, limited the development of members and obscured the line of site between tasks and the organization's value proposition. Different factions formed among the various subdepartments; collaboration was minimal.

Paul limited the time horizon of his managers to periods from days to weeks. Any plan they formed could quickly be nullified by a call saying, "I need this today!" As a result, the department did not address long term strategically imperatives. The fires of day-to-day crises consumed energy, hope, and engagement. "Do it early and do it over," became the department's mantra. And still Paul saw himself as an empowering, people-focused leader. "De Nile" was not just a river in Egypt; it flowed straight through Paul's self-perception.

Turnover was high—the department stumbled, relationships fragmented, and progress leveled.

Strong Leadership Stemming from a Strong Chain of Command: The Buck Stops Here

Consistently utilizing a well-defined chain of command ensures accountability. Empowering the manager to be fully responsible for his or her area leads to full accountability. If work is not accomplished or the quality is subpar, there is clearly a point of focus: the manager. Each employee knows where their direction comes from, and the managers are able to set priorities because they fully understand the breadth of work assigned to each individual.

As a manager, I try to think of my role as a "filter." I tell my employees that as long as you are working on the tasks I've assigned you, you have nothing to worry about. If my manager is unhappy about the pace of work in my department or the prioritization of the tasks assigned, I shoulder full responsibility. In the Navy, I had an engineering officer aboard one submarine who was an extreme micromanager. Whatever whim came to his mind, he would come down to the engine room and pull my sailors off of the jobs I had assigned them. Because the mechanic needs to get appropriate tools, lock out the systems, etc., stopping in the middle of tasks completely blows project schedules, as it takes again an additional half of the time as compared to starting a job and seeing it through to completion before starting on the next assignment. In addition, leaving a string of half-finished assignments leads to unsafe conditions and poor equipment reliability. To ameliorate the situation, I began a process of telling my sailors at our "6:00 AM muster, "Here are your assignments for today. Unless you're scheduled for duty, when you get your work done, you can go home. I don't care if you're done by 10:00 AM or 10:00 PM, as long as your work is done well and done safely." I also figured in port that the crew should maximize time with their families. At sea, we worked 12 hours on and 6 hours off in a three-shift 18-hour rotation: 6 hours of watch, 6 hours of maintenance or training, and

6 hours of rack time. In port, get the work done and get home. After a while of doing this, my engineering officer came down with an "urgent" assignment but couldn't find anyone to task so he came to my office, "Where is everyone?"

"Home, Sir."

"Why?"

"They were done with the work I assigned them. If there is something that needs to be done immediately, I'd be happy to help. But if it can wait, I'm preparing tomorrow's schedule and I'll incorporate it into the crew's work plans."

"I guess it can wait." He handed me the assignment and went back to his office.

After that, all tasks and assignments went through the chain of command. Productivity in our department greatly improved, as did morale. The schedule we laid out completed all required maintenance during our shipyard overhaul and allowed the crew to spend more time at home. We finished the overhaul on schedule and under budget. For our work, our engineer awarded every member of the department. I mention this story not to brag but to specifically make the point that you can lead upwards. It's not always possible, but by working effectively and courageously, you can be the manager and leader your crew is counting on you to be.

Committing Element 7: Individuals and Teams Hold Themselves Accountable

When an organization develops to the point where members begin to commit, when they embrace the organization's mission and goals as their own, they hold themselves accountable. At this stage, members understand the systems and drivers that affect a quality outcome. Motivation is high and members willingly take responsibility. An organization can only reach this point when they have successfully navigated the Forming and Focusing Stages.

Throughout both the Forming and Focusing Stages, we discussed laying the Framework of Organizational and Team Success. As shown again in Figure 4.17, the organization has disaggregated the strategies required to achieve the mission and vision into clearly defined behavioral expectations (goals), roles, and responsibilities. Structures, systems, and metrics have been created and are being implemented along with targeted training. At

Figure 4.17   Framework for organizational success.

the team level, the foundations for success were laid along with the team composition (shown again in Figure 4.18). Effective structured and deliberate communication added coordination. Mutual respect and effectiveness were instilled through the team's working approach. The development of systems and procedures improved the team's efficiency. Finally, the team is solidified as mutual accountability emerges in the Committing Stage.

Mutual accountability can only exist when all team members hold themselves and each other responsible for their individual as well as their collective performance, behavior, and quality. Mutual accountability stems from and helps reinforce an ongoing climate of trust. In order for mutual accountability and trust to emerge, each member must understand and consistently perform the roles and responsibilities for which they are responsible, and must concurrently have confidence that others will effectively and efficiently

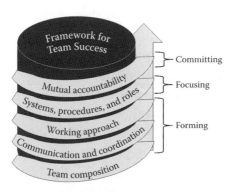

Figure 4.18   Framework for team success.

execute their assignments in a timely manner. In addition, the confidence created within climates of mutual accountability encourages members to take calculated risks. If a decision turns out poorly, individuals take responsibility; they don't pass the buck. Instead, the lessons from the decision are captured and shared to create a learning organization.

Compare the description of a culture of mutual accountability with cultures of entitlement or cultures of fear. Whether a culture of entitlement or a culture of fear the behaviors exhibited with both are surprisingly similar even though they lie on opposite ends of the spectrum. Within both climates of entitlement and climates of fear team members avoid taking responsibility. Both see accountability as another word for punishment. To avoid accountability (punishment) members are guarded, defensive, and afraid to take risks—frequently passing the buck to others or down onto subordinates. An air of caution pervades these cultures. It is better to settle for mediocrity through unanimity rather than taking a risk that might result in you being singled out as an example.

Regardless of whether the organization has a climate defined by entitlement, mutual accountability, or fear, remember that the climate or culture of an organization is only the manifestation of the multiple elements that drive behaviors. Climate cannot be directly altered; as such, a climate of *mutual accountability is an outcome*—not something that can be directly implemented or imposed. It must form naturally, and it does so only in the right environment—an environment defined by the limits of *logical consequences*.

Creating an Environment of Logical Consequences

Just as actions have reactions, behaviors have consequences. People tend to think of "consequences" in negative turns. When you say consequences, many people think strictly of punishment. In reality, consequences aren't solely negative, they can be positive as well. If I drop a glass, it shatters on the floor—a negative consequence. If I don't spend my entire paycheck, I have money left over at the end of the month and don't overdraw my checking account—a positive consequence. Some consequences are the natural result of cause and effect—dropped glasses that fall to the hard floor frequently shatter. Some consequences are imposed—additional penalties and bank fees aren't acts of nature; they are bank policies. Regardless of whether natural or imposed, consequences tend to alter behaviors. I may be more careful not to drop glasses, and I may pay closer attention to my spending during the month and stop assuming that having checks corresponds to having money.

Figure 4.19 shows a standard bell curve of normal population distribution. The vertical axis on the left represents the level of productivity from low to high; the horizontal axis represents the severity of consequences from few to dire. Where productivity is the highest is a region bounded by *logical consequences.*

A logical consequence is one that makes sense. Most of us grow up expecting consequences to be logical. If I work hard and honor my commitments, I am rewarded accordingly. Conversely, if I fail to perform, there is some cost I will bear. I won't be taken out and shot, but there will be some action commensurate with my failure to perform. An overdraft charge may not be natural, but it is logical. Natural consequences are inherently logical; imposed consequences can be or they can be wildly illogical. When looking to achieve maximum performance, it is important that the imposed consequences be logical.

In a situation where there are few if any consequences to behaviors, a climate of entitlement tends to emerge. When it doesn't matter if certain individuals work hard because they cannot be held accountable, productivity tends to drop off. The reason why individuals aren't held accountable for their individual performance doesn't matter. In general, the productivity of any protected or privileged group or individual tends to lag behind those where there are commensurate consequences given for individual effort and contribution.

On the other end of the spectrum where consequences are so severe they far outweigh any expected benefit, a climate of fear can emerge. Take balancing upon a narrow beam like a curb or railroad track for example. At one time or another, most of us have tried to walk along a narrow pathway

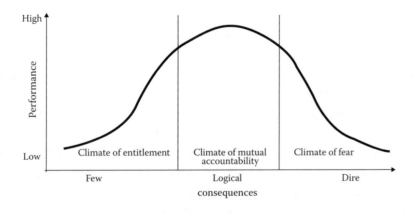

Figure 4.19   Consequences versus performance.

trying not to fall; it's kind of fun. Now imagine that same narrow path suspended across the Grand Canyon—would you risk walking across it? Unless you're one of the Flying Wallendas, you probably answered, "No way!" Why not? After all, the balance is no harder—you just have further to fall. That's the point; the consequence of losing your balance is so severe as compared to the relative satisfaction you might gain that it induces fear. When you work in an organization where the leaders frequently react in a manner far out of proportion to the triggering infraction, productivity drops off precipitously. For productivity to be at its peak, the consequences must be commensurate with performance. Here are a few common real-world examples. Imagine how motivated you'd be if you were in these situations:

■ You have been assigned to a joint project. Some of the team members rarely show up to team meetings and have yet to complete an assignment. To keep the project on track you and a few others have been putting forth the extra effort to complete every aspect of the project thereby ensuring success. At the project report dinner all of the team members are recognized by senior management for a job well done.—Entitlement

■ It doesn't matter how hard you work; the plant is probably going to close down, and there is nothing you or your team can do to change that.—Fear

■ For the past 10 years, you've been putting in long hours and really going the extra mile, sacrificing personal time away from family for the firm. Now you find that the choice position of Director of Operations you were hoping for is being given to the CEO's son who recently graduated from college.—Entitlement

■ Your firm has just been bought by a major competitor, you've heard from others that the new owners like to "clean house" and appoint their own management team.—Fear

■ Your area has been exceeding all production goals and consistently outpaces the other three shifts. When the position of Shift Lead becomes available, an operator off the shift with the lowest production levels is promoted because he has one month seniority over you.—Entitlement

■ Your new manager is really erratic: one day she is pleasant, talkative, and supportive, the next she is shrewish, insulting, and abusive. It's hard to tell which way she'll be from day to day, so everyone just tries to lay low and stay out of her way.—Fear

- Because of the tight economy, it's widely understood that pay raises will be limited. Instead of basing raises on individual performance and concentrating scarce resources to reward top performers, the management team gives everyone a flat raise of one half of one percent across the board regardless of individual performance reviews.—Entitlement

These are just a few examples. I'm sure you can think of dozens of others from your own experience. When you think of your organization, are the consequences logical? Is there a clear line of sight that exists between behavior and consequences?

Mediocrity for the Sake of Harmony

In Committing Element 6, it was stated that creating a clear chain of command enhances both leadership and accountability. Some would argue with me on this point by saying that matrix management organizations promotes consensus. This may be true in some cases, but consensus doesn't mean superior performance; how many poor decisions have been made by consensus with no one accountable? After all, if we all agreed, how can you hold me accountable for a decision we all made? Consensus can form a foundation for a "climate of entitlement." I once had a senior vice president actually tell me, "It doesn't matter if we come up with the best solution, as long as we all agree." How can any organization ever expect to be best in class with leadership willing to accept mediocrity for the sake of harmony?

The drive for consensus can also create a climate of fear. Studies of past management failures have found that when people are reluctant to stand up and voice dissent against the general consensus can lead to disaster. Though not the entire cause, the reluctance of dissenting individuals to voice their concerns were contributing factors in both the failure of the Bay of Pigs Invasion and the Shuttle Challenger disaster.

So how can the drive for consensus create both entitlement and fear? It's one of those paradoxes of management showing that, more often than not, climates of fear and climates of entitlement coexist within the same organization. Some members live in fear while others wallow in entitlement. Junior members without tenure don't speak up for fear that they won't be granted what they want; tenured members don't speak up because it doesn't really matter anyway. A National Union Rep once told me, "We know this plant is going to close, we just plan on getting the most we can for as long as we can before it does."

The intent of organizational development is to effectively combine all of the systems and technological elements with the human factors and then govern them through sound business acumen in such a way that the organization most effectively delivers on its value proposition. Elements that are not in alignment will need to be changed; change involves loss for some segment of the status quo. Attempts to keep everyone happy will more than likely limit the degree of organizational transformation you can effect. If you want to ensure consistent high performance, you must be willing to lead. Those aligned with the future vision must be empowered to act, willing to assume responsibility, and willing to be held accountable for their performance outcomes. Those who are opposed to the transformation must not be allowed to undermine the change initiative. Driving for consensus for consensus' sake can cause change initiatives to fail. When you see the change initiative stressing the organizational timbers, recognize that the group is fragmenting and needs intervention to keep the change initiative progressing. The forces stressing the organizational vessel won't simply fade away; the root causes need to be addressed by striking an effective balance of healthy dissent combined with collegial collaboration. This requires empowered management fueled through courageous leadership tempered by sound judgment and wisdom.

We'll discuss logical consequences more in Sustaining Element 10 (balanced rewards, opportunities, and consequences). For the purposes of understanding how to engender commitment within a developing organization, recognize that a climate of logical consequences must be fostered.

Committing Element 8: Individual and Intraorganizational Alignment and Collaboration

The power of teams is generally recognized as a formidable force that can accomplish more than any single individual could hope to—when it exists. But simply assembling a group does not necessarily form a team. For a group of individuals to gel into a team, an internal transformation must occur within each individual crew member such that they are willing to subsume their egos and individual volition to that of the team's; each must accept that their success is integrally tied to the success of the team, and each must commit to that success. This is not something that can be mandated; as was discussed in creating an organizational climate (Committing Element 7), teamwork too must form naturally, growing within the hearts and minds of individual team members.

At best, dictating teamwork will only achieve compliance. Depending upon the temperaments of the crew, the precursors, and the pervasive conditions, such edicts can give rise to malicious compliance. Having been enlisted and promoted from the bilge to the bridge, I am very aware that the individuals actually turning the wrenches and running the plays can make or break the success of an organization. I've seen more than a few petty dictators have their careers torpedoed by the crew. "We know what he told us to do won't work. But he's obviously so much smarter than we are; we're going to do it just the way that SOB told us to." When it all goes wrong and the tyrant has been dethroned, the "lowly" crew stands back and shrugs their shoulders, "We were only following orders. What could we do? We did it just the way he told us to." Successful managers engage and empower the crew. You can educate and you can legislate, but the only true control over any population is individual self-control.

Progression toward "Teamness"

For a fully functioning and cohesive team to successfully form each of the precursor elements need to have been established. The actions taken by leaders and managers to lay the Frameworks of Organizational, Team, and Individual Success during the Forming and Focusing Stages create an environment that is conducive to the emergence of cohesive teams.

- A clear vision has been set.
- The strategies have been defined and disaggregated into tactics.
- Systems have been developed.
- Each individual has been trained to perform their roles.
- Each individual and the group as a whole consistently fulfill their respective responsibilities within a climate of logical consequences.

Within these frameworks, the conditions become such that individuals embrace the mission as their own. They trust their leadership and their teammates. They begin to believe that acting in concert with the team will serve them better than acting alone—then and only then will individuals commit their fortunes and their futures to the team. Having set each well-crafted timber into the framework, individuals work together collaboratively as a team. Each is secure enough in their own abilities and is motivated to collaborate. At the same time that people support each other, they are also respecting the boundaries of each other's authority and accountability.

Without such mutual respect, personal and organizational boundaries can be crossed that undermine the basis of trust critical for teamwork. When these conditions are right, crew members become concerned with both getting the task done and getting each other involved and motivated.

Nonteam Players

The progression toward "teamness" can be outlined and flawlessly executed, but that doesn't mean that everyone will make the trip. Some will never make that commitment regardless of the conditions because they lack the fundamental ability to trust or they lack the humility to serve a cause greater than themselves.

THE REST OF THE STORY: In Committing Element 6, I described my contribution to a successful overhaul of a submarine's engine room. Here's the rest of the story. At that point in my life, I was more immature than I am today. I was ambitious, grasping, with a nasty temper edged with a sarcastic wit (I'm somewhat better today, thank you very much). I wanted to get commissioned so bad I could taste it. I had applied for commissioning programs four times before. On this, my fifth attempt, I was certain that the long hours and demonstrated success of the department would pay off. I believed my dedication, drive, and expertise would be recognized, and I would get the Captain's endorsement for a commissioning; it never came.

After I was rejected again, I made up my mind that I was going to transfer to shore duty, finish my degree on my own, and get out of the "Canoe Club." If I couldn't get promoted in the Navy, I'd get promoted in the civilian world. During my exit interview just prior to leaving the ship, I asked the Captain why he hadn't endorsed my package. He said, "You are one of the finest Petty Officers I've ever served with. You work hard and you really turned around the division. All your guys respect you and bust their asses. But despite all you accomplished, we never knew if you were doing it for yourself or you were doing it for the ship." Pissed, I responded, "What does it matter why I did it, it got done didn't it?"

Older now, I recognize that it does matter. No one likes to serve with an egoist. It's true that we accomplished a great deal, but I'll never know how much more we could have accomplished if my head and my heart had been in a better place.

P.S. I finally did get commissioned on my sixth attempt, and I never forgot the words of my submarine commander—"motivation matters."

When you think through the assessment of your team's performance, consider whether some individuals may lack the experience, humility, or motivation for collaboration.

Free Riders

Just as there are those who do things for their own purposes, there are those who don't do as much—again, for their own purposes. When assessing team performance consider whether there is a general feeling of imbalance in the amount of effort and the degree of involvement from some members of the group as compared to others. When there is a disparity in the application of logical consequences, some members can become "free riders" who don't pull their fair share of the load. Why they don't contribute and how they get away it invariably points to a single common factor—failure to manage. The lapse in effective management usually has one of five root causes:

1. Favoritism or protected status—The free riders hold some degree of invulnerability shielding them from consequences that puts them beyond the reach of performance management.
2. Conflict aversion—The manager lacks the intestinal fortitude to confront the behavior and would rather avoid a confrontation rather than directly manage substandard performance.
3. Apathy—The manager feels that it's just more hassle than it's worth and it's easier to work around the subpar performers, ride the good horses, or just do it themselves.
4. Enabling behaviors—Out of compassion, pity, or naivety the manager accepts or makes excuses for poor performance thereby allowing the behavior to continue.
5. Misdirection or manipulation—The manager remains oblivious to the free rider's behavior and its impact on the rest of the team because the individual is effective at flattery, misdirection, "flying below the radar," or taking undue credit for the work of others. This can happen more readily when managers are far-removed from the actual day-to-day work of the team and rely upon others to keep them informed.

Regardless of why the disparity in workload exists, it has a negative consequence on team formation and effectiveness. When one or more of the team doesn't fulfill their obligations, others in the team have to pick up the slack. The feelings of resentment and injustice fester and undermine the commitment of the team.

Despite the impact on team morale and performance, many managers wait too long until the problems have spun out of control beyond the hope of recovery. Managers may not intervene because they want to give people the benefit of the doubt or they believe the individual will come around. They may also not recognize how disruptive the behavior is. But like a cancer, it won't go away just because you don't want to believe it. Feelings of resentment created by the imbalance of labor distribution can greatly undermine the organization's effectiveness. Left unchecked, these feelings can propagate, feeding on themselves and cause organizational transformation to founder and potentially collapse entirely.

Courageous Leadership: Intervention

To intervene and directly confront inappropriate behavior requires courage on the part of leadership as well as appropriate management. It also requires a plan. Fortunately, we have one we've already outlined. Like all aspects of effective performance, appropriate team behaviors can be developed utilizing the Framework for Individual Success (shown again in Figure 4.20). To grow the capacity of individuals to become more effective team players reinforce the seven structural timbers:

1. Define acceptable performance
2. Set clear expectations

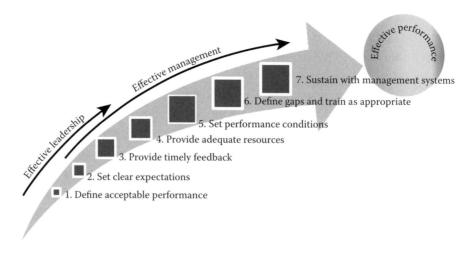

7. Sustain with management systems
6. Define gaps and train as appropriate
5. Set performance conditions
4. Provide adequate resources
3. Provide timely feedback
2. Set clear expectations
1. Define acceptable performance

Effective performance

Effective management

Effective leadership

Figure 4.20   Framework for individual success.

3. Provide timely feedback
4. Provide adequate resources
5. Set performance conditions
6. Define gaps and train as appropriate
7. Sustain with management systems

In tense situations, steps one through three require acts of courageous leadership. Once the conversation has been engaged and the expectations are clear, draw upon your management skills to guide the employee's behavior along a more productive path. Ensure you establish logical consequences for both compliance and failure to comply. Remember that all things yield to good management!

Incenting the Wrong Behaviors

Just as you can do the right thing for the wrong reasons, managers sometimes do the wrong thing for the right reasons. On many occasions, I've seen teams fall apart because managers with the best of intentions incent the wrong behavior.

THE LIMITS OF "HEALTHY COMPETITION": Dan was a sales manager for a consulting firm. He had three top producers on his team. Each traveled extensive spending more than 80% of their time away from home. Like many Americans, Dan believed in "healthy competition." He was always putting little carrots out for his team to scramble for. Entering the fourth quarter of a particularly profitable year, Dan offered a trip to the annual tradeshow to the top performer. No one accepted the challenge. When he asked why he was told, "A trip away is a trip away. As far as we're concerned, a tradeshow is still time away from family and we're not even generating sales." Dan wanted someone representing the firm at the trade show so he "sweetened the pot." Now recognizing how much time his sales reps spent on the road and how little time they spent with family, Dan offered an all expenses paid trip that included one guest to the tradeshow. With an incentive like that, Dan expected great returns; instead, he had a mutiny. Together the three reps marched into his office and opted out of the game altogether. "Look," the designated spokesman said, "we all bust our backs and are putting in hundreds of uncompensated hours. None of us can work any harder than we already are. In order for any one of us to look better, we'd have to work at making the other look worse—and none of us is willing to do that to each other. Therefore, you can go on the trip with your spouse, and we'll stay home with ours."

Dan was shocked. This wasn't the response he had intended. Not knowing what to say, Dan thanked them for their input and would consider what they had said.

Dan was an "S" by temperament and valued harmony. He had never wanted to create divisiveness in his team nor would he intentionally incent behaviors that undermined the team's cohesiveness. He thought about it overnight. The next day, Dan presented each of his top three performers with two airline tickets to the tradeshow and accommodations at a four-star hotel. The three reps felt valued; their spouses became more supportive of the long hours spent on the job, and the next year's profits more than paid for the trip.

When you're working to create incentives and build team cohesiveness, the results you get may not be those you intended. If the team doesn't have the desired level of alignment and mutual commitment, look first for the presence of the elements of organizational, team, and individual success established during the Forming, Focusing, and Committing Stages. If the three stages have been navigated well, look to the team's composition as well as managerial root causes, such as the failure to manage as well as mismanaged incentives.

Committing Element 9: The Organization Lives Its Values with Integrity

Committing Element 9 is so obvious that it is frequently overlooked and it is so egregious when it is lacking within an organization that there is little hope of implementing a solution. That being said, our discussion of the essential planks from which to construct your Vessel of Organizational Success would be incomplete without it. Quite simply put, if an organization seeks to engage its workforce to achieve a vision then the organization must strive to live up to its stated values. Just as you do not trust someone who doesn't "walk the talk," employees won't trust an organization that says one thing and does another. Recalling the four fundamental questions asked of all leaders, "Can I trust you?" was number one on the list. This is the other side of the concept of having a high degree of congruence between individual and organizational values discussed in Committing Element 1. Organizations, like individuals, spend their time and resources on what they value. If an organization says, "Our people are our greatest asset," but they don't invest in people by training and developing them, don't make opportunities for their people to be promoted from within, and lay off people early and often, do they really value their people?

Motivation Matters, but It Only Goes So Far

Like all things human, organizations can fail to deliver on their promises with sincerity or insincerity. I've worked with firms that genuinely wanted to live according to their espoused values, but due to circumstances, resources, or having a grasp that fell short of their reach, they failed to deliver. I've also worked with organizations that were so disingenuous at their very core; they would say all the "key words" and "catchy phrases" that investors wanted to hear without any intention of ever delivering.

It is more palatable for people to accept good intentions tripped up by failed execution more so than they can accept flat-out lies. The former is forgivable as long as it doesn't become an ongoing pattern; after all, "To err is human." However, regardless of good intentions failure to demonstrate your stated values will cause widespread dissent and a lack of commitment within your workforce. To illustrate consider the example of a very well meaning management team.

The Paper Mill versus the Saw Mill—The Expectation of Pain Is Often More Tolerable than the Pain of Expectation

I worked with a forest products company that operated both sawmills and a paper mills. Working conditions within the sawmills were very different than those found in the paper mills. The sawmills were covered by steel frames with tin roofs and no walls. When it was hot, you were hot; when it was cold, you were cold. The work was dirty, dusty, and noisy. On top of all of that, it's dangerous working around giant saw blades where occasionally planks were kicked back sending them flying through the air. Papermaking requires a consistent environment. True, it's hot and noisy, but each area had an air conditioned soundproof booth for operators to seek shelter. Paper machines can be dangerous as well, but their dangers generally involve sticking body parts where they shouldn't go—the dangers rarely came chasing you across the room. In addition to better working conditions, jobs in the paper mill paid almost double what you could make at a sawmill.

Every year the company conducted employee satisfaction surveys. Based upon the working conditions and pay at each location, can you guess which facilities had the higher levels of employee satisfaction? They are the dirty, dangerous, lower paying ones! Consistently, year after year, employees in the sawmills expressed greater degrees of job satisfaction than those working in the paper mills. Why? When we explored the reasons, we found that it was a matter of expectations.

Employees going to work in the sawmills were told in no uncertain terms that they could expect dirty and dangerous work. What they found was exactly what they expected—every day it would be dirty, dusty, and dangerous. The managers and supervisors of the sawmill didn't work to "empower" the employees; they were paid to do a job, and they were expected to get the job done. Employees did their jobs, got paid, and went home. Expectations were a straight honest business proposition—this is the job, do the job, get paid, go home—no surprises.

Compare the expectations of those in the sawmill to those in the paper mill. Every year the paper mill management pursued employee engagement by soliciting involvement. Hourly employees worked on special assignments, productivity improvement teams, safety committees, charitable fund raising, and employee morale events like the company picnic and annual safety fair. This work allowed extra overtime for everyone involved, those participating on the committees and those covering their shifts. Hourly employees attended many mill meetings and participated in most of the major decisions. So, what was the problem? It sounded like the managers were doing everything required to create a high-performing engaged workforce. The problem stemmed from two root causes: limits and sustainability.

The first reoccurring problem arose from managers failing to set clear expectations on the limits of empowerment up front. To the committees this implied a world without boundaries. Many suggestions arose from brainstorming sessions within various committees and task forces that lacked appropriate sponsorship, funding, or were otherwise resourced to insufficiently to be achievable. Consequently, high expectations consistently resulted in disappointment. If the managers had set clear limits within which the committees were fully empowered there would have been more likelihood that the employees could achieve satisfying outcomes. As it was, the resources poured into empowerment only fueled disappointment.

The second persistent problem was fueled by an unsustainable pace. Historically the paper industry was very cyclical in its boom and bust years. In the good times, money flowed and so did the improvement projects. When times got tight, the mills had to cut back. Training and overtime were always the first on the chopping block. This impacted employees financially and in their levels of involvement. Many employees spend what they make. When their pay was cut back to the base so was employee satisfaction. In addition to the very tangible loses the employees felt, they also experienced the loss of disenfranchisement. Where once they were involved and had a voice, they had none. You don't miss what you have never experienced, but having experienced the respect and involvement of working closely on projects and then going back to being "just an operator" fueled high levels of discontent.

Thus, despite the sincere desire for engagement on the part of the leadership, the employees didn't believe that management "walked the talk." Repeated patterns of engagement and disenfranchisement had left the majority of paper mill employees frustrated, cynical, and dissatisfied, even though the relative conditions were far superior to the lot of their counterparts working in the sawmills. The outcome of employee satisfaction surveys within the sawmills as compared to the paper mills illustrates that even with the best of intentions, efforts designed to create employee engagement can actually have the opposite effect.

Market Norms versus Social Norms

As it relates to behavioral expectations, a norm is a standard or pattern of accepted behavior. For instance, in Western cultures it is customary for men to greet each other by shaking each other's right hands. Different situations require different patterns of behavior. Behavior approved of in one situation will be met with various levels of disapproval in another. For instance, you generally don't toss the bouquet of flowers into the waiting crowd at funerals. As such, there are different expectations of behavior in social situations, social norms, as compared to the workplace, market norms.

In social situations, it is perfectly acceptable to ask a friend or neighbor to come over and help you move some furniture. The same friend who would happily spend a day lugging heavy objects for you for free would become indignant if you offered them minimum wage for the same task.

What's more is that you'd never consider asking such a thing. Market norms are rarely injected into social situations, but it's quite common for managers to draw upon social norms in common business situations. How often have you heard phrases thrown around the office such as, "We are one big family?" Businesses have potluck dinners and weekend "getaways" attempting to tap into that pool of discretionary effort stored within each individual in hopes that that last full measure will give the business a competitive advantage without any additional monetary exchange. This doesn't mean that managers are consciously trying to get more for less, but that is literally what is happening. And frequently, employees respond well to these overtures. They put in the additional hours and take on extra tasks out of a very real sense of camaraderie and familial commitment, and they feel good about it in the process. The problem comes when it's time to cut back. Then the same manager who once said, "We're family!" falls back on, "I hope you understand; it's nothing personal, only business." You can't have it both ways—you don't lay off your Cousin Winnie when fortunes change.

Eventually, mixing social norms with market norms will have lasting repercussions in the form of low morale and reduced productivity along with feelings of loss and guilt, anger, frustration, and righteous indignation that permeate the workplace after cuts. Because people see their colleagues as more than mere coworkers, their absence invokes very deep feelings of loss. At the same time that people are coping with the loss of a friend, they must now perform the tasks of absent coworkers as well as their own. Loss of manpower has a tangible impact on productivity. Now they feel angry and frustrated at having added responsibilities with no additional pay. Compounding all of this is the pervasive feeling of guilt. "Survivor's guilt" can consume the remaining employees such that productivity takes a double hit and the company and its remaining employees pay the added price. Cutbacks strike at the very heart of engagement, affecting hope, control, and equity. Attempts to squeeze more from the survivors through the infusion of social norms into the workplace usually results in lowered morale and increased cynicism.

If you can't sustain the expectations you set, it is much cleaner to maintain a strictly business proposition with employees. This is the job; this is the pay. By maintaining that clear segregation, the necessities of organizational realignment and other changes that companies must effect from time to time will be seen for what they are—necessities—and not as hypocrisy and a lack of integrity within the management ranks.

False Engagement through Manipulation

If employees are dissatisfied and accuse managers who honestly seek to engage them of hypocrisy, how much greater is their level of dissatisfaction when they are lied to by management that really doesn't have integrity? Unfortunately, there are firms that do engage in manipulation and misrepresentation. In those organizations, there is a widespread perception that the organization's true values are not aligned with its espoused values because it is, in fact, true. Leaders are viewed with cynicism and thought of as hypocrites because, in fact, they are.

If a firm makes minimal investment in training, research, and development while adding to their marketing, communications, and public relations, you may ask yourself, is this firm more concerned about what they actually are or only concerned with what they look like? If the firm puts the time and resources into achieving true excellence, they would have excellent products and services and won't have to hire scores of "spin doctors" putting "lipstick on the pig" attempting to make chicken salad out of chicken poop. Don't get me wrong, I recognize the value of marketing and publicity, but I firmly believe that a strong reputation can only be built on a solid foundation of truth.

If you find yourself in a firm such as this, what can be done? Unless you have the power, courage, and commitment to clean house—not much. There are ways to turn around such organizations; I've seen it done. But such reversals in culture require substantial commitment and a willingness to stay the course. It also requires truth and reconciliation to ameliorate the emotions and set the vessel on a productive course. We will talk more about this when addressing the Renewal Stage. For now, recognize that employees will see through false promises and cynical manipulations designed to induce engagement within the workforce. If there is a lack of integrity, it will be known.

Committing Element 10: Well-Defined Group Identity and Esprit de Corps

Esprit de Corps is the apex of workforce commitment. The term derives its origins from the French term literally meaning the "spirit of the body." It is commonly used within the military to refer to a shared feeling of comradeship among team members, enthusiasm for the mission, and devotion to the cause.

Some organizations shy away from using the term because of its military origin and some managers feel that it isn't applicable within a civilian context. I disagree. Don't underestimate the power of a well-defined group identity and pride in being a part of the organization. Incredible accomplishments can be made when people feel such a level of commitment that they proudly wear the company logo as a badge of honor.

For this level of commitment to exist, all of the precursors of forming, focusing, and committing need to be in place. In addition, the organization must consistently deliver on its promises to its people. When organizations do, leaders can solidify the growing commitment within their workers and build something that is a true differentiator between their organization and others that don't excite such pride in their workforce.

The Power of Symbols

Symbols have power. Religions, nations, and elite organizations know the power of symbols. Imagine the pride a golfer feels when given the green jacket for winning the Masters Tournament. You don't have to be an elite military unity or in professional sports to draw on this power, other organizations can as well.

PAPER ACES: As part of the discussion of Committing Element 2, I cited an example of Western Manufacturing Facility; one key aspect in the overall success of that initiative I didn't mention was the use of symbols. Part of the transformation we wanted to affect in the workforce was the development of a higher level of professionalism within the operators. To become qualified as a top operator, each employee had to successfully complete a rigorous multistep process. After demonstrating all the knowledge, skills, and abilities contained on the training checklist during their qualification period, the employee was then evaluated by senior trainers and the supervisors. Next, they were required to pass both a written exam and sit before the qualifications board made up of senior operators and managers. Upon successful completion of the oral board, the newly qualified operator was triumphantly given a leather bomber jacket with their name above the breast pocket and a custom embroidered patch on the back showing a winged playing card, the ace of diamonds and the words "Paper Ace" emblazoned across the back. Only operators who demonstrated the highest level of achievement could wear the jackets, and it was only given to them by those who had earned the right to wear it themselves. No one could buy a jacket; no manager could ever own one. Only professional papermakers who had earned their stripes could show those colors. The jackets became quite coveted and worn proudly around the town. Everyone who saw the jackets knew that it wasn't just given to the one wearing it—they had to earn it.

The symbols of professionalism don't have to be jackets; they can be as simple as pins or other trinkets. Members of sales departments who excel at customer service are often given stars and other symbols in recognition of their achievements. People wear them with pride and strive to add to their collections. The symbols themselves aren't as important as the significance ascribed to them. To make them coveted the award must have the following criterion:

1. It must be earned not purchased
2. It must be based upon high standards that are never compromised
3. It must reflect achievement, not simply based upon attendance or longevity

Be careful with undeserved group recognition. If the entire group in fact contributed, fine, but when there is a question of accomplishment where there may be free riders, the recognition could backfire. Too often managers give broad praise to diverse groups because they are conflict averse and don't want anyone to feel bad. These displays actually cheapen the value of recognition and are counter to creating a sense of Esprit de Corps—if everyone gets a trophy, the trophy means nothing.

Key Takeaways: Committing versus Fragmenting

Commitment is an outcome; it cannot be mandated, forced, or manipulated. It must be freely given and only arises when the conditions are right such that the three fundamental human satisfiers of hope, control, and equity combine with the three determinants of organizational commitment, inclusion, purpose, and congruence. When these six elements are effectively combined, they form the total equation for workforce engagement:

$$\text{Hope} + \text{Control} + \text{Equity} \rightarrow \underline{\text{Individual Satisfaction}}$$

$$+$$

$$\text{Inclusion} + \text{Purpose} + \text{Congruence} \rightarrow \underline{\text{Organizational Commitment}}$$

Yields:

$$\underline{\text{Impactful Outcomes}}$$

Resulting in:

$$\underline{\text{An Engaged Workforce}}$$

Commitment emerges from the complex ecosystem surrounding and pervading the organization. It is the resultant outcome arising from the culmination of all the efforts and activities involved in Forming and Focusing. The 10 elements of commitment we have discussed in this section can only enhance or reinforce what has been previously initiated; alone, none of them is sufficient to build commitment. Table 4.6 contains the key takeaways of the Committing Stage, including the desired outcome, team needs, indicators of effective and ineffective navigation along with effective leadership and management responses.

To help with your project planning, Table 4.7 shows a basic project plan to help navigate through the Committing Phase.

If you have reached the point of your project implementation plan where you are deploying the systems, processes, and procedures broadly across the organization and you don't see the signs of growing commitment, you must go back and explore the root causes, as shown in Figure 4.21. To intervene, you will need to retrace your steps to uncover which elements are insufficient or are lacking altogether within the Framework of Organizational, Team, and/or Individual Success that are resulting in inappropriate behaviors such as apathy, internal gamesmanship, poor communication, or failures in accountability. As you explore the seeds of discontent within the organization, you must maintain the courage to confront incongruent behaviors as well as demonstrate the humility to recognize that your plan may have flaws. Because there are so many moving parts, I'd be very surprised if any change plan were executed exactly as initially planned. There will always be

Table 4.6   Key Takeaways: Committing

	Focus	*Commit*	*Sustained Performance*	*Renewal*
Form	*Stumble*	*Fragment*	*Variable Performance*	*Level*

Committing: Occurs when team members embrace the team's mission as their own, become more engaged and commit to team success

Team Needs:

- Inclusion
- Training
- Opportunities to practice—growing mastery
- Timely feedback

The Change "Readiness vs. Response" Continuum	
Change Ready:	Collaboration
Change Resistant:	Compromise

Indicators of Effective Navigation	Indicators of Ineffective Navigation
• Growing skills • Clear integrated goals • Culture of inclusion • Building Esprit de Corps	• Apathy • Internal competition and political gamesmanship • Blocked team communication • Lack of accountability

Effective Leadership Responses:

- Transformational leadership living the values of the organization
- Reinforcement of fundamental satisfiers: hope, control, and equity
- Establish span of control and degree of engagement
- Foster inclusion among all team members in accomplishing the organization's purpose
- Courageously addressing organizational elements that are not congruent with the mission, vision, and values

Effective Management Responses:

- Reinforcement of the chain of command
- Mentoring including assignment of meaningful development opportunities combined with timely feedback

(continued)

Table 4.6 Key Takeaways: Committing (Continued)

	Focus	Commit	Sustained Performance	Renewal
Form	Stumble	Fragment	Variable Performance	Level

- Establishment of accountability through logical consequences
- Ongoing project management

Tools and Techniques:
- System deployment and targeted training
- Metrics: leading indicators and KPIs
- Effective feedback
- Span of control and behavioral triggers
- Establishment of group identity

Table 4.7 Committing Project Plan—Targeted Training

Project Step	Responsibility	Date Planned	Date Complete
(1) Establish appropriate spans of control and limits of authority for every position and aspect of organizational performance			
(2) Ensure each system is monitored via "timely view to the processes"			
1. Identify leading KPIs			
2. Identify trigger points			
3. Outline the appropriate responses to key triggers			
(3) Develop training strategy and process			
1. Utilize the strategy maps, process flowcharts, and any procedures, manuals, plans, and policies as well as other materials to conduct a DACUM to form the basis for training checklists			

(continued)

Table 4.7   Committing Project Plan—Targeted Training (Continued)

Project Step	Responsibility	Date Planned	Date Complete
2. Develop the essential elements of training (just enough—more formalized materials will be created to codify the final procedures during the Sustaining Stage)			
(4) Broadly roll out training throughout the organization. Utilize the SMEs and others integral in the design of the process as trainers			
1. Conduct principles and systems training to lay the foundation of solid understanding throughout the organization			
2. Analyze gaps between training checklists and individual performance to develop individual development plans			
3. Implement structured OJT to conduct targeted training as necessary to fill the gaps and build support—just in time and just enough			
(5) Continue to engage the management action teams (MAT) created during Focusing to monitor, mentor, and support the growing skills			
1. Establish consistent managerial norms regarding "logical consequences"			
2. Ensure ongoing engagement, involvement, and awareness of leaders in the fledgling processes, procedures, and the nascent culture growing within the organization			
3. Reinforce behaviors and demonstration of excellence, address lapses as they emerge through intervention			

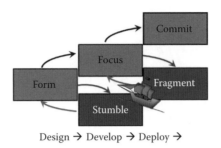

Design → Develop → Deploy →

Figure 4.21 Return to focusing.

those unknown and undiscovered aspects that are uncovered as the organization transforms. Only during a vessel's "sea trials" is its integrity proven and the effectiveness of its system design and construction revealed. Be prepared to return and readdress those elements laid down during Focusing or even Forming that are not "seaworthy."

If within your organization you see growing skills, alignment of goals, and team members mutually supporting each other and reaching out to include others, you may also begin to see a group identity developing. If these are the indicators you see, you can feel confident that you are on the right course and the team is becoming truly committed.

Chapter 5

Stage 4—Sustained Performance: Smooth Sailing

Overview and Assessment: Sustained versus Variable Performance

Thus far, we've explored how to lay the solid foundation to develop an aligned organization and a committed, engaged workforce. By the time you have moved from Forming through Focusing, you should begin to see the first fruits of your labors. If you've navigated your journey well, there is a high degree of alignment, growing commitment to the mission, the organization, and the team. The groups have moved through uninformed optimism, informed pessimism, and now hope is on the rise. This is fertile soil from which to reap the bounty you envisioned when you began your organizational voyage; this is the stage of Sustained Performance. Table 5.1 outlines the indicators and team needs observable within organizations that have successfully navigated to achieve Sustained Performance.

Sustained performance only occurs in those organizations that have formed well, have become focused, and are enjoying the commitment of their members (Figure 5.1). This stage is not labeled "high performance" because that term limits an organization; after all, how high is up? When we discuss Sustainable Performance, we mean consistent delivery on all goals and commitments in an efficient manner that manages to maintain a satisfying level of work–life balance and doesn't break the backs of overworked stressed-out employees. There are many organizations that haven't formed well, aren't focused, and have marginally committed employees that still

Table 5.1   Summary of Indicators: Sustained versus Variable Performance

	Focus	*Commit*	*Sustained Performance*	*Renewal*
Form	*Stumble*	*Fragment*	*Variable Performance*	*Level*

Sustained Performance: The organization is cohesive, skilled, and consistently achieves its goals

Team Needs: • Individual congruence with organizational culture • Growing autonomy and empowerment • Meaningful outcomes • Equitable treatment • Sustainable work–life balance

The Change "Readiness vs. Response" Continuum	
Change Ready:	Optimism
Change Resistant:	Skepticism

Indicators of Effective Navigation	**Indicators of Ineffective Navigation**
• High productivity • Focus on team achievement • Culture of excellence • Satisfaction	• Low/sporadic productivity • Missed deadlines/frequent mistakes • Culture of entitlement or fear • Focus on individual gains

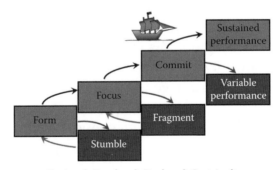

Design → Develop → Deploy → Sustain →

Figure 5.1   Moving beyond commitment to sustained performance.

consistently achieve their goals, but they do so at an unsustainably high cost. Organizations that haven't done the necessary work establishing the elements of Forming, Focusing, and Committing to lay a sound management foundation of aligned systems may accomplish their tasks, but only by running at a manic pace. And organizations that don't have engaged courageous managers that lead with integrity may also accomplish their objectives but only through great personal sacrifices and burning out their workforce. These organizations' performances are variable, as shown in Figure 5.1. Consider the unlikelihood that a chronic couch potato will wake up one morning and drag himself off the sofa to compete in and win a triathlon that afternoon. Our inspired couch potato may complete the event; he may even do well, but it is unlikely that he'll be able to sustain that pace without the disciplined conditioning required to be a triathlete; you simply can't jump into the middle and expect success.

So how sustainable is your organization's performance? Rank yourself on the 10 Elements of Sustainable Performance contained in Table 5.2.

Once you've completed the Sustained Performance Assessment, transfer your scores into the Sustained Performance Scoring Matrix contained in Table 5.3.

Table 5.2   Sustained Performance Assessment

For each of the paired statements or groups of statement below, decide which statement most accurately describes your experiences in the day-to-day work activities within your organization. For the statement that is chosen, check to what degree you believe the statement is either Most or Somewhat like your routine experience within your organization's work activities.

Check only one statement per paired question.

Assessment (Select One)			Choose the Statement that Best Describes Your Organization
1	+4	Most Like Us	Procedures are established for continuing to determine customer and stakeholder requirements and satisfaction including unstated customer requirements. When applicable, statutory and regulatory requirements related to products or services are incorporated and prompt notifications of changes are provided to all those impacted
	+2	Somewhat Like Us	
	−2	Somewhat Like Us	Information such as customer and stakeholder requirements, satisfaction, and/or feedback is hard to get or is so untimely that people operate in a void with many decisions made in a vacuum. The consequences of actions and decisions are not readily apparent or are inconsequential to the individuals responsible
	−4	Most Like Us	

(continued)

Table 5.2   Sustained Performance Assessment (Continued)

Assessment (Select One)			Choose the Statement that Best Describes Your Organization
2	+4	Most Like Us	The organization routinely develops new challenging goals or revises current goals as appropriate and then proceeds to consistently achieve those goals in a timely and efficient manner
	+2	Somewhat Like Us	
	−2	Somewhat Like Us	Development of goals is more of an administrative exercise rather than a strategic process to focus the organization's resources and activities. Goals are basically irrelevant; they are not updated and linger from year to year with little attention paid to them. Agreements are frequently ignored and deadlines are often missed with no accountability and no consequences
	−4	Most Like Us	
3	+4	Most Like Us	All members and leaders are well conversant in procedural requirements. Operational systems and critical procedures are formally documented. Materials are readily available for use and their use is expected and enforced
	+2	Somewhat Like Us	
	−2	Somewhat Like Us	Systems are not well documented. Understanding of operations and requirements are passed down through oral tradition. The resources and documentation have evolved "organically" rather than through "intelligent design." What procedures that have been developed are not routinely reviewed or updated and access to them is limited
	−4	Most Like Us	
4	+4	Most Like Us	Decisions are made applying a proactive, problem-solving approach. Regular input from those who will be affected both internally and externally by the organization's decisions is sought to identify, diagnose, and solve organizational problems
	+2	Somewhat Like Us	
			The financial impact of activities is understood and incorporated into the decision making process at all levels throughout the organization. The costs of inputs, processes, and activities are balanced against the value returned from outputs and outcomes
4	−2	Somewhat Like Us	Decision making is not proactive often resulting in limited options because the group has delayed taking action. Decisions are primarily made in a crisis and therefore not thought through and are often made by a select few with limited input from or notification to all those affected

(continued)

Table 5.2 Sustained Performance Assessment (Continued)

Assessment (Select One)			Choose the Statement that Best Describes Your Organization
4	−4	Most Like Us	The financial impact of decisions is not routinely nor widely considered and only by the leadership team—"That's management's job, not mine"
5	+4	Most Like Us	Team members keep each other informed of progress, problems, decisions, and changes. The group regularly reports the organization's progress to all interested parties internal and external to the organization
	+2	Somewhat Like Us	
	−2	Somewhat Like Us	Members work in isolation without briefing each other. Communications relies on informal networks resulting in miscommunications, lack of alignment, and lack of support
	−4	Most Like Us	
6	+4	Most Like Us	Progress toward goals is regularly monitored and routinely assessed; milestones are clearly established, communicated and adhered to. The use of a reporting mechanism such as a "Balanced Scorecard" ensures that the team maintains appropriate focus on all critical success factors maintaining key performance indicators (KPIs) for all priorities within required standards (customer/stakeholder, productivity/quality, financial, and human capital development)
	+2	Somewhat Like Us	
	−2	Somewhat Like Us	Measurement of progress is frequently based upon "gut feel," opinion and/or speculation. Those metrics that are available are typically lagging indicators that quantify activities that occurred in the past when it is too late to affect their outcome. Outputs are measured not outcomes (i.e., number of people trained measured instead of changes in behavior that resulted in process improvement)
	−4	Most Like Us	
7	+4	Most Like Us	Controls are in place to ensure inputs such as purchased products and services conform to requirements. Suppliers and service providers are evaluated and selected based on established criteria regarding their ability to meet requirements. Records of supplier evaluations and actions are maintained and form the basis of continuing utilization of suppliers and service providers
	+2	Somewhat Like Us	

(continued)

Table 5.2   Sustained Performance Assessment (Continued)

Assessment (Select One)			Choose the Statement that Best Describes Your Organization
7	−2	Somewhat Like Us	Few controls exist to govern the quality and consistency of supplied products and services. Little documentation is maintained on approved suppliers or vendors. Vendor agreements are often based on legacy relationships not on added value. The vendor and supplier performance is not routinely benchmarked and graded against "Best in Class." These vendor relations are often established in place of effective management—hire a consultant to tell you what your people should already know
	−4	Most Like Us	
8	+4	Most Like Us	The organization utilizes lean concepts and incorporates these elements into the ongoing activities of the organization. Value stream mapping is used to assess overall effectiveness and efficiencies of the organization's systems in accomplishing the mission. Appropriate control limits and system guidelines have been established and are used as a basis of process control. Members are capable of analyzing parameters and empowered to adjust processes based accordingly. 5S and visual management are widely used throughout the organization to promote consistency, efficiency, and cost savings
	+2	Somewhat Like Us	
	−2	Somewhat Like Us	Lean concepts are not incorporated into the organization's processes resulting in excessive waste and inefficiencies. The processes and procedures are informal and passed on through "oral tradition." There is a high degree of inconsistency from person to person or shift to shift
	−4	Most Like Us	
9	+4	Most Like Us	Nonconforming products and services produced by the organization are identified and controlled to prevent unintended use or delivery. Responsibilities and authorities for dealing with nonconforming products and services are defined and available in documented procedures. Nonconforming products and services are dealt with by
	+2	Somewhat Like Us	

(a) Taking action to eliminate the nonconformity

(b) Used by concession by appropriate internal authority or by the customer

(c) The nonconforming product or service is used for alternate, acceptable purposes

(continued)

Table 5.2   Sustained Performance Assessment (Continued)

Assessment (Select One)			Choose the Statement that Best Describes Your Organization
9	−2	Somewhat Like Us	No formal process exists to control nonconforming products and services. Without a consistent controls, products or services known to be out of compliance with organizational standards are sometimes furnished to customers and stakeholders
	−4	Most Like Us	
			Records of the nature of nonconformities and actions taken are not maintained. When nonconforming products or services are corrected, they are not reverified to ensure conformance to requirements
			When nonconforming products and services are detected after delivery or use has started, action is not taken in a timely manner that is appropriate to the effects, or potential effects, of the nonconformity
10	+4	Most Like Us	Rewards and opportunities are balanced between individual achievement and team success thereby encouraging team members to support each other
	+2	Somewhat Like Us	
			There is a clear and equitable linkage between rewards and opportunities commensurate with individual contributions. There is clear understanding of what it takes to be successful with well defined metrics based upon well understood and observable criteria
	−2	Somewhat Like Us	Rewards and opportunities are distributed inequitably based upon little known or little trusted criteria
	−4	Most Like Us	Rewards and opportunities are arbitrary and/or unrelated to individual contribution or everyone receives the same rewards regardless of individual contribution
			People are only rewarded for their own independent (and sometimes for self-serving) actions and efforts. The organization may say they value teamwork, but to get ahead, you have to look out for yourself

Table 5.3 Sustained Performance Scoring Matrix

No.	Score	Element of Sustaining	Effective Leadership	Effective Management	Tools and Techniques
1		Ongoing validation of customer and stakeholder requirements and satisfaction	Strategic relationship with customers and stakeholders bolstered by an uncompromising drive for quality	Maintaining a systems perspective with a broad view of outcomes and not majoring on the minors	Customer feedback Benchmarking Internal and external audits
2		Ongoing goal setting and revision	Continuous view of the big picture Balanced time horizon	Effective prioritization of tasks such that important long-term goals and objectives are achieved	Ongoing prioritization SMART goals Logical consequences
3		Availability and use of documentation for systems and procedures	Prioritization of documentation Courageous leadership and integrity by example	Assignment of documentation development and ongoing accountability toward its creation, utilization, and revision	DACUM process Training checklists Policy and procedure prioritization matrix
4		Proactive problem solving, decision making scope and impact	Open and engaging leadership—embrace the messengers	Avoidance of decision traps • Overconfidence • Groupthink • Inflexibility	Group decision making Improvisational change
5		Ongoing communications and reporting	Demonstrate and demand ongoing communication	Strategic and tactical cascading communications	Communications templates and matrices Internal and external lines of communication

6	Continuous balanced view of process outcomes	Stay the course—maintain focus on organizational priorities and goals Demonstrate and reward candor	Management by walking around Engagement of key organizational influencers	Balanced Scorecard Organizational dashboards
7	Ongoing control of vendors and suppliers	Adherence to quality standards—unwillingness to sacrifice quality for short-term gains	Framework of Vendor Management	Vendor and supplier audits and scorecards
8	Utilization of Lean concepts, 5S, and visual management	Demonstrated commitment to excellence	Adequately resourcing Lean initiatives Daily reinforcement of 5S	5S Value stream mapping Lean toolkit
9	Control of nonconforming products and services	Uncompromising commitment to quality	Refinement of spans of control and defined decision authority limits	Documentation of nonconformance and final disposition
10	Balanced rewards, opportunities, and consequences	Equitable rewards and establishment of a meritocracy Staying the course Challenge and support—leading sheep and driving goats	Reinforcement of logical consequences Shift from tactical to medium and long ranges goals Courageous management confronting and engaging the goats	Framework for Individual Success Situation analysis Performance contracting
——	Cumulative Sustaining Score			

Analysis: Sustained versus Variable Performance

Just like maintaining your new healthier weight after you've successfully dieted, sustainable performance requires ongoing discipline to continue the behaviors that have brought success to your organization. Judging by the sheer number of diet commercials that cloud the airways every New Year's Resolution season, it's easy to see why organizations backslide into the patterns that caused them to go astray. Sustainable performance requires organizational self-discipline to consistently apply and reinforce the foundational elements established during forming, focusing, and committing. Some of the sustaining elements are navigational aids; ongoing validation of customer and stakeholder feedback assure you that you are still heading on a true course. Some are progress checks; by consistently setting and achieving goals, you mark the progress of your voyage. As we explore the 10 sustaining elements, you will see some overlap between previous discussions. This is further illustration of the ebb and flow of organizational stages shown in Figure 5.2.

Sustaining Isn't Leveling

Although there is overlap between the elements of sustaining and many of the elements discussed in previous stages, sustaining performance is more than strictly continuing to do what you've been doing—there also needs to be further refinement and improvement of the processes and systems. Organizations that are sustaining performance are actually improving the consistency and quality of their products and services. It is within the

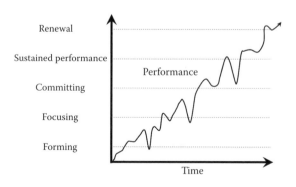

Figure 5.2   Ebb and flow between stages of organization development.

sustaining stages that concepts like 5S and Lean Six Sigma (LSS) are most impactful. By applying the LSS concepts, the organization is able to drill deeper, broadening understanding and reinforcing essential concepts and practices until they become consistent patterns of thinking and behaving, which results in greater mastery throughout the organization.

Sustaining Element 1: Ongoing Validation of Customer and Stakeholder Requirements and Satisfaction

In my view, systems thinking is the single most important mindset for leaders to maintain if they desire their endeavors to become and remain successful. Systems thinking promotes a holistic and dynamic view that enables the practitioner to consider the myriad of driving and restraining counterbalanced forces that maintain the status quo. As discussed in Focusing Element 8, increases or decreases in either set of opposing forces result in gains or losses in progress toward the goal. These forces are always in play, and the organization that loses sight of this fact can find itself drifting toward the rocks without even being aware of it. For this reason, the very first sustaining element is the ongoing validation of customer and stakeholder requirements and satisfaction. As the old sales adage says, "If you don't satisfy your customer, somebody else will."

Nothing Fails Like Success

If history teaches us nothing else it reminds us that there is no human enterprise that cannot fail. Of the Fortune 100 Best Companies of 1960, only 20 made the 2010 list. Just in the last five years, 18 companies have fallen out of the top 100 (derived from source data found at www.money.cnn.com). There are multiple reasons why companies fail, enough to fill shelves of business books, magazines, and tabloids, but when you boil them all down it comes back to the companies' ability to deliver on their value propositions. What they do or how they do it is no longer valued enough to compete within the marketplace. The companies that survive are able to adapt to changing conditions and changing market demands. They adapt their systems to the demands of the environment. To remain successful they need to consistently understand what customers want and remain focused on how well they satisfy that demand. This doesn't just happen; it must be planned, structured, and meticulously executed.

What exactly constitutes value and the many determinants that factor into how well your organization delivers is best understood by you and your customers/stakeholders so we couldn't go into any great level of depth here even if that was the intent. Therefore, we won't linger on this topic other than to stress the importance of customer feedback and the need for a sustainable organization to have consistently.

Ongoing Determination of Customer/Stakeholder Requirements and Satisfaction

To remain relevant your organization needs to have established procedures that regularly determine customer/stakeholder requirements and satisfaction. Like the odometer in the trunk analogy explained in Committing Element 4, too often this type of critical information is not available to decision makers or received too long after the fact for it to be of use. If a product has been in inventory for an extended period of time, defects will be difficult to trace back to the point of origin and even if it were possible, reconstructing the chain of events that resulted in the failure will be difficult and too late to be of any consequence. Without a clear, timely view to the process, its outputs, and its outcomes, decisions are calculated shots in the dark.

To be truly effective, the feedback should ascertain unstated customer requirements that help determine relative value compared to other suppliers and/or alternatives. One of the most effective methods is to establish and sustain strategic relationships with customers and other stakeholders. Members of the management team should be in ongoing contact with customers including regular site visits. Without these relationships, customers may not trust or value your organization sufficiently to give candid and timely feedback. In lean times of cost cutting, these relationships frequently suffer. Technology will never be an adequate substitution for human relations in business. Regularly schedule contacts and visits to nurture these essential relationships.

Sustaining Element 2: Ongoing Goal Setting and Revision

As Alice discovered in Wonderland, even a cat knows that goals are important:

QUOTE: "Would you tell me, please, which way I ought to go from here?" Alice asked of the Cheshire Cat.
"That depends a good deal on where you want to get to," said the Cat.
"I don't much care where—" said Alice.
"Then it doesn't matter which way you go," said the Cat.

Lewis Carroll
Alice in Wonderland (1865)

If goals are so important, why do so many organizations develop them merely as an administrative exercise?

GOALS IN A DRAWER: A good friend and mentor of mine helped me put the pointless administrative process of goals in perspective. It was fall harvest, time to pick goals. Valuing his wisdom, I asked for a copy of his annual goals to use as a template. Slowly and with great formality, he opened the lower right hand drawer of his desk and drew out a crisp, virtually untouched, manila folder.

"Here are my goals." He ceremoniously slid them back into the drawer and closed it reverently. "And there they will stay until next year at this time. But here…" he pointed to whiteboard behind him, "is what I'm working on." The handwritten, numbered "to do" list was extensive. It had circles and multiple colors underlining and highlighting. Some items were crossed off and other had exclamation points. "I can go year after year and never accomplish a single thing on my official goal sheet. But if I don't do these things, I'll be fired."

My friend and mentor was not overly cynical, he simply understood that every year the organization put everyone through their paces developing goals that would never be resourced or measured. But corporate demanded that every employee had an individual development plan with SMART goals and so they were written. "It's quite efficient really, think of it like perennial flowers, you only have to plant them once and they're good year after year!"

Through the years, I've encountered many organizations that go through similar pointless goal setting exercises. Some managers aren't quite as jaded about it; they have the best of intentions—they really do hope to accomplish the SMART goals they write—after all, goals are important—even a cat can tell you that! Alas, hope is not a strategy. Each new day one crisis or urgent priority follows the next and goals are steadily driven back into their dark drawers where they rest comfortably until they are dusted off and tweaked for the following year. As was discussed in Focusing Element 4, the "urgent" eclipses the important and organizations spend all their days scrambling from crisis to crisis continuously firefighting.

What I have found to be the case in most organizations that struggle with goal setting and achievement is that they are very effective at managing crises but ineffectual at remaining focused on the long-term priorities. They lose sight of their overall objectives; it's hard to remember you're trying to drain the swamp when you are up to your butt in alligators. Remember cardinal change sin no. 7, attention deficit management.

As you assess your organization be brutally honest; giving yourself unsubstantiated high marks is tantamount to cheating at solitaire. Ask yourself, "Is the development of goals just an administrative exercise?" If the organization frequently fails to achieve its stated goals, are there any consequences? To break the cycle the organization must systematically, methodically, and doggedly work to implement the systems and routines that constitute the elements of Forming, Focusing, and Committing. Like the conditioned triathlete, the organizational strength and discipline instilled during these stages will enable consistent goal achievement and the ongoing development of new and more challenging goals. If the assessment determines that goal setting is an ineffective administrative process than circle back to Focusing Element 6 (develop goals, action plans, and KPIs). If there are ineffective consequences, reexamine how individuals and teams hold themselves accountable as discussed in Committing Element 7. In Renewal Element 3, we will explore how to make the formal performance review and reward systems impactful.

Shifting Responsibilities from Team "F" to Team "P"

During the Forming Stage, we discussed the need to form two operational teams, Team "P" and Team "F" (Forming Element 3). Team "P" is responsible for ongoing running of the organization while Team "F" is crafting the future. Maintaining a dedicated team "keeping the wheels on the bus" is essential to providing organizational stability and ongoing cash flow that is funding the organization's investment in the future. For any change process to be considered a success a transformation has to occur whereby the future becomes the present. As such, it is important that the roles and responsibilities of the operations teams shift to adopt the new working reality. Being conscious of this need and deliberate in the transformation solidifies the visions of the future within the structures of the present. For some projects like new software or equipment, this transition is obvious. There comes a time when you turn off the old stuff and cut over to the new stuff. However, for some transformations the changes are not as clear-cut—changes in procedures, reporting, communications, etc., are changes that are not driven by physical infrastructures. These are the procedures that can be bypassed, undermined, and ignored if the organization doesn't deliberately make the shift. This is a major reason why multiple initiatives fail. One group adopts the changes while another continues on with business as usual. I've even seen changes that reduce the physical demands on individuals ignored for the sake of the past.

One driver that fuels the entrenched behaviors is failure to continuously engage Team "P" in the design of the future. During the hectic period of transformation, communications take a backseat to designing the new processes and solving the myriad of problems that arise during the change process. Once the problems have been worked out, Team "F" unveils the bright and shiny future to Team "P" where it is sometimes met with a "So?" or a "Did you consider?" or even an "Ain't never going to catch me doing that." I was once told by an operator in Alabama, "People would rather eat crap than have ice cream shoved up their butts." This crude piece of country wisdom reinforced in me the need to engage the entire plant as much as possible. However, engaging them too much can actually slow progress and derail the change initiative. This is the "art" behind the "science" of change management. A healthy balance must be maintained to keep it between the ditches.

To make a successful hand-off between Team "F" and Team "P," managers need to act deliberately to redefine the roles and responsibilities and reinforce the clear expectations with logical consequences.

Shifting Roles by Playing to Peoples' Strengths

In addition to the solidification of the new processes within the day-to-day operations, there is another very important reason for transitioning roles and responsibilities to Team "P"; it too links back to the elements laid down during the Forming Stage: temperament and capabilities. When we studied DISC, we outlined temperament types that thrive on change, challenges, and problem solving. The same individuals who were so critical to the change process can be detrimental to the sustaining process. The "D"s and "I"s of the world enjoy the fast pace and constant challenge of change. The "S"s and "C"s prefer a more measured pace and are most satisfied working with clearly defined procedures and processes. "D"s and "I"s frequently lack the attention to detail and the endurance to successfully sustain a process day in and day out, year after year. They become bored, restless, and look onward to their next challenge. Transitioning the responsibilities of running the new systems to the sustainers in the organization helps ensure that those changes will become the new norm. This transition of duties and responsibilities now frees up the "D"s and "I"s to direct their energies toward the next opportunity or threat facing the organization.

A WORD TO THE WISE: general temperaments are guidelines and not written in stone. Don't define people by a simple letter or title—this can limit their potential contributions and can also be demeaning and demoralizing. These general characteristics we are discussing are directional aids—not laws of physics. Thus, it is critical that managers know their people and make assignments based upon their individual strengths, preferences, change readiness, and their need for new challenges and growth opportunities. Continuously playing to someone's existing strengths does nothing to build their capacity and grow new competencies. The engaged mentor helps their people push past what they thought were the limits of their capabilities.

"Only those who will risk going too far can possibly find out how far one can go."

T. S. Eliot
American/English Poet (1888–1965)

Sustaining Element 3: Availability and Use of Documentation for Systems and Procedures

As the organization is forming, focusing, and committing it is deep within the creative processes discovering and inventing—it's all new, exciting, and very dynamic. Those who are there for the birth of the organization have firsthand knowledge of reasons why decisions were made and how the systems were designed. Busy building the organization, they don't have time to write anything down—yet another example of urgent tasks eclipsing important ones. Consequently, systems and procedures are not well documented. The resources and documentation that do exist have grown organically and out of necessity rather than through design. Once up and running, the procedures that have been developed aren't reviewed and updated to reflect "as built"; the organization continues to drive forward not taking time to document what has been done and why. This lack of documented procedures sets the process of generational competency decay in motion.

Written Documentation to Augment Training Checklists

When we discussed the need for a structured approach to training and qualifications (Committing Element 2), the use of training checklists was stressed as a way to minimize generational competency decay. The checklist is a comprehensive catalogue of essential knowledge, skills, and abilities. The availability of written procedures and similar documentation augments the checklists and enhances the training and qualification process.

Prioritization of Documentation Requirements

The training checklist developed through the DACUM process will list dozens of tasks required for each position. Documenting everything is expensive and time consuming. Do you really need a written policy or procedure for everything? The answer is no; attempts to do so may exhaust what resources are available that could have been used to create the truly important documentation. I've seen more than a few organizations start initiatives beginning at the top and consecutively writing procedure after procedure, working down a DACUM list until they run out of time, money, or ambition. The documentation project is abandoned halfway complete. To maximize the use of scarce resources and ensure documentation of the most important policies, processes, and procedures, prioritize them. There are two effective methods of prioritization: equipment functionality and operational criticality.

For organizations that have mechanical or electrical systems or equipment, functionality is a very effective method of prioritization. This method sets down the essentials of system operation. For each system, document the following at a minimum:

- Start up
- Shut down
- Emergency shut down

- Grade change or switches
- Essential maintenance

For other organizations that don't have machinery or equipment, where the operations logic dictates the prioritization of documentation, criticality to operations can be used.

The criticality to operations prioritization method is named for one of four elements used to rank the importance of documentation. This method ranks according to safety, criticality, difficulty, and frequency.

Safety: Any task that has a substantial risk of causing injury or equipment damage will be made safer with written documentation.

Criticality: Criticality is defined by how exacting the procedure or task must be done for safety or to conform to quality standards. For instance, if it is essential that a procedure be performed exactly in a certain order or with precise measures, tolerances, or timing, then you would rank its criticality has high. Analyzing blood or tissue samples requires precise measures and timing—this procedure is more critical than mixing a cocktail where the measures of ingredients can be varied according to the taste of the customer (although if you are serving James Bond, ensure that it is shaken and not stirred).

Difficulty: Difficulty is measured by the number and complexity of the steps involved in completing the task. A one-button or one-step operation such as pushing a button on an elevator is not too difficult and probably doesn't require a written procedure whereas launching the space shuttle does. Both will take you up, but one is clearly more difficult than the other. (NOTE: Some clients use the term *complexity* in place of *difficulty*.)

Frequency: Frequency is ranked in reverse order, with the more infrequent tasks being ranked higher. This is because the complex tasks that you perform routinely are committed to memory and are therefore less likely to be done incorrectly as a simpler task that you perform once a decade.

Apply these four ranking criteria to your DACUM task list to establish the priority ranking of documentation. I advise clients to rank each on a scale of 1–5, with one being low and 5 being high. Table 5.4 shows a partial sample

Table 5.4 Sample Prioritization Matrix Ranking Documentation Importance

Material Handler Tasks	Safety 1 = Little Chance of Being Injured 5 = Strong Chance of Grave Injury or Death	Criticality 1 = No Critical Issues 5 = Involves Extremely Critical Steps	Difficulty 1 = Simple Task 5 = Difficult and Complex Task Involving Multiple Steps and Coordination	Frequency 1 = Performed Multiple Times a Day 5 = Rarely Performed—May Be Years between Occurrences	Overall Ranking: Sum of Four Elements
1. Fill out clamptruck checklist	1	2	2	1	6
2. Demonstrate how to fuel clamptruck	4	3	3	2	12
3. Drive clamptruck	3	3	3	1	10
4. Roll identification	1	4	2	1	8
5. Prepare rolls for running	4	3	3	1	11
6. Run shredder	4	4	4	2	14
7. Unplug shredder	5	5	5	4	19

of rankings of the importance of developing documentation for the tasks of a material handler position in a paperboard converting facility.

According to this ranking, procedural documentation should be developed in the following order: 7, 6, 2, 5, 3, 4, 1. If you strictly followed the DACUM order, the most important procedures would have been written last, assuming they had time to get to them.

One final note on documentation: don't rely strictly on a mechanical score; apply judgment. If you believe that a task needs documentation, by all means develop it. For instance, the converting facility actually had more problems with quality and consistency from improper roll preparation than any other single source. Developing standards of operation for task no. 5 significantly improved the quality and contributed to the bottom line of the organization.

Documentation Is Readily Accessible and Regularly Used

Like many of these elements, it should be common sense that if there are procedures and other documentation developed, then those procedures should be made readily accessible for reference during the course of daily operations. Unfortunately, it's been my experience that this is frequently not the case. I've found procedural binders gathering dust on managers' shelves and locked inside of cabinets, closets, and trunks of cars. When I asked one manager why the binder wasn't out on the floor he looked at me as if I were as sharp as a pound of wet leather, "They'd only mess them up or lose them." To my way of thinking, this manager was obviously missing the intent of having procedures in the first place—unless the point of having procedures is strictly to satisfy some aspect of compliance. On more than one occasion the following conversation or one very similar to it has occurred when an auditor or inspector has dropped in for a visit:

> "Do you have safety procedures?"
> "Of course," the manager reaches onto the top shelf behind his desk, pulls down the nicely printed laminated book of procedures, blows off the dust and hands it over.
> "Very good, these are very good looking procedures."
> "Thank you, we are all about quality here at Acme Whosa-Whatsits."

To reiterate, unless you are more concerned with what you look like rather than what you actually are, a handwritten, coffee-stained procedure actually being used is infinitely better than a gold-plated tablet collecting dust on a shelf.

Procedures Need to Be Sufficiently Detailed

It is good to have documentation, it important to have it available, but it is absolutely essential that it mean something. Again, this sounds like common sense, but I have reviewed hundreds of examples of documentation that was so poorly written or so vague that it was meaningless. The operation would have been better off with nothing. Here is a verbatim example of a start-up procedure from a North American manufacturing facility:

1. Start power
2. Start air
3. Start equipment

That's it! If you were expecting more, there is none. It had a great header, footer, revision date, and six authorizing signatures, but I've left those all off to protect the guilty. When I first saw it, I thought it was a mistake. Perhaps it was a joke: the universal procedure good for starting anything from a chain-saw to the space shuttle. But it wasn't. This was only one of hundreds of other intentionally vague procedures created by this ISO-certified facility. When I asked the manager about the procedures, he informed me that the facility wanted to become ISO compliant to help them sell their products in the European market. To be compliant, they needed to have procedures that were consistently followed. By intentionally writing vague procedures, they were certified, and every operator on every shift was still able to operate as they felt appropriate. They had received certification by meeting the letter of the standard but had no intention of living up to the intent of the quality standard.

As you can imagine, this operation and its management team also ranked very low on Committing Element 9 (organization lives its values with integrity).

BEST IN CLASS: The very best example of documentation use and availability I have ever seen was in a chemical plant in Louisiana, U.S.A. Every procedure was available on line and in hardcopy (in case of power failures). It was expected that every operator print out a copy of the procedure to take with them for each task that altered system alignment or configuration. (NOTE: This policy did not apply to *emergency procedures*. They had to be memorized and practiced thereby preparing the operators to act quickly if necessary to put the plant in a safe condition.)

At the bottom of each procedure was the printed phrase, "This document valid for 24 hours after [print date and time]." This ensured that operators didn't keep copies pigeonholed in their lockers that may be out of date. As the operator performed the task, he or she would refer to the procedure in hand. Should the operator find an error or simply wanted to provide input or clarification they would mark up the hard copy and turn it in to their supervisor. If, after the supervisor, engineer, and other team members reviewed the proposed change, the procedure was modified, the change would be in ***bold underlined italics*** and the revision date would be changed. The procedure was also annotated in the Change Notification Log. A clipboard containing revised procedures along with its cover sheet that every affected person's name and a place for their signature and date. Each operator would review the changes, sign and date acknowledging understanding and commitment to compliance with the change. When everyone was notified, the procedure and its routing sheet were filed with the master procedures in the Quality Control Office. The hard copies available for use were also updated and documented.

Not only did this highly regimented process ensure procedural compliance, it also ensured a very high level of understanding in the operators and their involvement in the operation of the facility. When they had first implemented the process, few changes were submitted. But as operators began to realize that their input mattered and had an impact, they became involved and soon dozens of changes were submitted every week. After a time, the number of changes dropped off as the quality and applicability of the procedures improved. At the time of my visiting the plant, they only received one or two changes a month.

This was a very well run operation with extremely high safety and quality standards—I've never seen another facility that has compared before or since.

Sustaining Element 4: Proactive Problem Solving, Decision Making Scope and Impact

At its core, change management is a series of problems to solve and decisions to be made. The decision is made to change; during implementation, problems arise that must be solved in order to successfully navigate each stage and move to a higher level of performance. Problem solving is essential in every stage of the organizational change process and the ongoing effectiveness and efficiency of the organization's ongoing operation. Problem solving was discussed in depth in both Focusing Elements 7 and 8; we discuss it again because the problems encountered during the Sustainable Performance Stage require a slightly different approach.

Once an organization has reached the stage of sustaining, they have already solved many problems and made many decisions. They have navigated the challenges of forming; they moved through focusing after possibly stumbling for a bit before they created the systems, policies, and procedures; and they have established roles and responsibilities to which the employees are now committed. At this point, there is growing confidence, enthusiasm, and each employee is gaining increasing levels of mastery. It is here where many organizations fall into a common trap; they believe they are done. The trap is baited by overconfidence, groupthink, and an inflexible view of reality.

The Overconfidence Trap

When an organization has reached the point where they are performing well and achieving their goals, they become confident. This is a desirable state since confidence is essential to taking action. Without confidence, people and organizations can become paralyzed, unable to make decisions, constantly second-guessing themselves and seeking additional data that will definitively point to the one true path. However, in life, there are many paths and rarely do we possess complete information. Thus, confidence is a strength that enables forward progress; like any strength taken to excess, it can become a weakness. When a leader becomes overconfident and they reach a point where they believe the questions have been answered and everything is all sewn up in a neat little package they can fall into a decision making trap where they overestimate their abilities and underestimate the conditions—conditions they may not even be fully aware of from where they are sitting.

When a leader fails to maintain a healthy level of humility, they tend to make decisions that plunge them headlong into situations that can lead to disaster. They assume past performance guarantees future success; they assume that whatever they may encounter their skills will be sufficient enough to prevail. People heavily skewed toward the "D" temperament are vulnerable to this decision trap.

To avoid the overconfidence trap leaders need to be open to feedback. They must seek out information from all sources, particularly from those closest to the situation. Continue to value everyone's input, especially those who don't entirely agree and don't let the success achieved thus far be the downfall of the enterprise.

The other technique to help avoid the overconfidence is consistent utilization of a structured approach to problem solving that helps decision makers consider the multiple factors driving and restraining problems as well as considering the risks such that they can implement appropriate controls and develop contingency plans should the decision fail to yield the desired outcomes due to incomplete awareness of all factors.

The Groupthink Trap

The second decision trap organizations fall into during the Sustaining Performance Stage is groupthink. Irving Janis defined the concept as "a mode of thinking that people engage in when they are deeply involved in a cohesive in-group, when the members' strivings for unanimity override their motivation to realistically appraise alternative courses of action." (Janis, I.L. 1972. *Victims of Groupthink*. Boston: Houghton Mifflin Company.)

Organizations in the Sustaining Performance Stage have formed cohesive groups. Feelings of inclusion and mutual support have been forged in the fires of past trials where acting as a team has overcome adversity and brought with it a sense of pride and accomplishment. These tight-knit teams can reach consensus quicker and more easily than when they were first formed. Mutually shared trust and confidence minimizes each one's need to question the claims and assumptions of the others—after all, don't we all tend to trust the word of a friend more readily than that of a stranger? Cohesive teams tend to act quicker based on less information. In addition, the cohesiveness of the teams tends to dissuade dissenting opinions even when there are doubts or misgivings. It is uncomfortable being the lone voice crying in the wilderness. The desire for acceptance and unanimity is powerful and can cause people to set aside their difference for the good of the collective. Individuals with higher needs for affiliation, "I" and "S" temperaments, can tend to be predisposed in this manner. The ability to think critically, generates viable alternatives, and weighing the pros and cons of a given situation becomes impaired.

However, it doesn't have to be that way. Cohesive teams can make quality decisions provided that they are aware of the pitfalls of groupthink and are sufficiently self-aware that they recognize when they are in danger of falling prey to this decision trap. Janis offered seven strategies to minimize groupthink (p. 209–215):

1. Leaders should assign each member the role of "critical evaluator." This allows each member to freely air objections and doubts.
2. Higher ups should not express an opinion when assigning a task to a group.
3. The organization should set up several independent groups, working on the same problem.
4. All effective alternatives should be examined.
5. Each member should discuss the group's ideas with trusted people outside of the group.
6. The group should invite outside experts into meetings. Group members should be allowed to discuss with and question the outside experts.
7. At least one group member should be assigned the role of Devil's advocate. This should be a different person for each meeting.

Following these guidelines, groupthink can be avoided. Janis cited how the United States Government, under the leadership of President John F. Kennedy, avoided groupthink and made quality decisions avoiding a potential armed conflict with the Soviet Union (p. 148–149).

THE CUBAN MISSILE CRISIS: In October 1962, U.S. Military intelligence detected facilities being constructed on the Island of Cuba capable of launching nuclear ballistic missiles. Drawing upon the lessons learned from the failed Bay of Pigs invasion (April 1961), President Kennedy avoided groupthink by forming two separate teams to independently develop response strategies. The teams engaged in vigorous discussions with outside experts who shared their expertise and opinions on the crisis. Through all of this, President Kennedy remained deliberately absent from the proceedings because he did not want his views to bias the quality of the decisions. Though he was absent, he was not abdicating. He had given clear directions to the teams and then delegated to them the development of options. President Kennedy also clearly defined the limits of the teams' authority; they were to make recommendations, but the ultimate decision was his alone. The teams were held to strict timelines since intelligence reports confirmed that the missiles would soon become operational, thereby becoming a clear and present danger just 90 miles off the U.S. Coastline. When the teams had reached their separate conclusions, he had each critique the other's proposal. The two teams then presented their recommendations. One team advocated for swift military intervention to neutralize the threat prior to the missiles becoming operational. The other team recommended a naval blockade of the island nation. After listening closely and questioning each team, President Kennedy made the decision to try the naval blockade first; if it did not yield results within a set timeframe, he was prepared to authorize military action. Fortunately, the Soviets turned back, and the Cuban missile bases were dismantled and sent back to Russia without any escalation of hostilities.

This is a very effective example of utilizing a structured process to avoid the groupthink logic trap as well as a successful utilization of a situational approach to leadership. President Kennedy provided clear direction (S1), delegated to the group to develop potential solutions (S4), collaborated with the groups to explore the pros and cons of each potential solution (S3), and based upon the input of the team, made the decision (S2). The 1-4-3-2 pattern is as effective today as it was in 1962 and will serve you well whether you are saving your company money or saving the country from war.

The Inflexible View of Reality Trap

There is a myth that many organizations believe: the belief that after the work of organizational transformation is complete they will be done. Unfortunately, in our dynamic world, there are so many forces that shift and change the organizational ecosystem that, over time, or sometimes quite suddenly, solutions cease to be adequate. Think of it like swimming up a river: as soon as you stop, the current carries you back down again. The basis of this belief is part coping mechanism and partly the remnants of an obsolete change model.

Belief that there are green pastures ahead in which we shall take our rest helps keep us motivated. It's far too daunting to say to a recent graduate "Congratulations, here's your diploma. Now get out there and work like a dog until you die." I don't know why, but you just don't see that written in too many greeting cards. It is true that things can and do get better as organizations achieve a steady course of smooth sailing, but even in those halcyonic days, someone must always remain at the helm with a watchful eye toward the horizon and a steady hand on the tiller. Organizations founder when those entrusted to lead fall asleep at the wheel, lulled into a false sense of security by their current success. Leaders must remain alert for indicators of potential problems and consider organizational vulnerabilities. To achieve that essential mindset of constant vigilance it helps if leaders shift their patterns of thinking regarding the very nature of change which will improve their problem solving abilities.

Traditional Change Management versus Improvisational Change

The traditional view that has dominated the thinking about organizational change is a pattern whereby stable organizations can be unfrozen, changed, and then refrozen (Lewin, K. 1951. *Field Theory in Social Science: Selected Theoretical Papers*. D. Cartwright (ed.). New York: Harper & Row). This model helps reinforce the hope that there will come a day when things will be stable and unchanging. But this model is counter to the well-known axiom, "the one single constant in life is change." Hope for a stability that never comes leaves people frustrated and disappointed. Remember, it is our expectations that govern our degree of satisfaction with our outcomes. It is healthier for organizations to have an accurate view of the dynamic world they live in and create competencies appropriate to reality. In my experience, improvisational change methods significantly improve outcomes and attitudes within an organization.

The improvisational change model set forth by Wanda J. Orlikowski and J. Debra Hofman in their paper (Orlikowski, W.J., and Hofman, J.D. 1997. An improvisational model of change management: The case of groupware technologies. *Sloan Management Review*, Winter) outlines an adaptive methodology for implementing changes associated with software implementations. This model can be further adapted to expand an organizations view of virtually any change initiative, thereby preparing them to quickly adjust to changing conditions and thus stay on course as they navigate toward their objectives.

Successful planning, problem solving, and implementation of solutions cannot be a strictly linear progression, it must adapt to three variations of change:

■ Anticipated
■ Emergent
■ Opportunistic

Anticipated changes are those that are envisioned at the beginning of the project. The team expects the changes to occur and thereby can plan ahead. An example of anticipated change includes the known features of a system that require input. To be successful, the project will need to set forth procedures and train operators on their new roles and responsibilities.

Emergent changes are discovered along the way. As a project unfolds and the organization becomes more familiar with the vision, mission, and objectives, opportunities emerge that weren't planned but support the ability of the organization to achieve its goals in a more efficient and effective manner by adding capacity. One example of an emergent change occurred when a manufacturing plant implemented a distributed control system built on shared network architecture. Part of the anticipated capabilities of the system was the ability to save reports and screen shots to a common shared drive. The intended purpose was for reporting and troubleshooting. When operators encountered an error, they captured the event and saved it so that engineers could review it later. The change that emerged occurred when operators started using the shared database as an informal knowledge warehouse. They began to save lessons learned and best practices that they shared between shifts, trained new operators, and referred to later as needed. This use was not anticipated but became a value-added feature of the new infrastructure.

Opportunistic changes are those that the organization does not plan for specifically in advance but are purposely capitalized upon when they arise. These opportunities may become available based upon organizational readiness or timing. An example of this type of change could occur when the equipment breaks down and the supervisor takes advantage of the situation to train his crew on troubleshooting and problem solving thereby increasing her crew's competency and building capacity that will change how the team responds to future events.

Mastering the ability to respond to and navigate each of these types of change builds agility into the organization. A manager who sets out on an anticipated course and then refuses to alter the plan in response to changing conditions or adapt according to emergent or opportunistic circumstances risks not achieving optimal outcomes or outright failure. All four temperaments are vulnerable but each for different reasons: "D"s may be overconfident; "I"s inattention to details may lead them to miss opportunities for emergent and opportunistic changes; "S"s desire for stability may make them uncomfortable veering from the set course thereby missing an opportunistic change; and "C"s may be too inwardly focused that they become rigid in their views. Since every temperament may struggle with managing change, all of us can benefit from incorporating an appreciation of "Jazz." Orlikowski and Hofman use the analogy of a jazz ensemble compared to classical orchestra to illustrate how to gain mastery of improvisational agility.

Playing classical music follows established patterns. Beethoven's Ninth Symphony follows the same basic pattern that it has since it was composed in 1824. Certainly, each musician can add his or her own minor variations but the overall pattern of the notes remains the same. Compare this to jazz when musicians don't decide up front which notes will be played. Inspiration is the objective that guides each instrument as it plays off the patterns and melodies of the others, adding, modifying, and embellishing as the music emerges. Leading a jazz group applauds improvisation whereas impromptu spontaneity in the middle of a classical concert may get you banished like Lisa Simpson in the beginning of each of the cartoon episodes.

Sequences of Improvisational Change

Anticipated, emergent, and opportunistic changes aren't mutually exclusive; sometimes they occur in tangent with each other and sometimes in sequence. As depicted in Figure 5.3, an anticipated change is implemented from which an emergent change arises. This leads to an opportunistic change followed by an emergent change and so on.

Some changes may be anticipated in form, although it is not exactly known when the timing or circumstances will be for the organization to be able to act—these can be thought of as hybrids of "anticipated–opportunistic." The opportunity to acquire a competitor is an example of an anticipated–opportunistic change. The company must have anticipated that a desirable opportunity may become available and thus prepares by building its cash reserves and establishing policies and procedures for assimilation of the new acquisition; though anticipated, the opportunity must present itself before the change can occur.

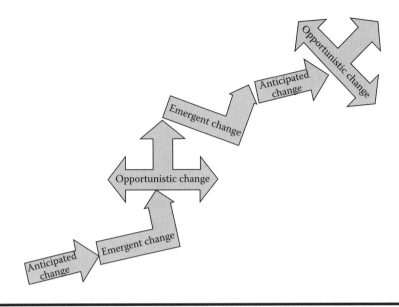

Figure 5.3 Improvisational model of change.

To take advantage of these three change variations leaders and managers must be able to manage creative chaos yet remain in control such that the organization continues on a path toward achieving its objectives.

1. Clearly articulate the team's span of control and limits of authority.
2. Ensure the change opportunity supports the overall vision and mission and is aligned to the organization's values.
3. Ensure that the initiative does not draw excessive resources away from the main objective thereby impeding progress. Unplanned changes can cause scope creep thereby overrunning the original initiative's budgets and timelines. If the emergent initiative is of value but the timing isn't quite right, have the teams capture their work thus far and shelve the project until the main initiative has been achieved. The new concept can be fully flushed out as an enhancement when time and resources can support it. This may not be possible for opportunistic changes. The window of opportunity may be open for a limited time. If this is the case, then management must make a tactical decision to either pursue or abandon the opportunity. This tactical decision must be made in full alignment with the organization's overall strategies. Otherwise the organization will suffer from the ill effects of either cardinal change sin no. 6 (failure to stay the course) or sin no. 7 (attention deficit management). Either one will derail the organization's change initiative.

4. Be alert for any unintended consequences; intervene promptly if negative consequences arise. Many emergent responses can be "work-arounds" that allow the change resistant factions of the organization to not fully participate in the change or to undermine the main initiative. Work-arounds that duplicate efforts or create secret secondary systems must be controlled.
5. Communicate the initiatives broadly such that other areas and teams can remain aware of the changes to enable them to take advantage of the benefits or observe any potential downsides as well as monitor and report results.
6. Incorporate the change initiatives into the overall strategic plan as they emerge, create documentation of the changes and incorporate them into plans and procedures to codify their use and ensure continuity of operations training one generation to the next.
7. Capture and share the lessons learned for future incorporation into future change initiatives.

Sustaining Element 5: Ongoing Communications and Reporting

Fueling the tendency to idle once a project's main objectives are complete and in place is the tendency to allow communications to wane. The broad reaching communications that organizations deploy during the initial push of the Forming Stage of the project tend to peter out. This reduction in the frequency and quality of communications gives rise to frustration of employees who were previously kept informed. The void in communications feeds the rumor mill. If an organization tends to only communicate well when it's embarking on a major change initiative, members will tend to view communications as propaganda designed to "sell them" on ideas that are not in their best interest. Ongoing communications on the status, successes, and challenges of the organization keep the fires of engagement stoked and the rumor mill at a minimum.

In addition to internal communications, messages outside the organization also tend to dwindle over time as well. Customers and stakeholders who were initially courted rigorously can be left out of the loop. Like a neglected spouse, they become vulnerable to courtship from competitors. This is particularly true if there are any issues with quality or service delivery that arose from the change in routine and procedures that haven't had all the bugs worked out. Lack of communications will lead customers and stakeholders assuming the change initiative is responsible for the quality issues. This can cause them to question the organization's ability to manage change as well as the management's commitment to quality and customer service. Without frequent ongoing communications, customers and other past supporters can withdraw their support from the organization. When this happens, it often catches the organization unaware because the lines of communication are down and the organization has had so much of its attention inwardly focused on affecting the change.

Ongoing communications maintains and deepens the relationship between the organization and its customers and stakeholders. These relationships allows the organization to take advantage of fresh opportunities that may arise and gives them ample warning when problems begin to sprout allowing time for correction or compensation without damaging the relationships.

To satisfy the elements of Sustained Performance continue to utilize and demonstrate the principles set forth in Forming Element 6: Leaders set the tone for effective, open, and inclusive communication. The principles of communication are the same; they just need to be continuously sustained. The messages will vary, shifting from an educational and marketing focus, to feedback gathering, and eventually toward growing alignment and reporting successes.

Life in the Clouds—The Executive Fogbank

Organizational effectiveness, like effectiveness in life, depends on having a clear and undistorted view of reality. Not seeing the car that hits you doesn't reduce the damage or even provide any comfort. As such, communications up are as important, if not more important than communicating down. For the uppermost echelon of many organizations, their view of reality is neither clear nor undistorted. Leaders are surrounded by their teams who report the progress and achievements of their assigned areas of operation. If their area is doing well, they look knowledgeable, competent, and effective. But what of those managers who really aren't engaged and aren't adding significant value yet receive undue credit? Because they control the message, managers have the opportunity to claim responsibility for the gains occurring within their areas. Time and time again I've seen the talents and toils of individuals go unrecognized by top leadership because the middle management tier minimized, and at times, completely negated, the contributions of those accomplishing the work. The executive's awareness and understanding of the true success drivers can be obscured by the cloud of individuals surrounding them—a cloud is just fog by another name. That cloud can distort the executive's perception of reality. Unless top executives seek alternate views to reality, they will only know the true value and worth of individual contributors if the manager accurately reports their contributions.

Don't get me wrong; it is the managers' due to receive credit for the accomplishments of their department, and, to be effective, every employee should work to make his or her boss look good—it helps to stay employed. Logic dictates that managers should value the highly competent because they make the department look good—but logic doesn't enter into the equation when cuts must be made through headcount reduction. Inept managers are more frequently intimidated and feel threatened by their highly competent staff—it's easier to look better when surrounded by those less competent then yourself. They will gladly throw another under the bus to maintain their own position. Many struggling companies lay off the ones accomplishing the work to save the jobs of management because the executives have a skewed view to the true value of their management team. Executives and managers who may be classified as "idea" men and women, described in the second cardinal change leadership sin, have a particularly hard time seeing beyond the fog of sycophants and schmoozers that swirl around them. Compound this with the personal relationships formed within the executive cloud it becomes easier to dispose of a faceless worker than an executive crony. Consequently, cuts are made, and the hidden talent pool is flushed, leaving an overpaid and underperforming organization.

There is a solution and we've already discussed it. If the organization has formed and focused well, having built systems directly supporting strategy maps they have defined the roles and responsibilities of every level. A clear and undistorted view of the organization's true inner workings will be apparent for all to see. This view can then be validated through the establishment of a continuous balanced view of process outcomes. So armed, leaders can remain sufficiently informed to make difficult choices regarding scarce resources.

Sustaining Element 6: Continuous Balanced View of Process Outcomes

We've stressed how systems thinking is essential to optimize and sustain performance throughout each section. In the initial stages of projects, there is usually very close attention paid to the process and outcomes from every level. Good results comfort the concerned and they shift their attention to the next summit to be climbed. With their gaze upward, organizations lose sight of conditions on the ground. Even a war zone looks better from 50,000 feet than it does from a trench. When managers consistently fly at a "high level," they only become aware of issues after they reach a critical mass. At 50,000 feet, only really big explosions get your attention. Reactively managing each subsequent organizational "explosion" creates the pattern of crisis management described in the seventh cardinal sin of change leadership (attention deficit management). Attention deficit management has two major contributing factors: insufficient data and/or inaccurate misleading data.

Avoiding Organizational Pinball: Reactive Management

Threats to organizational stability can come from any direction. They can originate inside the organization, from customers or stakeholders, from competitors, or obsolescence of the organization's products or services. To sustain the organization, managers must remain vigilant to each threat and constantly shift their focus and resources between multiple competing priorities while still managing to keep the organization on an even keel consistently focused on achieving the mission. Earlier we discussed how competing forces (tensions) are constantly driving or restraining progress; we also introduced the Law of Unintended Consequences. Competing tensions and unintended consequences can exacerbate each other to the point where organizations can feel as if they are caught in a pinball machine. You have a problem, you resolve the problem which leads to other problems; a vicious cycle ensues. Figure 5.4 provides an apt analogy to help illustrate the point.

Problem: Hunger → *Solution:* Eat → *Unintended Consequence:* Gain Weight → *Reaction:* Diet → *Problem:* Hunger → Repeat.

In business, we see similar patterns (Figure 5.5).

Problem: Poor Customer Service → *Solution:* Hire More Customer Service Reps → *Unintended Consequence:* High Operational Costs → *Reaction:* Lay off Service Reps → *Problem:* Poor Customer Service → *Repeat* …

These cyclical problem patterns are quite common in most organizations. Other frequently cited examples of the pattern include the following:

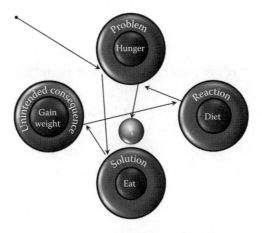

Figure 5.4   Yo-yo dieting.

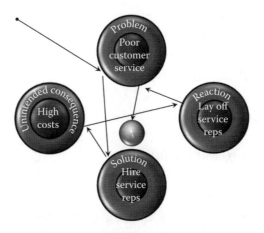

Figure 5.5   Organizational pinball.

training versus cost, quality versus production speed, maintenance costs versus equipment reliability, etc. Concentrating on one facet while neglecting another leads to unintended consequences. To break the cycle, managers must strike a happy medium—they must maintain awareness of the competing elements and balance them all within acceptable parameters. This is only possible if you have accurate and timely measures for each.

Avoiding "The Plan": The Need for Accurate Information

The analogy of gaining unwanted weight is one that most people can relate to; most of us are delighted if we step onto the scale and discover we've lost a pound or two. But what if the scale's inaccurate? What if you are relying on inaccurate information to gauge your progress? This can be the case when managers are too far removed from the process and rely on others to report and interpret the health of their organization. The same filtering can occur with autocratic managers who have a propensity for beating messengers. A photocopy of the following parable hung on the wall of a production engineer's office. I never found out who the original author was to thank him or her for putting such a humorous spin on how "happy talk" and "political correctness" allow poor plans to become policy:

"THE PLAN"

In the beginning, there was a plan,
And then came the assumptions,
And the assumptions were without form,
And the plan without substance,

And the darkness was upon the face of the workers,
And they spoke among themselves saying,
"It is a crock of s**t and it stinks."

And the workers went unto their Supervisors and said,
"It is a pile of dung, and we cannot live with the smell."

And the Supervisors went unto their Managers saying,
"It is a container of excrement, and it is very strong,
Such that none may abide by it."

And the Managers went unto their Directors saying,
"It is a vessel of fertilizer, and none may abide by its strength."

And the Directors spoke among themselves saying to one another,
"It contains that which aids plants' growth, and it is very strong."

And the Directors went to the Vice Presidents saying unto them,
"It promotes growth, and it is very powerful."

And the Vice Presidents went to the President, saying unto him,
"This new plan will actively promote the growth and vigor
of the company with very powerful effects."

And the President looked upon the Plan
And saw that it was good,
And the Plan became Policy.

And this, my friend, is how s**t happens.

Anonymous

If you want to know what is really going on in your organization, you can't shoot the messenger—embrace and encourage them! In addition to embracing the messengers, don't sugar-coat or "spin" the messages. It is important to craft the message in an effective manner such that the receiver is open to it, but don't alter the message to the point that the importance, urgency, or even the meaning is obscured. There is a world of difference between political savvy and political correctness.

To put into perspective the degree of "spin" that occurs within a facility, consider an analysis of 10 years of process improvement projects performed in a manufacturing plant. Based upon the sum total of all the percent efficiency gains each project claimed as part of its justification (10% for one, 15% for the next, etc.), the machinery should have been running at 190% efficiency—somehow the "happenings" didn't live up to the "hype."

If organizational reporting relies on unsubstantiated claims and anecdotal evidence, you might think you're making progress when we're actually losing ground. But in life, our clothes will tell us what the scale may not. Managers may fudge the numbers a bit, but in the end, the truth always comes out—if you don't believe me, ask Bernie Madoff.

You don't want to wait until a problem explodes before you notice it. Sustainable organizations maintain a timely view to validated KPIs that accurately reflect all facets of organizational health.

Organizational Dashboards and Balanced Scorecards

Long-term sustainability demands that the organization consistently deliver on its value proposition provided to customers and stakeholders. In its simplest form, this is determined by how efficiently the organization converts its inputs to outcomes and its ability to replicate that performance consistently over time. To maintain a view to reality, the outcomes of organizational activities and processes must be reported in an accurate and unbiased manner. This requires accurate metrics that cannot be massaged and engaged management. The most effective method I've seen to achieve this broad view is through the utilization of a Balanced Scorecard.

A balanced scorecard, sometimes referred to as an organizational dashboard, provides a comprehensive view of the multiple dimensions that define organizational success. Comprehensive dashboards usually include elements of four dimensions:

1. Financial results
2. Operational effectiveness
3. Customer satisfaction
4. Employee readiness and satisfaction

For each of these critical dimensions, KPIs are aggregated into a concise and easily understandable format. Sometimes these are represented as gauges (Figure 5.6), "spider" diagrams (Figure 5.7), bar charts (Figure 5.8), run charts (Figure 5.9), or multiple other variations depending upon the needs and desires of the organization. Regardless of the format, it is most important that each indicator be available in a timely manner to allow coordination of work activities and support tactical decisions, thereby allowing intervention before a flare-up becomes an all-out crisis.

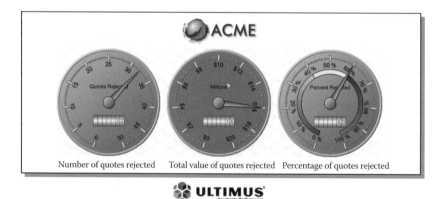

Figure 5.6 Dashboard gauges. (Courtesy of Ultimus, Inc. With permission.)

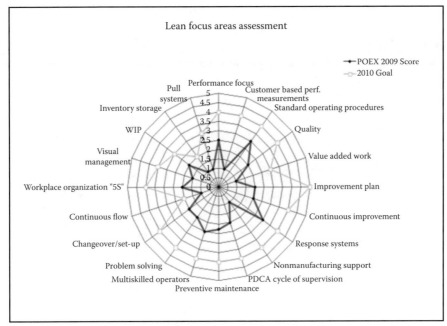

Figure 5.7   Spider diagrams. (Courtesy of Ultimus, Inc. With permission.)

The timely view to the process usually requires different views according to the position's specific roles and responsibilities. What is vital information to one business area may only be of mild interest to another. There are multiple technology solutions on the market such as the Ultimus Dashboard™ that provide near real-time access to information at the appropriate granularity of detail along with the capability to drill down into the details of each business process.

If all of this sounds a bit complex let me provide a nautical analogy that may help bring it into focus.

Course Corrections while Sailing into the Wind

Early we used the analogy of swimming upstream—when you stop swimming, you are carried back downstream. The same is true of a ship sailing in the windward direction. A sailing ship is unable to sail directly into the wind; it must alternate its course by tacking port and starboard turning its bow through the wind, sailing for a time slightly upwind and then tacking to

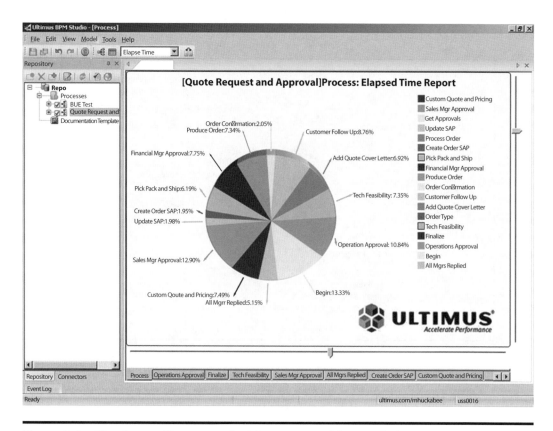

Figure 5.8   Pie charts. (Courtesy of Ultimus, Inc. With permission.)

sail slightly downwind. At any given moment, the ship is not headed in the exact desired direction, but when averaged out, the zigzag course arrives at the intended destination.

When making all these course corrections it is easy to overcompensate and end up sailing significantly off course. That is why it is essential for sailors to maintain a fixed reference that assures them they are still heading on course. Before the days of satellites and GPS, ships navigated by the sun and stars. By taking a "fix" on a known celestial body the captain could course correct throughout the voyage.

When sailing your organizational vessel your mission and your vision captured in your team charter provide your fixed reference points. Take the time to assess your progress toward those lofty reference points frequently to ensure that your multiple course correction along the way have not blown you off course. Doing so will assure you and inspire your crew that you are still maintaining a true heading toward your ultimate destination despite multiple course correction you'll need to make along the voyage.

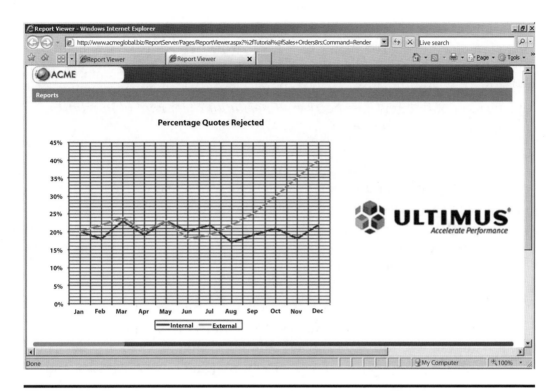

Figure 5.9   Run charts. (Courtesy of Ultimus, Inc. With permission.)

Sustaining Element 7: Ongoing Control of Vendors and Suppliers

Just as important as controlling the internal processes of the organization is the control of the inputs to those processes. Unfortunately, much of these inputs lie outside of an organization's direct span of control and can only be influenced. Further compounding the ability to control is a lack of transparency to supplier processes. Too frequently, organizations don't understand their supplier's processes and internal requirements. In addition, the organization may feel more like a victim than a customer, with the supplier dictating the terms and conditions instead of the other way around. The one absolute the organization does have in their favor is the power of the purse. Just as your customers can vote with their wallets, your organization can do the same to your suppliers.

To build an effective relationship with suppliers and vendors that provides as much control and consistency as possible, modify the seven planks of the Framework for Individual Success to build a Framework for Vendor

Management (Figure 5.10). As substance to each plank, we'll incorporate the criteria outlined by Chiang-nan Chao, Eberhard E Scheuing, and William A. Ruch for evaluating the effectiveness of purchasing departments (Chao, C., Scheuing, E.E., and Ruch, W.A. 1993. Purchasing performance evaluation: An investigation of different perspectives. *International Journal of Purchasing and Materials Management* 29(3): 33–39):

1. Define acceptable vendor performance
   a. Quality specs and standards for purchased items
2. Set clear expectations of the vendor's products and/or services
   a. On-time delivery
   b. Order accuracy
3. Provide timely feedback to the vendor
   a. Service levels
   b. Professionalism, standards of conduct, courteousness, and ethics
4. Provide adequate resources (access to information and processes)
   a. Cultivation of quality suppliers through teaming
   b. Knowledge of your business, products including trends, risks, and opportunities
5. Set performance conditions
   a. Delivery terms and conditions
   b. Price and quality

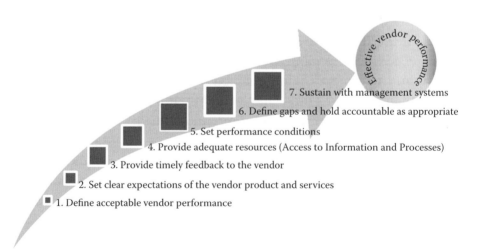

Figure 5.10   Framework for vendor management.

6. Define gaps and hold accountable as appropriate
   a. Negotiated discounts or charge-backs for gaps in on-time delivery, service, quality, and order accuracy
7. Sustain with management systems
   a. Integration of order and delivery systems
   b. Ongoing performance management and annual contract reviews, including benchmarking of quality, costs, and service levels

Adapting these seven elements implements vendor controls that will help ensure that purchased products and services conform to organizational requirements. Every supplier and service provider should be objectively evaluated and selected based on their ability to meet requirements and their willingness to establish partnerships that bolster the organization's mission. At times, this may require your organization to support capacity building of your suppliers. Once you have established a mutually beneficial relationship built upon trust with the supplier, your organization will need to share pertinent information that enables suppliers to meet your systems' requirements.

CAUTION: Be mindful of backdoor selling and information mining on the part of your suppliers, which may put you at a disadvantage during future contract negotiations. It is important to provide the information necessary for your vendors to meet quality and service levels; however, be careful not to provide information that is not strictly required to satisfy your organizational needs. Such additional information in the hands of your supplier may well erode your ability to manage your vendors. Train all employees who interact with suppliers and vendors in purchasing policies as well as legal considerations related to the purchasing process. I also strongly recommend that these employees receive training in "backdoor selling" and negotiating skills. The more they understand vendor management, the more leverage your organization will maintain to manage your vendors and suppliers.

For all interactions with suppliers and vendors, maintain accurate and complete records documenting supplier performance. These records will add to your leverage during negotiations.

The bottom line is that the same leadership and management required to build an effective organization is essential to establishing and sustaining the quality relationships needed with vendors and suppliers.

Sustaining Element 8: Utilization of Lean Concepts, 5S, and Visual Management

The LSS revolution has resulted in billions of dollars saved through process improvements and cost reductions. The systematic thinking and standardized tools can dramatically transform organizations by helping them rethink their processes and look with new eyes at their systems as well as their facilities. Yet, at the beginning, I made the critical statement that LSS was necessary yet insufficient to building an effective organization. I stand by that statement because I've seen organization after organization embark on LSS projects that fail to transform and fail to sustain their changes. So how can such excellent tools yield such disappointing results? The organization is unprepared. An organization can't very well optimize what is poorly defined, poorly understood, and poorly managed. Trying to control a process out to the degree of sixth sigma that can't even get operators to consistently follow the same procedure from shift to shift is a waste of time. Figure 5.11 has been added to reflect where LSS tools build upon the solid foundation built through the Forming, Focusing, and Committing Stages. Having laid the foundational timbers into the framework, the organization will have the essential understanding of the systems, requirements, and pitfalls of their operations and is ready to optimize and improve. The sophisticated and elegant tools held in the LSS toolbox cannot be a replacement for failures in management. Manage first; optimize second.

Figure 5.11   Framework for Organizational Success.

Overview of Lean Concepts

Once an organization has taken the time to form, focus, and has growing commitment within their organization, they can sustain their upward trajectory through the implementation of Lean concepts. For those not familiar with LSS, here is a quick overview of some of the most important LSS concepts.

Lean is a systematic approach to identifying and eliminating waste. Before you can get rid of waste, you have to identify it. Waste comes in many forms and fashions but can be broadly defined as any nonvalue-added activity. There are many ways of classifying nonvalue-added, i.e., wasteful, activities but my favorite is from Mark Eaton's excellent book (Eaton, M. 2009. *Lean for Practitioners: An Introduction to Lean for Healthcare Organisations*, 2nd ed. Hertfordshire, UK: Ecademy Press). (Although Mr. Eaton's focus in this work is the healthcare industry, his concepts are universally applicable to any LSS initiative.) Mr. Eaton defined waste using the acronym WORMPIT.

W—Waiting (when any part of the process is waiting, waste is generated)

O—Overprocessing (overproducing product or adding more activities/features than is required)

R—Rework (correcting poor quality mistakes)

M—Motion (inefficient movement—a mechanic that doesn't bring the required tools and has to keep returning to the toolbox mounted on the back of his truck is an example of excess motion)

P—Processing Waste (the excess materials from the process—cutting off a board and throwing away the excess or activities in a process that do not add value)

I—Inventory (excessive materials waiting to be processed, poor utilization of manpower—idle time, etc.)

T—Transport (the inefficient movement of materials, information, product, etc.)

Once you've identified your waste, LSS has many tools to help you reduce it. Of all the tools available, if you could only pick one, you should start with 5S.

A MOMENT OF IRONY: It's always struck me as ironic, and frankly annoying, that even though one of the key tenets held dear in the LSS world is simplification, practitioners of the craft insist on using foreign words, acronyms, and other obscure terminology that are not simple and do not simplify (unless the intent is to simply make things more complex and more confusing than they have to be). A few examples of complex and confusing terms that LSS uses to explain simple concepts include the following: "Muda" means waste, "Kanban" is a signal to order more inventories—an example of a trigger—a Kanban system is an inventory control system based on ordering when you get the signal—trigger. Granted, the terms are Japanese and make lots of sense to the Japanese, but just because a concept started in another language, we don't have to keep using the same terms. Louis Pasteur advocated for a system of cleanliness that prevented infection and the spread of disease. Like 5S, this was a great process that yielded many benefits. Though Lois Pasteur was French, we don't still say "Lavez-vous les mains, s'il vous plaît" unless you're in France, parts of Canada, or other places where French is widely spoken; we simply say, "Wash your hands, please." Much simpler and less confusing, isn't it?

5S and Visual Management

5S is a process where spaces and systems are organized and simplified. The term 5S comes from the five Japanese words that make up each step of the process: Seri, Seiton, Seiso, Seiketsu, and Shitsuke. Don't worry; there are five simple English terms that equate to the process, as shown in Table 5.5.

The five-step methodology establishes a place for everything and puts everything in its place.

Step 1: Sort—Remove all the items from an area that are not needed for current operations; leave only what is needed, only in the amounts needed and only available when it is needed!

Table 5.5   5S Terms—Japanese and English

Japanese	Translation	English
Seri	Organization	Sort
Seiton	Orderliness	Simplify
Seiso	Cleanliness	Sweep
Seiketsu	Standardized cleanup	Standardize
Shitsuke	Discipline	Sustain

Example: A small paper company in Wisconsin was "dark." The employees asked that additional lighting be installed. The company installed
additional lighting. Later, the company implemented 5S. During implementation, the company removed excessive inventory and excess junk.
They found a window hidden behind the accumulation of decades.
The natural lighting from window was sufficient to allow the additional
lighting to be turned off. The employees were happy and the company
saved money!

Step 2: Simplify—Arrange needed items so that they are easy to use and
label them so that anyone can find them and put them away! Simplify
typically uses a method referred to as visual management. Visual
management communicates where an item belongs, how many items
belong, what is the standard procedure, etc.

Example: Outlining your tools on a pegboard in your garage so you can
see where the hammer, wrench, saw, etc., all go and what is missing is
an example of visual management. Other examples include signboards,
painting, and color coding.

   A printing company color-coded their entire operating panel such
that each section corresponded with the portions of the press. They
also labeled and numbered each control in English instead of having operators memorize the hieroglyphic pictographs that the foreign
manufacturer installed. Clearly labeling each control and color-coding
it to the portion of the machine it was associated with minimized
errors and reduced the time it took for new operators to learn the
equipment.

Step 3: Sweep—Sweeping is an activity whereby you visually sweep the
space to ensure that everything is in its place and you then return
anything that is out of place. In addition, sweeping also entails the
physical act of cleaning, blowing off, wiping down, and generally
sweeping up.

Step 4: Standardize—Standardizing is a method used to maintain Sort,
Simplify, and Sweep. Related to all, but it's most related to Sweep!
Standardizing makes information about locations more recognizable.
If all labels on a shelf are formatted the same way, it is easier to visually
sweep through the labels. If procedures are uniform for retrieving and
returning items and information, it is easier for everyone in the teams
on all shifts to locate them quickly when needed.

Step 5: Sustain—Sustaining is the self-discipline to make 5S a routine
practice and a daily habit. Sustaining ensures that all team members do

their part to carry out the 5S actions they have agreed upon. The steps to sustaining include

1. Assign responsibility
2. Integrate 5S into all regular duties and responsibilities
3. Everyone conducts routine checks/inspection
4. Eliminate "spring cleaning" mentality—keeping it clean every day eliminates the need for major "clean ups"
5. Making a habit of properly maintaining procedures developed during the standardizing process to develop organizational self-discipline to maintain the gains of 5S

Once you've begun down the LSS path with 5S, other Lean concepts can be added and incorporated into the ongoing activities of the organization. The second concept I'd recommend implementing after the organization has mastered the simple concepts and has demonstrated the self-discipline to maintain the activities of 5S is *value stream mapping*.

Value Stream Mapping

During the Focusing Stage, you drew system process flow charts. This helped you design your systems, assign roles and responsibilities, develop procedures and reduce "fall points." Once you've reached the Sustained Performance Stage, the organization should have a very good understanding of the value delivery systems and how they are actually working as built as compared to the theoretical as designed. You now know enough to begin optimizing processes. As a practitioner, the most effective method I've seen for doing this is value stream mapping (VSM). VSM is a special type of process flowchart that uses Lean symbols and concepts to really analyze the systems as they currently work. Based upon this analysis, an "ideal" state can be determined. In reality, you will never reach the ideal state. An ideal process would have zero lag time, zero friction, and would run at maximum machine capacity 100% of the time. Though you'll never reach it, it is very important to quantify this perfect state to help you define "how high is up?" Within the gap between your "current state" and the "ideal state" lies your opportunity for process improvement.

The value stream map enables you to see the WORMPIT of waste within your processes. Once you've identified the sources of waste, you can work to improve the process and move toward that ideal by designing the "future state."

NOTE: If there is not a significant opportunity, don't even waste your time to improve the process. Focus on where you can get "bang for your buck." Reducing by 100% a source that contributes 1% waste won't add to the bottom line as much as reducing 10% of a source that causes 60% of your waste.

100% of 1% = 1% process improvement

10% of 60% = 6% process improvement

As you design the future state, be sure to indicate the milestones and other indicators that will signal the organizations progress. Mark the boundaries of acceptable performance through the establishment and utilization of upper and lower control limits (UCL and LCL). This helps ensure that the organization "keeps it between the ditches." Train each operator how to analyze parameters, the drivers of each, and empower them to intervene accordingly to control the process. As you work to improve your systems to more effectively, efficiently, and consistently convert inputs into outcomes, remember to continually think systematically and holistically. You must continue to refine the elements implemented earlier within the Forming, Focusing, and Committing Stages in order to have sustainable high performance.

Once you reached that future state, the organization can again turn back to VSM to explore how much closer they can move current operational reality toward the ideal and again crank the LSS lever to elevate the organization to the next higher performance future state. Each turn of the crank moves you closer to the ideal. We will talk more about this during the Renewal Stage.

Sustaining Element 9: Control of Nonconforming Products and Services

Despite best-laid plans, world-class systems, and a talented engaged workforce, occasionally you will produce products or services that aren't quite up to snuff. Since it's bound to happen, the question becomes, how do you manage these nonconforming products or services? Like everything else, you need to plan for them and have a system in place to identify, segregate/

contain, and manage them such that their impact on your operations and your reputation is minimized. There are four basic ways to minimize the impact of nonconforming products and services:

1. Dispose of the product such that it does not reach a customer or client
   a. The surest way to make certain nonconforming or substandard products or services don't impact the customer
   b. Expensive and generates the maximum waste
2. Fix the problem by taking action to eliminate nonconformity
   a. May not be possible once the service has been performed
   b. May be more expensive
3. Use it anyway after receiving permission from both appropriate internal authority and from the customer
   a. Customer may have the ability to compensate for the nonconformance thereby allowing them to utilize the product
   b. May generate lower revenue due to charge backs or allowances
4. Utilize the nonconforming product or service for alternate but acceptable purposes
   a. When possible, the substandard product may generate alternate revenue streams through sales in alternate markets

Defined Decision Authority

An important aspect of controlling nonconforming products and services is to clearly define with whom authority resides. What decisions does the line staff have authority to make? When should the supervisor be notified? The manager? Higher authority? This is all part of setting clear expectations and defining the span of control within the roles and responsibilities of each organizational area. Without clear guidance the gray areas between quality standards can be shifted day to day and shift to shift, adding variability to the products and services your organization provides. The reputation of your organization must be reconfirmed with every customer facing transaction—excessive gray leads to excessive risk.

Documentation of Final Disposition of Nonconforming Products and Services

Whichever of the four methods is utilized, it is important that the final disposition is recorded and appropriate documentation is maintained.

Understanding the various components that make up the products and thinking creatively can help determine appropriate alternative uses for substandard products as well as waste streams from the process. For example, the ash generated by power plant boilers can sometimes be used as an ingredient in catalytic converters. You and your organization are best qualified to explore alternate uses for substandard materials and waste streams generated through the course of operations. The important point being stressed here is to plan for these contingencies in advance and have systems in place that maximize the value added.

SYSTEMS LIMITED: Earlier in Focusing Element 1, we talked about the concept of *deckle* as the width of the paper manufactured on a paper machine. Ideally, a paper company can sell everything it makes; this is not always the case, and smaller width rolls of paper are created on the ends (referred to as side rolls). Side rolls are typically reprocessed and recycled back into the system. This is an example of the "O" in WORMPIT—overprocessing. Recycling utilizes the raw materials, but the process still generates waste from all the energy and raw materials used to create the rolls in the first place. The following are representative of the values inherent in this process:

1. High-quality paper = $500/Ton
2. Paper sold on the seconds market = $300/Ton
3. The value of recycling materials = $150/Ton

Selling the paper on the seconds market instead of recycling it generates an additional $150/Ton. Knowing this, a paper manufacturer firm I worked with located a broker willing to accept the side rolls. This new customer was willing to take all the side rolls produced and was even willing to send their own trucks to the mill such that the mill didn't pay for transportation. Sounds like a perfect business solution to dispose of a nonconforming product and generate twice the revenue compared to the next best alternative. Unfortunately, it never happened. The Enterprise Resource Planning (ERP) software system utilized by the mill had no codes for seconds and odd lots. Unique codes would have to be generated and entered for every odd size and grade. The IT Department was unwilling to create a generic odd lot code or work with the operations department to solve the system problem to capitalize on the potential new revenue stream.

THE BOTTOM LINE: Even though the company had a finished product and a customer willing to pay twice the value of the next best use, the business wasn't allowed to book the sales. This is another example of how a support department not only didn't add value—the systems they imposed actually lost revenue for the business.

Sustaining Element 10: Balance of Challenge and Support through Rewards, Opportunities, and Consequences

Having navigated forming, focusing, committing, and the first nine elements of sustained performance, the organization should be seeing real progress and productivity. As individuals have grown and adapted along with the organization's transformation, there should be greater understanding of the systems. Individuals should require less supervision at this point as they are now trained and the systems are well defined. This growing autonomy is a two edged sword. People acting independently in line with the organization's mission should free up managers shifting their time horizon to focus on more strategic long-range plans and goals. However, people acting autonomously who are not truly aligned can undermine the organization's ability to achieve its goals. To ensure that the former is true and not the latter, managers must regularly evaluate the driving incentives, rewards, opportunities, and consequences.

Equitable Rewards and Opportunities

With everyone contributing, logic implies that everyone should be reaping the benefits of the organization's success. These benefits include both rewards and opportunities. Rewards are not just monetary in nature—they also include a sense of security, stability, and recognition. Opportunities for continued advancement and growth will continue to inspire and motivate. A continuous view to the process with distinct success criteria in the form of KPIs helps keep the organization between the ditches. The organization should pride itself as a meritocracy where hard work, positive outcomes, and alignment with organizational goals are the standards for advancement.

Both rewards and opportunities need to be balanced to recognize the contributions of individuals as well as the achievement of teams. This dual micro–macro focus encourages both collaboration between team members and ongoing individual creativity and contribution. Rewarding one and not the other will invoke the law of unintended consequences such that free riders emerge, infighting and other self-serving behaviors begin to sprout and take root. Those opposed to the change may use the lull in organizational focus to roll back the changes to reestablish conditions as they would prefer.

Drivers of Variable Performance

By the time the first nine elements of sustained performance have been established organizations have a tendency to proclaim success and put the controls on autopilot. Unfortunately, when they do, the progress they've made begins to erode. Like all systems requiring the expenditure of energy, over time, organizational activities will flow entropically toward a lower energy stasis state. Two key factors contribute to this erosion: the Hawthorne Effect and the emergence of subtle saboteurs.

The Hawthorne Effect

At the very beginning of our voyage, we made the dismal claim that of the change initiatives that are initially considered successes, almost 90% failed to sustain their gains one year later. One of the principle reasons that so many initiatives backslide is that it is just so darn easy to get a quick temporary bump in performance. Theorists referred to this phenomena as the Hawthorne Effect, named after a series of research experiments done between 1926 and 1932 at the Western Electric Company's Hawthorne plant in Chicago, where they made equipment for AT&T. The researchers noticed that no matter what they did, there was an uptick in productivity which, over time, drifted back to the previous level. They increased lighting; productivity went up. They decreased lighting; productivity went up. And so it went (Parsons, H.McI. 1982. More on the Hawthorne Effect. *American Psychologist* 37: 856–857). There has been much analysis of the Hawthorne experiment since then, and many believe it is genuine while others say it is strictly a misinterpretation of the data. Parsons contends that observed increases are from the attention paid to the employees as part of the experiments causing them to work harder, knowing they are being monitored. I tend to agree with Parsons; when management becomes engaged, employees tend to respond to the added attention. People contribute a little bit more of their discretionary effort, but the improvement isn't sustained. From an implementation standpoint, a major factor contributing to these cyclical productivity trends relates back to cardinal change sin no. 7, attention deficit management and the concept of organizational pinball, discussed in Sustaining Element 6. Organizations manage as if they're in a dark closet with only a narrow-beam flashlight that focuses on one issue at a time. When the attention is concentrated on an issue, the issue tends to improve. At some point, attention shifts to the next emerging crisis; no longer in the spotlight, behaviors drift back to the point where the driving and sustaining forces reach equilibrium. Regardless of why it occurs, as a practitioner, the bottom line is that productivity seems to increase temporarily in response to focused attention in the workplace; however, over time, productivity tends to drift back to previous levels once the change becomes the new norm. To create another spike in productivity, another initiative is implemented. This pattern is frequently referred to cynically as "Program of the Month."

Learned Helplessness: The Organizational Cost of Program of the Month

The concept of logical consequences was introduced during the discussion of Committing Element 7. Let's continue that discussion by exploring the toll incurred by organizations trapped within a pinball machine and caught up in the Program of the Month cycle.

Earlier we showed a standard bell curve divided into three labeled sections: Climate of Entitlement, Climate of Logical Consequences and Mutual Accountability, and the Climate of Fear (shown again as Figure 5.12). If there are little or no consequences to poor performance, people tend to develop an entitlement mindset. People who have no security and little perceived control over their situations live in fear. When people feel they are empowered within a situation in which there is a direct correlation between their outcomes and their actions, productivity is at its peak. This is the area of logical consequences where mutual accountability can thrive. Imagine now the impact of "Program of the Month."

Organizations must balance multiple priorities. Within industry, safety, quality, and productivity are three of the priorities that get juggled. For some organizations, when safety is not an issue, the plant puts safety on a back burner. It is frequently spoken of, but with a wink and a nod, it is understood that productivity is king. If you have to cut a few corners here or

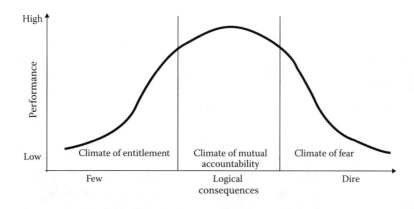

Figure 5.12   Consequences versus performance.

there, that's OK. There are no consequences for taking safety shortcuts; people become complacent about safety and it drifts into entitlement. Eventually, organizations with a laissez faire attitude about safety end up getting people hurt or killed. After an accident occurs, the focus shifts to safety with all hands on deck. Managers in the hot seat must rapidly change the organization's safety mindset or suffer the consequences. They go out to "kick ass and take names." Pity the fool who violates a safety rule. With safety as the focus, fear drives the numbers, and the safety indicators improve. While focusing on safety, the organization had special safety meetings, created safety teams, safety slogans, safety contests, and held safety fairs, etc., etc., etc.—productivity dropped off. "All hands on deck! Nobody rests until we get our productivity numbers up!" Complacency is replaced with fear, and productivity is driven back up. But wait, our quality has slipped The cycle continues, jumping through hoop after hoop in a never-ending oscillating three-phase cycle as the organization reacts to problem after problem, enacting program after program (Figure 5.13).

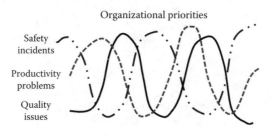

Figure 5.13   Reactionary management cycles.

Most of us can relate to being trapped in a reactionary cycle. But what's the cost of being continuously made to jump through hoops with apparently no end in sight?

The Dog in the Box: A Thought Experiment

NOTE: No dogs will be harmed conducting the following thought experiment! I would never condone doing this in real life so please don't take offense or write nasty letters to me. This is strictly an example to illustrate a point. I have a dog named "Bugsy" who is happy, healthy, and extremely spoiled. See Figure 5.14.

Suppose I want to train a dog to jump in response to a triggering event. Not that I would ever do this, but I could create a system made out of a box with a metal mesh floor as shown in Figure 5.15. There is a barrier dividing the box into equal halves that is short enough to jump over. A power supply is connected to the floor enabling me to run a small current through the floor. The current is not lethal, just uncomfortable. A light is mounted on the wall that flashes when one side or the other is energized. Within the box, I place a dog. When the light comes on, one side of the floor is electrified, shocking the dog. In response, he jumps over the barrier to escape; the light goes off. I turn the light on, shocking the dog again; he jumps back. Soon, with repeated practice I have taught the dog to jump to the triggering event of a light coming on; at this point, the negative reinforcement of electrical

Figure 5.14 Bugsy the dog living the good life.

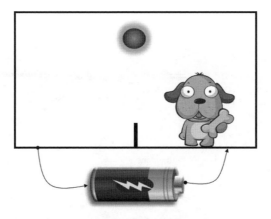

Figure 5.15   The dog in the box.

stimulus is not even required; the dog is trained. Light → Jump; Light → Jump.

NOTE: The use of a stimulus and response to modify behavior is called *operant conditioning* and was first described by psychologist B. F. Skinner.

Now, suppose I pull a fast one on the dog by energizing both sides of the box. No matter where the dog jumps, he is shocked. Soon the dog realizes that there is no way he can affect his own situation to escape discomfort. After a while, the dog gives up trying and just endures. Even if I open the box door and call the dog, he may not come because he no longer trusts that anything he does will make a difference, so why do anything? The dog has entered a condition known as learned helplessness.

Like the dog in the box, individuals and organizations that are whipsawed back and forth between programs can develop a sense of learned helplessness. Over time, the belief that "It doesn't matter what you do around here, nothing ever changes" permeates the organization. Figure 5.16 shows the relationship between performance and consequence in a reactionary culture. There is no standard bell curve. Individuals and entire departments jump from entitlement to fear and back again. There are very few "logical consequences" in a reactionary culture. Early in my career, a manager justified his learned helplessness to me by saying, "This is just our time in the barrel, wait a while and the spotlight will shift to another

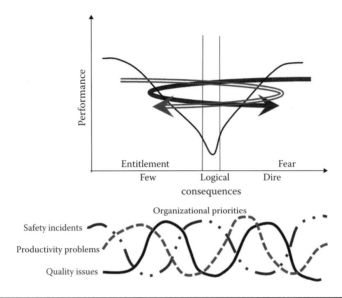

Figure 5.16   Relationship between performance and consequence in a reactionary culture.

department and we can return to business as usual." He didn't recognize it and I couldn't have put a name to it then, but looking back now, I can see that he was firmly trapped in learned helplessness. He had come to accept his situation as inevitable and unchangeable. Rather than trying to affect any positive changes, he gave the impression of busyness—doing enough to stay out of the barrel by majoring on the minors and rearranging deck chairs on the Titanic until the day he retired. The only satisfaction he took from his career was surviving long enough to get a pension.

Logical Consequences: Keeping It between the Ditches

We've discussed logical consequences many times now, but how do you establish such a culture? Figure 5.17 shows the same standard bell curve of performance versus consequences shown in Figure 5.12—only now, the area of logical consequences is bound between the "wall of complacency" and the "fine line of perception."

To move an organization out of entitlement you must break through the wall of complacency. Individuals and entire organizations must understand why they need to change. In his ground-breaking book, John Kotter explained the concept of a burning platform as the compelling reason (Kotter, J. 1996, *Leading Change*. Boston: Harvard Business School Press).

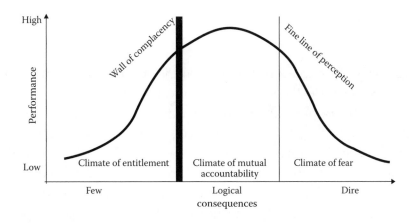

Figure 5.17   Barriers to logical consequences.

A burning platform could be negative, i.e., the threat of plant closure, or it could be positive, i.e., profit sharing. Creating a burning platform helps people understand they must change thus creating the momentum necessary to break through the thick wall of complacency. But when you do, be careful that you don't cross the "fine line of perception" and drive individuals and organizations into fear. This balancing act requires inspirational leadership and effective management. Let's drill deeper by tying in the earlier concepts of under- and overmanagement.

Establishing Logical Consequences through Challenging and Support

Transformational leaders are able to consistently apply a balance of challenges and support. They are trusted enough to be able to challenge ineffective behaviors while maintaining the trust of their subordinates through support. Managers who only provide support with limited challenging can enable stagnation within the organization by creating a climate of entitlement; they are undermanaging. Those that challenge too frequently without earning the trust of their subordinates are often overmanaging to the point of nitpicking, micromanaging, and dominating thereby creating a climate of fear within the organization. When we discussed under- and overmanagement, we used the analogy of "keeping it between the ditches"; those ditches now have names: complacency and perception.

To delve deeper into creating the climate of logical consequences we'll begin by breaking through the wall of complacency.

Breaking through the Wall of Complacency; Leading Sheep and Driving Goats

Every stage we've navigated through, Forming, Focusing, Committing, and Sustaining, has been designed to raise motivation and lead the organization to a higher level of performance. But what do you do if someone doesn't want to make the trip? For whatever reason, they are unwilling or unable to change. They are complacent. Complacency infers satisfaction with the current state. If one is satisfied, there is no reason to change. Perhaps the need for change is not understood (lack of motivation) or perhaps the act of changing is deemed unattainable or not worth the effort (lack of volition). To make any change individuals and organizations must gain both the motivation and the volition to change. These drivers can come from either internal or external forces; there are those who are willing to be led to change and there are those who must be driven to change. To help illustrate, here's a lesson in animal husbandry: the difference between sheep and goats.

To the uninitiated, sheep and goats appear to be two very similar creatures and in many ways they are; both are herbivores; both have cloven hooves, and both chew their cud. As a kid staying at my uncle's ranch in California what I found to be distinctly different between sheep and goats (besides one having wool and the other having hair) is their personalities. Sheep will generally follow; goats must be driven—and it has always been so. Biblical references describe how sheep follow a good shepherd. Nowhere does it reference goats following a goat herder no matter how good he or she is! I once saw a picture of a little boy on the Golan Heights with a sling and a bag of stones like David must have carried. When a goat got out of line, WHACK! The kid smacked him on the rump with a stone and the goat got back into line; he was a talented goat herder! The Bible advises that one must separate the sheep from the goats. This is still commonly done since problems arise among sheep and goats eating at the same trough. The goats tend to eat faster and aggressively dominate the troughs by pushing the sheep away with their horns. The sheep and goats are separated to ensure that the sheep received their fair share to eat and are not hurt by the head butting of the more aggressive goats.

This slight detour into animal behavior helps explain a common problem that causes frustration for many managers; they assume everyone is more like a sheep. An overwhelming theme in business courses and writings teaches that people will follow a good leader. They stress the need to inspire and lead—very little good is said about driving. If your people are more like sheep, you'll find the advice to be generally true—people will follow. But not everyone is a sheep and most organizations usually contain a mixed flock with plenty of goats mixed among the sheep. These more goat-like individuals won't follow the manager's lead because they are focused on following their own agenda. Though unwilling to be led, they may hang with the herd as long as it suits their purpose; but should the herd move left, and they think it should go right, these individuals, can work behind the scenes to undermine the change initiative and end up leading some of the sheep astray with them. The manager who fails to recognize the differences will have a very hard time managing the goats. Managing goats will be discussed in greater detail a little later.

Subtle and Not So Subtle Sabotage

The Hawthorne Effect assumes no ill intentions on the part of employees, supervisors, or managers, which is not always the case. With many change initiatives, particularly those that affect deep changes and shifts in power, pay, or responsibility, those that were opposed to the initiative are motivated to see the initiative fail either by withering away or going down in a blazing heap.

Sabotage may be too strong a word for most behaviors that undermine progress, though I've seen it happen on multiple occasions. Opponents to the change may contribute to an initiative's demise in more subtle, and in many respects much more insidious ways. The methods and timing of actions or inactions that undermine a change initiative will vary depending upon the ability to achieve the necessary degree of "plausible deniability." The early stages of implementing change initiatives usually draw the attention of senior management. Being visibly opposed to change can be detrimental to careers; you have to at least look like you care. But when attention shifts, the framework of changes can be dismantled with little fear of repercussions. Just how they dismantle the changes to restore the organization back to their desired state will depend upon where they lie along the resistance to change continuum and their perceived power base that shields them from accountability and negative consequences. They may simply underresource the initiative such that it slowly starves through benign neglect or they may aggressively deconstruct the systems, roles, and responsibilities in the name of "changing priorities."

What is important for anyone who genuinely desires progress is to recognize the inappropriate behaviors and then counteract their impact. Table 5.6

Table 5.6   Behavioral Responses to Unwanted Change

Emotional State	Behavioral Response
Avoid	Yupping
Deny	Malicious compliance or work slow down
Bargaining	Compromise–negotiation–manipulation
Anger	Conflict–attack
Sadness	Learned helplessness
Acceptance	Assimilation of the change • Thriving—bloom where planted • Coping—survival skills

summarizes the behavioral adaptations individuals display based upon their emotional response to unwanted change.

In the initial stages of a change initiative, individuals may be able to avoid the change altogether. One of the most common behavioral tactics used to avoid taking an unwanted action is something I refer to as "yupping." Yupping is a classic tactic whereby the person appears to agree, but has no intention of taking action. Consider George's response to his new manager's request:

Manager: "George, I need you to work with the process improvement team to develop procedures documenting how you change over the machines."
George: "Yup, that sounds like a good idea. I'll make sure I get with them."
Manager: "Great, I knew we could count on you."

The manager walks away feeling good and confident that George is onboard with the change initiative and will cooperate in developing procedures that will enable others to make machine adjustments that currently only George can perform. Weeks pass, and still the team hasn't been able to catch up with George.

Manager: "George, have you worked out a schedule to get with the team?"
George: "Not yet, you know how slammed we've been. It's on my list. I'll get to it as soon as we get passed this outage. You know how important that is. We wouldn't want to delay it."

Manager: "Yeah, I understand. Just try and work out some time to go over your procedures with the team."

George: "Yup, not a problem. But it will have to be after the outage."

Manager: "Thanks, George; you know how we all count on you."

And so it goes. George avoids contributing to the changes that he feels will undermine his power and worth with the organization. If he trains others, he may become replaceable so he feels that it is in his best interest to keep his knowledge to himself.

If the manager pushes George and insists that he cooperate with the team, George could shift to the next tactic, malicious compliance. The team could work with George to document the procedures, but George doesn't fully cooperate. He gives partial answers and omits key elements. A procedure is written, but it doesn't enable others to successfully perform the tasks. This actually adds to the perception that George is simply irreplaceable. And if George is ever questioned about the failed initiative he can simply deny responsibility.

George: "What can I say? I worked with them; they saw me make the changes. There are some things that simply can't be written down. It's an art; and not everyone is an artist."

George has avoided supporting the change again. Now he can go back to yupping for a while then a little more compliance followed by more yupping, and if he can hold out, priorities will change or the manager will transfer and George's life will remain as it always has. The status quo has been sustained.

If he is cornered, George could bargain or compromise and if pushed further he may explode in rage depending upon the depth of his convictions, his temperament, and the relative power he feels he has over his manager. Just because the manager has formal power, it doesn't mean that it will be sufficient to counter George's informal power of expertise and the power of relationships he may have established over the years with more senior managers. George could also be shielded by tenure or other HR policies that make him virtually untouchable and therefore, unwilling to comply with any change he doesn't support. As long as he doesn't cross an ill-defined line of insubordination, George can continue on indefinitely undermining the manager's desired change initiatives.

And as we discussed before, if one member of the team receives preferential treatment, seemingly immune to logical consequences, the productivity and morale of the entire organization eventually suffer. Failure to manage situations like these only reinforces the behaviors and exacerbates the problems. The "goats" within an organization know the rules probably better than the managers; they are adept at working within the system. Their power is derived from managers believing everyone is a "sheep." They play upon this belief to test the limits of their manager's abilities and resolve. When a manager continues to try and lead and never drives, the goats are empowered to further their own agendas. If confronted, they claim ignorance, overwork, confusion, or miscommunication. I've seen well intentioned managers even accept responsibility for the individual's poor performance due to their failure to provide adequate leadership or effective communication. When the pressure mounts, goats simply blend back in with the herd until the manager's focus is directed elsewhere and they are once again free to wander independently from the herd.

In addition to the goats causing dissent among the organization, goats are quite adept at leading others astray. The leadership qualities of goats can be inspirational to some sheep—particularly if there is a leadership vacuum because the manager hasn't been providing adequate direction and guidance to help them understand the mission, vision, and their individual roles and responsibilities. A sheep's need for affiliation will incent them to follow a goat to fulfill their need for inclusion. Failure to manage leads to fragmentation.

Situation Analysis: Understanding When to Lead and When to Drive

Managers need to manage. Unmanaged goats can be very disruptive to building a cohesive organization. But how do you manage those difficult and challenging individuals within your organization; how do you effectively separate the sheep from the goats? First, you must recognize that they exist. Denying their existence only cedes your power and ability to manage.

> GREAT MOVIE QUOTE: "The greatest trick the Devil ever pulled was convincing the world he didn't exist."
>
> **Roger "Verbal" Kint describing Keyser Söze,**
> *The Usual Suspects (1995)*

Before you can effectively confront inappropriate or ineffective behavior, you must first be able to identify and understand the drivers and sustainers of the behavior and then ascertain whether it is a matter of "will" or "skill." Throughout our discussions, we have referred back to the seven timbers within the Framework for Individual Success:

1. Define acceptable performance
2. Set clear expectations
3. Provide timely feedback
4. Provide adequate resources
5. Set performance conditions
6. Define gaps and train as appropriate
7. Sustain with management systems

The conceptual elements of each of the seven planks build successively upon each other. But having only a general conceptual framework of performance analysis will not always be sufficient managing the real world. You need substantive tools. The Performance Analysis Template (Table 5.7) builds the seven elements of individual success into an effective management tool that a will help you drill down to the root causes of each element.

RESOURCES CD: This and the other management tool templates are available for your use on the CD that accompanies this book.

The first portion of the Performance Analysis Template helps you define and document exactly what is or is not occurring and who is involved. Be as specific as possible and describe the situation in observable, fact-based terms. List the tasks that are not being accomplished.

Is It a Matter of Will or Skill and Who Is Responsible, the Individual or the Organization?

To be successful, individuals need both motivation and ability. Motivation is more than just interest and ability is more than just technical competence. As was previously discussed as part of Committing Element 6, each consists of four elements. Performance analysis requires consideration of each of these eight elements to ascertain the drivers of inadequate performance.

Table 5.7 Performance Analysis Template

Performance Analysis

Describe Performance Discrepancy:		
Team Member(s):		**Frequency**
Date(s):	**Location:**	

Tasks not Being Achieved

Task No: 1	
Task No: 2	
Task No: 3	
Task No: 4	
Task No: 5	

Element:	*Clarity of Expectations* *(Organizational Responsibility)*			*Individual Commitment* *(Individual Responsibility)*		
Motivation	Objectives and goals are clear?	Yes	No	Interest in task is sufficient?	Yes	No
	Metrics are aligned and available?	Yes	No	Confidence is sufficient?	Yes	No
	Feedback is appropriate, timely, and specific?	Yes	No	Willingness to assume responsibility is sufficient?	Yes	No
	Rewards and consequences are commensurate with actual performance?	Yes	No	Alignment with organizational goals is appropriate?	Yes	No

Element:	*Conditions and Drivers* (Organizational Responsibility)			*Individual Competencies* (Individual Responsibility)		
Ability	Resources are sufficient?	Yes	No	Technical skills are sufficient?	Yes	No
	Technologies are sufficient?	Yes	No	Interpersonal skills are sufficient?	Yes	No
	What reinforcers contribute to behaviors? (list)			Knowledge of job and organizational procedures are sufficient?	Yes	No
	What inhibits behavior? List			Appropriate degree of organizational power is sufficient?	Yes	No

Resources Needed

Time	Training	New Equipment	Other: |
Manpower	Authority	Technical Expertise	Other: |
Funding	Facilities	Access to Equipment	Other: |

Support Needed

Clear Expectations	Feedback	Flying Cover	Other: |
Mentoring	Coaching	Encouragement	Other: |
Decisions Made	Delegation	Consequences	Other: |

Overall Assessment of Situation:

Has the situation been over- or undermanaged?

Looking at individual ability and motivation is a good start, however, though necessary, it is insufficient to fully analyze performance gaps. To understand the full picture, we'll need to drill deeper still into the drivers of ability and motivation. Who is responsible? Is it really just a matter of individual accountability or is there an organizational component? For each of the eight individual elements there are corresponding responsibilities for which the organization is accountable. Table 5.8 shows a modified extract from the Performance Analysis Template listing the 16 elements of ability and motivation categorized according to whether they affect ability or motivation and whether they lie within the span of control of the individual or the responsibility of the organization.

Each of these 16 elements should look very familiar—each has been discussed previously. Now we are bringing them together to analyze how they interplay with each other as part of a holistic view of performance.

When diagnosing performance it is important to clarify where the breakdown(s) occurred. Does responsibility rest with the individual or with

Table 5.8   Organizational and Individual Determinants of Ability and Motivation

		Organization Responsibilities	*Individual Responsibilities*
	Element:	*Clarity of Expectations*	*Commitment*
Motivation		Objectives and goals are clear	Interest in task is sufficient
		Metrics are aligned and available	Confidence is sufficient
		Feedback is appropriate, timely, and specific	Willingness to assume responsibility is sufficient
		Rewards and consequences are commensurate with actual performance	Alignment with organizational goals is appropriate
	Element:	*Conditions and Drivers*	*Competencies*
Ability		Resources are sufficient	Technical skills are sufficient
		Technologies are sufficient	Interpersonal skills are sufficient
		Formal and informal behavioral reinforcers	Knowledge of job and organizational procedures are sufficient
		Formal and informal behavioral inhibiters	Appropriate degree of organizational power is sufficient

Table 5.9   Categories of Resources and Support

Resources Needed			
Time	Training	New equipment	Other: |
Manpower	Authority	Technical expertise	Other: |
Funding	Facilities	Access to equipment	Other: |
Support Needed			
Clear expectations	Feedback	Flying cover	Other: |
Mentoring	Coaching	Encouragement	Other: |
Decisions made	Delegation	Consequences	Other: |

management? Almost universally you will find that culpability rests with both. Even with goats, management must take some responsibility for undermanaging the situation and failing to provide logical consequences. As part of the analysis, consider whether management has provided adequate resources and support. Table 5.9 is another excerpt from the Performance Analysis Template with categories of resources and support essential for success.

Summarize the analysis with a conclusion and a determination of whether the situation has been over- or undermanaged. Defer back to the maxim: all things yield to good management.

As a practitioner, I'm not one to advocate paperwork for the sake of paperwork. The purpose of the Performance Analysis Template is to help you think through the drivers and restrainers of behavior. Consider the case study of the Administrative Department:

CASE STUDY PART I—MANAGING THE UNMANAGEABLE: As a very junior officer, I was assigned to be the Command Administration Officer even though the billet was slated for a much higher-ranking officer. I was tasked because no other officer was willing to take on the assignment in a department that was notoriously difficult to manage. Several other officers before me had tried and failed to manage the "unmanageable" department of three. But as a junior officer, I had nothing to lose. Though I was junior as an officer, I was still an experienced manager having served in enlisted leadership positions for years in other commands.

After a short time in the position, I found the problem. Ms. Stark, the most senior of the three staff and de facto supervisor, horded a treasure trove of secrets she kept locked and hidden from the other staff. She had password protected every file and folder on the computer systems. Neither of the other two staff members was allowed access. They couldn't access policies and the forms essential to performing their assigned tasks. Consequently, the command's administrative workload was backed up by this bottleneck creating delayed processing and reporting. The midlevel enlisted member had never been challenged on this behavior because other's believed her when she said, "I'm the only one qualified enough." It was true, the others weren't qualified; but that was by design. Her lack of cooperation and collaboration with the others prevented them from learning the tasks essential to their jobs. When Ms. Stark had been challenged by previous managers, she stood her ground—I'd even seen her yell in the face of senior officers. I didn't understand why they didn't bust her, but invariably, they'd back down because they needed the work to be done and she was the only one capable of doing the work. She wielded the power of expertise as both a weapon and a shield. What wasn't shielded by expertise she controlled through emotional tyranny. Having never been effectively confronted, she was firmly entrenched in her position, invulnerable and free to dictate over her little kingdom. In the DISC world, her temperament was "D" to the extreme.

Utilizing the Performance Analysis Template to think through the situation in the Administration Department helps identify which of the seven planks of the Framework for Individual Success was missing. To begin, start by listing the tasks not being accomplished:

1. Processing and reporting of administrative tasks in a timely manner according to established priorities and deadlines
2. Working collaboratively with other members to parse up the work to ensure equitable division of labor and opportunities to gain knowledge and experience
3. Providing access to tools and resources needed by other department members to perform their assignments
4. Training department members to increase their abilities to contribute and ultimately improving opportunities for career advancement

Looking at these four tasks that were not being accomplished; consider whether these were a matter of will or skill. Clearly, there is nothing physically stopping Ms. Stark from sharing the information with the other members of her team. The question was why.

All Behavior Is Rewarding on Some Level

If the goal of management is to optimize behaviors and resources then understanding why people do what they do as well as when and how they do it lies at the very heart of management. When examining behavior keep in mind that every behavior is rewarding on some level. Even severely dysfunctional behavior is satisfying a need at some level. The need could be healthy and productive or the need could be destructive to self or others. As a manager, it's not your job to psychoanalyze why people do what they do, just understand that there are reasons and your job is to set up the conditions that affect productive outcomes. With this in mind, as a practitioner, I've actually learned more about why people do what they do from my economics classes than I learned in my psychology classes. Psychology deals with theoretical drivers such as id, ego, superego, intrinsic motivation, drives, fears, phobias, neurosis, and psychosis, etc.; economics isn't as concerned about the why as much as it is the how based on the assumption that it is the consumers underlying values that governs the allocation of scarce resources. To effectively manage performance, there are two essential economics concepts every manager should know: the law of demand and indifference curves.

Behavior and the Law of Demand

The law of demand simply states that as the cost of something goes up, consumers generally demand less of it (Figure 5.18). Take cars for instance; a Lamborghini Reventon's list price is around $1.6M U.S. How many do you have in your garage? I don't have any because the price is a tad too high. However, if someone offered me one for $2K, I'd probably take a couple of them. The same concept applies for most purchased goods. So why is this concept important to managers? Because "cost" does not only imply monetary expenditure. Cost also relates to the degree of effort an activity requires. If the effort (cost) of any activity outweighs the perceived value, then people will expend less effort on that activity. For instance, if it is more work to get in the car and drive to visit my in-laws then the pleasure I receive from their

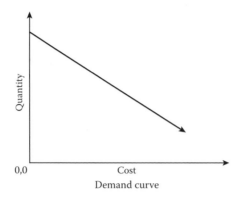

Demand curve

Figure 5.18   Demand curve.

company, then, I will be doing as little of that activity as possible. Similarly, if I want an operator to regularly tour the plant, this requires the operator to get up out of his air-conditioned control booth, leave the conversation he was having with his friends, and go out and walk around the hot, noisy plant, climbing up and down ladders and stairs and around and behind equipment. This requires effort on his part. If he doesn't perceive that the value of the activity exceeds the cost, there will be a minimum of that activity performed.

The law of demand restated for management is "as the effort compared to output increases—the quantity of the desired behavior decreases." As a manager, if you can help your employees understand the value of the behaviors, they will be more willing to expend the cost to perform the desired task. This is why establishing a line of sight between activities and outcomes is so important to creating engagement. Conversely, if the cost of nonperformance is greater than the effort expended performing the task, individuals are much more apt to perform the task. Ideally, we would prefer people perform their assignments because they want to just because they were assigned to do it. If this were the case management would simply be a matter of telling people what to do and when to do it. Anyone who has tried to manage knows that saying doesn't make it so. Effective managers have multiple tools to optimize performance and principles of economics are powerful levers that can move even intractable individuals into action.

However, continuous reliance on negative consequences creates a climate of fear; duress can lead to shoddy workmanship or malicious compliance. Negative consequences are often considered management options of last resort to be used after individuals fail to respond to more aspirational leadership approaches.

Indifference Curves

Indifference curves build upon the demand curve concept by comparing the balanced value of two goods such as beer and pizza (Figure 5.19). I like beer; I like pizza. If I spend all of my money on beer, I will have no pizza; if I spend all of my money on pizza, I will have no beer. To find my optimal level of satisfaction, I may like to have a little more pizza than beer— I'm balancing the value of having a certain amount of one item with having more or less of another. Now, apply this concept to behaviors.

Consider first your work–life balance. As shown in Figure 5.20, the more time I spend at work, the less time I spend at home and vice versa. Somewhere along the line, you strike the balance between the two. In order for me to spend one more unit of time on work, I need to get much greater return for my investment if I am to be enticed to sacrifice more time from home. There gets to be a point that the cost is just not worth the return. The same concept can even be applied to two unpleasant behaviors. Figure 5.21 shows the relationship between the time spent with in-laws as compared to the degree of spousal displeasure. The less time spent with in-laws, the more spousal displeasure is endured. If you like your in-laws, substitute any other activity which you dislike that your spouse greatly enjoys. People balance the time spent on one activity against the time enduring the grief of avoidance to find the most satisfactory point along the indifference curve.

The concept of balancing two activities or goods along an indifference curve can be applied to almost any other pair of conditions imaginable:

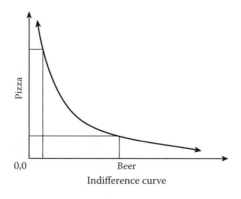

Figure 5.19   Indifference curve—pizza versus beer.

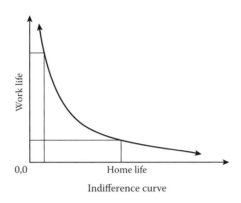

Figure 5.20 Indifference curve—work–life balance.

freedom versus security, debt versus material possessions, pleasing others versus pleasing self, etc. Each of these paired concepts requires a trade off whereby individuals strike a balance they find satisfactory.

Let's apply this concept to performance management. The time an individual spends on one task must be traded off against the time spent on another. As a manager, you must help determine this balance by setting priorities and clear expectations. If you are unengaged and lack a timely view to the day-to-day activities of your organization, your employees are determining their own level of satisfaction regarding the tasks to which they are assigned. If they find an aspect of their job less enjoyable, say thorough documentation, then, they will perform less of it unless you've established and enforce consequences that counterbalance their natural tendencies. This doesn't mean you should nag and whine, but it does reinforce the concept of logical consequences in balancing the necessary priorities and performance.

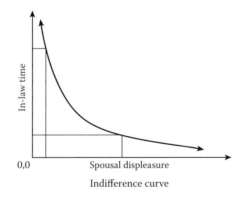

Figure 5.21 Indifference curve—time with in-laws versus spousal displeasure.

Given an understanding of these two fundamental economic principles, let's return to our exploration of performance analysis and effecting an appropriate response with *performance contracting*.

Performance Contracting: Setting Clear Expectations and Logical Consequences

A contract is a binding agreement between two parties; there are legal contracts, social contracts, written, oral, and unspoken or implied contracts. A performance contract is an agreement between a manager and an individual that outlines the roles, responsibilities, and expectations of both. These types of managerial instrument are usually thought of as tools of last resort used once an individual has consistently failed to perform. However, they can just as easily be used when initially making assignments as a means to set clear expectations. Early intervention and setting clear expectations of desired performance and required degrees of support greatly decreases the odds that performance contracts will ever become a condition of employment. Whether it is a case of addressing unsatisfactory performance or setting initial expectations, the principles and methodology are the same—only the degree of consequences varies between routine assignments and last chance agreements.

CASE STUDY PART II—MANAGING THE UNMANAGEABLE: Ms. Stark the administrative supervisor was balancing her desire to exert power and control against her responsibilities to train and develop the other staff. Heavily skewed in her temperament toward "D," she was much more inclined toward consolidating her power base by limiting the power and control afforded others she considered potential rivals. To shift her behaviors toward collaboration I needed to increase the cost of her dysfunctional behavior. I confronted Ms. Stark telling her to remove all passwords immediately and move all files to a shared drive the others could access. In a dismissive gesture not looking up, she replied casually as she continued to type, "I'll do that after these reports are done. Maybe next month, when I get some time."

Recognizing when I'm being blatantly "yupped" I stood my ground. "No, you'll do it now."

"I don't have time to do that."

"Make the time."

"I won't do it."

"OK, so let me get this straight," I took out a pen and began to write, "On this date, you disobeyed the direct lawful order of the officer in command…"

"What are you doing?" Ms. Stark stopped her typing and looked at me for the first time. I now had her attention.

"I'm filling out the report chit to take you to Mast for disobeying a direct order."

"You can't do that!"

"Yes I can, and yes I will. Now, on this date you refused to comply…"

"Fine, I'll take off the passwords."

"Thank you, and I've inventoried all the files so I know how many there are. Please ensure that they are all still available on the shared drive." I wasn't going to allow malicious compliance either.

It took a direct confrontation and an ultimatum that I was prepared to enforce to compel Ms. Stark to change her behavior. I didn't threaten her and I didn't raise my voice. I simply outlined the consequences of her behavior. If she refused to follow a direct lawful order, she would face formal disciplinary actions.

CASE STUDY—POST SCRIPT: The belligerent employee didn't take her loss well; Ms. Stark went around me and complained directly to the Commanding Officer. As he had done so many times in the past, he rewarded her behavior by "counseling" me to try harder to work with her. He was unwittingly enabling her bad behavior that had led to the dysfunctional unmanageable state of the department. "Sir, you assigned me with a clear mandate to improve the performance of this department. With all due respect, if you want me to improve the department, I must be allowed to manage without bypassing the chain of command." He left without saying a word. The next week he reassigned my problem employee to another area where she continued her bad behavior with an even greater sense of invulnerability and entitlement. She was empowered to be a little dictator and probably continues as such to this day, but not in my department.

In our area with one less staff, productivity went up, as did morale. Over the next two years, both of my staff were recognized as Sailor's of the Year, both received awards and promotions, and both thanked me for having the managerial courage to stand up for what was right. And although the Commanding Officer never took any responsibility for creating the problem, he did award me with a Navy Achievement Medal for greatly improving the performance of the Administration Department.

Avoiding "Democratic Ass Kickings"— Not Firing Blindly into the Flock

Direct confrontation is uncomfortable—so much so that many managers avoid it until the situation reaches an absolute crisis point. Instead of addressing the problem directly and personally, they hold group meetings and address the problems in the department by talking to everyone generally and no one individual particularly. Let's call these "democratic ass kickings," or DAKs. Instead of targeting the few individuals responsible, DAKs kick everyone's ass equally. I've endured so many of these over the course of my career that it's impossible to keep track of them all. Assemble everyone and complain about smokers not confining their smoking to the smoking areas—I don't smoke. Address the deplorable condition of the women's locker room—I'm not a woman. The night shift failed to properly restock the supplies—I'm on the day shift. People need to get their reports in on time utilizing the proper format—I turned mine in the day before it was due…and the beat goes on.

There are two major problems with DAKs: they anger, frustrate, and demoralize those not responsible, and they're ineffective at changing the behavior of those who are responsible. Assembling the group and chewing everyone out is tantamount to firing blindly into the flock. Some will be frustrated saying, "Why did they call me into this meeting? I'm not the one who did it and this is just taking time away from me doing my job. Now I'll have to stay late to finish up." At the same time innocent sheep are being fired upon, the goats are hunkered down in the back out of the direct line of fire. What's worse, these types of group discipline sessions are actually empowering to those responsible. A group setting allows the guilty to hide in the crowd. It's not much of a consequence and it's not logical.

For feedback to be effective, it must be specific, timely, and direct. DAKs are none of the above.

Action Planning: Preparing to Confront a Goat

When you encounter a situation with a "Goat" that you need to manage, prior preparation is essential. Directly confronting someone on their behavior will invoke all of the responses discussed earlier for compelling behavior—shown again in Figure 5.22.

Up to the point of direct confrontation, the individual has maintained the balance of power over the manager. As the manager tries to incent collaboration (Point 1), the individual follows their own agenda. When confronted (Point 2), the goat begins by minimizing the problem, misrepresenting or trying to misdirect attention, and even tries false promises by yupping.

As the manager stays the course and continues to keep the conversation focused, the individual may move to pity, "I've been really going through a lot these days...problems here or there...etc." They may move to guilt, "I can't believe you'd do this to me after all the time we've been together." They may even grow angry and try to intimidate the manager by threats of going around them, especially if they have relations with other senior managers (Point 3).

Ultimately, if the manager stays the course, is not dissuaded by distractions, and is not undermined by others in the chain of command, the individual will be compelled to conform or face the consequences.

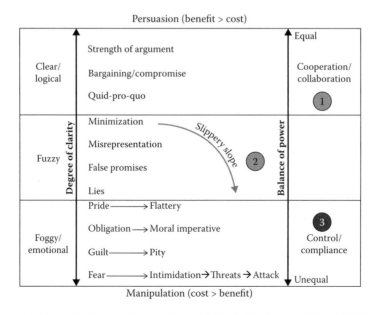

Figure 5.22   Compelling behavior of a goat.

Table 5.10   Action Planner/Performance Contract

Action Planner/Performance Contract			
Project Name		**Final Completion Date:**	
Team Member(s)			
Task:	**Description:**	**Responsibility**	**Due Date**
Task No: 1			
	Resources and Support Needed:		**Decision Authority**
Task:	**Description:**	**Responsibility**	**Due Date**
Task No: 2			
	Resources and Support Needed:		**Decision Authority**
Task:	**Description:**	**Responsibility**	**Due Date**
Task No: 3			
	Resources and Support Needed:		**Decision Authority**
Task:	**Description:**	**Responsibility**	**Due Date**
Task No: 4			
	Resources and Support Needed:		**Decision Authority**
Task:	**Description:**	**Responsibility**	**Due Date**
Task No: 5			
	Resources and Support Needed:		**Decision Authority**

Check Points and Milestones	**Due Date:**	**Key Metric**	**Target**	**Required Communications:**

(continued)

Table 5.10   Action Planner/Performance Contract (Continued)

Action Planner/Performance Contract			
What steps will be taken if performance does not achieve desired outcomes within the specified timeframe?			
Employee Signature	**Date:**	**Manager or Supervisor Signature**	**Date:**

Table 5.10 is an Action Planner/Performance Contract that will bring specificity to the situation and set clear expectations for both the individual and the manager.

This template will help guide the conversation through the cyclical communication process described previously shown again in Figure 5.23.

Begin the conversation having analyzed what has not been occurring and having in mind the desired outcome of the conversation. Frame the discussion around the need to improve performance outcomes and the desire to remove any barriers and provide the support necessary to address the performance gaps.

For each task, describe what is required along with who is responsible and due dates. During the conversation, the individual has the opportunity to request resources and support.

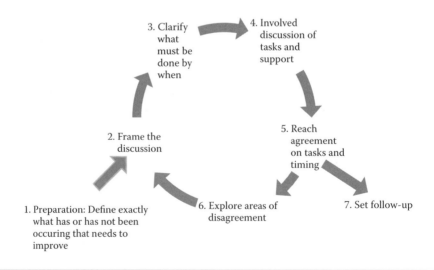

Figure 5.23   Communications process applied to performance contracting.

Another key element is defining the decision authority. State the limits of authority and who ultimately will make the decision.

The next section establishes milestones by defining the deliverables, key dates, metrics, targets, and channels of communications.

Finally, spell out what consequences will occur for failure to deliver. If you cannot reach agreement, you will need to cycle around again until you have reached agreement on actions, milestones, and due dates.

This guided dialogue eliminates confusion and eliminates all elements of plausible deniability. The individual has the opportunity to request the support and resources necessary for success thus eliminating the question of "skill." Failure to deliver on tasks at this point will clearly expose a lack of "will."

CASE STUDY: SHEEP LEADING THE GOAT: Keith had been a problem for years. In a textbook example of the Peter Principle, he had been promoted to manager where he was a conspicuous failure. Instead of the organization discharging him, Keith was demoted to a project lead position, though his pay was not affected. Angry and belligerent, Keith challenged his manager daily. He disappeared for hours at a time. When he could be tracked down, he would be found standing around in other work areas, bemoaning his situation, disparaging his manager, and generally spreading malcontent.

Keith's manager, Peggy, was chronically conflict averse. She looked for the best in everyone and believed that, deep down, everyone wanted to do a good job. Over the course of the two years since Keith was assigned to her department, she had tried to collaborate, inspire, entrust and engage. Each of which should have inspired Keith to follow Peggy's lead and align with the organization. Instead, Keith took full advantage of her good nature. Each failure on Keith's part was explained away or sidestepped to consistently avoid any accountability.

Overconfident in his invulnerability, Keith overstepped his entitlement zone when he failed to deliver on a multimillion-dollar opportunity. Peggy went to human resources to have him terminated. Unfortunately, her enabling behavior had resulted in no documentation from which a case could be built for termination. Peggy had to step forward and confront Keith face to face. Table 5.11 shows the action planner/performance contract that placed Keith on the short leash from which he might hang himself.

Table 5.11 Example of an Action Planner/Performance Contract

Action Planner/Performance Contract

Project Name	Real Estate Strategies 6 Month Probation	Final Completion Date:	9/30
Team Member(s)		Keith	
Task:	**Description:**	**Responsibility**	**Due Date**
Task No: 1	Respond to client inquiries in a timely manner	Keith	Verbally within one business day with written updates weekly on the status of their projects
	Resources and Support Needed:		**Decision Authority**
	None		Should response not be possible, notify Peggy
Task:	**Description:**	**Responsibility**	**Due Date**
Task No: 2	Be available during normal working hours	Keith	Daily
	Resources and Support Needed:		**Decision Authority**
	Documentation of times outside of office stating when, where, and with whom		Peggy to provide prior approval of all absences

Task:	Description:	Responsibility	Due Date
Task No: 3	Complete project reports	Keith	Within one week after assigned or prior to client due date
	Resources and Support Needed:		**Decision Authority**
	Client specifications of space and amenities requirements		Reviewed by Peggy prior to submittal to client / Client approval of final site packages

Check Points and Milestones	Due Date:	Key Metric	Target	Required Communications:
Weekly Project Status Updates	Every Friday	Completed project reports	Complete documentation of all projects	Meet weekly in Peggy's office 3:00 pm Fridays with project updates and action plan for following week
Approved Sight Packages	Per Project	Timely updates to clients	100% response to all client inquiries	Initial client meetings to set project goals, regular client follow-up on status of site selection, final approval of site recommendations

What steps will be taken if performance does not achieve desired outcomes within the specified timeframe? Failure to meet agreed upon performance expectations will result in processing for discharge with cause

Employee Signature	Date:	Manager or Supervisor Signature		Date:
Keith	9/30	Peggy		9/30

Taking the time to directly confront the behavior establishes clear expectations and outlines both positive and negative consequences of performance. Situations where someone is behaving outside the standards of performance and group expectations rarely resolve themselves. Typically, failure to address such situations only empowers those responsible and demoralizes and frustrates others.

In Defense of Goats—Don't Cull Them All

Managers, like everyone else, tend to take the path of least resistance. They often get into a mindset that great team behavior is when "everyone does what I tell them when I tell them." In contrast to Peggy's undermanagement, some managers would prefer to cull all the differences from their teams and surround themselves with compliant, easily managed employees. When they do, they typically have very weak teams with little creativity and little agility. If you want a high-performing team, you want to have motivated self-driven people, but you need them to be motivated for the right reasons and driven for the overall success of the organization and not just their own self-serving ambition.

Though it can be difficult, most performance situations can be improved by providing a balance of challenge and support. Challenge unproductive behaviors while providing support and timely feedback to reinforce desired performance. When it is done well, a poor performer can be brought back into the fold and become a strong contributor. To illustrate the strength of diversity, let's look again at the differences between actual goats and sheep.

Benefits of Goats over Sheep: Goats Can Flourish Where Sheep Cannot

1. Goats are hardier than sheep: Goats can survive with less water and on less grass. In addition, they are more productive giving more milk.
2. Goats can defend themselves better against predators: As the first colonist to the Americas discovered that goats are "…better able than sheep to protect themselves against wolves." (Larned, J.N. 1922. *The New Larned History for Ready Reference, Reading and Research.* Springfield, MA: C.A. Nichols Publishing Company.)

3. Goats are more creative and better problem solvers: By challenging the limits of defined boundaries, goats push the envelope in ways that sheep do not. They are better able to solve problems and think independently.

It is true that independent, driven, creative people are harder to manage, but they are vital to the ongoing vitality and success of the organization. If you seek to confine them such that great incongruence exists between the organization's freedom to act and the individual's self-efficacy and need for autonomy then the organization won't fully benefit from the strengths they can bring to the team.

Goats can be managed but only when there are clear expectations, rewards, and alignment between the individual's and organization's values and culture.

Key Takeaways: Sustained versus Variable Performance

To effectively maintain the organization on an upward trajectory of sustainable performance requires managers and leaders to understand and recognize the elements that undermine the changes they are working to implement. Once they understand these elements, they can more effectively work to institutionalize the balanced rewards and opportunities that will create the culture of "logical consequences" begun during Committing Element 7. They can employ tools like "situation analysis" and "performance contracting" to intervene and make course corrections along the way. If the organization doesn't sustain an even keel of logical consequences and rewards, employees can become frustrated and disengaged, falling into learned helplessness. Implementation of tools contained in the LSS toolkit is most effective at this stage of organizational development. Application of LSS tools in the absence of sound management yields only transitory results.

Sustaining organizational performance requires managers and leaders to step back and view the entire organization holistically. Is there an ongoing validation of customer and stakeholder requirements? Are systems becoming optimized? Is the culture of logical consequences widely embraced? As you step back to observe the operation, challenge your assumptions. Be aware of the forces resistant to change. Remember, failed initiatives exact

Table 5.12   Key Takeaways: Sustained versus Variable Performance

	Focus	*Commit*	*Sustained Performance*	*Renewal*
Form	*Stumble*	*Fragment*	*Variable Performance*	*Level*

Sustained Performance: The organization is cohesive, skilled, and consistently achieves its goals

Team Needs:
- Individual congruence with organizational culture
- Growing autonomy and empowerment
- Meaningful outcomes
- Equitable treatment
- Sustainable work–life balance

The Change "Readiness vs. Response" Continuum	
Change Ready:	Optimism
Change Resistant:	Skepticism

Indicators of Effective Navigation	**Indicators of Ineffective Navigation**
• High productivity	• Low/sporadic productivity
• Focus on team achievement	• Missed deadlines/frequent mistakes
• Culture of excellence	• Culture of entitlement or fear
• Satisfaction	• Focus on individual gains

Effective Leadership Responses:
- Maintain ongoing focus toward delivering on the organization's value proposition
- Empower members to take on more responsibilities and authority
- Challenge assumptions
- Proactive problem solving and decision making
- Embracing the messengers and maintaining multiple views to the organization

(continued)

Table 5.12   Key Takeaways: Sustained versus Variable Performance (Continued)

Effective Management Responses:

- Continuous process improvement
- Standardization of policies and procedures
- Vendor and supplier management
- Control of nonconforming products and services
- Courageous and consistent use of logical consequences

Tools and Techniques:

- Validation of customer and stakeholder requirements
- Ongoing goal setting and revision
- Documentation of policies and procedures
- 5S, visual management, and value stream mapping (VSM)
- Situation analysis and performance contracting

a heavy toll that has repercussions far beyond the financial and human capital expended on the project. Each time you start down a road that you don't finish you're worse off than if you had never started at all. You have wasted time, resources, and raised everyone's hopes and expectations but failed to deliver. As a result, the organization is less able to compete having wasted both time and money making the organization less prepared for future challenges and the feelings of frustration, cynicism, and learned helplessness have been further ingrained into the organizational culture. People will be less willing to expend their precious discretionary effort. They won't easily sign up for your next voyage of organizational change. Table 5.12 summarizes the key indicators of successful navigation of the Sustained Performance Stage along with essential management and leadership responses.

To help with your project planning, Table 5.13 shows a basic project plan to help navigate through the Sustainable Performance Stage.

Table 5.13   Sustaining Project Plan—Institutionalizing and Optimizing

Project Step	Responsibility	Date Planned	Date Complete
(1) Establish regular and ongoing evaluations, customer and key stakeholder requirements, and satisfaction			
(2) Implement process for regular verification and alignment department and individual goals to drive delivery of the organization's value proposition			
(3) Documentation of policies and procedures to include regular review and revision			
1. Prioritization of documentation requirements			
2. Ongoing procedural review			
3. Ready access to documentation			
4. Effective change notification process			
(4) Evaluate lines of communications— revise as needed			
(5) Ensure an ongoing and holistic view to the process			
1. Implementation of "Balanced Scorecard" reporting			
2. Implementation of "dashboard" technology to automate the view to the process			
(6) Establish/codify vendor and supplier review and feedback processes			
(7) Introduction and implementation of LSS concepts:			
1. Implementation of 5S			
2. Implement visual management			

(continued)

Table 5.13   Sustaining Project Plan—Institutionalizing and Optimizing (Continued)

Project Step	Responsibility	Date Planned	Date Complete
3. Conduct value stream mapping			
(8) Ensure managers and leaders maintain the cascading lines of communication within their areas and managing according to a climate of "logical consequences"			

Navigating out of Variable Performance

Like every stage before, there are many variables and unknowns that can cause you to blow off course from sustainable into variable performance. However, unlike previous stages, you simply can't course correct out of variable performance by circling back to the previous stage (Figure 5.24). In the earlier stages, if you found the organization stumbling, you reformed; if the organization was fragmenting, you refocused. But if your organization suffers from low or variable performance, you can't simply ask people to recommit. Commitment is an internal emotional transformation that occurs organically within each individual. It is an outcome of the combined elements of the Workforce Engagement Equation:

$$\text{Hope} + \text{Control} + \text{Equity} \rightarrow \underline{\text{Individual Satisfaction}}$$

$$+$$

$$\text{Hope} + \text{Purpose} + \text{Congruence} \rightarrow \underline{\text{Organizational Commitment}}$$

$$\text{Yields:}$$

$$\underline{\text{Impactful Outcomes}}$$

$$\text{Resulting in:}$$

$$\underline{\text{An Engaged Workforce}}$$

You can't demand it; it has to be given freely. I've witnessed how managers pound on the tables at a DAK, accusing their people of being

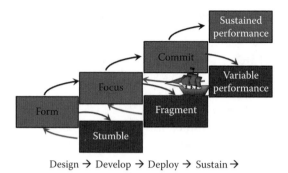

Figure 5.24 Navigating out of variable performance by refocusing.

uncommitted and demanding that people need to get on board or get off. These tirades may get compliance, but they will never garner commitment.

If the organization is experiencing missed deadlines, frenetic harried work schedules with some stressing out while others coast along, culture of entitlement or fear (these two are not mutually exclusive), and certain members focusing on individual gains at the expense of others then you have not achieved sustainable performance. You must circle back and look at the fundamental systems, processes, procedures that needed to be implemented during the Focusing Stage. And if the cancer of negativism and political gamesmanship of furthering personal agendas at the expense of others has spread so far that people no longer trust their managers or each other, you may have to go back and reestablish the elements that needed to be in place to properly form. Continuing the beatings until morale improves will not get you where you want to go.

Don't be surprised when you see some elements of each stage in your organization, there are so many multiple complex drivers that interact in unexpected and unplanned ways it would be surprising if you didn't see them. The key point is whistling past the graveyard won't address the problem. Courage, integrity, and genuine concern for the mission and the people are required. Staying true to your values and principles while maintaining your focus on achieving your vision combined with the humility to recognize the mote in your own eye will prove to be the truest compass that will safely navigate your organization through the most turbulent of times.

Chapter 6

Stage 5: Renewal— Refitting and Redeploying

Overview and Assessment: Renewal versus Leveling

An organization that has formed well, laid all the systems, and defined the roles and responsibilities of focusing, achieved the engagement and commitment of its members, established effective training, and maintains ongoing communications with its customers and stakeholders, resulting in a sustained upward trajectory of excellence supplemented with effective use of 5S, visual management, and value stream mapping can truly be said to be a world-class organization. This is an organization that deserves to celebrate its success! However (you knew there was going to be a "however"), just because a company is great doesn't mean that it will stay great. As evidenced by some of the 11 companies highlighted in the best-selling book *Good to Great* (Collins, J.C. 2001. *Good to Great: Why Some Companies Make the Leap...and Others Don't.* New York: HarperBusiness), Circuit City took a spectacular nosedive into oblivion; Fannie Mae also ran well off course during the great recession. My point here isn't to judge; I'm not qualified. The point to be made is the same disclaimer found within every company's stock prospectus: "Past performance *is not* indicative of future results." As we pointed out at the beginning of our Stage 4 (Sustaining) discussion, only 20 of the Fortune 100 Best Companies of 1960 made the 2010 list. If an organization is going to stay the course over the long term, it must regularly reinvent and renew itself. Without renewal, organizations can't regenerate, adapt, and reinvent themselves. In a very real way, organizations are living organisms.

Remember your high school biology classes when you learned that a living organism possesses the capacity to grow, reproduce itself, respond to stimuli, and adapt to the environment. Without these features, organisms cease to exist; they die. In his excellent book, *The Living Company*, Arie de Geus profiled 30 companies from around the world that had been in business for 100 years or more (de Geus, A. 1997/2002. *The Living Company*. Boston, MA: Longview Publishing Limited). Through his research, Mr. de Geus came to the conclusion that companies thrive over the long haul when they value people above the business; they believe that the business is a means to an end rather than an end in and of itself. It really is a matter of values. If managers place a higher priority on the production of goods and services than on the quality of life the organization provides to its employees and communities, chances are that organization is more apt to fail. If you value profits above people, the organization's lifespan is limited. In simple terms, sustainable businesses exist to serve the people rather than the other way around. And, like the goose that laid the golden eggs, the people must continue to be good stewards of the business or it won't survive to continue supporting them either.

In this section, we will explore the 10 elements that continue sustaining and improving the operation through organizational renewal (Figure 6.1).

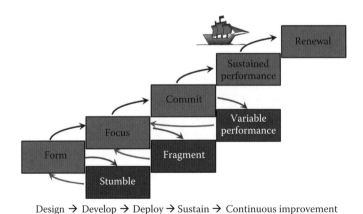

Design → Develop → Deploy → Sustain → Continuous improvement

Figure 6.1   Sustaining through renewal.

Table 6.1 Summary of Indicators: Renewal versus Leveling

	Focus	*Commit*	*Sustained Performance*	*Renewal*
Form	*Stumble*	*Fragment*	*Variable Performance*	*Level*

Renewal: A sustained culture of excellence, individual team members may change, but the organization continues to consistently achieve its goals

Team Needs:
- Fulfillment of purpose
- Celebration of accomplishments
- Increased opportunities and new challenges to overcome
- Increased levels of responsibility and mastery
- Effective integration and assimilation of new members
- Ongoing validation and adaptation of the value proposition

The Change "Readiness vs. Response" Continuum

Change Ready:	Celebration
Change Resistant:	Acceptance

Indicators of Effective Navigation	**Indicators of Ineffective Navigation**
• High productivity	• Frustration and burn out
• Celebration and good will	• Change resistance
• Low turnover	• High turnover
• Ease of recruiting top talent	• Unfilled positions
• Continuous improvement	• Ineffective improvement projects

Combined, these 10 elements give you a quick indication whether the organization is thriving, renewing, growing, and adapting or stagnating, and in decline. Left unchecked, patterns of stagnation and decline become the pervasive culture, and the overall vitality of the organization will decline to the point where it simply ceases to exist. Table 6.1 outlines the summary of indicators and organizational needs that differentiate a company that is capable of renewing itself.

Complete the Renewal Assessment contained in Table 6.2 by ranking which statement is most indicative of your organization for each of the 10 elements. Some of these elements are only symptoms that point to

Table 6.2 Renewal Assessment

For each of the paired statements or groups of statement below, decide which statement most accurately describes your experiences in the day-to-day work activities within your organization. For the statement that is chosen, check to what degree you believe the statement is either Most or Somewhat like your routine experience within your organization's work activities.

Check only one statement per paired question.

Assessment (Select One)			Choose the Statement that Best Describes Your Organization
1	+4	Most Like Us	Both individual and team successes are regularly communicated and celebrated reinforcing pride in affiliation with the organization and promoting a general feeling of purpose, accomplishment, and belonging among the team
	+2	Somewhat Like Us	In the midst of celebration, it is accepted that new goals will continue the drive toward further improvements. The organization is capable of celebrating the present accomplishments while still maintaining a drive for improvement
	−2	Somewhat Like Us	There is little communication regarding individual and team achievement. Celebrations are rare and what few occur are sometimes viewed cynically as a facade, a show for upper management, or a hollow attempt at improving moral
	−4	Most Like Us	When the team approaches a target, the goal is frequently moved just when it is within reach creating an overall perception that nothing the group accomplishes will ever be good enough
2	+4	Most Like Us	The organization is committed to continuous improvement as demonstrated by regularly benchmarking performance and the outcomes of their initiatives against "Best-in-Class" standards
	+2	Somewhat Like Us	Initiatives are impactful and directly contribute to the value proposition. The outcomes of initiatives are measured against stated objectives to assess the true impact and return on investment (ROI)
			People feel comfortable identifying ineffective team practices or behaviors and take timely corrective actions

(continued)

Table 6.2   Renewal Assessment (Continued)

Assessment (Select One)			Choose the Statement that Best Describes Your Organization
	−2	Somewhat Like Us	Leaders embrace and profit from the status quo. Individuals are complacent and give little consideration or questioning to how things could be made better. Problems are frequently ignored. Team members find ways to work around them rather than correct them
	−4	Most Like Us	Initiatives are superficial and/or self-serving. They arrive with fanfare then fade into obscurity with little impact or accountability
			Pointing out shortcomings is career limiting. It is better to remain silent than point out what everyone else is thinking. There is a general malaise and a belief that nothing really changes around here anyway, so why try?
3	+4	Most Like Us	Both internal and external auditing processes routinely validate performance and identify opportunities to improve based upon customer feedback, process performance, and product conformity
	+2	Somewhat Like Us	Records of reviews and review actions are maintained, process/procedure/system changes are communicated and relevant documents are amended, effective arrangements for communication with suppliers, customer, and employees are implemented
	−2	Somewhat Like Us	There is no effective auditing process. If and when an audit occurs, it is seen as a "witch hunt" meant to be endured, not an opportunity to improve
	−4	Most Like Us	Records are not maintained on process/procedure/system changes. Procedures and requirements are not maintained up to date and no standard process exists for process/ procedure/system changes requirement change notifications internally or externally
4	+4	Most Like Us	Meetings are impactful and well attended with punctual participants who genuinely feel that the time spent in meetings is valuable; they consistently add or gain value from their attendance
	+2	Somewhat Like Us	Meetings are efficient and task oriented, focusing on significant issues, not strictly routine administrative reporting

(continued)

Table 6.2 Renewal Assessment (Continued)

Assessment (Select One)			Choose the Statement that Best Describes Your Organization
	−2	Somewhat Like Us	The group does not routinely meet and/or meetings are often ineffective, rambling, and unproductive such that people come late, leave early, or do not attend unless mandated
	−4	Most Like Us	Meeting topics are frequently inappropriate for many participants who have little understanding of or influence with the topics discussed. Meetings cover routine information that everyone already knows, could easily get, or doesn't have a need to know
5	+4	Most Like Us	A climate of "logical consequences" is maintained through the ongoing use of an impactful performance review and reward systems
	+2	Somewhat Like Us	
	−2	Somewhat Like Us	The performance review process is strictly an administrative check in the box. A general climate of scarcity and/or inequity pervades the organization—there are not enough rewards or recognition to be shared so any success is coveted and horded—the organizational climate is either polarized or oscillates between entitlement and fear with little consistency
	−4	Most Like Us	
6	+4	Most Like Us	The organization has the expectation and opportunities exist for individuals to continuously grow their knowledge and skills
	+2	Somewhat Like Us	Career paths are defined and understood. Opportunities exist and are made available to be promoted within the organization or to cross-train to expand skills based upon individual aptitude and interest along with organizational needs and direction
	−2	Somewhat Like Us	There is neither expectation nor support for ongoing development. Once trained always trained such that any mention of ongoing development raises offense among incumbents creating a culture of entitlement and stagnation
	−4	Most Like Us	There is no clear path within the organization for the employee to be promoted. The organization experiences turnover of high performers with ambition as they leave the organization to seek opportunities, leaving the organization staffed by sedentary performers with low ambition/low confidence

(continued)

Table 6.2   Renewal Assessment (Continued)

Assessment (Select One)			*Choose the Statement that Best Describes Your Organization*
7	+4	Most Like Us	Training is a strategic priority—not an event, reward, or knee jerk reaction to the current crisis
	+2	Somewhat Like Us	A clear line of sight exists between the organization's vision, mission, and strategy and the training and developmental process
	−2	Somewhat Like Us	Training does not specifically connect activities to the mission and vision. Members are told what to do, not why it is important
	−4	Most Like Us	Members don't see the relevance in training so it is poorly attended and resented
8	+4	Most Like Us	The developmental process is well integrated and holistic covering the five spheres of development (Individual, Professional, Social, Managerial, and Leadership)
	+2	Somewhat Like Us	The content of training and development materials and qualification verification processes are task based and specific to the roles and responsibilities of the job. Content, policies, and procedures are kept current through an ongoing structured process
	−2	Somewhat Like Us	Training is not integrated with other requirements and is limited to the functional aspects of performing the job without additional linkage to other competency sets necessary for growth and advancement
	−4	Most Like Us	Training materials, policies, and procedures that are available are out of date
9	+4	Most Like Us	Roles and responsibilities are incorporated into skills hierarchies and competency maps to be used for preemployment screening, new hire orientation
	+2	Somewhat Like Us	Preemployment screening processes effectively utilize the competency maps to ensure the potential and motivational fit of individuals prior to bringing them into the organization
			There is an ongoing, effective and structured orientation and training program that ensures members joining the organization quickly integrate into the activities and culture of the organization

(continued)

Table 6.2   Renewal Assessment (Continued)

Assessment (Select One)			Choose the Statement that Best Describes Your Organization
	−2	Somewhat Like Us	New members in the organization frequently do not have the requisite skills and motivational fit to successfully acclimate and be promoted in the organization, resulting in high turnover of newer members
	−4	Most Like Us	Members joining the organization must seek out information and learn the organization's mission, vision, values, roles, responsibilities, and procedures on their own. There is frequently a feeling of frustration and isolation among new members that do not know where they fit in and how they can best integrate and contribute
10	+4	Most Like Us	Succession planning is performed in a proactive and effective manner. The highest performing individuals mentor others such that the culture of excellence is passed from generation to generation. The mentoring program is well structured with goals and activities. Being a trainer/mentor is seen as a position of honor and not another burden that distracts them from doing their job
	+2	Somewhat Like Us	
	−2	Somewhat Like Us	Succession planning is rare. Crisis staffing is the norm. When an opening occurs, the organization scrambles to fill the slot, resulting in losses in productivity and focus on mission accomplishment. The highest performing members of the organization are kept so busy performing the bulk of the work of the organization that they don't have time to mentor even if they had the desire to. Mentoring is nonexistent or left up to those with the most time on their hands — usually the lower-performing members of the organization
	−4	Most Like Us	

a loss of focus and drive; others reflect lack of renewal systems and processes. Whether a symptom or a system, these elements are key indicators of whether the organization is in renewal or in decline.

Once you've completed the Renewal Assessment, transfer your scores into the Renewal Scoring Matrix contained in Table 6.3.

Table 6.3   Renewal Scoring Matrix

No.	Score	Element of Renewal	Effective Leadership	Effective Management	Tools and Techniques
1.		Celebration and recognition of organizational and individual success	Regular, fair, and impartial recognition and rewards	Tracking and reporting projects, individual, and organizational outcomes	Impactful appropriate rewards and recognition Celebratory events
2.		Organizational commitment to continuous improvement	Continuous drive for improvement Courageous leadership Leading by example	Project management, resourcing, and tracking	Six Sigma ROI calculations
3.		Ongoing audits, records review, and change notifications	Encouraging and facilitating communications—embrace the messengers	Scheduling, resourcing, and following up on audits and benchmarking	Audits, bench marking, systematic process change notifications
4.		Relevant not robotic meetings with attendance for impact and development	Challenge meetings, Encourage involvement for communications, continuity, and development	Efficient meeting scheduling, planning, and execution	Meeting notifications, agendas, meeting evaluations
5.		Impactful performance review and reward systems	Challenging and encouraging the performance and review process for impact and outcomes	Timely and specific feedback Equitable and consistent rating	Application of logical consequences Performance reviews and contracting Progressive discipline

(continued)

Table 6.3   Renewal Scoring Matrix (Continued)

No.	Score	Element of Renewal	Effective Leadership	Effective Management	Tools and Techniques
6.		Developmental and promotional opportunities	Creation of a meritocracy climate Challenge favoritism, entitlement, and persecutory behaviors	Staffing and resourcing with a mind toward DISC temperaments, interests, aptitudes, and career pathways	Strategic staffing Reward and recognize team "P" as well as team "F"
7.		Training as a strategic priority that builds and maintains line of sight	Ongoing commitment to training Personal involvement and endorsement of training	Scheduling and staffing, prioritization of training Tracking attendance, involvement, and outcomes	DACUM aligned to value proposition creating line of sight
8.		Holistic and integrated training design	Ongoing endorsement of training Remaining teachable	Reinforce the line of sight, continuous learning—use of training checklists (TCLs) at every level	TCLs, procedures, job aids, dept of labor website
9.		Effective preemployment screening and structured new hire orientation	Reinforce the learning organization—everyone trains and everyone is trained Foster inclusion and enculturation of new hires	Use of the TCL for hiring and throughout the employment lifecycle, effective management of probationary employees	Preemployment screening and interviewing with TCL New hire orientation Management of employee development
10.		Proactive succession planning and mentoring	Consistency in leadership toward the organization's value proposition—not personal gain	Development and management of ongoing succession planning	Nine-box reviews Developmental assignments and opportunities Mentoring
	____	Cumulative Renewal Score			

Analysis: Renewal versus Leveling

Throughout our journey, we've been building a framework for organizational success that will allow the organization to navigate each stage to reach a higher level of consistent performance. The culmination of our activities, systems, structures, and processes is to reach a point where the organization can continuously renew itself to ensure its ongoing survival (Figure 6.2).

Merriam-Webster's Dictionary contains five definitions for the term *renewal* (July 2004, Revised Edition). Interestingly enough, all five are accurate when considering the Renewal Stage of an organization.

> *Definition 1: Renewal (Verb)—The act or process of renewing*—Renewal is an ongoing process; it never stops. Just like all living organizations, when they stop renewing, they decline and eventually die.
>
> *Definition 2: Renewal (Adj)—The quality or state of being renewed*—The ongoing process of organizational renewal becomes the state of organization and the defining quality of a thriving entity.
>
> *Definition 3: Renewal (Noun)—Something (as a subscription to a magazine) renewed*—Just as it is a conscious choice and an investment in resources with the understanding that there will be an ongoing investment in time when you buy a magazine subscription, it is a conscious choice for organizational leadership to invest in the organization's renewal along with the understanding that renewal will require an ongoing investment in time.

Figure 6.2   Framework for organizational success.

> *Definition 4: Renewal (Noun)—Something used for renewing; specifically: an expenditure that betters existing fixed assets*—The investment in renewal is an expenditure that improves the assets of the organization. *Definition 5: Renewal (Verb)—the rebuilding of a large area (as of a city) by a public authority*—Just as public authorities choose to renew an area to improve the quality of life of its people along with the economic viability of the region, renewing organizations choose to invest in their people and, through renewal, ensure the ongoing economic viability of the organization.

As we explore the 10 elements of renewal, we will explore renewal as an act, a process, an investment, and an ongoing state of being; above all else, we'll explore how renewal is a choice! Each element results from and reinforces the organization's ongoing commitment to excellence.

Renewal Element 1: Celebration and Recognition of Organizational and Individual Success

In order for an organization to consistently demonstrate sustained superior performance, it must have passed through Forming, Focusing, Commitment, and Sustaining while navigating around Stumbling and Fragmenting, and have broken the cycle of variable performance. The organization has designed and implemented effective systems, solved problems, engaged their team members, and overcome many obstacles and challenges. Above all else, the organization must have had the leadership foresight and courage to set and maintain a course toward an aspirational vision. Any organization that has successfully run this gauntlet has ample cause to celebrate!

Celebration is more than just a reward for a job well done; it has a powerful psychological benefit that satisfies a fundamental human need for recognition and closure. It is acknowledgement of the contributions and sacrifices that people have made. Celebrations bond people together. If an organization reaches its goals yet fails to celebrate the accomplishment, team energy and morale will tend to wane. What should have been a high point becomes anticlimactic. Once-high morale can morph into frustration and resentment. Too often, managers simply reward success with more work. "Congratulations, now, get back to work!" In effect, these managers move the goal just as the team is about to cross it. Just as the cartoon character Charlie Brown feels resentment when

Lucy pulls the football away when he is finally about to kick it, these managers breed resentment in their organizations. Even though it is important to be committed to continuous improvement, it is critical to celebrate the accomplishments of the team and the contributions of the individuals. Doing so will have both immediate and long-term impacts.

The immediate impact of celebration is to refresh and reenergize the group. The long-term benefits arise from having built the sense of community and mutual cooperation as well as reinforcing the belief within the group that all the efforts and sacrifices they have made are appreciated and, in the end, worth the price.

The best military commanders I served with were consistent about celebrating mission milestones and accomplishments. Halfway parties and steel beach bashes were great for morale and productivity.

Cost Does Not Always Equate to Value

Celebrations can also have a counterproductive effect when they are contrived or routine. I've seen organizations schedule routine celebrations so often that the events actually ended up contributing to the organization's climate of entitlement. Individuals no longer saw the events as special occasions to mark the achievement of a milestone—they expected them—they demanded them. The events were costly functions that further entrenched a dysfunctional culture.

Avoiding Mandatory Fun Events

Planning celebrations must be a thoughtful process. As impactful as effective celebrations can be, I've seen plenty having the opposite effect. Celebrations can be seen as cynical attempts on the part of management to manipulate overworked employees to give that last full measure. A celebration in an attempt to reverse poor morale will ring hollow when the underlying causes of poor morale are still pervasive. Remember, morale is a symptom—not a cause. If morale is poor, look to the elements that should have been put into place in the four preceding stages of organizational development. Without effective systems and all the other aspects that generate sustained performance, a celebration is nothing more than lipstick on the pig.

Even well-intentioned celebrations can be seen as punishment when they further encroach into the individual's already limited free time. Scheduling events after work or on days off such that people must travel to be with the same people they spend the majority of their time with throughout the week is not necessarily rewarding—it's just unpaid time at work. In addition, they may have to arrange for additional day care or incur other costs that actually make the reward punishing. Similarly, if they can't make it because of other obligations, they can feel left out or segregated. A smaller-scale event at lunch where people can partake without encroaching on their free time can be significantly more rewarding.

If you do plan an event outside of work, seriously consider making it a family event. This rewards those that support your employees, helping them to continue being supportive of the sacrifices that the family makes for the organization. Taking my wife to meet the people I worked with allowed me to spend time with her and put faces to the names of the people she heard me praise and complain about.

However you approach it, celebrations are essential when they are merited and when they are seen by the organization's members as sincere recognition—an outward demonstration of the genuine esteem that the organization holds for them.

Celebrations Aren't the End—They Are Transitions

When an organization has achieved sustained superior performance, there is a natural and understandable desire to rest, to say, "We are finally done." This tendency is compounded by the traditional view of change as an event rather than an ongoing process. As long as the world continues to change, the organization must continue to adapt. This requires that in the midst of celebration, it must be understood that new and challenging goals will continue to drive toward further improvements. This may seem contrary to the advice just given in Renewal Element 1, but it doesn't have to be—it's a matter of setting clear expectations up front. If the team has been led to believe that process improvement is an aberrant condition separate from their "real job," then they will approach it as such, with defined beginning and end points. When they reach the "end" and the manager springs another initiative on them, they will feel duped and become frustrated. However, if the team is versed in the principles of continuous improvement and improvisational change, they will recognize and accept that the celebration is a reward for reaching a significant milestone in an ongoing journey—like the "half-way" parties on ship, the voyage must continue. To sustain itself, the organization needs to be capable of celebrating the present accomplishments while still maintaining a drive for improvement. The celebration isn't the end; it's a transition.

Renewal Element 2: Organizational Commitment to Continuous Improvement

Organizations exist within the ever-changing flow of the world around them. When forward progress stops, the organization will be passed by or washed back downstream—thus the need for continuous improvement. Continuous improvement requires a choice and an ongoing commitment to invest time and resources. Renewal is a choice made by leadership to renovate, redefine, or completely remake the organization anew. If renewal is a choice to lead, why don't more leaders choose to lead? Recall cardinal change sin no. 1: the status quo exists to serve the status quo. Once a leader has reached the top, they too may have the expectation that, "They are done. They have arrived at their destination and their journey is over." As such, they may want to coast and lay back and enjoy the view as they ride upon the backs of the organization. Complacent, they are disinclined to exerting any more energy than is absolutely necessary to maintain their lofty perch. They have achieved their personal goals and choose to have the organization serve them rather than serve the organization. They are reaping the benefits of the system—so why change the system? Even if the change didn't potentially impact the perks they are enjoying, change requires effort that they are just not interested in expending. They fail to rise to the office to which they have been promoted.

The better leaders, the ones who are respected and admired, aren't satisfied with sufficient, they recognize and accept the special trust placed in them to be good stewards ensuring the longevity and security of those for whom they have been entrusted to lead. As such, they chose to lead—they choose to serve; they choose to renew. Their commitment is the catalyst that spurs the organization upward to new heights. Their vision inspires and compels others to strive for greatness. The question asked is not, "Can we get better?" but "How do we get better?" To answer the question, the organization looks beyond its own walls to others who have achieved excellence. If they are already the best, they look to the theoretical limits of perfection.

Defining How High Is Up: Benchmarking and Theoretical Constraints

Benchmarking is the process of comparing your own performance against that of others to gauge how well your organization delivers on its value proposition as compared to others. As a passenger in a closed cabin of an airplane, it is almost impossible to tell how fast or how high you are traveling. With the exception of a little turbulence, lying back enjoying the in-flight movie you may not even be aware of the sensation of motion—thus the need for benchmarking. Only when you can compare your speed relative to something else do you realize how fast or how slow you are traveling. Flying low over a freeway on approach for landing you may judge that you are traveling quite fast; being passed by an F-16 fighter jet you realize that you may be fast, but there is something faster. Organizations have the same tendency. The organization may be doing really well relative to past performance; but, when compared to others, the organization may be seen as too costly, providing poor quality or poor service. Organizations that are committed to continuous improvement regularly benchmark against "best-in-class" standards.

An organization committed to excellence regularly asks,

1. "How well is the organization performing as compared to the best in class?
2. What is the competitive space the organization occupies?
   a. Is it highest quality?
   b. Lowest price?
   c. Best customer service?
   d. Most convenient?

When looking outside your own four walls, don't limit your comparison strictly to other similar processes—compare your value proposition against substitutes and alternatives. Gauging the fastest horse is only beneficial in horseracing; even the fastest horse is slower than the least expensive car. Entire industries have succumbed to obsolescence—if the organization's goal is longevity, it must be willing to adapt to compete against substitutions and alternatives as well as nonalternatives. If the value proposition is insufficient, a consumer may choose to simply go without. Whether the loss of customers is to a competitor, an alternative, or to nothing won't matter to the organization—the bottom line is the customer chose not to favor the organization's products or services.

WARNING: The risk of obsolescence isn't limited to organizations. The same is true for internal departments and even individual contributors. If the services the department provides to internal customers can be outsourced or eliminated altogether, then its long-term sustainability is at risk. Similarly, if the organization can obtain more value from its limited resources outsourcing the work, the individual is equally at risk.

Six Sigma: How the Best Get Better

Benchmarking is an excellent tool to gauge how well you are doing against what is currently being achieved, but it does nothing to tell you the limits of how well you could be doing. What are the theoretical limits of the organization? The value stream mapping got to some of these questions, the tools contained within the Six Sigma toolkit can help you get the rest of the way.

NOTE: Like many of the topics we've briefly touched upon it is not the intent to provide a detailed explanation of Six Sigma. There are many fine resources dedicated to that purpose. The intent is to show when and how Six Sigma integrates into an overall organizational change strategy. Refer to other resources to gain a more detailed understanding and implementation strategies of Six Sigma.

A 60,000-Foot View of Six Sigma

Like Lean, Six Sigma helps identify waste. Specifically, Six Sigma is designed to reduce waste through the reduction in process variability. The more stable the process is, the more consistently a quality product or service is delivered to the customer.

Six Sigma is based upon the principles of statistical process control. In statistics, sigma, the 18th letter of the Greek alphabet (σ), is used to represents the standard deviation of a population. When looking at a standard bell curve (Figure 6.3), the distance between the average mean (μ) and the inflection point is the standard deviation (σ). Each standard deviation beyond the first is another sigma: one sigma, two sigma, three sigma, etc.

When producing a product or delivering a service, you typically have upper and lower specification limits (USL and LSL). For instance, imagine I

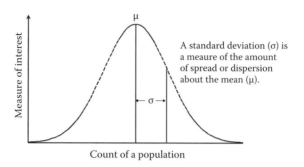

Figure 6.3   Sigma is a measure of variation.

produce a product that must weigh 100 lbs. 100 lbs is the target (T). Suppose that my customers will accept products within plus or minus 0.5 lbs. That means that I have acceptable quality if the product weighs between 99.5 lbs and 100.5 lbs. 99.5 becomes the LSL; 100.5 is the USL.

A process's sigma level measures the number of standard deviations that occur between the mean and the upper or lower specification limits. Figure 6.4 shows the standard deviation that occurs within a three sigma process. The total span between the LSL and the USL is actually twice the process's sigma level (i.e., a three sigma process has six standard deviations between the LSL and USL). When you control a process much tighter, there are more standard deviations between the LSL and the USL. Figure 6.5 shows the standard deviations that occur within a Six Sigma process. You can see that the bell curve is much narrower which means that more products are produced closer to the target mean and further away from the LSL and USL. Figure 6.6 overlays the three sigma control curve over the Six Sigma control curve. The difference between these two curves represents greater process variability.

So what's it worth? Well, if 99% of my product falls within the LSL and the USL, I would be at a 3.8 sigma quality level. If you got it right 99% of the time, you'd think that was pretty good. How much better would I be if I controlled at a Six Sigma level? 99.99966% of the time! Does 0.99966% more control really make that big a difference? If you made 10,000 units a day and 99% of them were within standards, that would mean that you had 100 units wasted per day. If you controlled at the Six Sigma level, you'd only waste one per month. On a monthly basis, you would be losing only one product to scrap as compared to 3000. That is a significant difference! It's easy to see why so many companies strive to achieve Six Sigma process variation. The company that controls their processes at the Six Sigma level has far less waste, lower costs, and more consistently satisfied customers.

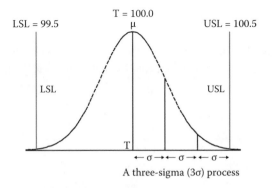

Figure 6.4   A three sigma variation in quality.

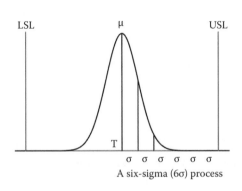

Figure 6.5   A Six Sigma variation in quality.

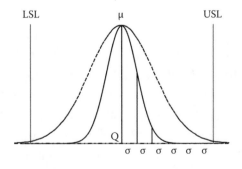

Figure 6.6   Six versus three sigma variation.

Three Limits of Six Sigma

As transformational Six Sigma is, it is not a panacea. In fact, there are times when it is not appropriate and actually counterproductive. Consider the following three rules of thumb when contemplating implementation of Six Sigma:

1. Six Sigma is not a substitute for effective management.
2. Could be better is the enemy of good enough.
3. Six Sigma does not lead to revolutionary discoveries.

Six Sigma Is Not a Substitute for Effective Management

I have worked with firms that set about implementing Six Sigma with the expectation that it would cure their organizational woes. They select champions and set about incurring all of the associated costs required to train and certify their staff in the Six Sigma process. They completed the training but saw only minimal gains in their process control. The problem wasn't with the Six Sigma principles, methods, or tools; the problem was that they weren't ready to make the quantum leap toward Six Sigma quality. It's the same problem discussed in the overview of sustaining versus variable performance; it is as difficult to go from extremely low control to Six Sigma as it is for an out-of-shape couch potato to win the Boston marathon.

VARIABILITY FOR VARIABILITY'S SAKE: Assigned to analyze the production operation, I wanted to talk to every shift so I made sure that over the span of a few weeks I attended all crew shift changes. Phil, assigned to Crew "A," relieved Nick, assigned to Crew "D." The machine had been running good product all night. After a brief turnover, Nick headed home and Phil headed out to the machine. "I hate the way that guy runs the machine." Phil set about adjusting the process the way he liked to run. He changed the water spray patterns and the machine tensions. Not long after, there was a breakdown. Phil cursed Nick's name, started up the machine the way he preferred to run it and then ran well the rest of the shift. The downtime wasted about an hour of production. Later on, I saw Nick repeat a similar pattern after he relieved Phil.

What was occurring between shifts in the example was the introduction of variability into the process. The machine process had so many variables that it could be run in slightly different manners and still make acceptable product. The problem arose when shifting from one pattern to another. The operators were introducing variability based upon personal preference not in response to system requirements. You can be going 100 mph north or you could be going 100 mph south; changing from north to south requires slowing, stopping, and restarting, resulting in a loss of momentum—waste.

The facility didn't need Six Sigma to tell them that operators were inserting variation. All they had to do was look at the downtime trends and see that a large amount of lost time and poor quality occurred around shift change. By holding the operators accountable and requiring them to agree that as long as the machine was producing good quality no changes should be introduced would have eliminated two hours of downtime and lost productivity per day—an easy 8% bump in productivity—no Six Sigma required. They were trying to engineer a complex solution to compensate for a lack of effective management.

Remember, 5S, Lean, Six Sigma, and all other process improvement tools are designed to minimize or eliminate waste. Recall the acronym WORMPIT to list the types of waste being targeted:

W—Waiting (when any part of the process is waiting, waste is generated)
O—Overprocessing (overproducing product or adding more activities/features than is required)
R—Rework (correcting poor quality mistakes)
M—Motion (inefficient movement—a mechanic that doesn't bring the required tools and has to keep returning to the toolbox mounted on the back of his truck is an example of excess motion)
P—Processing waste (the excess materials from the process—cutting off a board and throwing away the excess or activities in a process that do not add value)
I—Inventory (excessive materials waiting to be processed, poor utilization of manpower—idle time, etc.)
T—Transport (the inefficient movement of materials, information, product, etc.)

Before an organization endeavors to tackle their WORMPIT through the implementation of Six Sigma, their time and resources would be better spent implementing sound management principles, systems, metrics, and

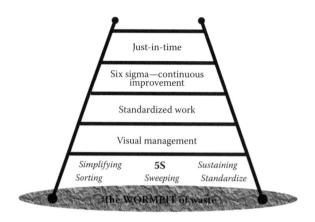

Figure 6.7   The process improvement ladder.

establishing a culture of logical consequences that consistently controls their processes. Prior to trying to control completely unstable processes to the Six Sigma level, implement 5S and Lean concepts such as visual management. Once the processes are in control and stable, refine them with additional tools in the Six Sigma toolkit. Think of each refinement as an additional rung on the process improvement ladder as shown in Figure 6.7. Each rung is more sophisticated in its approach than its preceding one. Visual management builds on the gains of 5S allowing the organization to then standardize the work. Once standardized, the DMAIC process uses data and statistical process control to further refine the analysis leading to continuous improvement. When these elements are mastered, the process can achieve the world-class standard of "just-in-time." Each step helps you climb further out of your organization's WORMPIT of waste.

Could Be Better Can Be the Enemy of Good Enough

There has been a bit of bad press around how Six Sigma can actually reduce a company's agility reacting to market trends. This can be true; like any strength taken to excess, Six Sigma can become a weakness if used dogmatically. Excessively strict compliance without questioning and judgment can lead organizations to become rigid and inflexible thereby hindering their ability to quickly adapt. Some organizations have missed market opportunities because the Six Sigma methodology slowed their speed to market. According to Brian Hindo's article "Motorola and the limits of Six-Sigma" (Domain-B.com, April 1, 2008), Motorola was one of the first firms to fully embrace the DMAIC methodology. They defined all their work practices accordingly and created a rigid culture built upon their Six Sigma methods. They codified degrees of expertise similar to martial arts by adding White, Yellow, Green, and Black Belts in the Six Sigma certification processes. By so fully inculcating a structured process improvement methodology, Motorola created a Six Sigma culture. Most, if not all, problems were analyzed and understood using the detailed DMAIC process. Motorola's defect rate dropped, their cost of poor quality (COPQ) fell, and they dominated their markets for years. The results were so impressive that business schools studied them, and other companies and some government agencies sought to emulate Motorola's success by adopting Six Sigma as their standard.

The problem with taking one element and building an entire culture around it became apparent over time. While Motorola was scrupulously following the DMAIC process to work out the details in digital wireless communications to the Six Sigma level, a small relatively unknown company in Finland called Nokia introduced a digital cell phone. Its reception wasn't the same quality as Motorola's analogue phones, but it was good enough. Nokia surpassed Motorola in market share and sales. Motorola learned the lesson the U.S. Military teaches—"Could be better is the enemy of good enough." Michael Abrashoff (Abrashoff, M. 2002. *It's Your Ship: Management Techniques from the Best Damn Ship in the Navy*. New York: Business Plus) discusses how the U.S. Navy has reaped significant benefits with Six Sigma but has also found that not all projects require the amount of effort a Six Sigma project demands. Speed of project completion for smaller projects fell behind as crews tried to gather all the specified details before implementing a solution. You don't always need to measure something to the 0.000001 level before deciding what needs to be done.

> INSPIRATIONAL QUOTE: "A good plan violently executed right now is far better than a perfect plan executed next week."
>
> **George S. Patton**
> *U.S. General (1885–1945)*

Six Sigma Won't Lead to Revolutionary Discoveries— Only Incremental Improvement

Other companies besides Motorola and the U.S. Navy have learned that the Six Sigma methodology has some unintended consequences. One reported drawback arising from a rigid adherence to a strict Six Sigma methodology is the loss of innovation and creativity. It has been postulated that Six Sigma can help you perfect what you already imagine but limits new discoveries. Earlier we discussed how 3M found that's its longstanding culture of creativity was being suffocated by the implementation of Six Sigma's disciplined problem solving approach (Hindo, B. 2007. At 3M, a struggle between efficiency and creativity. *Business Week*, June 11). Both the Navy and 3M came to the conclusion if you have to base all decisions on existing processes and measurable facts—you may not find the next revolutionary innovation.

> SALIENT QUOTE: "The quest for zero defects will quickly lead to zero innovation."
>
> **Sara J. Dunnigan**
> *Senior VP—Greater Richmond Partnership*

Like a crescent wrench, Six Sigma is an effective tool, but it shouldn't be your only tool. Sometimes you need a hammer and other times, a scalpel. Six Sigma is an excellent tool that can refine what is under control enabling the organization to take its processes to unprecedented levels of performance; but remember, it's only one piece of the puzzle. Six Sigma is not appropriate for every project and every situation and it can never be a substitute for sound judgment and effective management.

The Big "C" in DMAIC: Control and ROI

Projects utilizing the Six Sigma process follow the DMAIC process. However, far too often they really only follow the DMAI_ process. Control is left behind when the project disbands and the team returns to normal operations or on to the next project or promotion. Without Control, the ROIs are questionable and fleeting. Recall the audit of past projects discussed in Sustaining Element 6 (continuous balanced view of process outcomes); if all those projects had yielded the returns they had claimed the process would be running at 190% of capacity.

To help ensure the proper allocation of recourses apply the business concept of ROI to every project.

> NOTE: Some projects must be completed regardless of return to satisfy requirements or compliance issues. In such cases, the ROI should be utilized to determine the least costly alternative or least negative value. For other "optional" projects, the ROI should be calculated to select and validate the option which adds the most to the firm's value proposition.

There are various ways organizations justify projects. Some of the most common include project payback period, net present value (NPV), economic value added (EVA), and benefit to cost ratio. Let's explore some calculation of ROI before we consider when to use each.

Simple ROI

The simplest method of calculating the ROI is calculating the difference between Financial Gain and the Cost of the Investment divided by the Cost of the Investment.

$$ROI = \frac{(\text{Financial Gain} - \text{Cost of Investment})}{\text{Cost of Investment}}$$

This method may not be as beneficial for ongoing operations and doesn't lend itself to controlling the process. This simple formula is a snapshot in time that works well when selling stocks but isn't as useful as other more sophisticated calculations of ROI.

Net Present Value

Net present value (NPV) is a financial return calculation that examines the ongoing savings from a project standardized to what those cash flows would be worth at the present day value.

$$NPV = -\text{Initial Investment} + \frac{R_t}{(1+i)^t}$$

t = the time period of the cash flow (for capital projects, this is usually a three- to five-year period

i = the discount rate (the rate of return that could be earned on an investment in the financial markets with similar risk.); also called the opportunity cost of capital

R_t = the net cash flow (the amount of cash, inflow minus outflow) at time t

The NPV is particularly helpful in project alternatives. Calculate the NPV of a project and then calculate the NPV of an alternative investment of the same capital. The alternative investment could be another project or it could be an altogether different investment—say in stocks or bonds or sticking it in your mattress. This is a true business tool that helps organizations think like investors. Would a savvy investor put their money into this project or would they put their money into something else? Many industries use the NPV to compare their project returns against the average cost of capital. Traditionally, the rule of thumb was that the market returned 10%. If the project didn't return 10% or greater, then the money was better spent elsewhere. With the new realities of the stock market following the Great Recession, the cost of capital may need to be reevaluated to a lower level. I'm speculating that a solid return will be 5% in the domestic markets. But if you're thinking like an investor, overseas markets are an option that must be considered.

Economic Value Added

Economic Value Added (EVA)® is a registered trademark of Stern Stewart & Company that was first introduced in 1993. It is a popular calculation with companies that helps their finance departments determine the ROI above and beyond the company's cost of capital. This additional return is considered the profit that the company would make based upon the investment above and beyond their required operating costs. There are multiple ways to calculate EVA, but the most basic method is

$$EVA = \text{NOPAT} - \text{Total Cost of Capital}$$

NOPAT = Net Operating Profit after Taxes; sometimes referred to as Adjusted Accounting Earnings (AAE)

Total Cost of Capital = Interest Rate on Capital * Capital Borrowed

Standardize and Be Consistent with ROI Calculations

Each method of calculating ROI has pros and cons, the exploration of which is beyond the scope of our discussion. The main point to be made is that, regardless of the method you choose to calculate your ROI, be consistent with the assumptions, the metrics measured, and the calculation methods. Any analyst worth his or her salt can justify almost any project using various means and methods—all of which are mathematically valid. The running joke in one accounting department I worked with was, "What do you want the number to be Mr. VP?" And unfortunately, I've seen more than one project justified on the alternative EVA—that is, the good old "ego value added"! The executive wanted the latest and greatest with all the bells and whistles, so she got it!

If you are serious about creating a world-class sustainable organization, consistently apply a standardized ROI calculation to justify projects and hold project managers and their executives accountable for delivering on the ROI for the agreed-upon period after the project is completed. Otherwise, continue to put your money under a mattress—it will be safer there.

Renewal Element 3: Ongoing Audits, Records Review, and Change Notifications

Benchmarking is a very effective way to compare yourself against your competition, and Six Sigma can refine and improve your processes to stretch the limits of their capabilities; but neither benchmarking nor Six Sigma will help you if you become too focused on the fine details such that you lose track of the big picture. Companies can become so narrowly focused tracking the projects and initiatives under construction that other areas fall by the wayside. Remember that you must manage both Team "P" and Team "F" simultaneously; you've got to keep your eyes on both sides to stay out of the ditches. A well-formulated Balanced Scorecard combined with a management dashboard helps you maintain awareness of all the critical indicators for success. But like any other precision instrument, these tools need periodic reverification for accuracy and recalibration. This is best done through internal auditing and record reviews.

Ongoing audits and record reviews help the organization stay on course when done consistently based on relevant and reliable data. When performed as intended, internal audits validate how well the organization is achieving its stated goals and objectives, transforming resources into value-added outputs. Audits can ascertain whether the systems and procedures are effective and achieving the outcomes for which they were created and implemented. If not, analysis and problem solving can help you discover why not. Are the processes driving unforeseen behaviors and yielding unintended consequences? Are the metrics truly reflective of success or do they paint an incomplete or inaccurate picture? Is the organization achieving the metrics yet failing to deliver on its value proposition?

The Temptation of Inconvenient Truths

If we've learned nothing else from exploring the multiple elements entailed in navigating the stages of organizational change we've shown that there are many moving parts and degrees of complexity to achieving and sustaining high performance; and that is given the assumption that these elements are within your span of control or at least the reach of your influence. What if they're not? When you have accountability but no authority, an unfunded mandate, or conflicting priorities the projects and outcomes you are accountable for can fail to deliver despite your best efforts. When the future prospects for your career rely upon numbers that just won't add up it is tempting to bend or spin them. We've all seen individuals, companies, politicians, and entire countries selectively report their outcomes to put the best possible face on a "less than optimal" situation. Though understandable, creative reporting doesn't correct the problem and it leads to a very slippery slope. If you twist this number, how many more must be tweaked to keep the story straight? Where does it end? Remember the example discussed earlier regarding the audit of a manufacturing firm's efficiency gains yielded by capital projects over a 10-year period? If reality had matched the reported gains, they should have been operating at 190% of their actual capacity. The resources were spent but the process improvement didn't conform to the reported gains. The facility continued to lose money year after year. I don't believe that any project manager intentionally lied or manipulated the numbers; I believe the temporary improvement was based upon the Hawthorne Effect. Each project showed temporary gains which the project managers gladly report and attributed to their project. But, because the auditing was not consistently sustained, the productivity gains were temporary. As priorities shifted, the processes returned to their prior baseline levels of performance.

To improve the accuracy of audits and reporting don't rely strictly on manually calculated reports; items can be miscalculated and that which is manually tracked tends to be performed less and less frequently as time passes and attention shifts to the next crisis. Whenever possible metrics should be automated and based on tangible, quantifiable inputs. Also, include in your audits updates on the status of preventive, corrective actions, and follow-up actions from previous reviews and audits. Validate that the recommendations and plans from previous audits were acted upon and the productivity gains are being sustained.

One final word of advice, if you want honest reporting don't shoot, rather embrace the messengers. Adopt the Japanese axiom, "Fix the problem so there is no reason to fix blame." If the organization truly lives by this mantra people will feel freer to report the numbers as they truly are along with valid explanations of the drivers and restrainers preventing the achievement of the desired metrics. Encourage people to challenge the process and challenge the assumptions. Value candor. It's the only way for managers to gain a more complete and accurate view to the situation. As the view to the process improves there is greater opportunity and greater likelihood that the underlying performance can be improved—not just the reported numbers.

The Importance of Customer Feedback

Internal monitoring is important to validate your efficiency, but don't forget to check in with your customers to keep an ongoing pulse on your effectiveness. It is quite easy to get caught up in the day-to-day operations of your facility to the point that you don't have time to check in with customers. Often, organizations delegate the customer-facing portion of their businesses; existing customers interface with service representatives while the sales staff is excavating for new customers. If these are the faces and voices of your company to the customer, then it is paramount that these voices be knowledgeable of the products and services. Too often sales and customer service representatives are junior employees who have little knowledge of the product, its capabilities, or how it's manufactured. They can answer questions from a script, but lack a deeper understanding of the product. This puts your organization at risk of providing incomplete or inaccurate information to the customers. In addition, when the sales and customer service reps are remote from the manufacturing or servicing sector the feedback the customer does provide may never reach those who need to know. This is a clear case of not having timely feedback. Operators on the manufacturing floor may make decisions to ship products of questionable quality that are ultimately rejected by the customer; if they never get direct feedback regarding their decision, they are more apt to repeat that decision time and time again. As they do, they disappoint or anger customer after customer without ever being aware that their decisions are directly impacting sales. This is why it is critical to create as direct a line of sight between every individual in the organization and their impact on the organization's bottom line.

Timely Process Change Notifications

Along with the input your organization receives from customers and stakeholders, it is also important to proactively inform customers of any changes or updates to your product or services including any applicable statutory and/or regulatory requirements. This needs to be a formalized consistent process with set procedures and assigned accountabilities. The notification process should ensure prompt change notification to all those impacted including internal as well as external customers.

This may seem obvious, but I've seen some extreme examples of noncommunication. One firm I worked with consolidated manufacturing facilities—closing two plants and moving the equipment to a third without ever informing their customers. Their major customer heard about the shift by reading it in a trade journal. The manufacturing firm erroneously assumed that as long as the customers were being supplied it wouldn't matter from which location the product was produced; they were wrong. The plants were closed, the equipment was relocated, but unfortunately, the customers' orders weren't. The customers lost confidence in their supplier and transferred their entire orders to competitors. Having incurred the additional costs of moving while simultaneously losing revenue, the organization ended up closing the newly consolidated manufacturing facility and lying off the entire workforce. The moral of the story, don't assume customer relations are rock solid and never take them for granted. Communicate, communicate, and communicate.

Information Not Acted upon Is as Useless as No Information at All

Worse than having no information or feedback from the customer is an organization aware of feedback that fails to act. Far too many organizations understand the feedback provided by customers and stakeholders but don't respond. Failure to act sometimes stems from apathy on the part of the manager or from some protected status of the employee; regardless of the reason, the result of failing to act is the same and there is no point in seeking the information. Actually, it could be worse, if a customer took the time to provide the feedback and then finds that the firm knows about the problem but simply doesn't care; the disappointed consumer becomes an angry vocal detractor of the firm. Not only will they not use the product and services, they may actively work to get others to quit supporting the organization as well.

ANTICUSTOMER SERVICE: My wife was shopping in a major box store for a significant purchase. Over the course of the year, we planned on spending thousands of dollars on home renovations. As she was looking at products, several employees in the big box store walked by and none of them stopped to inquire if she had questions or needed help. Sadly, she wasn't too surprised or even offended by this because of the low expectations we've come to have of customer service in general. Suddenly, an employee came quickly around the corner and almost knocked her over where she stood. Instead of stopping, apologizing, and offering to help, the young man, dripping of attitude, snarled at her, "Watch where you're going!" Smirking, he continued on his way. Angrily, my wife gathered herself together and went in search of the manager. She found the inconsiderate employee and the manager joking with each other near the front of the store. "I want you to know that this employee is an extremely rude young man. He ran into me and nearly knocked me over and didn't apologize nor even ask if I was OK." The manager nodded and replied, "I'll talk to him." My wife walked off and as she looked back, the two were laughing even louder.

Needless to say, we don't shop at that store, nor will we ever shop there in the future. They have lost some very good customers for life. In addition, any time the subject comes up, my wife is a vocal detractor who will gladly try to convince other potential customers of her point of view. Customers vote with their wallets.

Though a single anecdote, the example illustrates how managers must be engaged as well as aware. The consequences of actions and decisions need to be readily apparent and governed by logic. If outcomes are inconsequential to the individuals responsible, entitlement will be the norm.

Renewal Element 4: Relevant Not Robotic Meetings with Attendance for Impact and Development

WHY SO MUCH FOCUS ON MEETINGS? You may be wondering why something as routine as meetings is stressed multiple times within the book. Like blood pressure, the conduct of meetings is a quick and reliable indicator of organizational health. In almost every low-performing organization, meetings are poorly run and ineffective. Meetings are critical communications, engagement, and problem solving tools but are treated as so routine that they often fail to be effective.

Effective meetings are important during every stage of organizational development; the focus and purpose of the meetings during each stage change, but they remain a principal tool for initial and ongoing success. During the Forming Stage, we discussed the importance of well-planned and well-executed meetings to communicate the vision, enlist involvement, and establish trust. During Focusing, meetings are used to clarify roles and responsibilities, guide the design and implementation of systems, and to solve problems that invariably arise. Meetings engage people and train them during the Committing Stage as well as give a strong indication whether the team is fragmenting or not. Meetings sustain the communications processes that are vital to ongoing operations. In the Renewal Stage, meetings are critical indicators of the overall health of the organization.

If you want to gain quick insight into how effective, cohesive, and engaged an organization is, attend some of their meetings; just sit back and observe. Is the meeting interactive or one sided? Is it well attended? Do people show up on time? Are the meetings focused and outcomes oriented or do they meander? Are they dominated by any one particular person or faction? Do they engage or simply report numbers and facts? Are they open or held behind closed doors, engaging only the elite few? Based on just a few meetings, you'll quickly learn a great deal about the values, priorities, and effectiveness of the organization.

SMALL TOWN POLITICS: My first meeting at a plant located in the heart of a small town began with the plant manager getting caught up on the latest gossip: who was seeing who and what was being said. It was clear where his priorities lay. Over the next few years, these initial impressions were confirmed as I watched the politics, relations, mystery, and intrigue of the local town folk regularly influence the decisions of the business. Who was hired, who was promoted, and who was vulnerably out of favor.

Are you in tune with what your meetings reflect about the organization? Over time, we become inured as routines become habits and second nature. In your next meeting, imagine how a stranger would judge your organization. What would she say you value? Are your people active, candid, and engaged, or are they simply going through the paces? Do people choose their words carefully, their meanings obscured in political correctness, making subtle points through inference and innuendo, maintaining their veneer of plausible deniability? Would they see that your organization was pursuing excellence or just doing time? The following list of 10 questions will help you take a pulse on the strategic health of your organization:

1. Yes ☐ | No ☐: Are there sufficient (not excessive) numbers and types of meetings to fulfill the ongoing need for communication and coordination as well as problem solving and process improvement?
2. Yes ☐ | No ☐: Are meetings planned ahead of time with ample notification of the purpose and agenda as well as any background information or preassignments with the expectation that people come prepared to contribute?
3. Yes ☐ | No ☐: Do people attend and show up on time?
4. Yes ☐ | No ☐: Are the right people at the meeting, sufficient to provide balanced input from the various stakeholders as well as sufficiently empowered to make decisions that will be enacted?
5. Yes ☐ | No ☐: Are the roles of facilitator, scribe, and timekeeper consistently and effectively fulfilled at all meetings?
6. Yes ☐ | No ☐: Do meetings start and end as scheduled, productively working through the agenda in a manner appropriate with each topic's complexity and importance (routine administrative items are efficiently processed allowing sufficient time to address significant matters)?

7. Yes ☐ | No ☐: Do meetings strike the right structural balance (free flowing and open enough as to not hamper creativity and engagement but not uncontrolled chaos dominated by the loudest and most assertive voices)?

8. Yes ☐ | No ☐: Does each member have influence on meeting outcomes or is attendance required to create the illusion of engagement?

9. Yes ☐ | No ☐: Do meetings end with documented decisions clearly understood as well as specific assignments and timelines for follow-up?

10. Yes ☐ | No ☐: Are meetings evaluated as to their effectiveness, efficiency, and whether continued meetings are supporting ongoing mission accomplishment and adding value?

Once you've answered the 10 indicator questions, review Table 6.4 for a quick snapshot of some of the underlying elements that may be missing or ineffective within your organization.

As Table 6.4 illustrates, ineffective meetings can be indicators of much deeper underlying issues that could emerge at any point within the organizations lifespan: Forming, Focusing, Committing, Sustaining, and/or Renewal. In this sense, meetings are a comparable organizational indicator similar to blood pressure. They can help determine overall heath, a sedentary and lethargic lifestyle, or a frenzied pace of manic high pressure. And, like blood pressure, if you don't regularly monitor meeting effectiveness and subsequently act to address the underlying issues that may be present, the organizational health will continue to decline.

Table 6.4 Meeting Evaluation Indicators and Organizational Elements

No.	What a "No" Response Could Indicate	Applicable Organizational Element to Review or Revisit
1.	(a) Lack of effective communications	Forming Element 3: Resource allocation and strategic staffing
	(b) Lack of effective prioritization of tasks	Forming Element 7: Communications are planned, deliberate, and broad reaching
	(c) Lack of structured organizational problem solving techniques	Forming Element 9: Meetings are well planned and prior notice is provided
		Sustaining Element 5: Ongoing communications and reporting

(continued)

Table 6.4   Meeting Evaluation Indicators and Organizational Elements (Continued)

No.	What a "No" Response Could Indicate	Applicable Organizational Element to Review or Revisit
2.	(a) Too many priorities—not enough resources (b) Ineffective meetings planning and preparation	Forming Element 3: Resource allocation and strategic staffing Forming Element 9: Meetings are well planned and prior notice is provided
3.	(a) Lack of or failure to adhere to ground rules (b) Lack of accountability (c) Lack of engagement	Forming Element 8: Clear behavioral norms are established and broadly observed
4.	(a) Lack of senior leader engagement (b) Lack of engagement and span of control (c) Inappropriate delegation	Forming Element 2: Senior leadership involvement Forming Element 4: Climate of trust, mutual respect, and mutual success
5.	(a) Ineffective meeting management (b) Failure to assign roles and responsibility (c) Lack of training	Forming Element 10: Meetings are well run, structured, and productive Committing Element 2: Structured approach to training and qualifications Renewal Element 6: Developmental and promotional opportunities Renewal Element 10: Proactive succession planning and mentoring
6.	(a) Lack of meeting management (b) Ineffective group problem solving	Forming Element 10: Meetings are well run, structured, and productive Focusing Element 7: Effective leadership towards problem solving Focusing Element 8: Organizational problem solving Sustaining Element 4: Proactive problem solving, decision making, scope, and impact

(continued)

Table 6.4 Meeting Evaluation Indicators and Organizational Elements (Continued)

No.	What a "No" Response Could Indicate	Applicable Organizational Element to Review or Revisit
7.	(a) Lack or failure to adhere to ground rules (b) Lack of mutual respect (c) Lack of engagement, delegation, and span of control	Forming Element 4: Climate of trust, mutual respect, and mutual success Focusing Element 3: Significant involvement of the crew Focusing Element 9: Tactical interpersonal communication and feedback Focusing Element 10: Healthy attitude about conflict Committing Element 3: Team members have and keep faith with their teams
8.	(a) Lack of engagement (b) Poor delegation and empowerment (c) Failure of organization to live its values	Forming Element 4: Climate of trust, mutual respect, and mutual success Forming Element 5: Team members and the team leader know and value each other's styles, strengths, and preferences Forming Element 6: Leaders set the tone for effective, open, and inclusive communication Focusing Element 3: Significant involvement of the crew Committing Element 3: Team members have and keep faith with their teams Committing Element 8: Individual and intraorganizational alignment and collaboration Committing Element 9: Organization lives its values with integrity
9.	(a) Poor leadership (b) Ineffective delegation/ performance contracting	Focusing Element 5: Gaining commitment and alignment of individual tasks and goals Focusing Element 6: Develop goals, action plans, and KPIs Committing Element 6: Strong leadership and appropriate delegation of authority Committing Element 7: Individuals and teams hold themselves accountable

(continued)

Table 6.4   Meeting Evaluation Indicators and Organizational Elements (Continued)

No.	What a "No" Response Could Indicate	Applicable Organizational Element to Review or Revisit
10.	(a) Lack of metrics and indicators (b) Not striving for continuous improvement	Forming Element 10: Meetings are well run, structured, and productive Sustaining Element 1: Ongoing validation of customer and stakeholder requirements and satisfaction Sustaining Element 6: Continuous balanced view of process outcomes Renewal Element 2: Organizational commitment to continuous improvement Renewal Element 3: Ongoing audits, records review, and change notifications

Meetings after the Meetings

We've stressed how meetings are essential tools for communication, alignment, and problem solving. Sufficient effective meetings are crucial to establishing and maintaining the cascading communication that creates line of site throughout all echelons of the organization as well as the conduit for timely feedback. Question 1 explores whether there are sufficient meetings; sufficient meetings include the meetings after the meeting. Too often limited meetings are held such that those in attendance are aware and aligned, but, the vital information and coordination doesn't subsequently flow down into the organization. It is incumbent upon every leader at every level to provide a conduit through which information flows to their areas. We just said that the measure of meeting effectiveness is comparable to blood pressure; it only stands to reason then that meetings are the organization's circulation system. An area that fails to have effective meetings is like an organ with inadequate blood supply—deprived of essential elements and allowing the buildup of waste product.

One of the primary reasons that meetings are not held within organizations is because they are seen as a waste of time—thus the importance of Question 5. Every leader, manager, and supervisor must have the appropriate skills to plan and conduct effective meetings. If they are ineffective, there will be insufficient circulation to their areas and the overall alignment and commitment of the organization will suffer.

Meeting Attendance for Communications, Impact, and Developmental Opportunities

In addition to the many organizational elements discussed throughout forming, focusing, committing, and sustaining, notice that there are some elements of renewal contained in Table 6.4, two of which we have yet to discuss: developmental opportunities and succession planning. When you consider who should attend meetings, don't limit your consideration to those who have a current need to know, valuable input to provide, and key decision makers; broaden your scope to include those who will benefit from attending for their professional development. Inviting a junior member into a meeting demonstrates your commitment to their career growth through involvement in the organization's business activities as well as allowing them to meet leaders and decision makers who will be beneficial to the individual's career development and advancement. An organization that doesn't utilize its meetings in conjunction with its development and succession planning strategy will consistently have gaps in the skill sets and readiness of its people.

Renewal Element 5: Impactful Performance Review and Reward Systems

Rewards are important. Rewarding people can reinforce desired behaviors and it can yield unintended consequences by reinforcing the wrong behaviors. The most common formalized tool that organizations possess to incent performance through recognition and rewards is the Performance Review System. We've just discussed how the effectiveness of meetings greatly impacts the organization—performance review and management impact even more. Think of the three components of individual satisfaction that drive the Workforce Engagement Equation: hope, control, and equity. The performance review and management process directly affects and reinforces all three of the fundamental satisfiers. No other single system has the opportunity to impact directly or indirectly the majority of elements of organizational success from the time the organization is formed throughout its ongoing renewal. As shown in Table 6.5, the performance review and management process drives, demonstrates, reinforces, and/or sustains over 60% of the 50 organizational elements (33/50).

As important as the performance review and management process is, in almost every organization I've had the opportunity to work with, the process is invariably a source of frustration and dissatisfaction. Though the

Table 6.5   Organizational Elements Significantly Impacted or Reinforced by the Performance Review and Management Process

Forming
Element 1: Setting a clear vision for the organization
Element 2: Senior leadership involvement
Element 3: Resource allocation and strategic staffing
Element 4: Climate of trust, mutual respect, and mutual success
Element 5: Team members and the team leader know and value each other's styles, strengths, and preferences
Element 6: Leaders set the tone for effective, open, and inclusive communication
Element 7: Communications are planned, deliberate, and broad reaching
Element 8: Clear behavioral norms are established and broadly observed

Focusing
Element 1: The vision, mission, and values of the organization are clearly defined and articulated
Element 3: Significant involvement of the crew
Element 5: Gaining commitment and alignment of individual tasks and goals
Element 6: Develop goals, action plans, and KPIs
Element 9: Interpersonal communication and feedback

Committing
Element 1: High degree of congruence between individual and organizational values and working approach
Element 2: Structured approach to training and qualifications
Element 3: Team members have and keep faith with their teams
Element 4: Performance feedback is appropriate and timely
Element 5: Leaders are engaged and act as mentors
Element 6: Strong leadership and appropriate delegation of authority
Element 7: Individuals and teams hold themselves accountable
Element 8: Individual and intraorganizational alignment and collaboration
Element 9: Organization lives its values with integrity

(continued)

Table 6.5 Organizational Elements Significantly Impacted or Reinforced by the Performance Review and Management Process (Continued)

Sustaining	
	Element 2: Ongoing goal setting and revision
	Element 5: Ongoing communications and reporting
	Element 10: Balanced rewards, opportunities, and consequences
Renewal	
	Element 1: Celebration and recognition of organizational and individual success
	Element 2: Organizational commitment to continuous improvement
	Element 3: Ongoing audits, records review, and change notifications
	Element 5: Impactful performance review and reward systems
	Element 6: Developmental and promotional opportunities
	Element 7: Training as a strategic priority that builds and maintains line of sight
	Element 8: Holistic and integrated training design
	Element 10: Proactive succession planning and mentoring

details varied from place to place, the primary complaints with performance review systems boil down to two:

1. The process is nonexistent, mechanical, and/or mindless
2. There is perceived inequity in the system

The first complaint is pretty obvious as well as pretty common. If there is no formalized structured manner in which employee performance is reviewed and rewarded, than the process is bound to be seen as arbitrary. When an organization relies solely on the manager–supervisor to reward performance when they deem appropriate; some employees who are favored will feel that the process works while others will experience growing resentment and frustration.

WHAT ABOUT BILL? To illustrate how an unstructured process can breed resentment and hostility consider the story of Bill. A new manager joined a small, privately owned, parts distribution firm. To familiarize himself, he requested to review every employee file. When he finished he asked the owner, "What can you tell me about Bill?"

"Bill? Bill's a solid performer, quiet, doesn't say much. Never complains. Just consistently does his job."

"I wouldn't have guessed that."

"Why?"

"Well, Bill hasn't had a raise in four years so I figured that he must be mediocre at best."

"He's never said anything—I suppose he's in line for a raise."

In the owner's defense, he outsourced his payroll to an accounting firm that processed the checks automatically so what Bill was paid was never really front and center for his attention. Many other employees had come and gone over the four-year period so most of his time spent on personnel matters was spent hiring and firing. Bill, a quiet, reliable individual heavily skewed toward a "C" temperament, continued doing his job expecting to be recognized for his performance and loyalty. Because the systems were manual, and no systems were in place for annual reviews and pay actions, the day-to-day dealings of the business overshadowed Bill. When the owner had approached him, Bill was happy to be recognized. With a little more insight, the owner found that Bill had been growing more and more frustrated and had begun looking to change employers. The company was about to lose its most dependable and consistent employee because of the lack of a systematic performance review system.

Bill's case is extreme, but, not that uncommon. Many employees expect that their hard work will speak for itself and that they will be recognized and rewarded. They become frustrated and disengaged when other more vocal, more aggressive individuals get the lion's share of the praise and compensation while they do the major lifting conducting the firm's business day in and day out with little recognition. Like all important processes, the performance review process should be systematized and regularly conducted to maximize its impact and ensure its effectiveness.

As a manager, look to reward the individuals who sustain the organization as well as those that seek to change it. Equal recognition needs to be given to members of Team "Present" as is given to Team "Future."

Impactful Performance Reviews

Assuming that your organization has a performance review system that is being utilized, it is equally important to ensure that the performance reviews

488 ■ *The Workforce Engagement Equation*

given are impactful and not just going through the motions to satisfy an administrative requirement. To be impactful, performance reviews should be timely, specific, and reinforce the climate of logical consequences—which means that the reward should be rewarding.

Impactful Performance Reviews Are Timely

During the analysis of Focusing Element 5 (gaining commitment and alignment of individual tasks and goals), the need for timely performance feedback was stressed. It is an essential component of the Framework for Individual Success, and, as highlighted in Figure 6.8, timely performance feedback is at the intersection that links effective leadership and effective management. Without giving effective timely feedback, you will be effective neither as a leader nor as a manager. As such, the annual performance review is not the time to provide new information. Nothing discussed during the formal annual session should be news to either the manager or the individual team member. The manager should be giving and the employee should be soliciting feedback regularly throughout the year. If the manager waits until the end of the year then he or she has not effectively managed during the previous 12 months. In the same light, if the individual waits until the final hour to let the manager know all the great things they've been doing to add value to the organization, there's a good chance that what they say will have little impact on their performance rating. Either way, last minute surprises reflects a profound lack of engagement on both the manager and the employee.

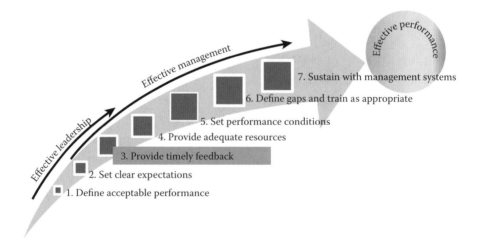

Figure 6.8   Framework for individual success.

Impactful Performance Reviews Are Specific

Just after the importance of timely feedback was introduced in Focusing Element 5, the importance of being specific was discussed in Focusing Element 6 (develop goals, action plans, and KPIs). As one follows the other, both form the basis of an effective and impactful performance review. After all, the primary basis for the individual's end of year performance rating should be how well they've achieved the goals they were assigned. And those goals needed to be specific to conform to the SMART (specific, measurable, achievable, relevant, time bound) goal criteria. The performance review conversation and justification of the employee's rating will be much more straightforward if the agreed-upon standards set forth were specific and measurable. At the end of the year, there shouldn't be any surprises—simply formal documentation of what was previously achieved, quantified, and reported.

Just as the individual's performance is measured upon specific standards, the manager's feedback should be specific as well. Too often managers provide fuzzy feedback that is hard to act upon. Here are some examples of manager's statements I've heard that really weren't helpful:

- "She's not a team player."
- "He doesn't have the right mindset."
- "She's too flighty."
- "He's just pissing me off!"

To be effective, you'll need to define in observable terms exactly why he or she is not a team player, what having the right mindset would look like, what flighty is, and why he is pissing you off. Incorporate the methods built into the performance contract provided in Sustaining Element 10. After all, a performance review usually sets forth the goals for the coming year as well as documenting the achievements of the past; what better way to set clear expectations up front than performance contracting?

Equitable Performance Reviews

We've spoken many times of the importance of logical consequences. Remember these simple principles that help determine whether the consequences are logical:

1. The reward for doing something must be greater than the reward for not doing it.
2. The consequences of not doing something must be greater than the consequences of doing it.

If everyone gets the same raise across the board, is it logical? Hope, control, and equity are the three fundamental human satisfiers—without all three, no amount of coaching, pep talking, or justification will make a person feel valued and satisfied in their situation. As such, the performance review process must be seen as equitable if it is to be impactful. But, what if there isn't sufficient capital to give everyone a monetary reward?

Rewards don't have to be monetary. In fact, money is a very short-term motivator. In the principles of formal logic, money is "necessary—but not sufficient." This means that if you never pay your employees, they probably won't be satisfied (volunteer organizations not withstanding). But just paying them is insufficient to make them satisfied. Once your individuals have sufficient pay to meet their needs and they feel that pay is equitable compared to others in similar situations, then pay ceases to be a motivator—there is truth in the old adage that "money can't buy happiness." When pay is sufficient, other factors become much more dominant in their impact on individual satisfaction. The use of these other factors can be more impactful in the establishment of a climate of logical consequences.

Figure 6.9 reveals the final planks in the Vessel of Organizational Success. When looking to reward consider the full spectrum of possibilities:

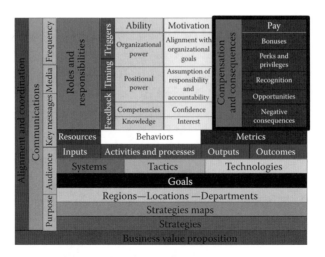

Figure 6.9　Compensation and consequences.

- Pay
- Bonuses
- Perks and privileges
- Recognition
- Opportunities

When you can't compensate with pay, provide other perks and privileges—time off, flex time, special parking privileges. The "key to the executive washroom" is a bit antiquated in today's corporate environment, but, it represents a level of distinction that people aspired to.

Recognition can be effective, but, it is a reward that can easily backfire as well. Some individuals dread being singled out. Recognizing them can have the opposite effect than was intended.

Opportunities are probably the most impactful yet underutilized form of reward. Giving an individual an opportunity to work on a special project or with the executive team where they can learn from and gain exposure to others can be a powerful motivator. But again, like recognition, be mindful of how it is received. Just as the example where "mandatory fun" events weren't rewarding, adding additional assignments onto someone as a reward is in fact a form of punishing hard work. You don't want to gain the reputation within your organization that "the more you work, THE MORE YOU WORK!" or "No good deed goes unpunished." And you don't want to be the manager that only "rides the good horse."

Application of Negative Consequences—Progressive Discipline

The final plank under compensation and consequences is negative consequences. Negative consequences are equally important and just as impactful as positive rewards. If there are no negative consequences, then there cannot be a climate of logical consequences. Most managers don't like to be the "bad guy." They'd just as soon avoid any discussion of, let alone imposition of negative consequences. But, to be effective, the manager must effectively utilize both tools. The "goats" run rampant and roughshod over managers within entitlement cultures without negative consequences.

To be effective, the negative consequences need to be logical, known, and anticipated. Just as there should be no surprises during the course of an annual performance review, anyone on the receiving end of a negative consequence should have "seen it coming." Negative consequences should build upon each other. This is the principle of progressive discipline. The first time someone does something invoking a negative consequence may justify verbal counseling, the second time may be written, the third results in time off, the fourth—termination. This progressive escalation of the severity of consequences allows the individual ample time to work through their cycle of individual change. At the same time, it maintains the pressure to continue to motivate the individual to continue pursuing a path of improved performance.

When a manager fails to address inappropriate behavior, the rest of the organization takes notice. It also takes notice if a manager invokes a seemingly arbitrary and disproportionately severe response. Both are ditches the manager can stay clear of through consistent utilization of feedback and the performance review process.

Shared Fortunes—A Rising Tide Shouldn't Swamp the Little Boats

The final point to be made about rewards and compensation is that risks as well as the rewards should be shared. There has been much said about the United States' Government response to the great recession of 2008–2009, where millions of individuals lost their jobs, but one overriding theme is the seeming inequity where profits were privatized and losses were socialized. Individual's retirement savings accounts were wiped out along with their jobs at the same time their taxpayer dollars were used to bail out the companies. To add insult to injury, millions of the bailout dollars went to executive bonuses. I make this point not as social commentary but as an example of how inequity affects engagement and organizational performance.

Employee satisfaction will always lag when there is a double standard embedded within the organization. It's hard to motivate employees whose leadership team has run the firm into bankruptcy, decimating both their livelihoods and their retirement savings, when those responsible are rewarded with promotions, golden parachutes, and lucrative buyout packages. When the fate of the leaders rises and falls along with that of those being led, there is much greater willingness to sacrifice and continue to engage. The finest example of this I've experienced is within the USMC officer corps. Marine officers are expected to live and eat among the enlisted and endure what they expect of their marines. Yes, rank has its privileges, but, no other executive staff is as integrated with their units as with the Marines. They live their core values of honor, courage, and commitment by sharing the fortunes and fates of their teams. As such, the enlisted make sacrifices for the organization that are unparalleled and are the greatest testimony to the power of the principles of equity.

Taking a lesson from the Corps' book, high-performing organizations demonstrate equity by sharing both the risks and rewards such that leadership shares the fate of those for whom they are entrusted to lead.

Renewal Element 6: Developmental and Promotional Opportunities

When examining development of a climate of logical consequence, opportunities featured prominently in the discussion. It is only logical that individuals seek out opportunities that expand their capabilities and further their careers. Without opportunities there can be no hope, and hope is the first of the three fundamental human satisfiers: hope, control, and equity. When a talented and motivated individual finds themselves in a position without opportunities, they seek to change their situation. The last thing any organization that wants to continue its ongoing success needs is the loss of its most talented and motivated people. Thus, it is absolutely critical to ongoing organizational success that opportunities exist for individuals to have increased levels of responsibility and mastery as well as opportunities for new challenges.

Those with the temperaments to change the world are very poor at sustaining the world as it is. Nothing is more frustrating for individuals who enjoy new challenges than to be bound by routine. Yet nothing is more disruptive to an organization than the upheaval caused by continuously modifying systems and procedures—this is called variability, and variability leads to waste, and waste is bad. Once again, the value of the different personality temperaments is demonstrated. Those that like challenges and changes can be freed to pursue new opportunities within the organization when they hand off the newly refined processes to those who enjoy stability and consistency. Team "F" passes to Team "P" and the organization *scores*!

To continue renewing and growing organizations must embrace this duality between stability and change. First, the organization should have the expectation that individuals continuously grow their knowledge and skills. In order to avoid raising expectations without providing resources, the organization should seek to create these opportunities. In maintaining a climate of logical consequences, opportunities needn't be afforded to everyone nor should they be. The limited opportunities should be given to those who have demonstrated the ability, motivation, and alignment with the organization's mission. These opportunities might be to get promoted within the organization or to cross-train to other areas. These opportunities benefit both individuals and the organization alike when individual aptitude and interest is aligned to the organization's needs and direction.

In the marketplace, talented performers are more sought after. Organizations that don't provide clear paths within the organization for promotions experience turnover of the high performers with ambition. Over time, the organization's overall staffing becomes dominated by the more sedentary performers with lower ambition and/or lower confidence. These are the ones who had no better prospects. This leads to a talent drain that allows the organization to drift into leveling.

> NOTE: Like all examples and rules, there are almost always exceptions. The concept presented here is general in nature—directionally correct as a concept—not meant to be an absolute.

Organizations can also drift into leveling when there is neither expectation nor support for ongoing development. Too often, the practice of "once trained always trained" is allowed to become the norm. Without the expectation of continuous lifelong learning among incumbent workers, stagnation and entitlement erode progress and the drive for continuous improvement. I've worked with organizations where any mention of ongoing development raises offense and indignation; "What? Are you saying I'm not good enough?!" For this reason, the expectation of continuous improvement needs to be built into each individual development plan as well as into the overall organizations process improvement strategies.

> REMEMBER: There is a significant difference between 10 years of experience and one year of experience repeated 10 times over.

Renewal Element 7: Training Remains a Strategic Priority that Builds and Maintains Line of Sight

Training is important—almost every organization says so and ostensibly believes it. Training most often plays a prominent role in the initial stages of organizational development or change management projects. Within the discussion of Committing Element 2 (structured approach to training and qualifications) effective training was shown to depend upon a structured systems approach utilizing training checklists (TCLs) developed through a DACUM process. Just as training is important in the initial stages of organizational development, it is equally important, and arguably more important, in the ongoing renewal of the organization.

Though training is important, it's very hard to determine the ROI of training. This is particularly true since training does not necessarily result in changes in behavior due to the multiple and often-conflicting determinants of behavior (shown again in Figure 6.10).

> For a review of the concept of Behavioral Determinants refer to the section on "Emotional, Cognitive, and Physiological Behavioral Drivers" discussed in the Focusing Stage as part of Focusing Element 10, in Chapter 3.

Once individuals have been trained, the perceived need for training is diminished and organizations shift their scarce resources toward other priorities. When the perceived need for training has passed, training materials

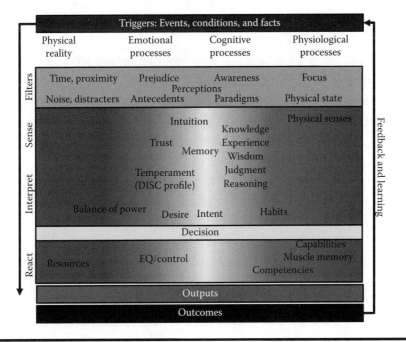

Figure 6.10   Behavioral determinants.

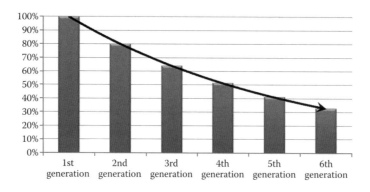

Figure 6.11   Decay of organizational competence.

and procedures often fall into disuse and become less and less accurate and relevant with each undocumented procedural and system change. Just as it is more expensive to rebuild a vehicle when it breaks down rather than consistently perform routine maintenance, it is more expensive to go back and refurbish neglected training manuals and materials than to maintain them as part of the ongoing process of management of change. Once training materials fall into disuse, it is often seen as cost prohibitive to revamp the training materials; inaccurate, the organization no longer utilizes the out of date materials and training devolves into unstructured on the job training, initiating the onset of the decay of organizational competence (shown again in Figure 6.11).

For an organization to sustain its journey of continuous improvement, it must resist the urge to cut training and must maintain the discipline to maintain its training procedures and manuals. Even when the organization has been successful in its navigation through the stages of organizational development, each new member joining the organization must begin at the beginning in their own Forming Stage. Each must make the journey through Focusing, Committing, Sustaining, and Renewal. Without a consistent structured formalized training process, each is dependent upon the informal process, and invariably, their level of understanding and depth of expertise will be lacking. For organizations that are committed to continuous improvement, training remains a strategic priority. It's an ongoing process not an isolated event. Every individual is expected to continue to learn as well as expected to train others. This strategic focus on training helps maintain the line of sight between the organization's vision, mission, and strategy and the tasks each individual performs.

A PARABLE ILLUSTRATING LINE OF SIGHT: A nobleman riding through a neighboring kingdom came across a man cutting down a tree.

"What are you doing?" he asked.

"Are you blind? Isn't it obvious? I'm cutting down this tree."

"I see, sorry to trouble you." The nobleman rode on. Soon he encountered a man laboring hard to split large granite boulder. "What are you doing?" he asked again.

"Are you blind? Isn't it obvious? I'm splitting this rock."

"I see, sorry to trouble you." The nobleman continued his journey until he came across a man deep in a hole, shoveling out the water and mud. Every laborious shovelful gained a little on the sliding mass and the hole slowly became a longer channel. "I see you're digging a trench," the nobleman said careful not to point the obvious."

"No, not a trench, I'm building a temple to God."

I don't remember when I was first told this parable, but, it has always remained one of my favorites. Though all three men were toiling to build a grand cathedral, only one kept the ultimate goal in mind. Helping people see the significance of their acts helps them remain focused and helps each maintain the motivation and engagement to build quality into their work. Without this line of sight, people can marginalize their actions and the resultant quality invariably suffers.

A REAL-WORLD EXAMPLE OF LACK OF LINE OF SIGHT: Working in a pharmaceutical packaging plant the entry-level position required the "Catcher" to remove pamphlets off the line and insert them into cartons. If you observed with casual eyes, you could say his job was to catch little pieces of paper and put them into a box with other pieces of paper. That's how the task was explained to him and that's the extent of thought he gave to his job. As I walked by the young man was drowsily picking and stuffing, picking and stuffing. He hadn't worked out his rhythm and occasionally dropped a few on the floor. Mechanically, he picked them up and stuffed them into the carton.

Like the rider in the earlier parable I asked, "What are you doing?"

"Putting these pieces of paper into the cartons."

"What about the ones you dropped?"

"I picked them up and put them into the cartons."

"If they came off the floor, are you sure they're the right ones?"

"I think so."

"What if the Catcher before you dropped some pamphlets? Might you pick them up and put the wrong one into the carton?"

"Maybe." He didn't show any level of concern for the possible error.

Obviously, the Catcher didn't think much of his job. I took him aside and unfolded one of the pamphlets; each contained the recommended dosage, drug interactions, and potential side effects of the drug. "Do you have kids?" He nodded. "Imagine if your child is sick and you had purchased one of the medicine packages you put the wrong information into. You read the wrong information and give the wrong amount. What could happen?"

His eyes grew a little wider with interest, "That would be bad."

"You see, your actions could have a profound impact on someone's life—maybe even kill them. So, you're not just putting paper into a package, you're providing a vital service ensuring that a customer has the correct information they need."

After that, the young man showed a little bit more care in doing his job. Establishing a line of sight through training helped.

Maintaining a strategic focus on training helps ensure that individuals understand the linkage between their tasks and the organization's mission and vision. Without a consistent approach to training, the development of people is left to chance.

The Absence of Leaders Undermines the Training

One final note about the importance of training as a strategic priority in high-performing organizations, it's hard to say how many hundreds of hours of training I've conducted over the course of my career for various clients and organizations. In all those hours of training, I can honestly count on one, maybe two hands, the number of senior leaders and managers that I've seen attending the training that they requisitioned for their organizations. And in almost every class, the question was invariably asked, "Have you trained our managers on this stuff?" The students learning about communications, conflict resolution, problem solving, or whatever, recognized that what they were being asked to learn, and presumably apply, were behaviors that they didn't see exhibited consistently by their leaders.

Managers asked about this consistently provide virtually the same answer, "I don't have time for that. It would be nice, but. . ." And of that handful of managers I've seen in training, few attend the entire training devoting their full attention. Phone calls and conflicting meetings invariably pull them away. What message does this send to trainees? "You don't need this stuff to get ahead in this organization." The lack of attendance also creates a double standard, "Do as I say, not as I do." If an organization wants to make lasting changes, then the behavioral expectations must be consistently and uniformly applied. Even if managers are well trained, their involvement adds credence that reinforces the importance of the changes. They can also add anecdotal support to the training that greatly enhances the real-world application of the classroom content building critical line of sight.

IF YOU APPLY THE TRAINING, YOU'RE FIRED! Working in a northwestern facility, the supervisors were trained in a communication process called Interaction Management (IM)® (Development Dimensions International, Inc.). In the training, the supervisors learned to empathetically listen and to engage their employees to work through problems to reach mutually agreed-upon performance agreements. The training was well received. One inspired supervisor had the opportunity to apply what he'd learned the day after class.

An employee came in late. Instead of his usual approach of chewing out the individual for being late and docking his pay, the supervisor listened. He found out that the individual had a reasonable explanation. The supervisor didn't allow the employee to just slide, he held him accountable with a contingency plan and a way to make up the time. Both felt respected and each one's esteem for the other was enhanced by the process.

When the department manager, who hadn't attended the training because "he already knew how to manage," heard that supervisor hadn't written the guy up, he was furious. He called the supervisor into his office and proceeded to chew him up one side and down the other.

> When he was finished, he issued the ultimatum, "Write him up and send him home or pack your things and go home yourself."
>
> Afraid for his job, the supervisor complied. I never observed that training utilized again in the facility by that supervisor or any other. The lesson was clear—training wasn't important. And if you did what the class taught, you were apt to lose your job.

This example is a clear indication of an organization that didn't live by its espoused values. As you can imagine, morale and productivity in the facility were both low as was its quality and profitability. Eventually, the plant closed; all the employees lost their jobs; the managers took positions elsewhere in the company.

Renewal Element 8: Holistic and Integrated Training Design

Committing Element 2 outlined that the organization needed to have a structured systems-based approach to training and qualifications; Renewal Element 7 stressed how training needs to remain a strategic priority that builds and maintains line of sight. So what more should be said about training? It can be structured, it can maintain a line of sight, but an organization won't get the maximum ROI in training unless the training is holistic and fully integrated. So what does that mean?

Something that is holistic encompasses all facets and not simply individual components. When I first learned naval propulsion systems, I studied the steam system, the condensate system, then turbines and drive shafts, and so on piece by piece. When I thought of a problem, I thought of it in isolation from others. Then one night, about 2:00 in the morning, I had an epiphany. My comprehension of the entire engine room gelled from individual systems into one integrated interconnected whole (this might have been lack of sleep, but it had a profound effect on me!). I pulled out a large sheet of paper and drew every system from memory and linked them all into one unifying diagram. Anyone else looking at it would probably say it looked like spaghetti, but to me, it was beautiful—it all finally made sense. What I had known, now I understood. I've been told the same thing happens for doctors. Going through med school, they learn the body system by system, organ by organ. Only after their residency do they begin to integrate the disparate parts into one inseparable whole (again, this might be lack of sleep).

Once a doctor is able to make that quantum leap of understanding, they no longer look at the patient as a series of parts; they treat the entire being—body, mind, and spirit. You'll immediately notice the difference in quality of care once you've had the benefit of being treated by a doctor who takes a holistic approach as compared to a doctor who is technically competent, but lacks a holistic perspective. Your organization will also benefit greatly from employees who have a holistic perspective.

NOTE: The entire focus of the Workforce Engagement Equation™ is to advocate for a holistic approach to organizational development working to build the multiple drivers, systems, and concepts into a single unified whole.

The first step to gaining a holistic perspective is to understand all the disparate parts. If you don't know the parts, you can't integrate what you don't know into a deep understanding of the whole. Having a rudimentary and simplistic understanding of processes causes leaders to create profound errors in judgment. If you don't understand the interrelation between the parts, you can cut out significant structural elements that undermine the entire system. More often than I'd care to count, leaders and managers looking to cut costs have eliminated essential elements of their organization because they were too removed from real-world operations and had no deeper understanding than an executive summary. Having only an "Executive Summary" of their organization's operation, they lacked a holistic understanding of the myriad of interworking elements that contributed to the overall functioning of the whole; refer to cardinal change sin no. 2: I'm an "idea man!"

NOTE: Do not confuse having a detailed understanding of the organization's operation with micromanaging and failure to delegate. It is having sufficient breadth of understanding to validate that each link in the chain has the appropriate skill set to effectively execute the mission.

To build a holistic view of the organization all five spheres of competence must be enfolded into training. (Refer to Committing Element 2 [structured approach to training and qualifications] to review the DACUM process and the creation of competency maps, skills hierarchies, and TCLs.) In addition to encompassing all five spheres, the training needs to be specific enough to be both observable and actionable. The elements need to be task based as well as specific to the roles and responsibilities of the job.

> DON'T REINVENT THE WHEEL: Throughout this entire book, I've advocated for simplicity and efficiency. I'm not changing that philosophy at the last minute. Though it is critical to have accurate and detailed TCLs, it's not necessary to reinvent everything from scratch. The U.S. Department of Labor has gathered many detailed competency maps and job and task descriptions and have made them available for free on their Workforce3One website. They call this the *Competency Clearinghouse*. I strongly recommend that you take as much as possible from what has already been developed and modify it to fit your specific needs. Before starting from scratch, check what has already been made available at https://ojttoolkit.workforce3one.org/page/training_plans.
>
> "Mediocre writers borrow; great writers steal."
>
> **T. S. Eliot**
> *American/English Poet (1888–1965)*

TCLs Aren't Just for Nonexempt Positions

Too few organizations implement and sustain the best practices of using competency maps, skills hierarchies, and TCLs; even fewer fully utilize the power of these tools for developing senior level management and leadership. There can be a bit of arrogance within some leaders and managers that make them assume their expertise in one sphere of competence makes them masters of all five. An organization committed to excellence will develop a structured developmental process for leadership, management, and business acumen as well as operational capabilities. The manager or leader who no longer remains "teachable" clearly communicates that continuous improvement is not important to ongoing success.

> MY OPERATIONS EXPERTISE MAKES ME AN EXPERT ON MANAGING PEOPLE—NOT! I attended a planning session at the corporate headquarters of a Fortune 500 company. My mentor, P.M., brought me along to provide me some exposure to the inner workings of the company. The focus of the meetings we attended was the

implementation of a comprehensive employee development and evaluation process called "mastery." During the course of the meetings, the senior VP of Operations made multiple demands on the process. P.M. listened attentively until the VP finished his laundry list of changes to how the program would be rolled out and administered. P.M., who had designed the program, responded after the VP had finished his diatribe. "We can do everything you're suggesting, but I want you to be aware, if we alter the program as you are suggesting, these are the consequences that will result." Barely three minutes into P.M.'s response, the VP cut him off with a few expletives that barred further discussion. P.M., whose calm demeanor I wish I had one-tenth of, said, "So, what you're saying is, although I have over 20 years of experience in this area, several advanced degrees, and have been specifically hired because of my expertise, you know more about managing people because you can make the product?"

"Now you F***ING understand!"—The meeting was over.

The program was rolled out just as the VP of Operations insisted, a few million dollars were spent, and it was a colossal failure.

POST SCRIPT: Not long after that meeting, P.M. left the company to join an organization that valued his experience and holistic view of human behavior where he continues to thrive to this day.

Leaders who are unwilling to learn aren't really qualified to create a "learning organization." It's like the Zen saying, "If you meet the Buddha on the road, kill him"—when you believe that you are so enlightened that you are chatting it up with Buddha and sharing fashion tips, etc., you are actually so far from enlightenment that you need to kill your self-important self-image and return to a teachable state.

Renewal Element 9: Effective Preemployment Screening and Structured New Hire Orientation

Training is important; it keeps skills sharp and facilitates growth that leads to promotional opportunities. As members are promoted up or out, others must be available and prepared to replace them; someone must stand ready to fill their previous role and satisfy their responsibilities. Just as your body's cells are constantly being replaced, the organizational body must replace members to ensure its ongoing effectiveness and its very existence. In the body, DNA maintains structural and functional continuity generation after cell generation. If the replication is incomplete or inaccurate, mutations occur—some of which can be deadly. What is the basis of your organizational DNA? If it's left to chance, it's probably mutable generation after generation; its clarity may diminish over time.

The Architects of Your Organization's Future if Left to Chance

In its most simplistic terms, performance comes down to ability and motivation. Placing these two elements on a vertical and horizontal axis, respectively, and scaling them from low to high produce the simple two-by-two matrix shown in Figure 6.12. Painting in very broad strokes, this two-by-two matrix allows us to classify every member of an organization within one of four boxes. Obviously, this is a gross generalization, but it is highly instructive.

What kind of employees do you want in your organization? Those high-ability and high-motivation employees of course! We'll call these "ideal" employees and we'll show them in the upper right-hand box. Then we have those highly motivated employees who lack abilities; they don't know what they're doing, but, by gosh, they're going to do something! Represented

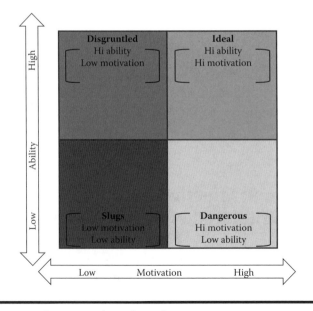

Figure 6.12   Four generic categories of employees.

in the lower right-hand box, they are definitely dangerous. Next, we have those low ability, low motivation employees. Let's call them *slugs*, and we'll store the slugs in the lower left-hand box. Finally, we have those highly skilled employees who lack motivation. Shown in the upper left-hand box, these employees could do a great job if they would only apply themselves. Unfortunately, for whatever reason, they don't. They are disgruntled. In the Navy, we referred to these people as CAVE dwellers.

CAVE = Citizens against Virtually Everything!

Shifting from Box to Box

When someone joins an organization, they are typically very motivated but lack ability and experience. High motivation combined with low ability makes them dangerous. They need training and they need experience. Ideally, we'll maintain their motivation and they will grow into ideal employees (Figure 6.13). Who do we want training our new employees to make them "ideal?" Why, the ideal employees of course. But do ideal employees have the time to train new people? Sadly, the answer is frequently "No." The ideal employees are too busy. They are getting the work done, responding to crises, and carrying the lion's share of the organizational load. It's the old

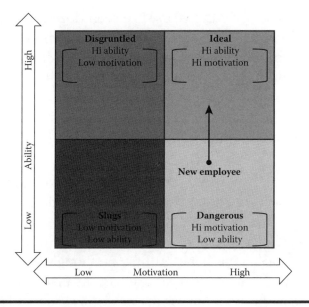

Figure 6.13   New employees can be developed into ideal employees.

80–20 rule: 80% of the work is being done by 20% of the people. So, who has time to train? Why, the slugs do.

SLOW DOWN, YOU'RE MAKING US LOOK BAD: After a few years of having my mail delivered late in the day I suddenly started receiving my mail by 10:00 AM. I was curious, but didn't give the matter much thought; I figured it was probably a route change or something. The trend continued. One Saturday, I met the new mailman. He was a young and extremely fit marathon runner. Instead of driving the truck, he was running his route. He loved his new job because he could get the entire route done by early afternoon and then have the rest of the day to do whatever. This went on for a few months when suddenly it ended as quickly as it had begun. "They must have switched postal workers again," I thought. On a subsequent Saturday, I saw the young man come running up in the late afternoon. "I was wondering what had happened to you."

"I do my route in two shifts now. Some of the other guys were bent out of shape. They said I needed to slow down because I was going to give management the idea that they didn't need as many workers. So now, I do half my route in the morning, take a break, then finish the other half in the afternoon. The others are much happier with me now."

This is one example; over the years, I've seen dozens of similar situations where slugs transfer their DNA of bad habits and slipshod workmanship to the next generation by being allowed to train new employees—drawing them from "Hi Motivation–Low Ability" into "Low Ability–Low Motivation" (Figure 6.14). Because the ideal employees don't have the time to train, it is left to those with plenty of time, slugs. You will also find that disgruntled employees will make the time to train new people.

WELCOME TO HELL! One fine day, a young man went to work at a west-coast manufacturing plant. He reported to work excited and eager to go. He was motivated. On his first day of the job, he was greeted by three seasoned plant workers on the loading platform. "Welcome to hell. You're going to hate it here." At first, he thought they were kidding. They assigned him to clean up. He got his first assignment done efficiently and sought them out for the next. "Slow down kid, this is a career, not a job. Take this form to the supply shack and bring back the parts bag." The new guy briskly walked off. When he returned, the plant was in chaos. The machine was making poor quality and everyone was scrambling. "Don't have time for you right now. Take this radio and go find a place to hide out. We'll call you when we're done."

This example is so extreme that people sometimes think I'm making it up; unfortunately, it's true. On his first day on the job, that new employee learned to not work too fast and where the best places to slack off and hide are—two essential elements for becoming a slug. The employee was an apt pupil and became a slug par-excellence.

We've discussed how we'd like new employees to grow into ideal employees and how new employees can drift into "slugdom," but, how do disgruntled employees develop? New employees don't become disgruntled employees, and slugs are rarely motivated enough to gain Hi Abilities. Ergo, disgruntled employees must have been ideal employees at one time (Figure 6.15).

What makes an ideal employee disgruntled? Poor leadership and bad management. You might say that disgruntled grows out of malignant dissatisfaction. Dissatisfaction results from lack of one or more of the fundamental

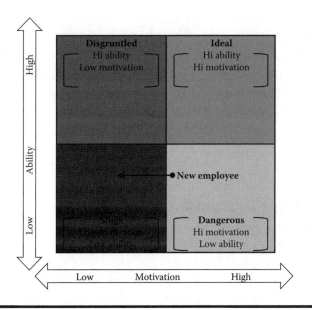

Figure 6.14   New employees may drift into slugdom.

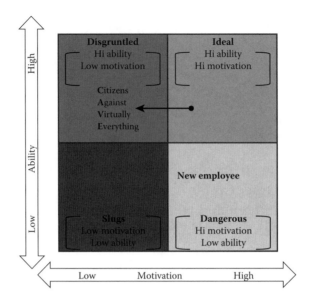

Figure 6.15 Ideal employees can become disgruntled.

satisfiers: hope, control, and equity. When the conditions are such that the individual continuously feels a sense of hopelessness, when they don't feel that their future is within their power to affect a positive change, or when they experience what they feel is profound inequity in the system, their dissatisfaction grows and metastasizes until they devolve from being a productive ideal employee into an angry and disaffected CAVE dweller.

Personality and temperament certainly play a factor in how and when someone becomes disgruntled. But under the right circumstances, anyone can become dissatisfied, frustrated, and angry. Some will leave the organization to affect a positive change in their lives—others will check out but never leave. They stay and brood over their situation creating a toxic environment that can propagate spreading their bad attitudes to others whenever possible.

Architects of Your Organization's Future When Not Left to Chance

Exploring how new employees grow into ideal employees or drift into "slugdom" should provide ample motivation for not leaving the development of new employees to chance. Fortunately, if you have developed a consistently high-performing organization you have all the tools among your arsenal to prevent the decay of organizational talent if you choose to consistently apply them. The main tool is structured systematic training the basis of which is the TCL (refer to Committing Element 2).

Use of the TCL throughout the Employee Lifecycle

As we've discussed training is most effective when it is systems based and holistic; to maintain its effectiveness and thereby deliver maximum ROI, training must be fully integrated into the employee lifecycle as shown in Figure 6.16. When we speak of the employee lifecycle, we are referring to six passages an individual will encounter working for an organization:

1. Hiring
2. Orientation
3. Competency development
4. Promotion to next level
5. Annual performance reviews
6. Management of change

The use of training materials is commonly reserved for stages three and four.

> NOTE: In many organizations, formalized training is reserved for new equipment installations or major systems revisions. The training material developed as part of those projects is not maintained and not integrated into ongoing operations or new employee orientation.

Figure 6.16   Integration of TCLs into the employee lifecycle.

Utilization of the TCL within every stage will yield far better outcomes for every stage of the employee lifecycle.

Use of the TCL for Hiring—Decision Analysis

The typical hiring process entails the posting of a job description, review of applicant resumes, interviews, and selection. Since the downturn in the economy that began in 2007, there have been multiple applicants for every posting. With so many candidates to choose from, it would seem that employers would have an easier time picking up the talent they need. Yet according to a 2011 survey by CareerBuilders, employers still experience difficulty making the right hiring decisions. Two-thirds of the responding companies reported that bad hiring decisions had negatively impacted their business within the previous 12 months. Eric Presley, Chief Technology Officer at CareerBuilders stated, "Hiring the wrong IT talent for a position can have a significant effect on an employer's bottom line, so IT employers are making an effort to improve their recruitment strategy, especially as they look ahead to 2011." (Lawinski, J. 2011. Bad Hires Are Costly Mistakes. *Baselinemag.com*, 2011-01-12). What is true for the information technology industry is equally true for every other business. Bad hiring decisions are costly in terms of time, money, and productivity. To avoid a bad hiring decision, it helps to examine all the aspects of the five spheres of a candidate's competence.

A skills hierarchy in the form of a competency map provides a detailed analysis of the multiple facets required to be successful in a position. The competency map becomes the basis for the TCL. Once you have screened your applicant pool, have each candidate evaluate their abilities against that hierarchy. During the interview process, discuss their specific accomplishments that demonstrate mastery in each area. If you are conducting a panel interview or a series of interviews, assign each interviewer specific spheres of competence to focus on. After the interview, compare and contrast each interviewer's observations and insights to paint a more complete view of the applicant's portfolio of competencies. These perspectives can be recorded and weighed against the significant success criterion required for the position in a decision analysis matrix using the decision quality methods discussed in Focusing Element 8. Since hiring decisions are rarely clear-cut and straightforward, decision analysis is an appropriate tool.

Following the decision analysis approach, organize your decision process by first considering the objective that you hope to reach. Think of this as the value proposition of the prospective employee. Based upon that value proposition, state the decision that needs to be made in clear concise terms. Enumerate the core competencies from each of the five spheres that form the essential (musts) along with the useful (wants) hiring criteria. Each essential criterion is a deal breaker. If a candidate doesn't have it, the decision is obvious. Prioritize the useful criteria from the most important to the least. These will become the grading criteria for the hiring process.

Evaluate and rank the alternative candidates interviewed against these criteria to determine the most viable. Clearly, any alternative that does not have all of the essential criteria can be immediately ruled out. If no candidate has the essential criteria, you will either have to widen the applicant search or reevaluate what is essential. Rank the remaining candidates according to the useful criteria you have established. Validate your decision by weighing any risks a candidate may pose. The risks in hiring are really centered on competency gaps. If hired, these gaps will need to be filled through an individualized development plan. Using decision analysis tools you should have a pretty clear indication of the best hiring decision. Once a hiring decision has been made, the depth of experience within the five spheres of competence of the individual candidate can be used as the basis for the starting salary.

This holistic approach to interviewing does take more time than the typical approach to hiring, but consistently yields substantially better results and is ultimately less costly than less comprehensive hiring methods.

The Use of the TCL in Orientation: Satisfying the Individual Needs of Forming

Once hired, the skills hierarchy and TCLs support new hire orientation. Remember, even if the organization is well established and consistently achieving its goals new members joining the organization must traverse each of the stages of development others have already navigated. Each must have their individual needs satisfied that others achieved during the Forming, Focusing, Committing, Sustaining, and Renewal stages. Individuals joining a new team need the following:

- Orientation
- A sense of purpose
- Building trust

The TCL provides an efficient and effective way to orient new members to all five spheres of competence for all aspects of their jobs. This

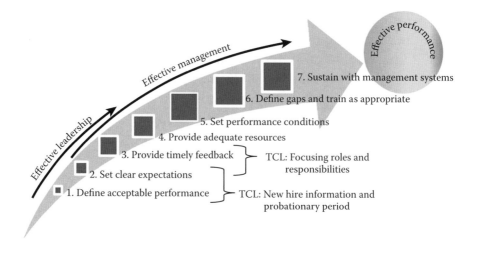

Figure 6.17 Integration of TCLs into the framework for individual success.

is particularly true if the organization has built them using the systems approach incorporating the vision, mission, principles, policies, and procedures, problem solving, and analysis. This methodical approach, when supported by current documentation ensures consistent orientation thus preventing the degradation of employee capabilities. This process further bolsters the framework for individual success we've been systematically building within the organization (Figure 6.17).

The Use of the TCL in Orientation: Effective Use of the Probationary Period

Another significant benefit of utilizing competency maps and TCLs for orientation is the tracking of individual progress during the probationary period of employment. When an employee interviewed, they represented their competencies and experience to be at a particular level. If, during the probationary period, the individual fails to demonstrate the skills and competencies they purported to have during the hiring process, there is a logical consequence that either their pay or their employment status should be affected.

Too frequently, the probationary period of employment is not effectively used to screen out employees who ultimately prove ineffective. The employee maintains a veneer of engagement until they feel they have safely slid into the protected status of permanency. Utilizing the TCL stringently during the probationary period to support frequent progress reviews by the supervisor provides valuable insight during that short window of opportunity where the organization can mitigate a poor hiring decision.

The Use of the TCL in Competency Development: Satisfying the Individual Needs of Focusing

Once an individual understands the vision and mission, they can focus by learning their new roles and responsibilities. The TCL enumerates the competencies associated with each. During their training process the TCL tracks their progress and measures the remaining competency gaps ensuring the employee attains the requisite levels of mastery in each of the five spheres of competence.

The Use of the TCL in Promotion to Next Level: Satisfying the Individual Needs of Committing

New employees that quickly become acclimated and demonstrate their skills and abilities are more trusted and more readily accepted into a standing team than someone who struggles and routinely demonstrates a lack of competence. In this way, the TCL facilitates more rapid inclusion and integration into the previously formed team. The team's cohesion remains more consistent because every member understands their own as well as others' defined roles.

In addition to initial training, once an employee has completed the TCL for their current position, they can look to the next level for promotion opportunities. When they understand what is expected to advance, they can work to gain those essential competencies that will prepare them for promotion when the opportunity is available. It is easy to see how utilization of the TCL bolsters hope, control, and equity within a climate of logical consequences. Each individual knows what is expected of them and what is required to advance. If someone is advanced who has not satisfied the clearly defined criteria, it will be readily apparent in such a transparent system.

The Use of the TCL in Annual Performance Reviews: Satisfying the Individual Needs of Sustaining

Just as the use of TCLs structures the hiring, training, and promotion process, it equally facilitates effective performance reviews. A supervisor or manager can sit with the individual and discuss factually how well the individual has achieved the requirements of the position. When combined with clear metrics and a continuous view to the process, performance reviews should never degrade into "he said–she said" discussions based solely on opinion and anecdotal hearsay. The facts will speak for themselves.

The Use of the TCL in Management of Change: Satisfying the Individual Needs for Renewal

To achieve renewal, individuals need to experience fulfillment of purpose, celebration of accomplishments, and be afforded increased opportunities and be afforded new challenges. The widespread availability and use of TCLs enables and documents all of these.

Another aspect of utilizing a TCL is tracking changes. When a policy or procedure is added or revised, the TCL is updated. All future trainees will receive the benefit of training on the revision. What's more, utilization of the TCL will ensure all existing employees are trained on the revision as well. When the TCL is modified, the percent trained of the existing employees will drop. Where they were at 100%, the addition or modification of a task line item drops their status to less than 100%. Once trained, their records will be updated to show them returning to 100%, thereby ensuring that all current and future employees remain current on the organization's operational requirements.

The TCL Is the Vehicle—Effective Trainers Are the Drivers

The use of TCLs and associated training materials, procedures, and job aids are essential elements of a systematic approach to training that will help sustain and renew high performance within an organization; they are proven best practices. However, no matter how elegant, a tool is only effective when wielded by a competent craftsman. TCLs can be misused or falsified as well as anything else. Like all other systems, effective training needs competent trainers and ongoing audits and reviews.

Training others should be a core competence as well as an ongoing expectation. In order to promote up, the TCL should include the training of others among the social and team skills sphere of competence. In order to promote to the next level, each individual should be trained in the basics of "Train the Trainer."

NOTE: Training should never be reserved as part of the domain of the elite few. Every person is capable of training given the proper incentive. All it really takes to be a trainer is to know more about the subject than the person you are training and a willingness to try. If the organization has effective standardized procedures and TCLs then the training received from one should be essentially the same as the training given by any.

Too often organizations have designated trainers. Though it is true that some people may be better at communications and have a natural flare for training, this practice has multiple unintended consequences that outweigh the benefits.

Consequence No. 1: Designating trainers creates a bottleneck that limits access to training and advancement thus building inequity into the system.

Consequence No. 2: Crowning someone with the mantle of "trainer" can alienate others and give them an excuse for not sharing their knowledge or skills: "I'm not the trainer so I won't teach you" or "If you want me to train, it will cost you."

Consequence No. 3: Having only designated trainers limits crosspollination of ideas and capabilities. You can learn something from everyone. Having designated trainers leads to limited approaches in problem solving and limits the propagation of best practices.

Consequence No. 4: Having only a few trainers removes the training of others from the widespread development of all. You never have to know a subject as well or as deeply as when you have to train someone else. You may think you know something well, but, when you train someone else, you'll quickly learn that there are many things you don't know.

Consequence No. 5: Having designated trainers leaves the organization vulnerable to gaps in continuity with no succession plan.

The requirement to train your replacement prior to your promotion is a powerful incentive. Including the development of others as a line item in every annual performance review inculcates training as a core competency of the organization that facilitates the final element of Renewal: proactive succession planning and mentoring.

Renewal Element 10: Proactive Succession Planning and Mentoring

Examination of organizations that are able to consistently sustain high performance reveals that the faces change, but the intensity of focus doesn't. The elements that made them successful are consistently utilized and adapted as the competitive landscape evolves. This ongoing cycle is perpetuated with the infusion of new members through a structured selection and orientation process as described in Renewal Element 9 and built upon through the processes of succession planning and mentoring (Figure 6.18). The organization continues to deliver on its value proposition to customers and stakeholders achieving the mission and vision through strategies, goals, and objectives by implementing initiatives. This process is sustained even in the face of employee turnover.

Too often organizations lose focus when a new leader is driven to "make his mark" with little regard to what has been done prior to their arrival. Remember cardinal change leadership sin no. 3: manager of the month. If an organization is going to sustain, then it must ensure that future leaders will remain true to the principles, values, and vision of the organization. This is best accomplished with a structured succession planning process.

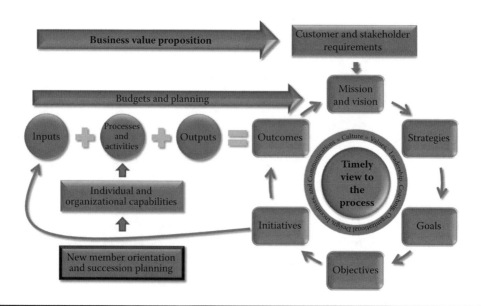

Figure 6.18 Sustainability engine in renewal.

Growth of Successful Leaders: Know Yourself, Know Your Business, and Know Your People

An ancient proverb states, "He who seeks to manage others must first learn to manage himself." This saying is just as true today and will remain true for as long as people are people. To help chart out an effective path of leadership growth, consider the development of a seventeenth-century sea captain.

> THE TYPICAL SEVENTEENTH-CENTURY NAUTICAL CAREER PATH: In the seventeenth century, before commanding a ship, the typical nautical career path began as an ordinary seaman, sometimes called a deckhand. After two years experience and having gained competence and a solid understanding of the ship's routine, they could be considered an able seaman. With time and increased skill, they might be promoted to first mate. Finally, with any luck, they might be selected to become a captain. Of course, some captains were political or financial appointments who may not have possessed the required experience and skills and consequently did not have the respect of the crew.

When considering a modern leadership growth path, the principles that applied then still apply today. The skill set required to lead in today's world is quite different, but you still find that the most respected leaders have risen up through the ranks. Inherited positions and political appointees may be feared for the power they wield, but they are not always respected.

Regardless of your profession, the first step to becoming an effective manager and respected leader begins by successfully managing yourself as represented in the five spheres of competence introduced in Committing Element 2. Figure 6.19

Figure 6.19   The upward spiral of development through the five spheres of competence.

illustrates how an upward spiral of development winds through the five spheres of competence.

To Be Successful You Need Four Things

Throughout the course of our discussions, we have stressed the importance of training as well as the need for opportunities for advancement. However, training and opportunity don't guarantee any particularly individual will successfully leverage those opportunities. Everyone knows (and many of us believe we are) frustrated geniuses that the world has failed to recognize and reward. Just like the example of Bill given in Renewal Element 5, some individuals spend their days laboring well below their self-assessed potential living lives of quiet desperation. As they see others afforded opportunities and given the promotions they covet, they wonder, "What's that guy got that I don't have?" Well, here are the secret four keys to success:

1. Professional competence
2. Emotional intelligence
3. Opportunity
4. A mentor

NOTE: Like having the treasure map to the Lost Dutchman's Mine but not the means to finance an expedition, this knowledge won't guarantee your own success. Just like the disclaimers on late-night paid infomercials, "Individual results may vary." I'm telling you what took me years to discover and I still haven't been able to fully apply.

Success Factor 1: Professional Competence

Unfortunately, and as much as it pains me to say it, in the case of individual advancement competence is the least important of the four. Almost anyone who has a work history knows someone who promoted up with very little professional competence (refer to the Peter Principle described in cardinal change sin no. 3 [manager of the month]). However, individuals need sufficient competence to not fall on their own sword. It is also critical for organizations that sincerely seek to become world-class to have employees with professional competence.

Growth in the ability to manage and lead expands the span of influence and control (introduced in Committing Element 6 [strong leadership and appropriate delegation of authority]). Be aware that the span of influence expands much faster than the span of control. Understanding that true power lays more in influence and less in absolute control will start new managers out on a solid footing. Without this understanding, many aspiring leaders quickly become frustrated and proclaim in exasperation, "Why don't people just do what they're told!" It doesn't take long to learn that, unless someone wants to do something, forcing them will only yield very iffy results ranging from half-hearted attempts to malicious compliance.

REMEMBER: You can hire someone's hands, but they have to give you their head and their heart.

As individuals promote up they rely less on their own professional expertise and more on the competence of others. Each promotion requires a greater understanding of people and the broader business and each step requires a larger, more effective, span of influence. Figure 6.20 charts how the span of influence grows along with the growth of professional and managerial competencies. If personal competence keeps pace with the growing span of influence, individuals will be ready to progress up the organizational ladder from being an individual contributor toward becoming a manager as opportunities present themselves.

Managing the enterprise and leading the business	• Preparing for what's to come • Delivering on the value proposition by establishing the vision, values, and strategies
Managing locations and leading business units	• Strategic development • Deploying strategy to achieve business sustainable results
Managing departments and leading leaders	• Translating strategy into tactics • Building capabilities, business acumen, and functional expertise
Managing others and leading teams	• Execution of tactics • Coordinating activities to efficiently execute the plans, communicating with and developing others
Managing self and leading by example	• Controlling the process • Safely and efficiently executing tasks to add value within each activity

Figure 6.20   Growth as a leader.

NOTE: To remain in balance, the degree of responsibility and account-ability must also continue to expand along with the span of influence. Great power with little accountability is, and always will be, a recipe for the abuse of power.

The first tier of individual growth involves performing tasks, controlling processes, and the ability to manage yourself. This level is often referred to as the individual contributor. It is important for individual contributors to understand the importance of the tasks and their impact on quality—maintaining their line of sight to the value proposition of the organization. Effective individual contributors draw most heavily from the "management of self" and "professional and technical skills" spheres of competence. Individual contributors can lead by example, inspiring coworkers by setting a good example, demonstrating professional skill, dedication, and appropriate team behaviors.

SALIENT QUOTE: "No matter how insignificant the thing you have to do, do it as well as you can, give it as much of your care and attention as you would give to the thing you regard as most important. For it will be by those small things that you shall be judged."

Mahatma Gandhi
Leader for Indian Independence (1869–1948)

Those that prove effective as individual contributors are likely to be promoted up to supervise and manage others. This second level of organizational activity revolves around the execution of tactics rather than the development of strategies. This level of leadership involves coordinating activities. To be effective, managers must be extremely effective at face-to-face communications. To sustain at this level, managers must be adept at developing others to become effective individual contributors. Avoiding becoming an example of the Peter Principle requires growing competence in all five of the spheres of personal and professional competence. Simply becoming more adept in a single sphere will limit a manager's effectiveness.

The third level of leadership entails managing a department and managing other managers. This level of management is really about translating strategies into tactics. Understanding the big picture and having the capabilities to design systems, divide the activities across work teams by defining the roles and responsibilities that accomplish the business goals within the organization's day-to-day activities.

As one grows further in their leadership capabilities, they will have to set their sights beyond the walls of the organization to look across multiple locations for accomplishment of the goals. Here is where strategies that cascade down through multiple organizations are developed. This level of leadership requires a greater vision and continuous persistent communications.

The apex of organizational leadership entails leading the enterprise. At this level, leaders not only have to be looking beyond the walls of the organization, they need to be looking well into the future. The leader must ensure continuous delivery on the organization's value proposition while planning ahead to how that value proposition will change as the technology, competition, and the economy reshapes that proposition. Just as Wayne Gretzky contrasted the abilities of hockey players when he said, "A good hockey player plays where the puck is; a great hockey player plays where the puck is going to be," the ability to skate to where the organization will need to be in the future will determine the individual leader's success and the success of all the many individuals and their families and communities counting on them to lead.

ONE FINAL NOTE: The ability to affect outcomes rarely results solely from a single person's efforts and influence—especially as they seek to influence the broader organization. Multiple factors affect outcomes in the chaos of the work environment. Consider again the pond analogy discussed in Committing Element 6, *the more waves on the water, the harder it is to observe the ripples from a single stone.*

Success Factor 2: Emotional Intelligence

Emotional intelligence (EQ) is often defined as "the ability to perceive, regulate and communicate emotions—to understand our own emotions and the emotions of others." Daniel Goleman further refined the concept (Goleman, D. 1996. *Emotional Intelligence: Why It Can Matter More than IQ*. New York: Bantam Books), defining EQ as a measure of an individual's competency in four key areas: self-awareness, self-management, social awareness, and relationship management.

- Self-awareness: The ability to recognize your emotions and their effect on your thoughts, decisions, and actions.
- Self-management: The ability to control your emotions and reactions, and to exercise leadership, particularly during times of stress, duress, and conflict.
- Social awareness: The ability to sense, understand, and empathize with the emotions of others, and to effectively function within social structures.
- Relationship management: The ability to develop healthy relationships, influence others, and effectively manage conflict.

Since the span of influence exceeds the span of control managers must cultivate their emotional intelligence to successfully thrive when promoted. A high level of emotional intelligence enables effective engagement of others to fully commit and contribute to the success of the organization. Having a high level of emotional intelligence is essential to every manager's ongoing success.

Success Factor 3: Opportunity

It's not enough to have the ability; to be promoted you'll need to be in the right place when an opportunity presents itself. You'll also need the courage to act on the opportunity. When prior preparation meets opportunity, success follows. Don't get discouraged and don't expect you'll capitalize on every opportunity that comes along—you will stumble along the way.

> SALIENT QUOTE: "I don't measure a man's success by how high he climbs but how high he bounces when he hits bottom."
>
> **George S. Patton**
> *U.S. General (1885–1945)*

Providing Opportunities through Structured Succession Planning

Succession planning is the process by which organizations systematically build capabilities into the leaders of the future. Too often succession planning is performed in a reactionary crisis mode when a key individual unexpectedly leaves. This lack of future planning causes severe losses in productivity, quality, and even customer confidence. To avoid these potential disruptions in performance, the organization should adopt a succession planning process. We'll discuss two common approaches their benefits and their potential drawbacks.

One common methodology is "train your replacement" (discussed in Renewal Element 9). Limiting someone's ability to promote motivates them to pass their knowledge and skills on to the next generation. And, if the trainee will be working for the trainer, the trainer is more likely to strive for a quality outcome. However, if the individual is moving beyond the department, they may be driven to train as quickly as possible and report success sooner than would otherwise be warranted to facilitate their own promotion. Even if they are not moving beyond the organization, the train-your-replacement methodology may not yield optimal results because of the tendency for like to promote like. Refer back to the Forming discussion on DISC temperaments. People often admire traits in others they themselves tend to exhibit. The tendency of like to promote like left unchallenged and unchecked can create homogeneous organizations heavily skewed toward one set of traits. As such, the ongoing practice of train-your-replacement can produce organizations with all the strengths of a particular temperament along with all its weaknesses.

"YOU'LL GO FAR IN THIS ORGANIZATION—BECAUSE YOU'RE JUST LIKE ME!": One Fortune 500 company I worked with relied almost exclusively on train-your-replacement. Over time, 9 out of 10 of their top management team had been staffed with severely introverted analytical "C" temperaments. This firm became mired in analysis and innovation lagged others in their industry. In addition, communications were very limited leading to lack of alignment in and among the various business units.

To temper the potential ill effects of train-your-replacement succession planning teams or committees can be used to good effect. These teams are made of senior managers from across the organization. Each manager attends a succession planning conference where they become the advocates

	Low Performance	Medium Performance	High Performance
High Potential		Cher lo	Toni T. Iger F. Loop
Medium Potential	P. T. Oastie (New)	W. Eatie	C. Crunch S. Bears
Low Potential	P. Tart (Performance Plan)	O. T. Meal C. O. Wheat	R. C. Ispy

Figure 6.21   Nine-box succession planning.

for their succession choices. To manage such teams it is helpful to structure their discussions utilizing a nine-box matrix (Figure 6.21). The nine-box matrix pairs two traits, performance versus potential, each rated as either low, medium, or high.

Prior to attending the conference, each manager ranks every member of their department on a copy of the nine-box matrix. The names of each individual are placed in a box based upon their manager's assessment of where their performance intersects with their potential. Each is scaled between Low, Med, and Hi. If someone has consistently demonstrated both high performance and high potential, they're name would be listed in the upper right-hand box. Conversely, names in the lower left-hand box reflect consistently low performance and low potential. To promote consistency, define the characteristics that define Low–Med–Hi. Clearly, these characteristics should align with the TCLs that have been developed for the positions reflecting each of the five spheres of competence. It is also a good practice to base the assessments on three years of performance reviews. If someone is new to the organization or new to their position, that should be annotated as well. Similarly, if someone is on a performance plan, that too should be flagged.

During the nine-box discussion, managers explain their assessments to their peers and to the executive leadership team. The discussions that follow confirm or contradict each manager's assessments based on the experiences and observations of other managers. Group consensus determines which box each individual name ultimately resides. The results of this group ranking can then be used to develop performance plans for every member of the organization. Those who are slated for promotion as part of the succession plan should receive the training and the exposure requires preparing them for advancement. This methodology helps guide the allocation of scarce resources to yield the highest return on the investment in employee development.

As useful as the nine-box methodology is, it can have some severe unintended consequences for an organization that is not mature in its development or management processes. If managers are prone to gossip the final rankings of the organization will quickly become known. This can be quite divisive. In addition, individuals will question why they weren't ranked higher. If the development process within the organization is well structured around a TCL process, then the results should come as no surprise. Anyone falling in the lower left-hand quadrant should already be on a developmental plan. The process can also fail to recognize the strength of members of Team "P"—those individuals who are outstanding at their current jobs and have little desire or aptitude to promote. The organization still needs them to keep performing the vital day-to-day tasks that consistently deliver value. Too often rewards are limited to those on the promotion track. Individuals are driven to promote even though they could remain quite content in their current position thus sowing the seeds of the Peter Principle. There is also no guarantee that using a nine-box committee will promote diversity in the leadership team. The only systematic approach to building diversity into the organization's succession planning process is to ensure the strong attributes of each DISC temperament is incorporated into the appropriate spheres of competence. Thus, each position will reflect the elements from each sphere and each corresponding temperament attribute to the degree it is appropriate for each role and responsibility within the organization. This built in balance can be complemented by asking each manager to play devil's advocate for those that they had previously sponsored. This balanced approach tends to counter the imbalance inherent within every system and yield outstanding results. Done consistently, the nine-box process can build substantially deep bench strength into the organization.

Success Factor 4: A Mentor

The fourth and final success factor, mentoring, is by far the hardest to consistently and systematically develop within an organization. It's difficult to overstate the value of effective mentoring; almost all successful people have had at one time or another someone who was there for them, someone who took the time to teach them, gave them honest feedback, gave them a chance (see opportunity above), and who flew cover for them when they made a mistake. This mentoring relationship allows them to survive their mistakes, learn, and continue to grow.

The reason that mentoring is so difficult to foster and sustain is because it depends upon two transitory situations to be impactful: the mentor–mentee relationship and the teachable moment. The most effective mentor relationships exist when there is a genuine bond between the two. Because mentoring is so time intensive, it is difficult to mentor anyone you don't have a genuine regard for. You can council, you can direct, you can coach, and you can reprimand anyone if you are a good manager, but you won't be as effective as a mentor if you don't esteem them—and the esteem must be mutually reciprocal. It goes back to the essential elements of why someone follows a leader: Can I trust you and do you care about me? Without these, the lack of trust essential to mentoring won't allow the mentee to lower their defenses and receive the feedback they need to hear.

CHINESE PROVERB: A closed fist cannot receive a gift.

Anonymous Fortune Cookie Author

The second key element for effective mentoring is catching someone at that teachable moment. The impact of a mentor is heavily dependent upon the individual's ability to accept and to apply the feedback they receive. If they are not at a place or in a condition that enables them to capitalize on the mentoring relationship, it will be of little value. Mentoring builds upon the Framework for Individual Success that had been built throughout each stage of organizational design (Figure 6.22). You might say that mentoring supercharges the developmental process. This can only be done when the mentor is available to observe the mentee and give specific and timely feedback. This is why mentoring is so time intensive. Just as a smattering of "quality time" is incapable of replacing the necessary quantity of time, both mentors and mentees need to make a substantial investment of a precious resource into the relationship or it will be of little impact.

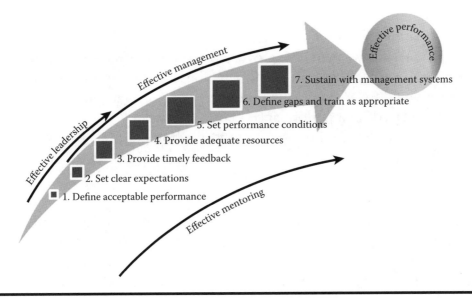

Figure 6.22   Mentoring and framework for individual success.

WARNING: BE CAREFUL WHO YOU ADOPT AS YOUR MENTOR—A PAINFUL EXAMPLE: A mentor is important, but be selective—your reputation and your future career opportunities may hang in the balance. When you first join an organization, you have no way of knowing how those around you are truly seen by their peers and managers. Falling into formation with the first person willing to "take you under their wing" may just brand you with whatever reputation that person has and may quickly limit your future prospects. Recall the lessons of Renewal Element 9—the slugs and the disgruntled employees are frequently eager to recruit you into their ranks.

When I first joined one firm, a very likable coworker offered to show me the ropes. Being new and wanting to make a success of my new job, I welcomed his advice. Unfortunately, I later came to learn that my savior was an anchor. He was frequently late turning in his assignments and his projects routinely came in overbudget and behind schedule, leaving a trail of angry customers in his wake. His offer to support and train me was, in reality, a cunning strategy to get me to do his work for him. After a few months on the job (and many long hours completing both his and my assignments in the name of my training and development), a manager pulled me aside and shared his growing concern. It seems that the quality of my mentor's work had improved since my arrival. After a few hours going over my work products with the manager, he discerned the truth of the situation. I was reassigned to another project where I was eventually promoted to a principal, and my "mentor" was placed on a performance plan.

LESSON LEARNED: Be careful of those who offer to help you move *their* furniture.

One final note about mentoring, if mentoring is to be built into the succession planning process, the mentor must be willing to invest in the individual, sharing their secrets and key relationships with the mentee. This includes establishing relationships with key customers and stakeholders—to do any less isn't really preparing someone effectively and completely to fill the next higher position. This degree of disclosure requires a great degree of self-assurance on the part of the mentor. The mentor must have absolute trust that what they say will not be used as a lever to push them out of the organization. More than one driven young employee has gunned for their next promotion by putting crosshairs on their mentors back. And more than once, self-preservation on the part of the mentor has limited the advancement potential of up and coming stars. This is the reality of the world. Successful mentoring lies somewhere between these two ditches.

Renewal versus Leveling: The Need to Reform

Organizations either renew or they level out and begin to decline—there is no middle ground. We began our journey with a quote from Will Rogers that's worth repeating as we near our destination; "Even if you're on the right track, you'll get run over if you just sit there." When organizations fail to consistently apply the elements that brought them success while maintaining a critical eye on their SWOTs (strengths, weaknesses, opportunities, and threats), they expose themselves to the risk of losing their competitive advantage to other more strategic, innovative, and progressive organizations that overtake them and drive them out of business. Given the dire consequences, it would seem that managers should have sufficient motivation to keep a close weather eye on the horizon looking for the telltale signs of Leveling.

- Frustration and burn out
- Change resistance
- High turnover
- Unfilled positions
- Ineffective improvement projects

In previous organizational development stages, if your navigation blew off course, you could simply backtrack a stage or two and resume your forward progress—not so with leveling. If the organization is experiencing frustration and burn out, if people have become entrenched in their ways such that they are resistant to change, the organization needs to be reformed (Figure 6.23).

Reforming the organization doesn't mean that you have to blow it all up and start over from scratch. And it certainly doesn't mean that you allow productivity to return to a level comparable to before you had worked out systems, assigned roles and responsibilities, etc. It means that the organization must initiate a major intervention that reinvigorates and reignites the flames of engagement. The team has developed its talent, built systems to deliver on its value proposition and has learned many lessons through the process of building the organization. Knowing then what they know now they'd probably do things a little differently. This provides an opportunity for creative destruction. Through collaboration, the organization can recreate itself. Shake up the organization by giving people new opportunities and new challenges. Let them rethink their processes, their roles, and their responsibilities. This can be accomplished by retraining, reassignment, or bringing in some new talent. Benchmarking others, including those in

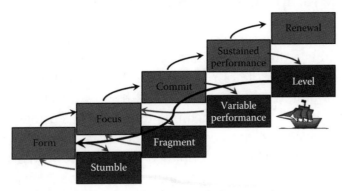

Design → Develop → Deploy → Sustain → Continuous improvement

Figure 6.23   Reforming the organization.

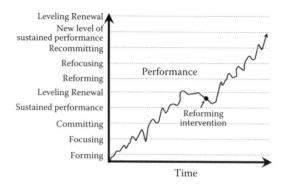

Figure 6.24 **Reforming the organization to achieve a higher level of sustained performance.**

entirely different industries, can often infuse new ideas into the organization. The Disney Institute is an excellent example of how "different" can be transformational. Leaders, managers, and designers from every industry have attended the institute to learn to think differently by reimagining the "Art of the Possible." Graduates return to their organizations eager to adapt new ideas into their organization to take it to the next level. An example of how productivity within a leveling organization can be propelled to higher levels when the organization Reforms → Refocuses → Recommits → to reach a new higher level of sustained performance is shown in Figure 6.24.

Key Takeaways: Renewal versus Leveling

The process of renewal is vital to all living entities, including living organizations. Renewal is a time to celebrate past successes and transition to the next phase. Renewal is a rite of passage that must be acknowledged and embraced. Without it, the emotional heart of the organization languishes. Remember, our emotions assign meaning to events (Focusing Element 10). When an organization fails to recognize and celebrate its achievements, energy levels will falter. High performance with little rewards is not sustainable over the long haul. Table 6.6 summarizes the key takeaways of Renewal versus Leveling.

To help with your project planning, Table 6.7 shows a basic project plan to help your organization continuously renew.

Table 6.6 Key Takeaways of Renewal versus Leveling

	Focus	*Commit*	*Sustained Performance*	*Renewal*
Form	*Stumble*	*Fragment*	*Variable Performance*	*Level*

Renewal: A sustained culture of excellence, individual team members may change, but the organization continues to consistently achieve its goals

Team Needs:

- Fulfillment of purpose
- Celebration of accomplishments
- Increased opportunities and new challenges to overcome
- Increased levels of responsibility and mastery
- Effective integration and assimilation of new members
- Ongoing validation and adaptation of the value proposition

The Change "Readiness vs. Response" Continuum	
Change Ready:	Celebration, Engagement, and Commitment
Change Resistant:	Acceptance and/or Compliance

Indicators of Effective Navigation	Indicators of Ineffective Navigation
• High productivity • Celebration and good will • Low turnover • Ease of recruiting top talent • Continuous improvement	• Frustration and burn out • Change resistance • High turnover • Unfilled positions • Ineffective improvement projects

Effective Leadership Responses:

- Ongoing validation and adaptation of the value proposition
- Distributed delegation and empowerment
- Creative destruction and recreation through collaboration
- Focusing the team for self-critical auditing and analysis
- Decision making and continuous improvement
- Mentoring and leading by example

Effective Management Responses:

- Effective process improvement
- Customer and supplier partnerships

(continued)

Table 6.6   Key Takeaways of Renewal versus Leveling (Continued)

	Focus	Commit	Sustained Performance	Renewal
Form	Stumble	Fragment	Variable Performance	Level
• Ongoing continuous development • Delegation and empowerment • Succession planning				

Tools and Techniques:
- Continuous benchmarking and improvement
- Six Sigma process improvement
- Effective new hire orientation
- Ongoing commitment to training and development of current and new members
- Succession planning—nine-box evaluations

Table 6.7   Renewal Project Plan—Refitting and Redeploying

Project Step	Responsibility	Date Planned	Date Complete
(1) Evaluate your communication processes and practices. Ensure individual and organizational successes are broadly shared and documented			
(2) Celebrate organizational successes in a way that is significant to whomever is being recognized			
(3) Evaluate internal and external auditing processes. Ensure that there is appropriate documentation and follow-up to audit findings			

(continued)

Table 6.7 Renewal Project Plan—Refitting and Redeploying (Continued)

Project Step	Responsibility	Date Planned	Date Complete
(4) Benchmark competitors as well as customer alternatives. Incorporate findings into goals and action plans			
(5) Review the ROI of past process improvement projects and initiatives. Ensure ROI is consistently used as a justification and validation of projects			
(6) Utilize meeting assessments to gauge the effectiveness of meetings. Address shortfalls and ineffective practices			
(7) Review and evaluate the performance review and reward processes to ensure consistency and the judicious application of logical consequences			
(8) Evaluate the organization's learning climate, processes, and degree of engagement. Verify career pathways are planned and utilized			
(9) Audit the effectiveness of the training process and practices			
(10) Review the hiring process to ensure it effectively incorporates the elements of TCLs			

(continued)

Table 6.7   Renewal Project Plan—Refitting and Redeploying (Continued)

Project Step	Responsibility	Date Planned	Date Complete
(11) Evaluate the process and outcomes of new hire orientation. Ensure ongoing enculturation and inclusion of new hires to establish the line of sight to the value proposition			
(12) Review and evaluate the succession planning process. Benchmark mentoring and adapt into the organization			

Chapter 7

Putting It All Together

Our journey has taken us through five stages of building an effective organization. Each stage contained 10 elements. Exploring these 50 elements, we've covered many, many topics; it all may seem a bit overwhelming. Now, it's time to step back from the trees and consider the forest—when you do, understanding the intertwined elements of organizational success should become quite clear—almost simple. As the American physician, author, and poet Oliver Wendell Holmes Sr. is attributed to having said, "I would not give a fig for the simplicity this side of complexity; I would give my right arm for the simplicity on the far side of complexity." Figure 7.1 illustrates how the human factors of optimization combine to drive sustained performance:

1. Engaged leadership with vision leads to:
2. Competency development and mentoring supported by:
3. Documentation, feedback and accountability facilitated by:
4. Ready access to resources, references, policies, and work instructions that empowers an:
5. Engaged workforce utilizing:
6. Work systems, practices, and processes validated by a:
7. Continuous view of processes and key metrics benchmarked against:
8. World class standards

The well-run organization seamlessly combines these human factors to consistently deliver on the organization's value proposition. The work you've done to assess the 50 individual elements within the five stages helps paint

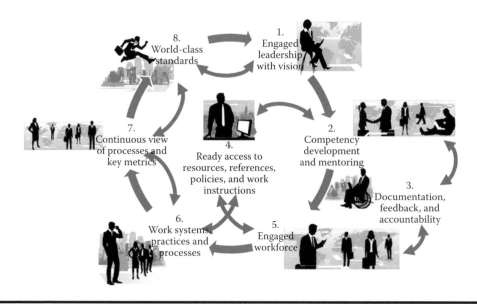

Figure 7.1   The human factors of organizational optimization.

a composite picture of how well your organization has optimized the human factors. To view the whole at a glance, record each of the 10 element scores you rated for the five stages you assessed within the Composite Scoring Matrix Table 7.1.

Total your score. The final score for each stage will fall between +40 and −40. Place the overall score for each organizational stage in the corresponding block at the bottom of each column. Any column with an overall score between 30 and 40 represents a well-navigated stage. A total of less than 30, but more than 20, indicates that there are areas that need improvement. The lower your organizational score, the stronger the indication that there are profound aspects of the organization's operations, communications, and structures that are impeding achievement of its mission and vision.

The rating scale is not divided into even quartiles because the scale of assessment is based upon a forced choice scale. There is no "undecided." This is intentional because "undecided" is frequently used to sit the fence and remain uncommitted and thus unaccountable. For good or bad, it's either somewhat like you or most like you. If there are multiple elements within any stage that are not navigated well, those elements will have broad-reaching ripple effects throughout the organization and probably unseen and unintended consequences. As we pointed out, when the fundamental human satisfiers of the Workforce Engagement Equation were first introduced, organizations are one indivisible whole. As you consider the whole,

Table 7.1   Composite Scoring Matrix

	Stage 1	Stage 2	Stage 3	Stage 4	Stage 5
	Scores	*Scores*	*Scores*	*Scores*	*Scores*
Element 1					
Element 2					
Element 3					
Element 4					
Element 5					
Element 6					
Element 7					
Element 8					
Element 9					
Element 10					
Range	*Overall Score*	*Overall Score*	*Overall Score*	*Overall Score*	*Overall Score*
30 to 40	Well Formed	Focused	Committed	Sustained Performance	In Renewal
20 to 29	Forming	Stumbling	Fragmenting	Variable Performance	Leveling
19 to –19					
–20 to –40	Profound Gaps	Profound Gaps	Profound Gaps	Profound Gaps	Profound Gaps

don't forget to weigh the perceptions from all the echelons—what's your view of the parade; the vantage point of the blimp, or the limited and obscured perspective among the crowd? Where elements exist that are counter to the espoused values of an organization or incongruent with mission accomplishment, the ill effects of those negative elements will impact other areas of the organization. Just as a single hole may well sink a ship, one or two profound gaps may derail an organization's quest for excellence of mission accomplishment through engagement.

> SALIENT QUOTE: "One man cannot do right in one department of life whilst he is occupied in doing wrong in any other departments. Life is one indivisible whole."
>
> **Mahatma Gandhi**
> *Leader for Indian Independence (1869–1948)*

Interpreting the Composite Scoring Matrix

Looking at your scores recorded in Table 7.1, do you see a pattern? If you have profound gaps in an earlier stage, chances are you have low scores in subsequent stages. You can't build high performance on an infirm foundation. To interpret any gaps, consider the initial premise of the Stages of Organizational Development Model—intuitive and directionally oriented. Don't fall into the paralysis of analysis—use your intuition. What is the root of the matter?

1. While forming, was the orientation toward the mission and vision adequate to build the new organization's trust?
2. Were systems created and problems solved through an inclusive process that focused individuals on their roles and responsibilities?
3. Was the training adequate with sufficient opportunities to practice along with timely feedback to build individual mastery and inspire commitment?
4. Is the organization consistently achieving meaningful outcomes within a climate that is congruent with individuals' values and sufficiently empowering to their needs for autonomy?
5. Does the organization celebrate its successes while making opportunities for individuals to advance in their careers opening opportunities for new team members?

This five simple questions sum up the long and arduous journey to sustained organizational excellence. Answering the five questions helps ascertain if you've navigated each stage of organizational development well. If you have, you'll have impactful performance at each of the five organizational tiers. As shown in Figure 7.2, the five organizational tiers correspond to growth as a leader (Figure 6.20). When we explored the five leadership rungs to be climbed, we started at the bottom and worked our way up; conversely, transforming an organization starts at the top and cascades down.

1. Drivers of impactful business performance
   a. Compelling value proposition delineated into a clear vision and strategies
   b. Sustainability of profits + people + planet
2. Drivers of impactful facility performance
   a. Strategy deployment through tactics
   b. Complementary organizational structures, goals, incentives, and rewards
3. Drivers of impactful department performance
   a. Internal and external process alignment
   b. Clear roles and responsibilities supported by enabling technologies
4. Drivers of impactful process performance
   a. Well-defined management operating systems, metrics, and timely view of process
   b. Lean and sustainable design

Figure 7.2   Five tiers of organizational impact.

5. Drivers of impactful individual performance
   a. Clear expectations, feedback, and consequences
   b. Individual competencies, organizational congruence, and adequate resources

Orchestrating the interaction among and between these five tiers is a clear line of sight created though alignment, communications, and coordination. The five tiers of an impactful organization's performance are created through the effective navigation of the five stages of organizational development:

Forming → Focusing → Committing → Sustained Performance → Renewal.

To stay the course of your organizational journey, chart your progress regularly by gauging the performance indicators and responsively make leadership and management course corrections. Table 7.2 summarizes the individual needs/indicators along with effective leadership and managerial responses for each of the five organization development stages.

The key attributes of successful practitioners of organizational development and process improvement is continuous engagement and a questioning outlook. Don't accept subpar behaviors as "just the way things are." Always remember these two key management principles:

1. Every behavior is rewarding on some level.
2. All things yield to good management.

SALIENT QUOTE: "Intuition will tell the thinking mind where to look next."

Dr. Jonas Salk
American Medical Researcher—Cured Polio
(1914–1995)

Conclusion: Transformational Leadership Requires Courage

We began our journey delving into the dark side of leadership by exploring the reasons why things don't change, consolidated into Seven Cardinal Sins of Change Leadership. It was important to begin in those dark places to

Table 7.2 Summary of Individual Needs and Effective Leadership and Managerial Responses for Each Organizational Stage

	Team Needs	Effective Leadership	Effective Management
Forming	• Orientation • A sense of purpose • Building trust	• Set a clear vision and mission • Communicate organization's mission and vision	• Define the strategies that will accomplish the mission and vision • Comprehensive approach building a vessel of organizational success • Coordinate resources with timing and needs • Goals alignment with customers and suppliers
Focusing	• Understanding of how the mission and vision are to be accomplished • Inclusion and involvement • Initial training • Assignment of roles and responsibilities • Development of Processes and Procedures	• Mutual regard and inclusion • Cascading organizational mission to individuals • Problem solving • Conflict resolution	• Meeting facilitation that maintains the crews focus on the tasks at hand and minimizing tangents that distract from the focusing process • Development of systems and processes • Assignment of roles and responsibilities • Allocation of resources • Scheduling and coordination of work

(continued)

Table 7.2 Summary of Individual Needs and Effective Leadership and Managerial Responses for Each Organizational Stage (Continued)

	Team Needs	Effective Leadership	Effective Management
Committing	• Inclusion • Training • Opportunities to practice—growing mastery • Timely feedback	• Transformational leadership living the values of the organization • Reinforcement of fundamental satisfiers: hope, control, and equity • Establish span of control and degree of engagement • Foster inclusion among all team members in accomplishing the organization's purpose • Courageously addressing organizational elements that are not congruent with the mission, vision, and values	• Reinforcement of the chain of command • Mentoring, including assignment of meaningful development opportunities combined with timely feedback • Establishment of accountability through logical consequences • Ongoing project management

Sustained performance	• Individual congruence with organizational culture • Growing autonomy and empowerment • Meaningful outcomes • Equitable treatment • Sustainable work–life balance	• Maintain ongoing focus toward delivering on the organization's value proposition • Empower members to take on more responsibilities and authority • Challenge assumptions • Proactive problem solving and decision making • Embracing the messengers and maintaining multiple views to the organization	• Continuous process improvement • Standardization of policies and procedures • Vendor and supplier management • Control of nonconforming products and services • Courageous and consistent use of logical consequences
Renewal	• Fulfillment of purpose • Celebration of accomplishments • Increased opportunities and new challenges to overcome • Increased levels of responsibility and mastery • Effective integration and assimilation of new members • Ongoing validation and adaptation of the value proposition	• Ongoing validation and adaptation of the value proposition • Distributed delegation and empowerment • Creative destruction and recreation through collaboration • Focusing the team for self critical auditing and analysis • Decision making and continuous improvement • Mentoring and leading by example	• Effective process improvement • Customer and supplier partnerships • Ongoing continuous development • Delegation and empowerment • Succession planning

heed the wisdom provided by Sun Tzu in *The Art of War*—"Know your enemy." Taking another page from Oriental thought, we know that within the Yin and Yang of life, every dark force has a counterbalancing light. The Seven Virtues of Change Leadership can overcome the Seven Cardinal Sins if we choose the path of light. This path is not easy—maintaining the light requires a continuous expenditure of energy—without energy, darkness rushes in.

> MOVIE QUOTE: "All that is necessary for evil to triumph is for good men to do nothing."
>
> **Sergei Bondarchuk's adaptation of Leo Tolstoy's *War and Peace***

We Need Heroes: Seven Transformational Leadership Virtues

To some, the idea of a hero is passé. A cynical workforce has seen their benefits cut, jobs outsourced, and firms and factories closed while those most culpable for these failures have been rewarded. For many, integrity is relative. One company I worked with believed that "excessive honesty" was a detriment that limited an employee's upward potential. One performance review derided an employee for "complicating business decisions with excessive ethics." Are the days of "voluntary virtue" gone? Don't people do the right thing just because it's the right thing to do? In Machiavellian terms, do the ends justify the means?

The best-performing and sustainable organizations equitably cultivate a culture of logical consequences. Great organizations are meritocracies guided by an uncompromising quest for fairness—a rising tide should lift all boats. The world needs another Milton Hershey.

Milton Hershey was one of the finest heroes that this country has ever known. I learned of him when living in Pennsylvania and traveled to Hershey Park (www.hersheypa.com). The town with streets lined with "chocolate kiss"–shaped lights is a living legacy to a leader who exemplified the Seven Virtues of Transformational Leadership.

1. Transformational leaders value equity.
2. Transformational leaders are realistic and willing to do the hard jobs.
3. Transformational leaders choose to lead.
4. Transformational leaders have far-reaching vision.
5. Transformational leaders have integrity and humility and remain teachable.

6. Transformational leaders are determined, persistent, and resilient.
7. Transformational leaders are courageous.

1. **Transformational Leaders Value Equity**

For many, the name Hershey is synonymous with chocolate. The Hershey Chocolate Company has remained consistently one of the most successful companies since its opening in 1894. Milton S. Hershey founded Hershey's Chocolate as a subsidiary of his successful company, The Lancaster Caramel Company, which he started in 1883. His talent for making candy, marketing, and distribution made Hershey a wealthy man. But unlike some successful people then and now, Hershey saw his wealth as a profound responsibility; as the proverb says, of those who are given much, much is expected. Hershey gave back to his workers, his community, and to the world. As part of his commitment to his employees, Hershey built a model town for his employees that included comfortable single- and two-family homes, an affordable public transportation system, and a quality public school system. If this were not enough, he felt his workers' quality of life would be improved by providing recreation and diversions, so in 1907, he opened Hershey Park, PA. His benevolence not only benefitted his workers and their families, it generated a thriving tourist industry for the town. Then and now, thousands of out-of-town visitors flock to the park every year, bringing more revenue to the town.

2. **Transformational Leaders Are Realistic and Willing to Do the Hard Jobs**

Born in rural Pennsylvania in 1857, Milton S. Hershey was no stranger to hard work. He grew up helping work the family farm. To learn his trade, he apprenticed himself to a confectioner in Lancaster, PA. Knowing the business first hand allowed Hershey to innovate new processes and systems in which he then trained others to increase the capacity of the systems. He valued hard work and didn't ask anyone to perform a task he was not willing to perform himself.

3. **Transformational Leaders Choose to Lead—Leadership Is a Choice!**

With his wealth, Milton Hershey could easily have retired and lived a life of leisure, and no one would have blamed him, but he never shirked his responsibilities. In addition to running a successful company, he and his wife, Catherine, founded the Hershey Industrial School for Orphan Boys in 1909. Even after his wife died in 1915, Hershey continued to remain active, leading the school while continuing to manage his company and remaining active in the affairs of the town. He shouldered the burden of leadership throughout his life up until his death in 1945.

4. **Transformational Leaders Have Far-Reaching Vision**

   We have stressed throughout the book how leaders are going places. Leaders have a vision. Think of it like an airplane. If you are a passenger, you don't want the captain back in the cabin checking on the number of peanuts and drinks being given to passengers; you want him or her in the cockpit focusing on the destination and scanning the horizon for turbulence and storms. Just so, Milton Hershey continuously sought opportunities. Not satisfied with the success of the Lancaster Caramel Company, Hershey bought a new piece of equipment he saw at the 1893 World's Fair. With the new equipment, Hershey added new candies to his sales line: chocolates, chocolate-covered caramels, baking chocolates, and cocoas. His vision secured his own prosperity as well as the prosperity and security of those who trusted him to lead.

5. **Transformational Leaders Have Integrity, Humility, and Remain Teachable**

   Even though his own formal schooling was limited, Hershey believed deeply in education and remained teachable his entire life. Beyond his apprenticeship, Hershey learned to make caramels from a confectioner in Denver, chocolates from a German confectioner, and discovered innovative advancements working with the U.S. Military. He valued education as much as he valued hard work. He passed that love of learning on to his employees as well as children less fortunate than himself. The Milton Hershey School continues that tradition today.

INSPIRATIONAL QUOTE: "If I ever become rich, I am going to use my money to build schools to give every boy and girl an opportunity to get an education."

Milton S. Hershey
American Entrepreneur and Philanthropist
(1857–1945)

6. **Transformational Leaders Have Determination and Are Persistent and Resilient**

   As important as vision is, determination, persistence, and resilience are crucial. It was Milton Hershey's determination, persistence, and resilience that were the initial ingredients of his success. Hershey's first shop in Philadelphia wasn't successful and neither were his next two attempts in Chicago and New York. But he never gave up on his dream. Leaving his failures in his wake but carrying the lessons he'd learned with him, he returned to his native Pennsylvania. His fourth business enterprise was successful.

7. **Transformational Leaders Are Courageous**

Of the seven leadership virtues, courage is the only one at par with equity. Leadership requires courage at every turn. Courage to start—Milton Hershey's father wanted him to be a printer. It took courage to follow his dreams. It took courage to start his own company and restart others when his first efforts didn't bear fruit. Courage to endure—Hershey's courage led his company through the Great Depression—that courageous leadership inspired his company and his town to persevere through bleak times. Where a man of less courage and conviction might have pulled back from his commitments to others in order to protect himself, Hershey remained faithful to those who trusted in him. Throughout the Great Depression, he continued his building efforts to provide good jobs to those not working at the chocolate factory.

The Investments that Pay Dividends for Generations

Milton Hershey is an exemplary example of transformational change leadership. It is true that Milton Hershey was a generous man who gave away millions of dollars, but it is one of life's great paradoxes: the more you give, the more you receive in return. Mr. Hershey lacked for nothing. As his community prospered, he prospered. His investments in people yielded dividends throughout his lifetime and continue to this day, long after his passing. The world is a better place because of Milton Hershey, and there is little doubt that the world would be far better off with more like him.

Today's Opportunity

I write these words on September 11, 2011. As I write about leadership on the 10th anniversary of the deadliest attack on U.S. soil, I am convinced that the need for leadership is greater today than it was 10 years ago and even greater than it was in Milton Hershey's time. We face global competition and global terrorism and are in the grips of the worst economic downturn since the Great Depression. We need transformational leaders.

Now is the time, just when it seems most bleak; just as the savvy broker maximizes his investment in a down market, now is the golden opportunity to sow the seeds of business success on solid foundations. The workforce has been hit hardest by the economic downturn. Much of today's workforce is disillusioned, disenfranchised, and distrustful. But even among the economic ruin, today's workforce hasn't given up. They retain the hope of a better tomorrow and the resilience to follow their dreams; they are ready to

QUOTE TO LIVE BY: "The reasonable man adapts himself to the world; the unreasonable man persists in trying to adapt the world to himself. Therefore, all progress depends on the unreasonable man."

George Bernard Shaw
Irish Author, Playwright, Nobel Laureate for Literature, Oscar Winner
(1856–1950)

make changes; they are ready to follow a leader. Will you be the one to rise up and lead? Are you ready?

Just as it took courage and vision for Milton Hershey to follow his dreams and lead others, and it took courage and vision to rebuild Seattle from the ashes and lift it out of the muck, if you decide to rebuild, that too will take courage, vision, committed leadership, and a committed workforce—but most of all, courage. Equity is crucial, but like freedom, it can't be won without courage. For every person who wants to change the future, there are hundreds who want to keep things the way they are and thousands more whose timidity breeds anxiety-fueled apathy. The status quo exists to serve those who benefit from it. When you make changes, you'll alter the dynamics of the status quo; the current beneficiaries will oppose you to maintain the system. Stand up; make that change. The realists among us will tell you that in order to survive, you must fight and scrape for your piece of the pie, but why fight for a small piece? Why not make a bigger pie? If you have a vision, if you care for those around you, if you are committed to excellence, and if you can be trusted, then . . . RISE UP, YOU WORTHY BASTARDS AND FOLLOW ME!

Finish
September 11, 2011

Index

Page numbers followed by f and t indicate figures and tables, respectively.